The Lean Entrepreneurship Playbook

A Practical Guide to Innovation in the Modern Enterprise

George Watt

The Lean Entrepreneurship Playbook: A Practical Guide to Innovation in the Modern Enterprise

George Watt
Ottawa, ON, Canada

ISBN-13 (pbk): 979-8-8688-0121-1					ISBN-13 (electronic): 979-8-8688-0122-8
https://doi.org/10.1007/979-8-8688-0122-8

Copyright © 2024 by George Watt

This work is subject to copyright. All rights are reserved by the Publisher, whether the whole or part of the material is concerned, specifically the rights of translation, reprinting, reuse of illustrations, recitation, broadcasting, reproduction on microfilms or in any other physical way, and transmission or information storage and retrieval, electronic adaptation, computer software, or by similar or dissimilar methodology now known or hereafter developed.

Trademarked names, logos, and images may appear in this book. Rather than use a trademark symbol with every occurrence of a trademarked name, logo, or image we use the names, logos, and images only in an editorial fashion and to the benefit of the trademark owner, with no intention of infringement of the trademark.

The use in this publication of trade names, trademarks, service marks, and similar terms, even if they are not identified as such, is not to be taken as an expression of opinion as to whether or not they are subject to proprietary rights.

While the advice and information in this book are believed to be true and accurate at the date of publication, neither the authors nor the editors nor the publisher can accept any legal responsibility for any errors or omissions that may be made. The publisher makes no warranty, express or implied, with respect to the material contained herein.

>	Managing Director, Apress Media LLC: Welmoed Spahr
>	Acquisitions Editor: Susan McDermott
>	Development Editor: Laura Berendson
>	Project Manager: Jessica Vakili

Distributed to the book trade worldwide by Springer Science+Business Media New York, 1 New York Plaza, New York, NY 10004. Phone 1-800-SPRINGER, fax (201) 348-4505, e-mail orders-ny@springer-sbm.com, or visit www.springeronline.com. Apress Media, LLC is a California LLC and the sole member (owner) is Springer Science + Business Media Finance Inc (SSBM Finance Inc). SSBM Finance Inc is a **Delaware** corporation.

For information on translations, please e-mail booktranslations@springernature.com; for reprint, paperback, or audio rights, please e-mail bookpermissions@springernature.com.

Apress titles may be purchased in bulk for academic, corporate, or promotional use. eBook versions and licenses are also available for most titles. For more information, reference our Print and eBook Bulk Sales web page at http://www.apress.com/bulk-sales.

If disposing of this product, please recycle the paper

Table of Contents

About the Author xix

Acknowledgments xxi

Chapter 1: Introduction 1

   Why I Wrote This Book 3

   Do I Have to Do Everything in This Book? 4

   How to Read This Book 7

      What's in This Book 8

      Chapter Sequencing 15

      If You've Read *Lean Entrepreneurship* 15

      Use of Fictitious Names in Real-Life Stories 16

      Quickly Find Tools 17

   Let's Go! 17

Part I: Before You Begin 19

Chapter 2: Why Innovation Fails in Established Organizations 21

   1. People Build Things Nobody Wants 22

      No One Is Immune 26

   Why Even Good Ideas Fail in Established Organizations 27

      "Project Sisyphus" and Beyond 27

   2. New Ideas Are Managed Like Mature Businesses 29

      Heavyweight Processes and Process Pageantry 30

      Rise and Grind: The Hero Culture Myth 31

TABLE OF CONTENTS

    Friction 33
    Great Works of Fiction 34
    NoOp: How Over-Investment Killed a Startup 36
    The Bottom Line 38
    Fallout: How Heavy Internal Process Crushed an External Supplier 38
  3. There Is No Consistent Approach to Help New, Innovative Ideas Succeed 39
    Stephanie and Dinesh: A Story of Innovation Pageantry 40
    Michael: A Tale of Bad Timing and Inconsistency 41
    Consistent, Deliberate Decisions 42
  4. Loss of Executive or Sponsor Interest 44
    Cognitive Overload 45
    Quarterly Cadence 45
    Short-Term Measurements and Incentives 45
    Lack of a Common Vocabulary 46
    Insufficient Communication 46
    Inadequate Alignment on Time Requirements 47
    Budget Pressure 47
    Reorganization 48
    Innovation's "Messy" Nature 49
    Battle Fatigue 49
    Failed Committed Bets 50
    Internal Competition 50
  A Failure Ecosystem 51

Chapter 3: Why Innovation Programs and Initiatives Fail 53
  1. Underinvestment 54
    Initiative Funding Is Not Set Aside 55
    Failure to Budget for Success 55

TABLE OF CONTENTS

2. Poor Strategic Choices 57
   Not Having a Deliberate Strategy 57
   Building the Wrong Type of Initiative 58
   Part-Time Innovation 58
   Casting Too Narrow a Net 59
   Building the Initiative in Isolation 60
3. Use of Innovation Funnels 60
   Focus Only on the "Left Side" of the Funnel 62
   Funnel Fatigue 64
4. Bias 64
   HiPPO-Centric Bias 65
   Cliquetocracies 66
   Perception of Bias 67
5. Misalignment 67
   Absence of a Common Vocabulary 68
6. Unhealthy Culture 69
   Performative Innovation Culture 69
   Unhealthy Internal Competition 70
7. Execution Errors 71
   Ambiguous Ownership and Accountability 71
   Lack of Follow-Up 72
   Failure to Inspect and Adapt 72
   Process Subservience 73
   Inadequate Reorganization-Proofing 74
8. Poor Incubating Team Composition 75
   Absence of Minimum Viable Teams 75
   Placing People in the Wrong Roles 78

TABLE OF CONTENTS

    Importing Bad Habits 79

    Insufficient Training and Support 80

  Why Bother? 82

Chapter 4: Lean Entrepreneurship and Why It Matters 83

  Don't Give Up! 83

    Onward! 84

  1. A Brief Introduction to Lean Entrepreneurship 85

    Lean Experiments 86

    Words Matter 89

  2. Lean Entrepreneurship Principles 90

    Lean Governance Is *Not* an Oxymoron 91

  3. The Benefits of a Lean Approach 93

    "*Does One Degree Matter?*" 94

    Small Errors Are Compounded Over Time and Become Large Errors 95

    Bringing New Ideas to Life Through Lean Navigation 99

    Lean Innovation Reduces Risk and Waste 101

  4. Avoiding Wasteful Committed Bets 101

    So Much Waste! 104

  5. Leveraging the Lean Advantage 106

  Let's Get Started! 108

Part II: Preparation 109

Chapter 5: Assessing the Current State 111

  You're Almost Ready 112

    It's Not Time-Intensive 113

    Don't Skip This Step! 114

TABLE OF CONTENTS

1. What Is an Assessment? 114
2. Benefits of an Assessment 116
   - Trust Is Essential 124
   - Assessments Deliver 125
3. Begin with Goals 126
   - Leverage Your Primary Contact's Knowledge 128
   - Don't Feel Overwhelmed 129
4. Design with a Purpose (Optional) 129
5. Leverage Existing Knowledge Bases 132
   - Where to Find Secondary Research Information 135
6. Plan and Estimate Time Requirements 136
7. Create an Interview Guide 138
   - Structure 139
   - Go Deep 147
   - Prioritize 147
   - Set Landmarks 148
   - Interview Guide Template: Putting It All Together 149
   - Learn Fast and Iterate 152

Chapter 6: Conducting Assessment Interviews 153

1. Select Interview Participants 154
   - *"How Many People Should I Interview?"* 154
   - *"When Should I Stop Interviewing?"* 155
   - Diversity Over Quantity 158
   - Additional Considerations 159
   - Finalizing the Participant List 159
   - Choosing Your First Interview Participant 160
   - Leave Time for Adjustment 161

TABLE OF CONTENTS

- 2. Prepare for the Interviews 161
  - Scheduling Interviews 162
  - Rehearse 164
  - Learn About the Organization and the People 165
  - Have an Initial Hypothesis 167
  - Check Your Bias 167
  - Be Well Rested 168
  - Prepare Your Environment 168
- 3. Conduct the Interviews 175
  - Respect Participants' Time 176
  - During the Interview 177
  - Taking Notes 182
  - Thank the Participants! 185
  - Ethics Matter 185
  - Pseudonyms 186
  - Back Up Your Data 187
  - Enjoy the Experience! 188
- 4. Review and Cleanse the Data 189
  - Be Deliberate, Make Time 190
  - Automatic Transcription 191
- 5. Update Stakeholders (Don't "Go Dark") 192
  - Stakeholder Conversations Are Always Valuable 193
- 6. Prepare the Findings 194
  - Begin at the End 197
  - Review, Reduce, Repeat 197
  - Schedule "Quiet Time" for Preparation 198
  - Why Progressive Disclosure? 198

TABLE OF CONTENTS

Don't Wait, Iterate! 199
Themes and Discovery 199
7. Finalize the Findings 203
Additional Considerations 204
Become a Member of the Team 206
What's Next? 207

Chapter 7: Designing Your Approach 209

1. Decide What You Are Building 210
   Decision 1: Toolkit, Framework, or Initiative? 215
2. Be Deliberate About Inputs and Outputs 216
   Decision 2: What Will Enter the Initiative? 218
   Decision 3: What Will Exit the Initiative? 226
3. Select the Initiative's Structure 229
   Structure 1: Seed–Series 230
   The Need for a New Structure 233
   Structure 2: Explore–Experiment–Transition (Public Sector) 234
   Structure 3: Incubate–Startup–Accelerate (Private Sector) 237
   Alignment with Desirability–Feasibility–Viability 238
   Decision 4: Select a Structure 239
4. Prepare a Detailed Design 240
   Stage Overview 242
   Detailed Stage Checklists 243
   Ceremonies 244
   Tools and Artifacts 246
   Design Workshops 248
   Be Roughly Right, Not Precisely Wrong 253

ix

TABLE OF CONTENTS

    5. Engage Cross-Organizational Teams 253

        The Impact of the Different Archetypes 254

        Nuances Matter 258

    The Impact of Portfolio of Initiatives 258

    Additional Considerations 262

        Investment or Funding, What's in a Name? 263

        Public Sector Lean Canvas 264

    It's Time for Action 264

Chapter 8: Finalizing Objectives 265

    1. Be Deliberate, Be Intentional 266

        Confirm Alignment 267

        Be Unambiguous 267

        Pause for Introspection 268

    2. Objectives and Key Results (OKRs) 268

        What Are OKRs? 268

        How OKRs Work 270

    3. Setting Objectives with OKRs 270

        Three OKR Horizons 273

    4. Set Your Initiative's Objectives 274

    5. Establish Ownership 281

        The Initiative Must Be Its Owner's Top Priority 281

        External Ownership 282

        Internal Ownership Advantages 282

    6. Establish a Heartbeat (Cadence) 283

        Set a Deliberate Cadence 285

        Weekly Rhythm 286

        Don't Set Monday Deadlines! 287

TABLE OF CONTENTS

7. Obtain Alignment and Buy-in 287
    Broader Alignment 288
What's Next? 290

Chapter 9: Communicating 291
1. Broaden Your Communication Scope 292
    Don't Go Dark, Be Deliberate 293
2. Refine Your Communication Needs 295
    A Structure for Informal Communication 297
    You Won't Need a Massive Team 298
    Leverage Existing Channels 298
3. Get Help 299
4. Communicate Proactively 300
    Clearly State Your Intentions 300
    Inspect and Adapt the Messaging 303
    Set Expectations for Long-Term Gains 304
5. Communicate to Preempt Threats 307
    Embrace Other Initiatives 307
    Be Transparent About Restrictions and Timing 308
    Be Aware of Innovation Killing Personalities 309
    Beware of Overoptimism 310
    Prepare People for the "Chaos" 311
    Hardening Against Reorganizations 311
Additional Considerations 312
Summary 315

xi

TABLE OF CONTENTS

Part III: Build–Measure–Learn 317

Chapter 10: Laying the Foundation 319

   Not a Cast of Thousands 321

   1. Form the Initiative Team 322

      The GEFN Advantage 323

      A Lean Mindset 324

      How Many People? 325

      Start Small and Evolve 326

      Stay Small but Mighty 327

      Additional Considerations 328

      Who May Matter More Than How Many 329

      Characteristics of Good Initiative Team Candidates 329

      Initiative Team: The Bottom Line 330

   2. Form the Governance Team 332

      Diversity Is Key 333

      Build a Pipeline 335

      Lean Governance Is Lightweight, Responsible Governance 336

      Governance Is About People 337

      Characteristics of Good Governance Team Candidates 338

      Governance Team Time Requirements 339

      Governance Team: The Bottom Line 342

      Extended Governance Teams (a.k.a. Investment Teams) 343

   3. Engage Advisors and Allies 344

      The Advisory Team 345

      Advisors Become Allies 346

      Caveat: Adding Bench Expertise 346

      Advisors Can Prevent Consequential Errors 347

TABLE OF CONTENTS

  Characteristics of Good Advisory Team Candidates 348

  Advisory Team Time Requirements 349

  Advisory Team: The Bottom Line...349

  Incubation Team Advisors..350

 4. Consider a Maker Team 352

  Shared Maker Team...352

  Characteristics of Good Maker Team Candidates 353

 Team Relationships..353

 5. Prepare a Budget 354

  Consider Expenses Across Major Categories, Groups, and Functions.........354

  Team-Level Budget Considerations 361

  Second Order Thinking 363

  Understand When Expenses Occur, and Forecast Monthly or Quarterly......366

  Unfair Advantage: Organizational Programs 366

  Modeling Your Initiative 367

  Priming the Initiative 368

 Additional Considerations 369

  Group Development 371

 Summary..375

Chapter 11: Launching the Initiative 377

 1. Capture and Select Ideas..379

  Ten Steps for Capturing Ideas 379

  Designing a Pitch Ceremony..380

  Creating the Information and Material Candidates Need to Prepare for Their Pitch..382

  Providing a Mechanism for Candidates to Submit Pitch Requests..............383

  Promoting the Initiative and Recruiting Participants 384

  Accepting and Triaging Pitch Candidates 387

xiii

TABLE OF CONTENTS

    Selecting and Sequencing Pitches 388
    Scheduling Pitches 388
    Directing and Guiding the Governance Team 391
    Adjudicating Ideas via a Pitch Ceremony 393
    Informing Pitch Teams Whether or Not Their Ideas Are Selected 395
    Priming the Pipeline 396

  2. Onboard Incubating Teams (Entry) 398
    Eliminating Waste by "Testing Out" 400
    Welcoming Incubating Teams 401
    Tools and Resources 404
    Developing Good Habits and Guiding Principles 405
    Consider the Impact of Cohorts 406

  3. Allocate Initiative Team Time for Removing Obstacles (Unblocking) 408

  4. Use 3P Reviews to Assess and Facilitate Progress 409
    3P Review Format 410
    Transition Request 3P Reviews 412
    Scheduling 3P Reviews 413
    Guiding the Governance Team 416
    Keep It Light, Keep It Lean 417

  5. Reward Participants 417

  Final Considerations 419

  Summary 420

Chapter 12: Measuring Performance and Impact 421

  Where Do I Begin? What Can I Measure? 422
    Two Measurement Classes 423

  1. Measure Incubating Ideas 423
    A Continuum of Measurement 424

2. Measure the Initiative's Performance 428
Measuring Flow 428
Initiative Performance Data 434
Automating Data Capture 442
Putting It All Together 447
Performance Metrics and OKRs 449
3. Measure Impact and Value 450
Value Migration 457

Putting It All Together 458
Additional Considerations 459
Summary 461

Chapter 13: Continuous Learning and Improvement 463
Beyond the Metrics 464
1. Retrospectives 468
Easy to Prepare, Easy to Conduct 469
Capture and Manage Actions 470
Learn Everywhere 471
A Few Things I Learned from Initiative-Focused Retrospectives 472
2. Proactive Learning 473
3. Leadership Development 474
4. Summits and Off-Sites 477
Team Lead Summits (Founder Summits) 477
Governance Team Off-Sites 483
5. Introspection 488
When We Are at Our Best/When We Are Not at Our Best 490
6. Role Clarification and Alignment 492

TABLE OF CONTENTS

    7. Incremental Learning 494

    Additional Considerations 496

    Summary 497

Part IV: Conclusion 499

Chapter 14: Conclusion 501

    You Don't Have to Do Everything at Once 501

    Start Small, Build Incrementally 502

    Get Help 503

    Be Opportunistic 504

    It Is Always About People and Trust 504

    Communication Is Paramount 505

    Good Governance Is Also Good Guidance 506

    Be Willing to Let Go 507

    Watch for Drift 508

    Never Stop Learning 509

    Take the First Step! 509

Part V: *The Lean Entrepreneurship Toolkit* 511

Appendix 1: Initiatives-at-a-Glance, One-Page Stage Overviews, and Stage Checklists 513

    How to Use This Section 513

    Seed-Series Model–Private Sector Product or Service Scenario 515

    Incubate–Startup–Accelerate Model–Private Sector Product or Service Scenario 530

    Explore–Experiment–Transition Model–Public Sector Program or Project Scenario 547

Appendix 2: Ceremonies **565**

Appendix 3: Tools and Artifacts **661**

Index **745**

About the Author

George Watt is passionate about solving unsolved problems and applying technology in innovative ways to improve people's lives. Over his more than thirty years in the technology industry, George discovered innumerable obstacles to bringing new ideas to life in established organizations and, more importantly, how they could be overcome.

As VP of Strategy for a multibillion-dollar technology company – and faced with a challenge to design, deploy, operate, and evolve an innovative start-up accelerator program – George created what became the foundation of the Lean Entrepreneurship approach to enable others to overcome those obstacles.

Throughout his career, George delivered innovations of his own such as a knowledge base for a neural network-based predictive performance management solution, one of the earliest private clouds (2005), and a lightweight event management agent. George was also awarded a patent for securing protected content by identifying recording devices.

George has a broad range of experience, including leading global scientific research, worldwide innovation initiatives, and an innovative start-up accelerator for a multi-billion-dollar technology company; holding many national and global leadership positions and leading global teams spanning North America, Europe, Asia, and Australia; serving as a Technology Evangelist; and holding many technical roles such as Systems Programmer/Sysadmin and Systems Engineer.

ABOUT THE AUTHOR

George has shared his experience overcoming obstacles to innovation and new idea incubation in established organizations in two previous books: *The Innovative CIO* and *Lean Entrepreneurship*.

Acknowledgments

Nobody writes a book alone, even when they are the sole author. There are countless people who contributed to this book in a broad variety of ways. First, I would like to thank my family, Lee Anne, James, and Heather, for their unwavering support and encouragement. Always patient, always supportive, and always my bedrock. I appreciate your patience and enthusiasm the many times I said, "Hey! Can I show you something?" I am especially grateful to Lee Anne for agreeing to be my "Proofreader in Chief" and reading, correcting, and commenting on countless drafts.

Special thanks to Scott Morrison, who agreed to read the early drafts and has given me candid and invaluable feedback that has made this book exponentially better. Thank you for your patience and candor.

I am grateful to Laura Berendson and Jessica Vakili of the Apress team for their patience, direction, and guidance. You made the difficult things easy. Thank you as well to Susan McDermott of Apress who listened to my idea and shepherded this book through the proposal and approval process.

I would like to thank the many people who have contributed to the experiences that led me to where I am, the many colleagues, clients, and customers who gave me their trust and created the opportunities that enabled me to learn and test these concepts. I have been exceptionally fortunate to have worked with you all, and I appreciate your confidence in me. To the Accelerator team with whom I built the first Lean Entrepreneurship accelerator, thank you from the bottom of my heart. You exemplified what a high-trust, high-performance team should be and demonstrated the magic a team like that can deliver. I appreciate your trust, I enjoyed our time together more than you could imagine, and I carry you all with me every day.

There are pieces of every one of you in this book. Thank you.

CHAPTER 1

Introduction

This book is about choices.

If you've read Charles Dickens' classic story, "A Christmas Carol" – or if you've seen one of the many movies, plays, and other works of art based on it – you probably remember the pivotal scene. Having been confronted by two ghosts who showed him how the choices he made impacted his past and present, Ebenezer Scrooge was confronted by the spirit he feared most: the ghost that would show him the not-so-pleasant future his choices had designed. But then something very interesting happened.

Like a great lean practitioner, he asked an amazing question. "Are these the shadows of things that will be, or are they shadows of things that may be, only?"[1] Is this the future that *shall* be? The future that *must* be? Or is this simply the path that I am currently on? *Can* it be changed?

Though he did not get a direct answer to his question, he developed a falsifiable hypothesis that if he became a better person, his future *could* be changed. Then, like the great lean practitioner that he apparently was, Scrooge ran a series of experiments which largely consisted of doing good things for people and being a good citizen.

Fortunately for Scrooge, his hypothesis was confirmed. He had changed his approach, and his future. He had become, "as good a man as the good old city knew."

---

[1] A Christmas Carol, Charles Dickens, Chapman & Hall, 1843

CHAPTER 1   INTRODUCTION

This vignette from a story written in 1858 hints that we've known about the benefits of a lean approach for a very long time. Long before Charles Dickens wrote his classic story. (I'll expand on this in Chapter 4.) Scrooge's success – his happy ending – began with a choice. That choice was the result of one great question – "Are these the shadows of things that will be, or are they shadows of things that may be, only?"

So, I will extend my opening statement. This book is about choices. Choices and questions… and answers. It is filled with questions, examples, artifacts, and tools to help you make *your* choices as you develop a way to ensure new ideas in your organization have the best possible chance to succeed. It includes information, experience, and anecdotes that will help you identify, anticipate, and overcome not only roadblocks to bringing those ideas to life but also obstacles to the initiative itself. It contains frameworks and archetypical examples that will help accelerate your deployment. More about that in a moment.

Terminology   Throughout the book, I will refer to the thing you create to nurture new ideas and bring them to life as an "initiative," regardless of whether it is a toolkit, framework, mandatory or optional approach, incubator, or accelerator. The reason for this is twofold. First, it simplifies the reading. If I had to type all those things each time I referenced an initiative, this book would be longer than *War and Peace*. Second, though this type of thing is often referred to as a "program" (in fact, that's what I called the first one I built), as I will explain later, that word sometimes has a very specific meaning to certain groups. Using it might create confusion or misconception.

CHAPTER 1   INTRODUCTION

Why I Wrote This Book

It's hard to believe it's been five years since Howard Abrams and I wrote *Lean Entrepreneurship*. Its publication opened a lot of doors for me. It led to me meeting many amazing people and resulted in my working on some very interesting projects and assignments. People responded very well to *Lean Entrepreneurship*, but they wanted something more. The irony isn't lost on me that they brought this to me in the form of a question: "Is there anything out there that tells me *how* to do this?" "Is there something that explains how to create an initiative like the one described in the *Lean Entrepreneurship*, step-by-step?" There wasn't.

There were a lot great of books about how to become creative, how to be an innovative company, how to generate ideas. But what happens then? What do you *do* with those ideas? How do you give them the best possible chance to succeed – or not – based upon the ideas' own merits? How do you create the conditions for repeatable new idea incubation and/or innovation in an established organization?

That feedback provided me with two reasons to write this book: (1) People asked me to break the lean entrepreneurship concept down into additional detail and provide step-by-step guidance. (2) There wasn't anything like it. I wasn't certain that was enough, but as I engaged with people who were building lean entrepreneurship style initiatives on their own, I discovered additional needs.

First, it was not well understood that the span and scope of these initiatives can vary widely. They can be broad, full-service initiatives as was described in *Lean Entrepreneurship*, they might be smaller and more focused, bringing a single idea at a time through customer-problem fit validation, or they could even be a set of self-service guidelines that individuals or teams could follow on their own. This variety of choice is great, but things can go off course when different people in an organization have differing ideas of what the initiative will be, or when those responsible for the initiative set out to build the wrong thing. The results can be catastrophic.

Second, I saw unnecessary stress, false starts, and failures because people had not made the right choices early on. They had not asked the right questions. They had done too little, or done too much and made their initiative too heavy. They had built the wrong thing, or had built the right thing but it wasn't what others expected.

At times these setbacks were not the result of making the *wrong* choices. *Crucial decisions had not been made at all.* The people building the initiatives were not always aware of the questions to ask and decisions to make to ensure they were building the *right* thing. What made that situation more unfortunate was that even the "wrong" choice (or a suboptimal choice) would have been better for many of them. These initiatives are not immutable. They can be adapted. They can intentionally start small and hyper-focused and evolve as needed.

I discovered many additional reasons over time, but I will share only one other so we can get on to the topic at hand.

I am passionate about the success of others. It energizes me. *Anyone* can create an initiative like this. It would be incredibly disheartening to learn of people who could have but did not, or whose initiatives did not deliver to their full potential – or were shut down – because of a choice they did not make or a step they did not take. I want you to succeed. I want you to be aware of choices you can make, questions you can ask, steps you can take, and pitfalls you can avoid. I will explain how in a moment, but first let's address an important question.

Do I Have to Do Everything in This Book?

No.

That's the short answer. You don't have to do everything in this book, and you probably won't; at least initially.

CHAPTER 1 INTRODUCTION

This book covers a broad variety of design options and nuances, but you don't have to do everything in it to deliver a successful initiative. This is true across all elements of your initiative, from its size, to its scope, to its team composition, to the composition of the stages of the initiative, to what is selected to enter the initiative and the kind of thing that will exit. You could create a simple initiative that may only *find* ideas through what I refer to as the "pitch" stage. You could select ideas, bring them through one or two stages of incubation (i.e., the steps necessary to first determine whether an idea is worth pursuing and then to validate whether people would be interested in the solution you envision), not build a solution at all, and then send those validated customer problems or potential solutions elsewhere to be brought to life. The choice is yours, but it doesn't stop there.

Even if you wish to build a full-service initiative that encompasses everything discussed in this book, you don't have to build it all at once. You can build it incrementally using the same lean approach that you would encourage each of the initiative's participating teams to use. You could begin by creating a pitch mechanism alone. When you're satisfied with that you might create the resources necessary to enable participating teams to confirm people actually have the problem the team is trying to solve, that the problem is painful enough people would take an action to adopt it, and – if appropriate – that they would pay for a solution. As you are doing that, you could work to improve the pitch mechanism you built earlier. Then you could build a second stage that enables teams to develop and validate potential solution ideas for that problem; and do an even better job building that stage because of what you learned building the first two elements of your initiative. You could continue to build your initiative incrementally and inspect, adapt, and improve what you built until you have a full initiative.

Done that way, you may not even need to build some of the elements of your initiative for a year or more. You don't even have to set out to build the entire initiative that you envision. You could intentionally build something much smaller in scope and evolve it as your needs change, and as you become better prepared to deliver something new. You could build an initiative that consists only of idea competitions or pitches. That's it. Later on you could evolve that to a more moderate initiative that might include de-risking, but not building, the solution. Then later build upon that.

Finally, even if you decide to build *all* of the components of an initiative described in this book, you don't have to build all of the parts of each stage or component initially. You can build a minimum viable version – perhaps more appropriately a minimum valuable version – of each stage at the outset, and then enrich one or more of those stages as your initiative matures. You could even have some fully developed stages initially, while others remain minimum viable versions.

In the interest of not filling the book solely with the breadth of possibilities, I'll stop enumerating them now. The bottom line is:

- You do not have to do everything outlined in the book.
- You do not have to complete every aspect of anything you choose to do.
- You can begin with a minimum viable version of anything you plan to include.
- You can start small and iterate, regardless of your final objective (do this!).
- You can begin with a smaller initiative and evolve it into something larger later.
- You could build an initiative that enables one team to incubate at a time, or you could welcome a dozen, or dozens of teams.

- You could create a toolkit, framework, or guideline that you make available in a self-service shared location so individuals can use it as they please.

The choice is yours. You can build the initiative that will best accomplish your objectives, and that will be the best cultural fit for your organization.

You can also leverage things you have already done. For example, if you already have a way to find and select ideas, and it's working well, use it. If you're not happy with what you have, you still might be able to preserve some or all of it. (Chapter 13 has some tips regarding how you might do that, and the Toolkit includes a step-by-step guide for performing retrospectives that will help you improve what you have.)

This book was written to help you build the initiative that's best for you. So, I wrote it so you can read it as you like. Let's look at what's inside, and how you can use it.

How to Read This Book

Just as you do not have to *do* everything in this book at once, you should not have to *read* everything in this book at once. Though it was written so it could be read in order, from start to finish, it was also written so that each chapter can be read on its own, in any order. If you have already performed some of the steps, you can skip those and get right to what you are interested in. In addition, I have included many section headings within each chapter so you can quickly skim through and find the information, questions, examples, or checklists you are interested in.

CHAPTER 1 INTRODUCTION

What's in This Book

This book consists of five major parts.

Part 1: Before You Begin

Part 1 of this book contains context and information that will be helpful before you begin your journey. It provides an updated introduction to lean entrepreneurship concepts, describes the reasons the approach is needed, reviews why innovation fails in established organizations, explores the most common causes *initiatives* like this fail, and provides a brief overview of the lean entrepreneurship approach. If you have read *Lean Entrepreneurship*, some of the concepts in Chapters 2 and 4 will be familiar to you, though each chapter contains information that was not included in *Lean Entrepreneurship*. I have noted the areas which were covered in *Lean Entrepreneurship* at the end of this chapter so it will be easy for you to find the sections you may want to skip.

Part 1 consists of three chapters:

1. **Chapter 2, "Why Innovation Fails in Established Organizations,"** describes the many reasons established organizations struggle to bring new ideas to life, especially those that are novel. It breaks each reason down and includes new case studies that demonstrate why organizations fail to innovate.

2. **Chapter 3, "Why Innovation Programs and Initiatives Fail,"** introduces the major classes of risk to innovation and new idea incubation initiatives. It breaks each risk down and describes why the initiatives themselves often fail so that you can recognize and mitigate those risks as you build your own.

3. **Chapter 4, "Lean Entrepreneurship and Why It Matters,"** introduces the lean entrepreneurship approach and its principles, and explains why a lean approach works. It also includes an example that I have found very useful in helping people understand the value of a lean approach by explaining how people have been using similar approaches to other problems for hundreds, perhaps thousands, of years.

Part 2: Preparation

Part 2 is focused on the activities and preparation that must be done before you begin building or deploying your initiative. It discusses what must be done to ensure you understand the problem you are solving with your initiative, how to determine what to include, and what must be considered prior to deciding upon a final design. It provides design choices and archetypes, and explains how to do the groundwork necessary to ensure you build the right thing and are adequately prepared to deploy it successfully.

Part 2 consists of five chapters:

1. **Chapter 5, "Assessing the Current State,"** provides a guide to performing a simple, lightweight assessment of your organization's needs to ensure you build the right initiative. It discusses the importance of performing an objective assessment of the organization's current state, its needs, and the expectations of stakeholders and influencers before you decide upon an initial design. It also describes the many benefits of an assessment beyond its obvious value, discusses the steps necessary to conduct one, and provides tips regarding what to

CHAPTER 1   INTRODUCTION

do and where to find the information that will help you design a successful initiative. In addition, it includes guidance on preparing an interview guide – including sample questions – so you can perform your own primary research.

2. **Chapter 6, "Conducting Assessment Interviews,"** provides a step-by-step guide to conducting your own primary research via interviews. It shares information on how to structure them, how to schedule them, how to select participants, how many you will need, and how to know when you've done enough. It also provides tips for conducting effective interviews online, discusses the importance of trust and anonymity, and provides guidance regarding how to prepare the interview's findings.

3. **Chapter 7, "Designing Your Approach,"** discusses how to take everything you learned from the assessment and other sources and incorporate it into your design. It provides archetypes for public sector and private sector initiatives, describes the impact of each, and steps through the major decisions you will need to make as you finalize your design. It also covers what to include in your basic design artifacts to ensure each stage is well understood and effectively executed, and that participants, stakeholders, and the governance bodies are aligned.

4. **Chapter 8, "Finalizing Objectives,"** discusses the need for, and value of, setting explicit objectives as you build your initiative. It introduces Objectives

and Key Results (OKRs) as a simple and effective way to establish and capture goals and ensure the actions you are taking are achieving those goals. It also introduces the benefits of having a common cadence and the need for alignment and buy-in; and includes a simple tool for analyzing and managing stakeholder relationships.

5. **Chapter 9, "Communicating,"** discusses the need for regular and broad communication to various groups and constituents as you prepare to build the initiative. It reviews the benefits of communicating, and enumerates a range of people and groups which should be considered when planning your communication strategy. It also includes two simple tools you can use to develop a communication plan and ensure key relationships are appropriately managed. The chapter also offers strategies to improve your communication abilities and infrastructure that do not require bringing those skills into your team.

Part 3: Build–Measure–Learn

Part 3 focuses on the deployment, operation, and continuous improvement of an initiative. It begins with a discussion of the teams and roles required to lay a foundation that will support a successful initiative. It discusses how to launch the initiative, find creative people and their ideas, and successfully bring them into the initiative. It includes tips on how to prime your initiative and give it a running start that may even be a potential source of funding. It then moves on to a discussion of how to measure the initiative to ensure the actions you are taking are having the desired impact and advancing the initiative, and concludes with a

CHAPTER 1   INTRODUCTION

discussion of how those measures, and other techniques, can be used to ensure you are learning from the experience of a broad range of people and applying that information to continuously improve the initiative.

Part 3 consists of four chapters:

1. **Chapter 10, "Laying the Foundation,"** discusses how to leverage all the groundwork covered in Part 3 as you begin bringing others into the initiative and prepare for its launch. It describes each team you will require and their roles, provides tips for selecting people for those roles, and discusses how you can, and should, start small and evolve. It also discusses the dynamics of teams as they evolve, and how each of the teams interacts with, and supports, the others. Chapter 10 concludes with a discussion of what you will need to consider as you prepare a budget for your initiative, if one is necessary.

2. **Chapter 11, "Launching the Initiative,"** covers the activities required to prepare and launch your initiative. It includes tips for capturing ideas and bringing incubating teams into the initiative, and for priming the initiative to give it a running start and, potentially, some additional funding. It also discusses the key ceremonies required for idea selection, ongoing operation, and supporting and governing incubating teams.

3. **Chapter 12, "Measuring Performance and Impact,"** introduces two classes of measurement that are required in order to ensure the initiative is executing well and is driving the value it was created to drive. It begins with a discussion of the

application of a measurement continuum to help incubating teams advance, and introduces the types of measurement that will help ensure the initiative itself is evolving and performing well. It includes several examples of detailed metrics and measures that can be used to identify where the initiative is performing well and what might need attention, and that can be used to communicate progress, status, and goal achievement to stakeholders and interested parties.

4. **Chapter 13, "Continuous Learning and Improvement,"** explores techniques for learning and improvement that go beyond metrics and measures. It explains how a combination of retrospective, proactive, and introspective learning can help your initiative advance, evolve, and improve; and how they can be used to maintain and confirm alignment and communicate progress. It also includes a discussion of group learning and improvement through summits and off-sites, why they are useful, and steps to take to ensure they are successful and not painful.

Part 4: Conclusion

As you likely guessed, Part 4 ties it all together and offers some additional tips on how to create a successful initiative.

Part 4 consists of one chapter:

1. **Chapter 14, "Conclusion,"** offers additional context and a few final thoughts to help ensure your initiative's success.

CHAPTER 1   INTRODUCTION

Part 5: The Lean Entrepreneurship Toolkit

Part 5 contains tools, artifacts, and ceremonies that will help you deploy your own initiative and ensure it is successful. It includes:

- For each of the initiative archetypes covered in the book:
    - A one-page initiative-at-a-glance that covers all stages of the archetype
    - A one-page stage overview for each of the five or six stages of the archetype
    - A checklist that provides guidance regarding the types of activities that should be conducted at each stage
- Step-by-step guides that will help you lead each of the ceremonies discussed in the book
- Additional tools and artifacts mentioned throughout the book with instructions regarding how to use them
- A list of the top ten errors I most commonly encounter when reviewing public sector lean canvases
- A list of the top ten errors I most commonly encounter when reviewing private sector lean canvases

The overviews and checklists in Part 5 can be used on their own, as starters to accelerate your initiative, or as inspiration for your own checklists. It should be noted that **they are intended to be directional, not directive**. Some of the items in those checklists and overviews may not apply to your initiative, and you may want to add your own items. The assessment and design outlined in Chapters 5–7 will give you much of the information you need to make those decisions, and the continuous learning and improvement ideas from Chapter 13 will help you to maintain them.

Chapter Sequencing

This book was written so that it can be read from start to finish. Reading it that way will provide you with a comprehensive understanding of what is required to design, deploy, and operate an initiative of this nature. However, it was also written such that each chapter or section can be read selectively or in a different order.

The chapters in Parts 2 and 3 of the book are written in the order you will likely *begin* their execution. However, you may find executing more than one step at a time, overlapping one step with its predecessor, can accelerate your progress. For example, you may be conducting interviews (Chapter 6) before you have completed your assessment in full (Chapter 5). You may begin thinking about your design (Chapter 7) before you complete your interviews or even your full assessment (Chapters 5 and 6). Once you've built the initiative (Chapters 10 and 11) you will begin a virtuous cycle of build–measure–learn (Chapters 10, 11, 12, and 13) that will continue throughout the life of your initiative.

As mentioned earlier, depending upon your objectives and your own experience, you might find yourself reading part of a chapter, moving to another, and then returning to the first later as you evolve your initiative and need more information. The chapters and sections were structured to accommodate that.

If You've Read *Lean Entrepreneurship*

If you have recently read *Lean Entrepreneurship: Innovation in the Modern Enterprise* **some of the material in Part 1 may be familiar**. Figure 1-1 provides recommendations regarding which sections of Part 1 to read even if you have recently read *Lean Entrepreneurship*. If you have not read it, or it has been a while since you've read it, I recommend reading Part 1 in its entirety.

What to read in Part 1 if you've read *Lean Entrepreneurship*

Chapter 2: Why Innovation Fails in Established Organizations
1. Section 1: "People build things nobody wants"
2. Section 2: The "Rise and grind: The hero culture myth" subsection
3. Section 4: "Loss of executive or sponsor interest"

Chapter 3: Why Innovation Initiatives Fail
1. The entire chapter

Chapter 4: Lean Entrepreneurship and Why it Matters
1. Section 3: "The benefits of a lean approach"
2. Section 5: "Leveraging the lean advantage"

Figure 1-1. *What to read if you have read Lean Entrepreneurship: Innovation in the Modern Enterprise*

Use of Fictitious Names in Real-Life Stories

I share several real-life stories throughout this book. I used real names and companies in the few stories that are already publicly available and broadly known. Elsewhere I have used fictitious names to protect the identities of those involved. I have placed an icon to the left of each story's initial paragraph, as I have done here, to help you easily identify these shadows of the past.

CHAPTER 1   INTRODUCTION

Quickly Find Tools

 I have placed a hammer icon to the left of the tools, artifacts, and checklists in each chapter so you can easily find them.

Let's Go!

That brings us back to choices. Choices and questions. Questions and answers. Your first choice might be where to begin reading this book. I would like to suggest you start with Part 1, and look both at why innovation and new idea incubation fails in established organizations (Chapter 2) and why the initiatives that are designed to help bring those ideas to life so often fail (Chapter 3). Understanding the pitfalls and obstacles outlined in those chapters will help you to identify those threats as they approach you, take action to avoid them, and design *your* initiative to prevent them from happening.

Whatever your choice, thank you for reading this book. Now, let's go build something great!

PART I

Before You Begin

CHAPTER 2

Why Innovation Fails in Established Organizations

Scrooge's analysis of what the spirits in Dickens' novel showed him, and his subsequent transformation to becoming "as good a man as the good old city knew" demonstrate how invaluable understanding the past can be to those charting their own course to a better future. People who have previously attempted to nurture innovation and bring new ideas to life in established organizations have encountered a myriad of setbacks and roadblocks. Understanding those shadows of the past before you begin will enable you to select, design, and deploy the initiative that will drive the most value for its participants, and your organization, in *your* future.

Fortunately, unlike Scrooge, you do not have to make all the mistakes yourself. In this chapter, I will introduce you to the "shadows" I most commonly encounter (Figure 2-1).

CHAPTER 2 WHY INNOVATION FAILS IN ESTABLISHED ORGANIZATIONS

> **In this Chapter**
>
> Why Innovation Fails In Established Organizations:
>
> 1. People build things nobody wants
> 2. New ideas are managed like mature businesses
> 3. There is no consistent approach to help new, innovative ideas succeed
> 4. Loss of executive or sponsor interest

Figure 2-1. *What's in this chapter*

Let's begin by looking at the most common reason innovation fails, both inside established organizations, and elsewhere.

1. People Build Things Nobody Wants

In March 2019, I joined the heavily attended Convergence Keynote session at the world-famous SXSW conference in Austin, Texas. Meg Whitman, former President and CEO of both eBay and Hewlett-Packard, and Jeffrey Katzenberg, former CEO of Dreamworks Animation and former Chair of Walt Disney Studios, were the featured panelists (Figure 2-2). They were promoting their new – and at the time not yet available – service, Quibi.

CHAPTER 2   WHY INNOVATION FAILS IN ESTABLISHED ORGANIZATIONS

Figure 2-2. *South by Southwest Convergence Keynote, March 8, 2019. Left to right: Keynote host/moderator Dylan Byers, Senior Media Reporter for NBC News/MSNBC; Meg Whitman, CEO Quibi, and; Jeff Katzenberg, Co-Founder, Quibi. (Photo credit: George Watt)*

Whitman and Katzenberg explained that Quibi, short for "quick bites," would deliver premium digital entertainment in six-to-ten-minute episodes. They asserted that people between 25 and 35 years old spent five hours each day between 7:00 AM and 7:00 PM watching content on their phone; 70 minutes of which was spent watching short-form content like you might find on YouTube. They believed that if they created premium short-form "snackable" content – for example, breaking up what would be a two-and-one-half-hour episode into smaller six-to-ten-minute snippets – Quibi would take a share of those 70 minutes. They also believed Quibi would be so compelling it might even take a share of the time their prospective customers were spending consuming video entertainment of longer durations.

I understood **the Quibi thesis** as follows:

1. People commuting to work on public transit do not have time to consume long episodes, such as those on Netflix or other streaming services.

2. Due to those time constraints, commuters either do not watch long-form content when commuting or they try to watch it in smaller blocks, but find that terribly annoying.

3. Those annoyances are painful enough that commuters will switch to an alternative service.

4. Quibi, formatted specifically for mobile devices, will be that alternative.

5. Once Quibi viewers become accustomed to the quick bites, customers will replace not only some of the short-form content they are watching (e.g., YouTube videos) with Quibi episodes, they will prefer those snackable bites over some of the long-form episodes they currently watch.

The combined power and intelligence of these industry icons, billed as a "marriage of Hollywood and Silicon Valley," raised US$1.75 billion in funding for Quibi.

The service launched in April 2020. It shut down a little more than six months later.

In an open letter to employees, investors, and partners, Katzenberg and Whitman admitted Quibi failed **because "the idea itself wasn't strong enough."** They also felt timing may have played a role. Either way, it was clear **they had built something nobody wanted.**

Think about that. Two of the world's most successful, most experienced businesspeople spent more than one billion dollars building something nobody wanted.

Let's consider the reasons why it is so easy to fall into this trap. As illustrated in Figure 2-3, **to be successful a new, innovative idea must be**:

- **Desirable:** People must want it, must believe it delivers value to them, and the value they experience must be sufficient to entice them to switch from any existing alternatives.

- **Feasible:** It must be possible to build, deliver, and operate the solution and, in a public sector context, it must also be possible to build it while respecting applicable policies, mandates, regulations, and/or legislation.

- **Viable:** It must have sufficient traction to meet a business's objectives and generate enough revenue to cover the expense of making and delivering the solution while generating sufficient profit (private sector), or deliver sufficient benefit to a government department or program's beneficiaries while making a sufficient contribution to the organization's mission and mandate at a reasonable cost (public sector).

CHAPTER 2   WHY INNOVATION FAILS IN ESTABLISHED ORGANIZATIONS

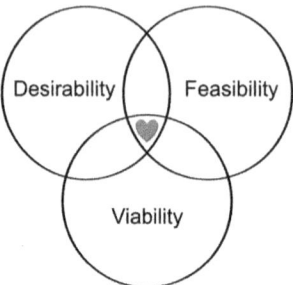

Figure 2-3. *Successful new ideas are found at the intersection of desirability, viability, and feasibility*

Quibi failed the desirability test.

If you are a regular observer of new, innovative ideas, I would bet you are not surprised by this. Innovative people tend to focus on their solution hypothesis first and foremost. Focusing there often puts them in the space where they are most comfortable, especially if they are technical practitioners. Thus, **they can unwittingly become feasibility-myopic – focused only on whether they *can* build something, not whether they *should*** – as appears to have happened in Quibi's case.

No One Is Immune

The reason I like to share the Quibi example is that it demonstrates that *anyone* can fall into this trap. Even people with an amazing track record of long-term success, like Whitman and Katzenberg, can build something nobody wants. Such maniacal solution focus can be tricky, subconscious, and insidious. (I will explain this further later in Chapter 4 when I introduce you to the "committed bet".)

Stories like this make many executives skittish about innovation, and reluctant to support innovation initiatives. Therefore, any approach we create must address it head on. But we cannot stop there. **Even *good* ideas can fail in established organizations.** Let's explore why.

Why Even Good Ideas Fail in Established Organizations

The Quibi story highlights the most likely reason *any* innovative idea is likely to fail, regardless of where it is brought to life. But it does not address other, equally important, questions such as **"Why do ideas fail in established organizations, even when they are desirable, feasible, and viable?"**, "Why do they fail there, when they should, and might otherwise, succeed?" "Why do they sometimes succeed, just not for the organization that conceived them?"

I have often seen an idea fail in one organization and later become a resounding success for a different, sometimes competing, organization. In some cases, the innovators, frustrated with an organization's innovation impediments, resigned and created new startups. Some of those are still active, vibrant companies. In other cases, I have seen frustrated, creative people leave one organization so they could bring their innovative idea to life for a different well-established organization. Adding insult to injury, those who brought the idea to life were not always those who conceived it.

Why does this happen? **Why do established organizations let ideas slip through their fingers, never to live up to their potential, or to be delivered elsewhere?**

"Project Sisyphus" and Beyond

In *Lean Entrepreneurship*, I shared the findings of a research project codenamed "Project Sisyphus." During that project I was mandated to determine whether new ideas generated in a large, well-established organization were consistently afforded sufficient opportunity to succeed. The terms of reference of the project included investigating:

1. Whether new business ideas had *any* chance of succeeding
2. Whether *all* new business ideas were consistently afforded the *same* probability of success
3. The root causes of the failure of any businesses that had not succeeded, and identification of any common root causes of failure across all failed ideas

During Project Sisyphus, we discovered two primary conditions that cause innovation failure in established organizations: (1) New ideas are managed like mature businesses. (2) There is no consistent approach to help new, innovative ideas succeed. Since *Lean Entrepreneurship's* publication, an element of Project Sisyphus' second category has increased sufficiently in frequency, impact, and nuance to justify its own category: Loss of executive or sponsor interest.

With that addition, **the top three reasons established organizations struggle to bring new, innovative ideas to fruition, *even* in cases where those ideas *should* have succeeded, are:**

- New ideas are managed like mature businesses.
- There is no consistent approach to help new, innovative ideas succeed.
- Loss of executive or sponsor interest.

It is essential that *all* of these potential pitfalls be considered and addressed. The remainder of this chapter explores each one in additional detail. Let's start with the first.

2. New Ideas Are Managed Like Mature Businesses

Project Sisyphus found innovation was failing in established organizations because they were falling into a classic management trap: managing everything the same way. Small teams were being crushed under the weight of heavy processes and procedures designed for large, mature businesses. Application of measurements used by their mature counterparts – and inappropriate or meaningless so early in their idea's life – was also resulting in unrealistic expectations and/or unfair or inaccurate assessment of their progress. In Chapter 1 of *Lean Entrepreneurship*, we presented 16 detailed root causes in this category:

- Fiction, frustration, fiction
- No pivots, please
- Unconscious bias toward current business models
- Value proposition conflict
- Overlapping business models
- Turf wars
- Intractable systems
- Organization structure constraints and silo-focused measures
- Heavyweight processes and process pageantry
- Solution focus meets builder mindset
- Emphasizing revenue too early
- Failure to consider the true cost of new businesses
- Resource constraints

- Skill deficiency
- Mature business budget pressure
- Intrapreneurial fear

I will not expand on every item listed here, since they have already been discussed in detail in *Lean Entrepreneurship*. I will, however, elaborate on a couple of these topics so you will have the context you will require to read and understand the remainder of this book, and to provide you with an adequate foundation for the creation your own approach to innovation or new idea incubation.

Heavyweight Processes and Process Pageantry

We discovered the most prevalent reason new, innovative ideas failed in established organizations was that processes, procedures, measures, and KPIs that were designed for large, mature, successful businesses – sometimes with tens or hundreds of millions of dollars in annual revenue – were being applied to small teams in the very early stages of new idea incubation. Those teams, sometimes composed of one or two people, were being crushed under the weight of those processes.

Incubating teams were expending an enormous amount of energy and effort toward process adherence. They were participating in meetings that were nothing more than process pageantry. They were filling out forms and completing checklists, many of which were irrelevant and unhelpful to the organization. All for the sake of feeding the process beast. In some cases, these creative people were putting *more* time toward satisfying a process's requirements than they were spending bringing their new idea to life.

The consequences were soul crushing, even for the people who, teeth gritted, managed to satisfy the process requirements. This process pageantry squandered an enormous amount of time and effort. None of it brought any value to the incubating teams or to the organization. What's worse, application of those heavy processes often necessitated after-hours work and extended work weeks of 60 or 70 hours or more, resulting in exhaustion and risk of reduced creativity.

Rise and Grind: The Hero Culture Myth

Some people can carry on a 70- or 90-hour work week for a short period. Fewer can do so for an extended period. Almost nobody can sustain it over the long term. Nobody should. What's worse?

Those extended hours don't matter. They don't make you *more* productive. They make you *less* productive.

You may be thinking, "that's obvious!" But, if you've ever been through periods of 70-, 80-, or 90-hour work weeks, you may remember how those increased hours crept up on you insidiously. You may recall that you were unaware that *you* were the metaphorical lobster being slowly boiled. In addition, I am confident you will recall how unbelievably exhausted it made you feel, especially after sustaining it for a few weeks. Though there is an upside, right? There are the accolades that often accompany the "Herculean" effort. The corporate hero worship.

It's all an illusion. Here's why.

Research has shown that "after fifty-five hours (of work in one seven-day work week), productivity drops so much that putting in any more hours would be pointless."[1] I remember how deflated I felt when I first encountered that research. One such study continues to conclude that, "those who work up to seventy hours per week are only getting the same

---

[1] "Stanford professor: Working this many hours a week is basically pointless. Here's how to get more done—by doing less", CNBC, March 20, 2019, Kabir Sehgal, Deepak Chopra www.cnbc.com/2019/03/20/stanford-study-longer-hours-doesnt-make-you-more-productive-heres-how-to-get-more-done-by-doing-less.html

amount of work done as those who put in the fifty-five hours." I've certainly hit that number more than a few times. My deflation turns toward anger when I think of it. But it's even worse.

A 2021 study by the World Health Organization concluded that "working 55 or more hours per week is associated with an estimated 35% higher risk of a stroke and a 17% higher risk of dying from ischemic heart disease, compared to working 35-40 hours a week." Furthermore, the adverse health impact of overworking is rising. According to the same study, "between 2000 and 2016, the number of deaths from heart disease due to working long hours increased by 42%, and from stroke by 19%." This prompted Maria Neira, director of the WHO's Department of Environment, Climate Change and Health to declare, "Working 55 hours or more per week is a serious health hazard."[2]

The lesson is clear. **If you buy into the hero culture mythology, especially for sustained periods, you're at best fooling yourself and at worst harming your health and well-being**, *and perhaps that of others.*

Forcing people testing new ideas, that have small levels of inherent risk, to use over-engineered processes designed for the risks of large, mature businesses or programs, wastes their time and effort, and can be hazardous to their health and well-being. It truly gives a chilling and more sinister new meaning to the phrase "death march," which is often used to describe this type of workload.

Consequently, developing an approach, framework, or initiative to help bring new ideas to life that *includes* those heavy processes is usually no better than telling people to just work the idea off the corner of their desk. We know that rarely works.

---

[2] "Long working hours increasing deaths from heart disease and stroke: WHO, ILO," World Health Organization, May 17, 2021 www.who.int/news/item/17-05-2021-long-working-hours-increasing-deaths-from-heart-disease-and-stroke-who-ilo

There are no reasons to adopt a hero culture approach, and countless reasons not to.

Friction

The downside seems obvious, yet over and over we encountered the misapplication of inappropriate, irrelevant, heavy, mature processes and procedures. The primary symptom of this is often the "seventy-page business case" that frequently greets would-be intrapreneurs. Their inaugural conversation often goes something like this:

"Hey! It's great that you have a new idea! At *Fictitious Corp* (or the *Department of Fictitious*) innovation is a core value." Thwack! "Here's our business case template. Bring it back here once you've filled it out. Oh! And don't leave anything out or we'll just reject it and return it to you without reading it."

The document they present, usually electronically, has sections for nearly every imaginable aspect of a business or program. Technological overviews, multi-year sales or adoption projections, multi-year cost projections, marketing plans, multi-year product or service release plans… At this early point in their nascent idea's life, the innovators may not even know what their final solution will be or how they will build it. Yet they are being asked to deliver detailed estimates on its cost, delivery, communications, and marketing over multiple years.

Often created for mature, well-staffed teams, the business case usually contains a combination of detail that no one intrapreneur would likely have the skills to complete. It requires an enormous amount of effort, and **it leads to the most common of reasons I have seen *even good* innovative ideas fail in established organizations. They never get started.** "Forget it!" to quote *Lean Entrepreneurship*.

Recipients of these templates become overwhelmed. The workload is huge, they don't have all the skills they need to complete everything, and it's not usually the kind of work that interests them. They would rather be creating something than filling out forms and templates. So, they metaphorically say, "forget it." They either stop pursuing the idea, work on it in their own time, or leave and take it with them. Or worse, they complete the business case. Why is that worse?

Great Works of Fiction

Some innovators *do* get past the sticker shock of the business case and decide to complete it. Since much of the data typically requested in these cases would be unavailable to *anyone*, they often fabricate it. They make it up!

That's not to suggest they all intend to intentionally mislead or outright lie. They simply make their best estimates for things they cannot be certain of, or for which they lack sufficient domain knowledge. They estimate things like how much of a solution people will buy over time and how much customers will pay, when they are not yet certain what they will actually build and whether anyone will ever want or use it. They estimate how long it will take to build their solution and what it will cost before they are even able to fully describe it in detail. And so on.

Realistically, it's complete fiction. That's why many of those business cases contain projections that look like Figure 2-4.

CHAPTER 2   WHY INNOVATION FAILS IN ESTABLISHED ORGANIZATIONS

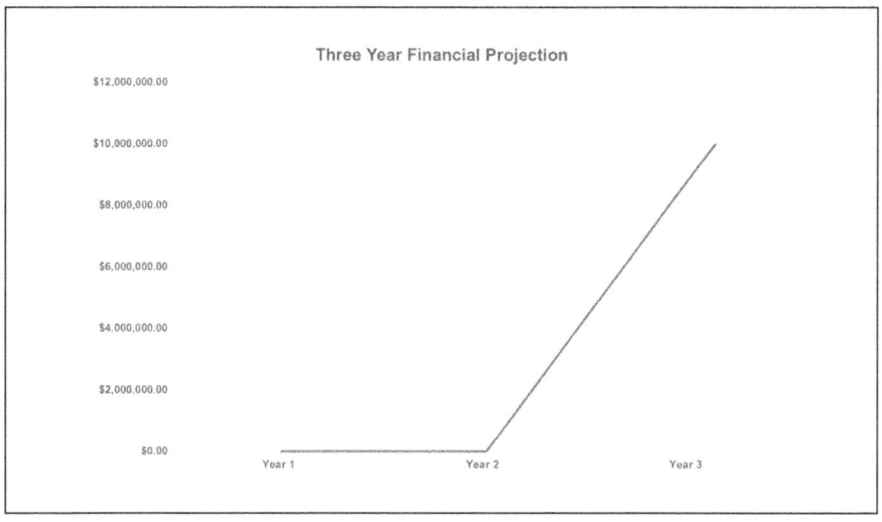

Figure 2-4. *Overly optimistic fictitious three-year financial projection*

"Year 1 revenue or benefit projection: $0. Year 2: $0. Year 3: $10,000,000!"

In my experience, this type of estimate often has less to do with a thoughtful financial analysis than it is the result of someone hearing an executive say something like "I'm not really interested in ideas that have revenue (or benefits) of less than $10,000,000."

The result is a business case that tells a great story. In reality, it is a work of fiction. What's worse is that these "projections" are often accepted by operations teams at face value. They are included with the organization's mature products and/or services projections, and often given equal weight.

If that happened with the projection shown in Figure 2-4, three years from the commencement of the new idea's incubation an executive would be responsible for $10,000,000 in additional benefits or revenue that may not – likely would not – exist. Unless it is one of the fortunate few miracle cases, that estimate has just become a serious problem for a senior executive who must then find a way to make up a $10,000,000 shortfall. Such a shortfall can have serious consequences in both public and private sector settings, and possibly legal implications.

We also discovered that **business case templates and accompanying processes were often optimized to support existing approval processes, as opposed to being optimized to drive value and positive outcomes for the innovative ideas and appropriately mitigate their risks.** Furthermore, those existing processes were often designed to simplify the lives of people who administered them, as opposed to being designed to increase the probability new ideas would be properly selected, nurtured, and brought to life.

To make things worse, teams whose ideas were selected were often forced to follow every aspect of their initial business case *exactly as it was originally submitted*. Even when a team discovered they were on the wrong path and a pivot was necessary, process administrators rejected any changes to the team's plans. The innovators were told things like, "You said you were going to take [these specific actions] on [these specific dates], and that's what you'll do. Otherwise we'll make your life very difficult. We may even pull your funding." So, the incubating teams relented and stayed on their original – known to be off-target – plans.

Maniacal subservience to a process can force a team to build the wrong thing – even when they know what the right thing is – or to build something that is not as good as what they could have otherwise built.

It's not always over-taxing a team that crushes a new idea. Ironically, new ideas can sometimes be crushed when they are given too many resources.

NoOp: How Over-Investment Killed a Startup

NoOp had the largest team of any of the incubating ideas in our accelerator, but it was making the least amount of progress. They were moving at a snail's pace, and it made no sense.

In hindsight, the reason was straightforward. NoOp had dozens of engineers developing a product before they had achieved customer-problem or problem-solution fit. The team had found a problem space that truly resonated with customers, but their *product* was not resonating.

The incubating team knew they were on the wrong path but continued to develop their product anyway. Since their solution had not yet developed traction, we had expected them to be extremely active with customer outreach, customer sensing, and customer-problem fit exploration. Yet none of those things were happening.

As a member of the accelerator's governing body, during two consecutive monthly updates I had asked in frustration, "If you don't know what to build, why are you still building it?" Eventually we learned the answer. **They had a large team of engineers building a solution that they knew nobody wanted because managing that large team was taking so much of their time they had no time for customer outreach, or anything else.**

Notwithstanding the enormous amount of waste, **imagine how demoralizing it was for the team's engineers to learn they had been spending their creativity and effort, likely sacrificing some of their personal life and time, building something that their leaders knew nobody would ever use.** Something that would be thrown away.

Many of us have been there. Learning you've been wasting your time and passion is horrible. Knowingly putting someone in that position is irresponsible. It became clear that over-optimization and over-funding could be just as damaging as over-burdening with process.

CHAPTER 2   WHY INNOVATION FAILS IN ESTABLISHED ORGANIZATIONS

The Bottom Line

In summary, Project Sisyphus found the primary reason innovation fails in established organizations is that new ideas are too often managed like mature businesses. For example:

- Processes are optimized for mature businesses and programs.
- Teams are given unrealistic traction, revenue, and/or benefit targets.
- New business cases are optimized for existing approval processes.
- New initiatives are funded and staffed like mature businesses.

We also learned that these heavy processes could have an impact outside the organization that uses them.

Fallout: How Heavy Internal Process Crushed an External Supplier

During their monthly update, one of our startups informed us that their marketing strategy was in jeopardy. They were distraught that a small, innovative marketing company – which was creating a pivotal campaign for them – had just called to end their business relationship. The marketing company's representative reported that we had as many people "red lining" their contract proposal as the marketing company had employees. They could not keep up, and they could not afford to have the incubating team as a customer.

Given we designed our initiative to prevent things like this from occurring to *our* startups, how could this happen?

Out of corporate habit **we had been applying the same processes and standards to this several hundred, or couple of thousand, dollar contract that we would apply to a multimillion dollar marketing contract**. It made no sense. **The risk mitigation was not commensurate with the actual amount of risk.** The administration work that resulted might have cost the marketing firm as much as the contract's entire value. It certainly would have consumed their margin.

This event opened our eyes. It was clear that we were not always conscious of the full impact of at least some of the pitfalls we had designed the initiative to address. Fortunately, this discovery presented us with both an opportunity to rectify our approach to working with the marketing company, and to set the stage and tone for working with other small suppliers and partners from that point forward.

Making adjustments like these, and being deliberate about breaking the habit of managing everything the same way, is a great start. But it's not enough. Which brings us to the next reason new ideas which should succeed, often fail in established organizations.

3. There Is No Consistent Approach to Help New, Innovative Ideas Succeed

Our Project Sisyphus research found that some intrapreneurs *were* able to overcome the obstacles summarized in the previous section. However, those that did were often thwarted by the second most common reason innovation fails in established organizations: There was no consistent approach to help new, innovative ideas succeed. I will further explain by introducing you to Stephanie, Dinesh, and Michael.

CHAPTER 2   WHY INNOVATION FAILS IN ESTABLISHED ORGANIZATIONS

Stephanie and Dinesh: A Story of Innovation Pageantry

Stephanie and Dinesh were elated. Their company had created a CEO-sponsored innovation fund. One million dollars had been allocated to the fund, with hope the amount would grow as the program gained momentum.

The fund's first activity was a competition to find the "most innovative" idea. The winner would be awarded tens of thousands of dollars of funding to help further explore their idea. Stephanie and Dinesh were amongst the many who submitted their ideas and competed in the run-off. In a pleasant surprise, *both* had been selected as winners.

The selection of Stephanie and Dinesh had an immediate, and enormously positive impact on the morale of the thousands of engineers and technical employees throughout the global organization. Until then, people in the organization's technical and field groups had been extremely frustrated that they had no avenue for their creativity. They didn't expect every idea they generated would be a winner, but they thought there should at least be an outlet for their ideas to be heard. This new competition appeared to be just that.

Both Stephanie and Dinesh were very well known and universally respected. They had each built and launched extremely successful industry-leading products. The competition had been perceived as fair, and it made sense to all participants that two of the best, most respected engineers would have generated winning ideas. The impact was so positive it is difficult to describe. Until...

Several months had passed, and neither Stephanie nor Dinesh had received their funding. They had not been given time to spend on their ideas. They had not been allotted resources. People had not been assigned to help them bring their ideas to life. There was no follow-up whatsoever.

"Forget it!"

CHAPTER 2   WHY INNOVATION FAILS IN ESTABLISHED ORGANIZATIONS

Following up and chasing the innovation competition team became too exhausting for Dinesh and Stephanie and, in the end, their ideas were never pursued. Not in any way. Worse, the technical employees felt they had been misled. People throughout the company had become excited about Dinesh and Stephanie's ideas and were interested in their progress. But word soon spread that nothing had been done.

It was an abject lesson in the consequences of performative innovation. The innovation award had been seen as a promise from the CEO, not only to Dinesh and Stephanie but to the entire technical community. Whether it was well-intended, as I believe it was, did not matter. The negative impact of this broken promise was orders of magnitude greater than the positive impact of the initiative's launch. The company had sent a clear message that the initiative had been mere innovation theater and, implicitly, that its leadership did not value the technical community's ideas.

This would have had a negative impact under any circumstances. The fact Stephanie and Dinesh were universally known, universally well respected, and universally liked made the impact much worse. Morale was low. People were angry. And much productivity was lost.

The company had found two good, perhaps great, ideas. But they did not know what to do with those ideas once they found them. They needed a consistent approach to objectively bring those new ideas to life.

Stephanie and Dinesh were not alone.

Michael: A Tale of Bad Timing and Inconsistency

Michael's team had developed a novel way to secure connected environments. In hindsight, their solution was many years ahead of the state of the industry. It was beginning to get traction with customers, but it had not yet generated a lot of revenue because it had only recently been released.

As often happens in established organizations, especially large ones, Michael's team was impacted by a company reorganization that placed them in a much larger business unit. As it happened, that business unit was predicting a budget shortfall for its already-established, mature business that amounted to a seven-digit dollar figure. Unfortunately for Michael's team, that shortfall happened to be nearly identical to their yearly expenses.

Predictably, Michael's team was shut down and their budget was allocated to the mature business. The decision was "easy" for them.

Should they have shut Michael's team down? It's always difficult to predict what a parallel future might have brought. Though the evolution of their market suggests it may not have been the best decision. Either way, I believe that the method used to make the decision – the amounts matched – was suboptimal and overly simplistic. The challenge was that the business unit had insufficient context within which to decide whether Michael's team should persist. They had no consistent approach to evaluating the merit of the new idea, and no way of insulating it from "easy" decisions like this one if it had merit.

Consistent, Deliberate Decisions

In each of these cases, the problem was not whether people were able to generate good ideas. All three of them had very good ideas. The challenge these teams, and those that managed them, faced was that **they did not know what to do with great ideas once they found them**.

It is critical that such decisions be made *deliberately*, and with data. Yet, there was no consistent approach to help ensure all new ideas were given the best chance to succeed, while also ensuring that unsound ideas were detected and shut down as early as possible.

Project Sisyphus discovered many detrimental characteristics of inconsistent approaches. For example, process and governance were often too heavy for new initiatives. Customers were involved too late in the incubation process – if at all! And the time required to get new ideas off the ground was not well understood, especially by senior executives and sponsors who spent a lot of their time focused on the short term, usually the current quarter. (More on that in the next section.)

There are many more reasons lack of a consistent approach to helping new and innovative ideas succeed can lead to failure. If you would like additional detail or background, Chapter 1 of *Lean Entrepreneurship* expands upon this discussion and explores several other root causes, including:

- Inconsistent idea triage
- Organizational myopia
- Failure to set realistic executive expectations
- Failure to focus on customers early
- Absence of deliberate customer selection and experimentation
- Customer myopia
- Tactical misalignment
- Mature business model gravity
- Failure to effectively capture or communicate the value proposition
- Failure to consider existing alternatives
- Insufficient attention to strategic control
- Failure to focus on a profit (or benefit) model early enough
- Absence of business model discipline

Project Sisyphus' characterization of the key impediments to innovation ended here. Though, as mentioned earlier, in the years since writing *Lean Entrepreneurship* I have discovered a rise in the frequency, nuance, and impact of another significant impediment – originally identified in Project Sisyphus as executive "attention span" – that justifies its promotion from an element of "Failure to set realistic executive expectations" to its own, and our final, major category: Loss of executive or sponsor interest.

4. Loss of Executive or Sponsor Interest

Interest in innovation initiatives, internal incubators and accelerators, and incubation frameworks has been growing in both the private and public sectors. People seem to be increasingly determined to identify and overcome their organizations' obstacles to organic innovation and incubation, and they appear to be willing to invest in a solution.

In *Lean Entrepreneurship*, we discussed how failure to set, and reset, executives' expectations can result in their loss of patience or interest, ultimately leading to a loss of sponsorship, funding reduction, or the complete shutdown of an innovation initiative. Since we published the book, this loss of interest has increasingly become one of the most common reasons I have seen initiatives stall or fail.

With so many things competing for their attention, it can be easy for an executive to lose interest in "smaller" things or "secondary priorities." Especially something new like an early stage innovation initiative that may not yet have delivered any tangible benefits, revenue, or returns. It is important to structure your initiative and change management activities to manage this risk.

The patience or attention span of executives, senior leaders, sponsors, or champions can wane for many reasons. Let's briefly explore the ones I most commonly encounter.

Cognitive Overload

Senior leaders have a lot of competing interests and crises to deal with. They must process a lot of, often complex, information every day. The higher their position, the greater their span of control, the more their brain will be taxed. Overburdened executives sometimes address this cognitive overload by shutting down small or low-priority initiatives, or handing them off to subordinates, some of whom may not be well-suited or equipped to sponsor an innovation or incubation initiative.

Quarterly Cadence

Processes, procedures, reporting regulations, and organizational cadence can cause an executive to develop a short-term focus, especially in the last month of a quarter. Most innovation or incubation initiatives have a significantly longer time horizon. This dissonance may result in conflict or loss of executive interest.

Short-Term Measurements and Incentives

Often measurements, KPIs, and incentives assess short-term results. Whenever we measure something, we cause the behavior of people subject to those measurements to change. Thus, short-term measurements can drive short-term focus. New, innovative ideas may require a longer view and different measures. (We'll discuss this in Part 3.) Use of the wrong measures can result in faulty decision-making, create conflict, and drive behavior that is incompatible with the successful incubation of new ideas.

Lack of a Common Vocabulary

I frequently encounter different people using the same words to describe something, but interpreting the words in dramatically different ways. I have found this to be a common occurrence for words like "innovation," and many other terms used in the context of bringing new ideas to life. I have even seen different people who define terms in the same way, but become misaligned in a nuanced way. That can be even worse.

Insufficient alignment of this nature can result in unrealistic and/or unachievable expectations, or cause an executive to perceive something as having failed when it did not. A senior executive is likely to quickly lose interest in an initiative that consistently fails to meet their expectations, and it won't matter that it's because of a semantic misalignment.

Insufficient Communication

As with any new initiative, especially one that is transformational in nature, communication with stakeholders, sponsors, partners, and beneficiaries – in their own language – is crucial. I'm sure it is obvious that senior leaders must have a clear understanding of the objectives, characteristics, and milestones of your initiative. What may be less obvious is that **you may need to regularly *remind* them of the conditions they agreed to**. For example, if your initiative is accepting nascent ideas your sponsors may need to be reminded several times not to expect revenue or benefit from them in the early months of incubation.

It is also possible to overwhelm your executives and sponsors with information, as discussed in the "Cognitive Overload" section. Establishing and setting expectations for a communication cadence early, and sensing, inspecting, and adapting it is critical to ensure executives and sponsors do not lose interest.

Inadequate Alignment on Time Requirements

The time required to bring new ideas to life is not universally well understood. Furthermore, the level of maturity ideas must reach before they can enter your initiative will dramatically impact the time it takes to advance each new idea to a specific state (e.g., a functioning MVP, a fully operational program, initial revenue). The more nascent the idea, the more time it will take to bring it to life. Other factors such as the nature of what you are creating (e.g., hardware vs. software) can also impact timelines, activities, and resource and expense requirements.

Executives who do not understand your initiative's parameters at the outset may come to believe that progress is taking too long, even when teams are exceeding reasonable expectations. In the worst cases, executives may develop unfavorable perceptions and beliefs about incubating teams or your initiative such as, "the team is slacking off," "the team is not serious," or "this approach is not working."

Budget Pressure

Senior leaders almost always want to accomplish more things than their available resources and funding can support. They are constantly reprioritizing and making choices regarding where to allocate their organization's finite resources. Adding pressure to that are the inevitable expense overruns, underestimates, and unforeseen events that jeopardize budget forecasts, margins, or public sector program scope and capabilities.

Such circumstances can thrust executives into, often complex, rebalancing and planning exercises that can lead them to lower the priority for an innovation initiative, placing it and/or some or all of its funding at risk. When funding for an innovation initiative is not segregated or protected from being allocated to other purposes it can become a tool of convenience, as was the case for Michael's team earlier in this chapter.

The risk of such funding reallocation is especially high when the innovation initiative is in its early stages and it may not have had an opportunity to gain sufficiently broad momentum and traction across the organization, and when it may not have had time to advance one or more ideas to the stage where its value is widely understood.

Reorganization

The Greek philosopher Heraclitus wrote, "Change is the only constant in life." That is especially the case in established organizations. Almost every organization changes eventually, and some change frequently. **This may be the greatest risk discussed in this section.**

If the value of your initiative is not broadly understood, if you have not sufficiently extracted and prepared its unique value proposition, and if you are not able to communicate it succinctly and in the language of your current and prospective sponsors, your initiative will likely be at very high risk of getting lost or shuttered in a reorganization. This risk is especially high in the initiative's early days, when it may not have had a chance to experience some early wins and demonstrate its value.

During a reorganization, leaders and executives are typically processing a mind-numbing amount of information and making scores of decisions every day. Therefore, it is easy for an innovation initiative, which is likely relatively small in comparison to everything else the leaders must deal with, to get lost.

Teams must be ready to explain the value and relevance of their initiative at a moment's notice. They must find a way to get on the reorganization team's radar early and stay there.

Innovation's "Messy" Nature

Innovation is messy. It can involve experiments that deliver counterintuitive results, pivots, low fidelity mock-ups, and restarts. Not every idea will survive, and some that do will look dramatically different than originally envisioned as they exit. These things are especially true for breakthrough or nascent ideas.

This rapid experimentation and iteration, and inspection and adaptation, is normal and should be expected when bringing new ideas to life. However, this can appear to an outsider as if things are disorganized, sloppy, chaotic, irresponsible, and unmanaged or ungoverned, placing the initiative – and possibly the initiative team's reputation – at risk. Teams building innovation and new idea incubation initiatives must ensure executives and sponsors understand innovation's messy nature from the outset.

Battle Fatigue

I have encountered many innovation initiatives throughout my career. The majority of them failed. Some left spectacular craters as they self-destructed. Thus, it is very rational for leaders and executives who may have seen such failures, or that have had their career damaged or set back by a failed innovation initiative, to be weary of new schemes with a similar moniker.

Some executives may see innovation initiatives as all risk and no reward. That can cause them to deprioritize those initiatives or quickly lose interest when things get challenging. Initiatives can be especially susceptible to battle fatigue risk during a reorganization.

Failed Committed Bets

In a committed bet, a large team is deployed very early in the life of an innovative idea, before the team knows whether anybody actually wants what they are building. (I will further explain committed bets in Chapter 4.) Committed bets often lead to expensive, visible failures. Just think of the case of Quibi discussed earlier in this chapter. They spent more than one billion dollars very publicly building something nobody wanted.

Most committed bets do not leave as impressive a crater as Quibi did. But they can visibly waste resources, and they often damage the reputations of anyone involved. Therefore, leaders who have witnessed, or fallen victim to, a failed committed bet may be reluctant to take on additional innovation initiatives.

Internal Competition

Many executives and aspiring leaders believe in the value of innovation. Some are passionate about it. Others like to foster a perception of themselves as being innovative because they believe it will help advance their career or position. As a result, when one leader in an organization launches an innovation initiative, others may decide to develop parallel or competing initiatives. This is not always bad. Healthy competition can raise performance standards and morale for everyone. However, unhealthy competition can lead to widespread failure.

Where healthy competition exists, resources and expertise can be pooled and leveraged to the benefit of all of groups, teams, departments, or business units. The competing initiatives can learn from one-another, and even work together. When unhealthy competition ensues, not only are opportunities for efficiencies, resource pooling, collaboration, and shared learning missed, teams often take deliberate steps to harm the progress of competing initiatives. It can get ugly. It can get personal. It can seriously damage morale, careers, or people's well-being.

Unhealthy competition of this nature often arises when people believe that the existence of the new program means they will no longer be permitted to innovate anywhere else. When they come to believe that innovation can *only* happen in the new program. That should never be the case. If it is, you need to inspect and adapt your program immediately.

Given the potential for a bad outcome, many leaders will lose interest in, or work to distance themselves from, initiatives subject to unhealthy competition.

A Failure Ecosystem

This chapter explored some of the most common causes of innovation failure in established organizations, and how they can be broadly categorized as follows:

1. People build things nobody wants.
2. New ideas are managed like mature businesses.
3. There is no consistent approach to help new, innovative ideas succeed.
4. Loss of executive or sponsor interest.

By now you may have realized that these root causes are frequently interrelated, and that often many of the previously discussed conditions are simultaneously present. Critically, any one of them might result in loss of sponsorship, funding, or executive champions on its own. Thus, it is important to keep them top of mind as you design, build, and operate your initiative.

So, just design an initiative with those in mind and you're in good shape, right? Not quite. There are many risks inherent to how the initiatives themselves are structured and deployed. Understanding those risks will help you to avoid missteps, delay, escalations, false starts, or worse, failure. The next chapter will help you understand these initiative-related risks.

CHAPTER 3

Why Innovation Programs and Initiatives Fail

Understanding why new and innovative *ideas* fail in established organizations is essential to the successful design and delivery of innovation and new idea incubation initiatives. But it's not enough. There are a multitude of potential risks related to the *initiatives* themselves. Failure to anticipate and mitigate those risks can lead to an initiative's rapid, and potentially spectacular, demise. In this chapter, I will share the initiative related risks I most commonly encounter (Figure 3-1), so that you can plan for, identify, and mitigate or eliminate them.

CHAPTER 3 WHY INNOVATION PROGRAMS AND INITIATIVES FAIL

> **In this Chapter**
>
> Why Innovation Initiatives Fail:
>
> 1. Underinvestment
> 2. Poor strategic choices
> 3. Use of innovation funnels
> 4. Bias
> 5. Misalignment
> 6. Unhealthy culture
> 7. Execution errors
> 8. Poor incubating team composition

Figure 3-1. What's in this chapter

1. Underinvestment

Innovation and new idea incubation initiatives are not free. Whether an organization is making a toolkit available, establishing a framework, approach, or guidelines, providing lean startup training, or creating an incubator or accelerator, these initiatives require some amount of time, effort, and resource. Sure, the amount of investment required varies greatly. Establishing a toolkit may only require a few software licenses and a minor slice of a person's time. Running a multi-business accelerator may require full-time staff, equipment, and maybe even a location. But there is *always* a cost.

This may seem ridiculously obvious, but I have lost count of the number of times I have witnessed initiatives fail – or come close – because of a failure to plan for their costs. What may surprise you is that initiatives like this can fail due to financial constraints even when they *are* included in an organization's budget. Let's look at two of the most common causes of this.

Initiative Funding Is Not Set Aside

Lack of bespoke, protected funding is one of the most common causes of innovation initiative failure I encounter. I have seen many cases where initiatives have stalled, delivered less than expected, lost momentum, and/or ultimately ceased to exist because funding was not set-aside for their exclusive use. As Michael's team discovered in Chapter 2, an innovation initiative or project can easily fall victim to unrelated near-term budget pressures if its funding is not protected. Frequently a target of convenience, innovation initiatives are often the first to lose pooled funding when an organization's leaders are searching for ways to address unrelated short-term needs, crises, or opportunities.

Ironically, an initiative's sponsors can become frustrated and/or confused when the initiative fails to meet their expectations as a result of their own repurposing of its funding. This can lead to circular discussions where the sponsor expresses frustration with the lack of progress, the initiative's team explains progress was dampened because funding was pulled, and sponsors state they are not inclined to fund things that aren't making progress. It does not always get to this point, but it is never pleasant.

The risk of funding reallocation is higher when other risk factors are present, such as a quarterly focus, short-term measurements, or many of the other risks discussed in Chapter 2.

Failure to acknowledge an initiative's costs and deliberately allocate funding for them can predetermine its failure. It is a near guarantee for underachievement and disappointment.

Failure to Budget for Success

One of innovation's dirty little secrets is that the more successful an idea is, the more it will cost. In addition, the funding required to advance an idea from one stage to the next stage (e.g., from problem-solution fit to a minimum viable product) will, at times, exceed linear growth. Let me explain.

Work early in an idea's life might primarily involve speaking with potential customers or beneficiaries to determine whether they actually *have* the problem the idea solves, or finding out whether those customers or beneficiaries would be willing to adopt a new solution and/or pay for one. Completion of that work might only require one or two people working for several weeks or a couple of months. Most established organizations would not consider that to be a large investment.

If the team's idea resonates, they will need to *build* the product or service. Building it may require engaging a development team of five to ten people, for example. That is a steep cost increase. Perhaps as much as 500% or more. In addition, the development phase may require new equipment or resources that necessitate additional spending. If the idea gets traction and is further pursued, cost increases will continue throughout its life.

Without budgeting for this reality, an incubating team might have just enough time to prove their idea resonates with potential customers before they run out of funding and are forced to stop working on it. In addition to the missed opportunity, that can have a massively demoralizing impact. The team is forced to abandon an idea they are passionate about, and that they have proven is worth pursuing. Disheartened and frustrated, one or more of a team's innovators will often leave the organization, sometimes to pursue their idea elsewhere.

Initiatives that fail to plan for the success of their new ideas may face budget pressures and be forced to slow the pace of their incubation efforts, or even shut one or more of them down. This can result in market and competitive risks, demoralization of personnel, loss of potential revenue, reduction in market relevance or position, or missed opportunity to better the lives of citizens through new program offerings.

2. Poor Strategic Choices

A colloquialism states, "if you don't know where you're going, any road will take you there." In this context, I strongly disagree. That road will take you *somewhere*. If you have unbelievably good luck, it may take you somewhere near where you want to go. But "we will rely upon good fortune" is never a good strategy. Be deliberate and intentional about your strategic choices.

Great strategies are about making *deliberate choices* about what something will, and will not, be. I have frequently seen poor strategic choices lead to suboptimal outcomes, or even the failure of new initiatives. But the greatest and most damaging strategic error I encounter most often is the failure to actually make strategic choices.

Not Having a Deliberate Strategy

To be successful, an innovation initiative requires a *deliberate* strategy. There must be alignment on things like what the initiative will be designed to create, and what things it will not create. There must be clear decisions regarding whether the incubator will deliver products, services, internal systems, and/or government programs. If they are to be products and services, the team must decide what kinds of products or services they will be. There must be a hypothesis regarding which part of the organization will become responsible for products, services, or programs that have successfully completed their incubation, and who will be responsible for their ongoing growth and operation.

Failure to develop a deliberate strategy will leave your team directionless and hamper your ability to make decisions and properly set expectations. Without an explicit strategy, potential participants, sponsors, champions, and executives will each assume it is whatever they would like it to be, and you will be held accountable for delivering all of their assumptions. As was discussed in the previous chapter, these mismatched expectations can lead to a quick, often spectacular, end to an initiative.

Building the Wrong Type of Initiative

Initiatives aimed at bringing different types of ideas to life require different design choices. For example, an initiative aimed at delivering commercial products will have different requirements than the one that targets delivery of government programs. While those differences can, at times, be minor or nuanced, they can also be critical to the initiative's success.

Making the wrong design choices – or making no deliberate choices at all – and building the wrong *type* of initiative can be disastrous. It can dampen the progress of incubating teams or, in worst cases, make it difficult – or impossible – for them to succeed. It can cause incubating teams to focus on the wrong activities and waste time. In the worst cases, the wrong type of initiative might cause incubating teams to deliver suboptimal or misaligned solutions, or build things nobody wants.

The bottom line is that the wrong type of initiative may not be able to deliver the right types of outcomes. Frustrated sponsors may decide to shut the initiative down if it is too far off track or does not quickly produce the desired outcomes. If you're lucky and teams *are* able to build the right solutions through the wrong type of initiative, doing so will likely result in increased delivery times, higher cost, waste, and stress.

Part-Time Innovation

New idea incubation takes time and effort. Yet organizations frequently expect employees to innovate during their "spare time." I have heard people describe their management's position as, "You can innovate any time you like after 6:00 PM and before 8:00 AM." Few people can innovate this way.

Commitment to a part-time approach is an unspoken proclamation that innovation will never be anyone's highest priority, and often drives innovators to unhealthy and unsustainable 70-, 80-, and 90-hour work weeks. The productivity declines and health risks that accompany such an extended work week (as introduced in the "Rise and Grind" section of Chapter 2) mean part-time innovation may not be the "productivity hack" some believe it to be.

A part-time innovation posture limits the potential pool of innovators, constrains the number of ideas available to an initiative, sends the message that employees' personal time is not valued, and demonstrates that a company's belief in innovation is performative. Worse, it sends a clear message that innovation is not *truly* valued by the organization and its leaders.

Casting Too Narrow a Net

Opening an initiative to the largest possible candidate pool will increase its chances of finding the best and most innovative, untapped ideas. So why would someone limit their candidate pool and reduce their chances of success? The most common reason I encounter is fear that the initiative's team will be overwhelmed by the number of ideas they receive, especially early on. That is a reasonable concern, but it can be addressed.

If you are worried you will become overwhelmed by the potential volume of ideas, you can start with a smaller pool, or focus and filter ideas to simplify the selection process as you shake down your initiative. For example, you might initially focus on a specific group of people, a specific technology, or a specific geographical region, and expand your candidate pool once you are comfortable your approach is working.

Limiting entry can lead to assumptions of unfair or unequal treatment of candidates. So, if you do decide to start small and expand, make sure to be transparent about how and why you are narrowing your focus, what criteria will determine whether and when the pool of potential participants will be expanded, and what circumstances might lead you to delay or cancel its expansion.

In addition to increasing the probability you will find great ideas, casting a wide net will also increase your opportunities to identify and recruit innovative employees, experts, mentors, governance team members, sponsors, and champions. The wider the net, the better.

Building the Initiative in Isolation

As we will discuss in additional detail later, an innovation or incubation initiative is often only one component of a broader ecosystem of related future-focused activities that may include things like scientific and applied research. When such an ecosystem exists, its components can support one-another (e.g., a research project can become the foundation for a new idea which is then brought to life in an incubator or accelerator).

Leveraging a broad ecosystem, while not strictly necessary, will enhance the value an innovation initiative delivers. Failure to consider such an ecosystem not only squanders potential synergies and opportunities, but it may also result in broader inefficiencies or unnecessary competition with other ecosystem participants.

3. Use of Innovation Funnels

It is highly likely you have already seen an "innovation funnel" like the ones in Figure 3-2, or are familiar with the term. These diagrams show how organizations that wish to innovate usually begin by generating a large number of ideas and filter those ideas through several stages until a small number are selected and developed. Most also depict how ultimately very few of those developed become successful in a production or market context.

CHAPTER 3   WHY INNOVATION PROGRAMS AND INITIATIVES FAIL

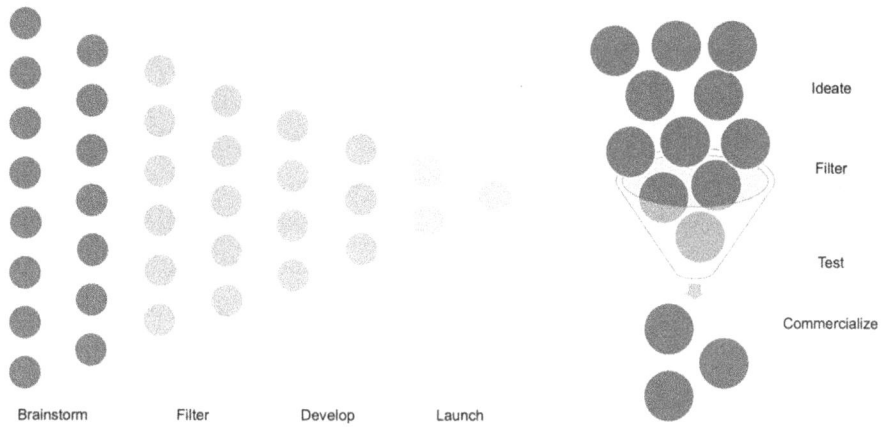

Figure 3-2. *Sample of simplified innovation funnel diagrams*

These representations of the innovation lifecycle are ubiquitous. As I was writing this, a Google search of the term "innovation funnel" returned approximately 28,200,000 results. Most of the innovation funnels I encounter place the stages of the funnel into very broad categories such as "Brainstorm => Filter => Develop => Launch" or "Ideate => Filter => Test => Commercialize." Some are more aspirational, beginning with core value terms like "Creativity," "Knowledge," and "Collaboration" as input to "Innovation" which delivers some sort of success.[1]

There is nothing wrong with these diagrams. Most of them *do* provide an accurate depiction of how innovative ideas flow through an organization. The challenge is that they usually represent a very high-level view. When creating an innovation initiative, we must look more deeply inside the funnel. The details matter.

---

[1] My characterizations of these funnels are meant to be archetypical and are not in reference to any specific funnel diagram. Any resemblance to existing funnel diagrams is purely coincidental.

Though these funnels can be accurate, the level of detail they present can over-simplify a person's understanding of the amount of effort required to bring a new idea to life. This can lead to misalignment and stakeholder misconceptions of the type of work which must be done and the amount of time required to do it.

Some of these innovation funnel diagrams can leave their reader with the impression that *all* ideas that pass the selection stages and move to development will be successful and deployed or sold at scale. **That is not usually the case**, especially if you plan to accept breakthrough or disruptive ideas. Your success rate may be higher if your initiative focuses only on very near-term innovation (e.g., 6–18 months). But innovation funnel diagrams can also create overly optimistic expectations in those cases.

Such a simple outlook can lead to very unpleasant surprises, and risky misunderstandings. Executives may expect a much higher rate of short-to-mid-term success than can reasonably be delivered, and any mismatch of expectations can put an initiative like this at risk. The "damage control" exercises that are often required can be enormously stressful and time-consuming. In the worst cases, diversion of resources and attention to damage control exercises can contribute to – or cause – an initiative's failure. Ironically, this type of misalignment often peaks in the mid-term time frame, just before an initiative is about to deliver results that will please its sponsors.

Focus Only on the "Left Side" of the Funnel

Most innovation funnels depict a flow from left to right or top to bottom. The beginning of this flow – shown as the leftmost or topmost item in the funnel (Figure 3-3) – is usually something related to ideation or some form of idea cultivation. **While capturing ideas is certainly a necessary first step in bringing them to life, it is *only* the first step.**

CHAPTER 3 WHY INNOVATION PROGRAMS AND INITIATIVES FAIL

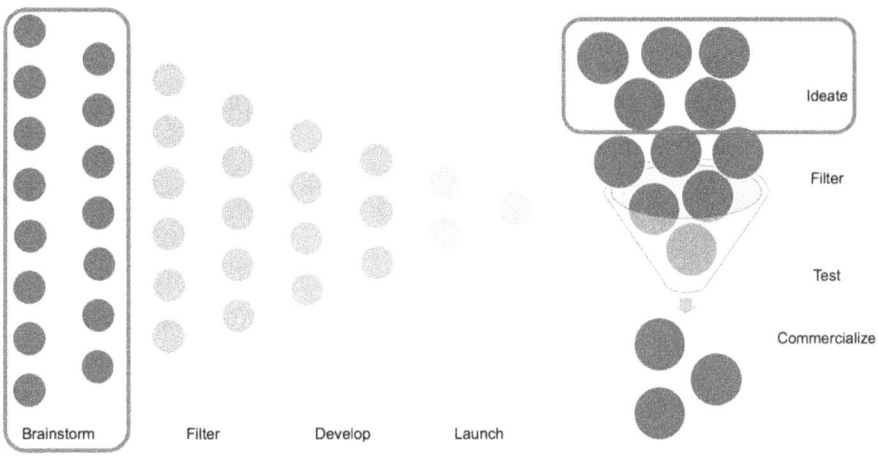

Figure 3-3. *Idea capture shown at the left or top of a simple innovation funnel*

Many innovation initiatives focus heavily, or solely, on ideation techniques such as brainstorming, gamestorming, serious play, and brainwriting. These techniques are great, but what happens *after* you find an idea worth pursuing? How do you ensure potential users, customers, or beneficiaries care about the problem it solves? How do you know they would adopt it? How do you make sure you are solving problems in a way that will make their lives better? How do you go about delivering your minimum viable product or service? How do you know when to shut something down?

Approaches that focus only on the "left side" of the funnel can generate great ideas, but they give no structure or support to the *execution* of the ideas. They produce exciting, promising ideas that never progress, even if they should. **Successful approaches to innovation must address the full spectrum of activities required to bring new ideas to life, which is often far more than innovation funnels convey**.

I do not want to leave you with the wrong impression. I very much like ideation and idea capture approaches and techniques. They are an obvious, and necessary, early step. Limiting your scope to these activities is fine *if* that has been a deliberate choice. It may even be a good place to begin building a broader initiative. But, if your initiative is designed solely for helping people with ideation and idea capture, make sure everyone knows that is where your assistance ends.

Funnel Fatigue

Some people just don't like innovation funnel diagrams, regardless of their level of detail or accuracy. They have seen innovation funnels before and have heard all their promises, but believe "They. Just. Don't. Work." It's not surprising. Innovation funnel diagrams have been around for decades, and many executives have developed "funnel fatigue." They just don't want to hear about them.

Executives who have previously sponsored an unsuccessful innovation program or initiative can be especially weary of funnels. In fact, one of the primary reasons we wanted to find a different way to graphically depict the accelerator we described in *Lean Entrepreneurship* was our belief that our own executives were suffering from funnel fatigue. (I will introduce to you that diagram in the next chapter.)

4. Bias

Bias – whether conscious or unconscious – can quicky destroy an initiative. Unfortunately, it often finds its way into the idea or team selection process. For example, I have seen people responsible for selecting ideas favor candidates in their own social circles. I have also seen adjudicators select ideas based upon their personal interest in a specific technology or domain, as opposed to prioritizing the interests of the organization or focusing on the initiative's mission and objectives.

While an initiative may fall victim to many forms of bias, I would like to highlight two damaging and potentially difficult-to-detect types I frequently encounter.

HiPPO-Centric Bias

HiPPO is a short form of the phrase "<u>h</u>ighest <u>p</u>aid <u>p</u>erson's <u>o</u>pinion" or "<u>h</u>ighest <u>p</u>aid <u>p</u>erson in the <u>o</u>ffice." In our context, it is usually the most senior person involved with an innovation initiative, or the most senior person present when a decision is made.

A HiPPO-centric bias occurs when the people building and running an initiative bend to the will of the HiPPO regardless of whether it conflicts with the initiative's strategy or priorities. HiPPO-centric bias can affect almost any aspect of an innovation initiative. Quite often – perhaps most often – it manifests itself when the HiPPO directs idea selection *solely* based upon their personal preferences.

Ironically, sometimes a team's *perception* of a HiPPO's biases can constrain an initiative even when the HiPPO is not present or has not shared their preferences. I have encountered situations where ideas were selected for incubation because the team selecting them simply *believed* a leader or senior executive had an interest in them, or in the domain to which the ideas belonged. The HiPPO had not said anything. They had not taken any action to influence the outcome. They had not even participated in the decision. Yet, the team made key decisions based upon what they *thought* the HiPPO would have preferred. What's more incredible is that in some cases, their assumptions were wrong. The HiPPO had no preference or bias.

Regardless of whether the bias is perceived or real, HiPPO-centric execution can lead to poor decisions, which can be devastating to an initiative.

CHAPTER 3   WHY INNOVATION PROGRAMS AND INITIATIVES FAIL

Cliquetocracies

In *The Innovative CIO*, I defined a "cliquetocracy" as a social construct which rewards people largely for whom they know, as opposed to solely for what they have accomplished. For example, you may have been part of an organization where a company's discretionary benefits and perks (e.g., conference participation, honors, prestigious titles, awards) were largely or exclusively given to employees who were friends or relatively close colleagues of those choosing the recipients. While that type of bias is often easy to detect, cliquetocracies possess an important nuance that makes them potentially more dangerous and much harder to recognize.

A cliquetocracy does not necessarily reward people *solely* based upon their personal relationships. I have seen cases where cliquetocracies had very high standards for reward recipients. In such cases, everyone who was presented with a reward was well qualified to receive it, and some were widely respected across the organization. Those conditions can make a cliquetocracy undetectable because there are no cases where the *only* rational explanation for a recipient being chosen is their connection to the cliquetocracy's members.

Cliquetocracies can make it difficult – or impossible – for people unknown to a clique to receive an organization's awards or honors (e.g., to have their idea selected for entry into an innovation initiative). They can be extremely difficult to detect because, though they are sometimes intentional, members of the clique are often unaware of its existence. The clique itself can be the result of an unconscious bias. Its existence could be a manifestation of what psychologists call the "familiarity principle of attraction" or "mere-exposure effect," describing people's tendency to prefer things they are familiar with or have been previously exposed to.

The presence of a cliquetocracy can severely, and undetectably, constrain your initiative. It creates a blind spot that can limit the initiative's potential by curtailing the diversity of its pool of ideas and participants and lowering the number of ideas that *truly* have a chance to be selected.

It will likely be difficult to detect the presence of a cliquetocracy, especially in the short-to-mid-term. Once discovered by employees who are not members of the clique, a cliquetocracy can be profoundly damaging to an initiative.

Perception of Bias

It is not enough that an initiative be fair, unbiased, and functioning "as advertised." Everyone in the organization must also *believe* **it is unbiased.** If not, those who feel like they are not in the "favored" cohort (e.g., not close enough to a perceived clique, not in a favored team, not in a favored location) may decide not to bring their ideas or talents to the initiative. Furthermore, they may consciously or subconsciously campaign against it and discourage others from participating in, or supporting, it.

Most people have seen at least one bad innovation initiative, so even the perception of bias can feed any preconceptions your initiative is just another case of innovation theater.

5. Misalignment

Most experienced executives have likely seen more than one unsuccessful innovation initiative. To those that have, mitigating the risk of a new one often means a bias toward shutting it down at the first sign of trouble. As a result, mismatched executive or sponsor expectations can be a fast path to the end of an initiative.

Sponsors, executives, and champions need to clearly understand things like the initiative's objectives, what it will produce, the outcomes that are expected, the time horizon during which to expect the outcomes, and how progress toward the initiative's outcomes will be tracked, measured, and reported. Sometimes those seeking executive sponsorship might be tempted to inflate those expectations while selling their vision. Don't! Setting unrealistic expectations will immediately jeopardize the initiative and damage your own credibility.

Failing to set expectations regarding when *updates* on the initiative's progress and current state will be delivered is also a pathway to peril. As we will discuss in a later chapter, there are a lot of parameters to consider. Not providing sufficiently frequent updates, or failing to deliver an expected update ("going dark"), will likely lead to a management escalation and, possibly, loss of confidence in the initiative, its leader, or its team.

Expectations must be clearly communicated, explicitly agreed upon, and periodically reinforced.

An initiative is potentially one meeting away from a crisis until it gains momentum. The more senior the executive, the more quickly they are likely to lose interest or to decide the initiative is not worth the risk or their time. If expectations are not clearly established, sponsors and executives will conceive their own and the initiative will be measured based upon those implicit and unspoken expectations. That almost always leads to a poor outcome or, at best, a crisis management exercise that takes time, resources, and focus away from helping bring new ideas to life.

Absence of a Common Vocabulary

As mentioned in Chapter 2, a common vocabulary is essential when launching innovation and incubation initiatives. Even people who work closely together can have vastly different understandings of things like what innovation is, what incubation is, what comprises a minimum viable product, and what is expected at each stage of bringing a new idea to life. Such differences can lead to inconsistent delivery across teams, confusion both inside and outside a group, misaligned expectations, delays, waste, and/or frustration. It can also lead to loss of confidence in an initiative's team, unnecessary tension, unhealthy internal competition, low morale, or withdrawal of sponsorship or funding. It is a path to misalignment, unmet expectations, and unnecessary risk and stress, and can be a key factor in the demise of an initiative.

6. Unhealthy Culture

As with any transformational activity, cultural norms and habits must be reflected in the design, development, and deployment of your initiative. This may mean adapting the initiative to some, probably most, of the organization's norms. But success may also necessitate your helping the organization to unlearn an unhealthy or unproductive habit. I commonly encounter two that require attention when present, so let's explore each briefly.

Performative Innovation Culture

You may have visited (or worked at) an organization where ubiquitous posters and signs declared, "We are an innovative company," "Innovation comes from everywhere," or simply, "Innovation." Sometimes those declarations are included in the organization's core values. In a performative innovation culture, there is nothing beyond those posters. No action is taken to turn the slogans into reality.

While posters and slogans may make people feel good initially, eventually everyone comes to understand they are empty promises. It's a betrayal. In the worst cases, employees might also learn that those who engage in innovative activities – those who try to bring new ideas to life – are putting their own jobs at risk. I have encountered many cases where a team tasked with bringing a new idea to life was shut down and its members were punished by being given difficult, unglamorous assignments that would not contribute to their career growth or advancement. We referred to that as "being sent to the doghouse."

People who were sent to the doghouse were lucky. They could eventually put their careers back on track if they accepted their hardship assignment and were successful. Others, not as fortunate, were laid off. In some cases, people widely known to be top performers were let go. Obviously, those conditions make would-be intrapreneurs think twice about whether they want to join an innovation project. Worse, top performers are often amongst the first to learn these assignments are best avoided.

While the term "performative innovation culture" may appear to be pejorative, that is not my intent. There are many cases where organizations genuinely intend to foster and nurture innovation and "become an innovative company," but unwittingly fall victim to the risks and influences discussed elsewhere in this book (and in *Lean Entrepreneurship*). Well intentioned, they are oftentimes unaware they have become performative because of the insidious nature of many of these potential pitfalls.

Unhealthy Internal Competition

In established organizations, there is usually more than one group, team, department, or business unit interested in becoming better innovators. Many see it as necessary for the sustained relevance – or survival – of their department or business unit, or the entire organization. Because of this, other teams may already be running initiatives of their own when you launch yours, or may be planning to start one. This can result in unhealthy competition or political posturing that can crush one or more of the initiatives.

Ironically, those different teams or initiatives may not be trying to solve the same problems, and the threat each perceives may not be real. In many cases, the work of the "competing" initiatives is actually complimentary, and an opportunity for collaboration and synergy is missed.

Taken to an extreme, the destructive behavior that results from unhealthy internal competition can lead to the demise of one or all of the active or planned initiatives. (Or lead to some of the "Unintended Consequences" discussed in Chapter 2 of *Lean Entrepreneurship*.) At best it creates the need for unnecessary damage control activities that drain resources and energy from each, and can delay or dampen their results and progress.

7. Execution Errors

Every transformational initiative has inherent execution risks. Innovation and new idea incubation initiatives are not immune. Fortunately, most of these are easily addressed. Here are a few you should be aware of before you begin.

Ambiguous Ownership and Accountability

Creating the conditions for repeatable innovation and incubation in an established organization usually requires cross-organizational support and collaboration. When that happens, responsibility for an initiative's success is often assigned to more than one person, or even more than one group. That rarely works.

When everyone is accountable, no one is accountable. In the absence of a single, accountable owner, incubation and innovation initiatives can languish, stall, and fail to deliver value.

It is not enough to simply assign one person as the initiative's owner. That person's success must be tied directly to the initiative's success (e.g., it must be part of their OKRs, PMAs, or MBOs). Furthermore, the initiative must be the owner's highest priority assignment. If it is not, key tasks might always be "next on their list," leading to missed deadlines and lost momentum. Not making the initiative a high priority item for its owner can also give others the impression that it is not *truly* valued by the organization, or that it is innovation theater.

Lack of Follow-Up

One of the fastest ways to have potential participants lose interest in your initiative is to fail to follow up, even on the smallest of commitments you made to them. I once witnessed an innovation competition where the winner was to receive $25,000 in funding to pursue their idea. There was a chance the idea would be further supported if it showed promise, though it was clearly communicated that there was no promise of funding beyond the initial prize. The sponsor got that part right.

Sadly, the competition's organizers failed to follow through with the funding. This resulted in a decrease in morale and a complete loss of interest in all innovation activities sponsored by that team. Employees concluded that, though the sponsors and their team *said* the right things about innovation (e.g., "innovation comes from everywhere," "we are an innovative company," "we value innovation"), it was just innovation pageantry. This single failure to follow up brought an end to all of the group's innovation programs.

Failure to Inspect and Adapt

It is extremely unlikely that anyone could design and deploy a perfect program, initiative, approach, or framework from day 1. They may get close, but nuances missed early on can be the difference between an OK initiative and an outstanding one. They can also be the difference between an initiative that experiences long-term success and one that ether fails or becomes irrelevant and fades into oblivion.

Even if your initiative *is* perfect on its first day, the world around it will change. The organization will evolve, objectives will change, citizen needs will change, and markets will change. New approaches, tools, and technologies will present new opportunities, and possibly render some older tools and approaches ineffectual.

Your initiative must be adaptable. Initiatives that do not include retrospectives, introspection, and adaptation at a reasonable cadence will eventually decrease in value and will be at risk of falling out of favor or becoming irrelevant.

Process Subservience

In Chapter 2, I discussed how heavy processes burden and application of the wrong types of process are among the most common reasons even good, innovative ideas fail in established organizations. What surprises me is how frequently even people who are aware of this pitfall deploy new initiatives that fall victim to it. In some cases, their new approach is more burdensome than the process it replaced.

Artifacts, checklists, tools, and other resources must be accelerators and force multipliers. They must help teams to focus on the most important activities and give their new ideas the best possible chance to succeed. They must make the team's progress easier and/or simpler.

Even when tools or processes are good, lack of clear instructions, failure to adequately communicate the intent of tools or resources, or simple misinterpretation of their purpose can overburden incubating teams. For example, I once worked with a team that mistakenly thought they were required to complete every artifact in a large flipbook which contained the initiative's entire toolkit. They used every tool and created every artifact available for every stage when one or two of the tools and artifacts would have been sufficient. They were miserable.

Three things happened as a result of that team's misinterpretation: (1) The team performed an enormous amount of non-value work which consumed valuable time that could have been spent advancing their idea; (2) it delayed their progress and delivery, creating sponsorship risk; and (3) **the team came to believe the incubator was just another process-heavy initiative, and that it was the same old approach with a new logo.**

Furthermore, the team's members shared their negative perceptions with people outside the team, placing the initiative's momentum at risk.

Fortunately, this misstep was caught in time. (Just in time.) Even so, correcting the perception of the team, and those with whom they had shared their frustration, required a substantial communication and interpersonal networking exercise.

Processes, tools, procedures, and artifacts should never be an incubating team's primary focus or objective. Their objective should be bringing a valuable new thing to life. If you find incubating teams are speaking more about the artifacts than about beneficiaries or customers and their problems, that should serve as a warning that your initiative might be drifting in a bad direction.

Inadequate Reorganization-Proofing

If you have ever worked in an established organization, you are likely no stranger to reorganizations. These can be frequent occurrences, and it seems the larger the organization, the more frequently they reorganize.

Initiatives that serve multiple departments or business units – often referred to as "Headquarters initiatives" or "common services" – are frequently shuttered during reorganizations. This often occurs because the people executing the reorganization are unaware of the initiative and/or its value. Initiatives without sufficiently broad traction or reputation are the most susceptible.

When initiatives are shuttered, the people designing, deploying, and/or maintaining them are either redeployed to teams with different missions and priorities or, worse, terminated. Once the people passionate about the initiative are no longer there to advocate for it, the initiative's resurrection is much less likely.

8. Poor Incubating Team Composition

It's probably obvious that incubating teams without an adequate skill set are much less likely to succeed. Even though members of incubating teams are often high performers, and each tends to wear many hats early on, no one person can do everything. (OK, there are some exceptional people who can, but those are extremely rare.) Ensuring teams are properly balanced is as important, perhaps more important, than any individual's skills. But you cannot stop there. Bringing the wrong type of person into an incubating team can lead to disaster. Incubating teams can even stumble when they have great people with great skills who bring bad habits. Let's further explore each of these potential risks.

Absence of Minimum Viable Teams

Achievement of any worthwhile objective requires a minimum set of skills. The initial size of an incubating team is usually very small (one to three people), so ensuring those skills are identified and acquired early on is especially important. Without a sufficiently well-rounded skill set, an incubating team will miss potential opportunities and suffer through potentially avoidable or easily solved problems. Worse, they will not likely be able to deliver to their idea's true potential.

In his 2012 SXSW session, Rei Inamoto introduced the concept of a "minimum viable team" (MVT) to describe the minimum skill set teams require in order to successfully bring new ideas to life.[2] The nimble team Inamoto described included three key personas:

---

[2] "Why Ad Agencies Should Act More Like Tech Startups," South by Southwest 2012, March 13, 2012, https://schedule.sxsw.com/2012/events/event_IAP10319

1. The Hipster
2. The Hacker
3. The Hustler

We explained in *Lean Entrepreneurship* that we intentionally moved away from the "Three H's" since some people found them offensive. Thus, **I prefer to describe MVTs as consisting of**:

1. **The Developer:** The builder of the product, service, or program's components

2. **The Designer:** The person, usually with user experience and design thinking skills, who can translate the customer and sponsor needs into a specification of what must be created

3. **The Dealmaker:** The person who deals with the "outside world," communicates, networks inside and outside their immediate organization, connects people, creates partnerships, and finds and manages customers or beneficiaries and the team's relationships to them

In addition to purging any potentially offensive terms, I believe the "Three D's" are more accurately descriptive. It should also be noted that the word "Developer" above does not necessarily refer to a software developer. In those cases, it might help you to think of the first "D" as a "Deliverer."

The terms you use are less important than the overall concept they convey. You can, and should, use terms that are compatible with your organization's culture and local norms, and that are easily understood and inoffensive.

CHAPTER 3   WHY INNOVATION PROGRAMS AND INITIATIVES FAIL

Public Sector Minimum Viable Teams

Since public sector MVTs frequently build solutions that cross major organizational boundaries, there is often the need for a fourth "D":

1. **The Developer:** The builder of the product, service, or program's components

2. **The Designer:** The person, usually with user experience and design thinking skills, who can translate the customer, beneficiary, and sponsor needs into a specification of what must be created

3. **The Dealmaker:** The person who deals with the "outside world," communicates, networks inside and outside their immediate organization, connects people, creates partnerships, and finds and manages customers or beneficiaries and the team's relationships to them

4. **The Decider:** A person with business or operations acumen, who normally works in an organization outside the incubating team, and is usually a member of the sponsor organization, who: knows the sponsoring organization's mission and mandate; understands the beneficiaries and their needs and mindset; understands the problem to be solved; and is passionate about the problem and the value a solution will bring to the beneficiaries

The Decider is frequently, perhaps most often, a part-time assignment. The Decider normally remains in their original department or business unit, where they can communicate and influence as an insider, and where they can remain aware of that group's state of mind and evolving needs and priorities. In cases where a separate Decider is not necessary, the Dealmaker usually performs the activities a Decider would otherwise perform.

Private Sector Deciders

There are also times where it may make sense to include a Decider in a private sector MVT, such as when the team is incubating an internal program or project, or is working on a new offering predestined for a specific business unit. Private sector Deciders may also be useful when business units or departments are seconding innovation activities to an internal incubator or accelerator.

MVTs Matter

MVTs are essential, but they are often incomplete. I have found that incubating teams almost always include someone in the Developer role early in their life, but are frequently missing one, or both, of the other D's. The impact of this can be fatal.

Without a Designer, a team is more likely to build something that nobody wants, or that people cannot or will not use. Without a Dealmaker, a team may lack the relationships necessary to gain interest and support in their solution, gain approval for deployment, maintain sponsorship, or may be incapable of communicating the solution's value and driving adoption. Of course, if there is no Developer, nothing will get built.

Placing People in the Wrong Roles

Some people are *extremely* comfortable with the ambiguity that is often present when an idea is nascent. They are happiest when presented with an empty whiteboard and a substantial problem. They like it when the stakes are high, and the outcome is unknown. For others, that level of uncertainty results in an enormous amount of stress that, ironically, stifles their creativity and may even negatively impact their health.

For the former, your incubation initiative is a dream job. For the latter, it is a nightmare, and potentially a reason to resign. Thus, care must be taken when choosing an incubating team's members, especially early on when the team may consist of one or two people. Bringing in a toxic or terrified team member, or placing someone in the wrong role, can be disastrous for your idea... and for the team's well-being.

Some people may never get to a point where they can become an effective contributor to a team working to solve an ambiguous and substantial problem. This does not mean an incubating team can never leverage the skills of someone who is risk-averse. It simply means you must take care to bring them in under the right conditions (e.g., onboard them later in the idea's life, ensure the team includes a risk-taker capable of coaching and mentoring their more risk-averse colleagues and making them more comfortable).

Importing Bad Habits

When people who have been working in established organizations for a long time move to an innovation initiative, they bring with them habits that were formed in their former roles. It makes sense. Those habits helped them to cope and succeed thus far, so why wouldn't they have the same positive impact on their new role. Some of those habits may be helpful. Others may be harmful.

 To help you to understand how bad habits can negatively impact your initiative, let me expand on an earlier example. You may recall that in our accelerator we had compiled a massive collection of tools and artifacts (the "flipbook") so teams could

select specific tools that might help them execute their current stage of incubation. You may also remember how one team completed every page in the flipbook in preparation for one of their initial monthly reviews.

When asked why they had done so, they informed us they had completed the dozens of artifacts because that is what would have been expected of them in the organization they came from. We learned they had been accustomed to preparing for rote quarterly business reviews where every page, form, and artifact of a long slide deck template, and every box in a large checklist, was to be completed. Our accelerator team referred to bad habits like these as "bad muscle memory," as most of the time people were not conscious of their existence.

You may recall that most of the material they prepared was completely irrelevant to the stage they were in. Much of it did not make any sense. Many artifacts were, as you might expect, complete works of fiction. Worse, preparing the material took an enormous amount of time away from doing work that would have helped bring their idea to life.

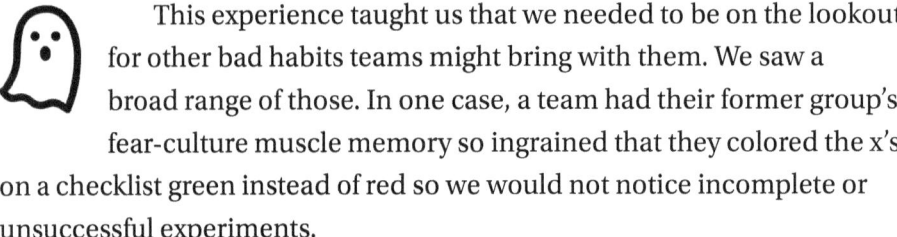

This experience taught us that we needed to be on the lookout for other bad habits teams might bring with them. We saw a broad range of those. In one case, a team had their former group's fear-culture muscle memory so ingrained that they colored the x's on a checklist green instead of red so we would not notice incomplete or unsuccessful experiments.

In the best cases, application of bad muscle memory creates waste in an innovation or incubation initiative. Often the consequences are much more dire.

Insufficient Training and Support

Finally, it is unlikely that all your initiative's participants will arrive with every skill they require. For example, you will likely find that many, or most, participants have little or no experience bringing new ideas to life. To ensure their success you may need to provide training and/or support to incubating teams in one or more essential areas such as:

- Basic skills training
  (e.g., solution domain expertise, agile development)
- New idea incubation fundamentals
  (e.g., falsifiable hypothesis creation, running experiments)
- Evaluating experimental outcomes and determining next steps
- Understanding when to experiment, when to optimize, when not to optimize, and when to pivot
- Recognizing when a team is building something nobody wants

Training requirements will vary depending upon the nature of your initiative and what is being built within. There will also be times when incubating teams need assistance or access to expertise to stay on track, such as:

- Help unblocking organizational impediments to progress
  (e.g., addressing unique procurement requirements)
- Leadership mentoring and coaching
- Team management guidance
- Specialized domain expertise
  (e.g., Legal, Human Resources, Procurement, Budgeting)

The scope and objectives of your initiative will determine the level and type of assistance that should be offered, but the first item on the list above is vital.

CHAPTER 3   WHY INNOVATION PROGRAMS AND INITIATIVES FAIL

Why Bother?

Thus far we have explored the most common reasons innovation fails in established organizations, and why initiatives aimed at addressing those impediments also fail. If you feel overwhelmed, don't despair! None of these challenges is insurmountable. Furthermore, you are unlikely to encounter every one of them, at least initially.

Understanding these challenges and pitfalls, and being able to identify them when you encounter them, will help you to deliver a more robust, more valuable innovation initiative. But that's enough time on the downside. The next chapter will introduce you to the lean entrepreneurship approach, and help you understand how it addresses those impediments and roadblocks so you can deliver a successful innovation approach, framework, initiative, incubator, or accelerator.

CHAPTER 4

Lean Entrepreneurship and Why It Matters

Don't Give Up!

After reading Chapters 2 and 3 you may be thinking, "Forget it! Innovating and incubating new ideas in established organizations is too hard. It's not worth it." Don't give up! Innovating in established organizations is incredibly rewarding. It can be a lot of fun, and it's definitely "worth it."

Understanding the potential pitfalls described in Chapters 2 and 3 will help you design a robust initiative that will prevent many of them from occurring, and that will counteract those that are unavoidable. It will also help you steer clear of avoidable hazards as you build your initiative. Avoiding those hazards – or knowing what to do when they occur – will result in the smoother, faster delivery of your initiative, and may even increase stakeholder and sponsor confidence in both the initiative and your ability to deliver it.

CHAPTER 4 LEAN ENTREPRENEURSHIP AND WHY IT MATTERS

Onward!

Now that you are familiar with the major reasons innovation fails in established organizations, and the hazards facing people building innovation initiatives, it is time to briefly introduce the lean entrepreneurship approach and how it addresses those challenges (Figure 4-1).

> **In this Chapter**
>
> 1. A brief introduction to lean entrepreneurship
> 2. Lean entrepreneurship principles
> 3. The benefits of a lean approach
> 4. Avoiding wasteful committed bets
> 5. Leveraging the lean advantage

Figure 4-1. *What's in this chapter*

In this chapter I will use the model originally introduced in *Lean Entrepreneurship* to illustrate the lean entrepreneurship approach. In Part 2 I will expand upon that model, discuss how it can be used in private and public sector settings, and explain the changes required to apply it to the delivery of different types of solutions (e.g., commercial products vs. government programs).

CHAPTER 4 LEAN ENTREPRENEURSHIP AND WHY IT MATTERS

1. A Brief Introduction to Lean Entrepreneurship

The lean entrepreneurship approach to innovation and new idea incubation combines an angel/venture capitalist (VC) style investment strategy with lean, agile, and lean startup operational principles to ensure teams minimize waste, concentrate on the activities that are most important at each stage in their new idea incubation, and focus on building things that people actually need and will use (Figure 4-2).

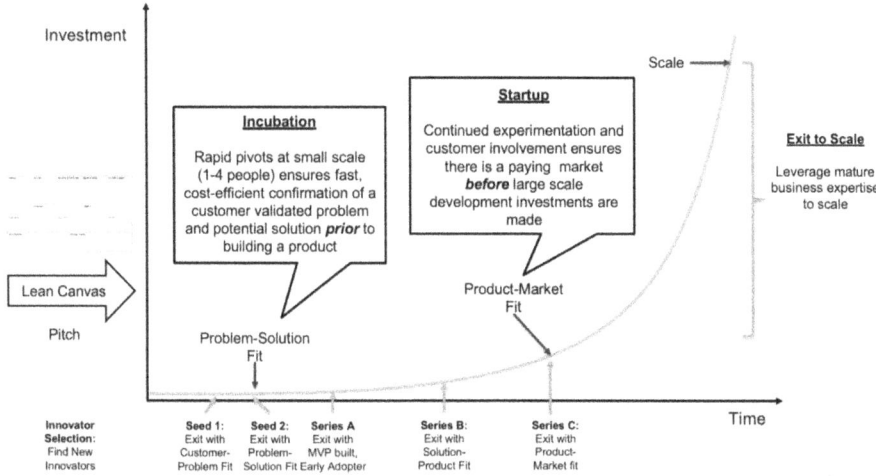

Figure 4-2. The original lean entrepreneurship approach

If you look at Figure 4-2 you will notice that the horizontal axis represents a timeline. The lean entrepreneurship approach begins at the far left of that time axis with a **maniacal customer or beneficiary focus,** even as teams first pitch their ideas. This maniacal focus continues throughout the entire life of the idea and persists until a solution exits as a product, program, or service, or is shut down. This **is the most pivotal principle of lean entrepreneurship.**

Lean entrepreneurship teams tend to be very small at the outset, normally ranging from one to three people. While some might state small team sizes are a characteristic of lean entrepreneurship, I prefer to think of the approach as having teams that are the *right* size for their current stage and objectives. Since a team's early activities usually include speaking with potential customers, beneficiaries, or users, confirming hypotheses, and getting themselves established and equipped, the right size at that early stage is usually one to three people.

Starting small dramatically reduces an organization's financial risk, minimizing the outlay required to perform early idea vetting. Limiting the number of participants early on also reduces the inherent personal risks of people who leave their established career paths to join an incubating team. Finally, sizing the teams based upon their current stage and activities helps avoid killing an idea by over-burdening its leadership, as happened to the NoOp team discussed in Chapter 2.

Lean Experiments

Once a team begins to bring their idea to life, their work consists of the rapid iteration of lean experiments. The nature of these lean experiments can vary broadly, from interviewing customers to researching or testing technology to building a minimum viable product (MVP), for example. In lean experiments, teams strive to learn as much as they possibly can about their current objective using the least possible amount of effort, time, and resources. The output of each experiment is then used as input to the next experiment, and the iterations continue. Each step builds upon the team's previous learning and advances them toward bringing their new idea to life (Figure 4-3).

CHAPTER 4 LEAN ENTREPRENEURSHIP AND WHY IT MATTERS

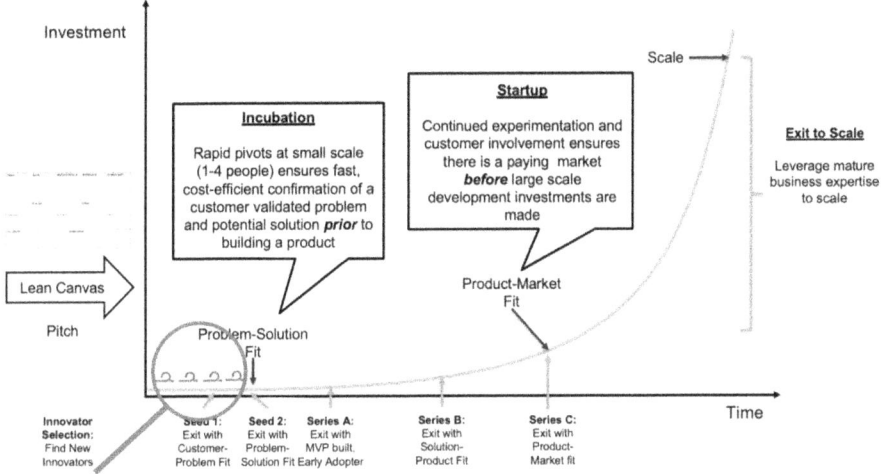

Figure 4-3. *Every stage of lean entrepreneurship consists of a series of rapidly iterated lean experiments designed to deliver the greatest amount of learning using the least possible amount of effort, time, and resource*

Pivot, Pause, or Persevere: The North Star

Through lean experiments, intrapreneurs and entrepreneurs determine the desirability, feasibility, and viability of their idea. To minimize waste and ensure they are building things people want, teams use what they learn from each round of experiments to decide whether they should "pivot," "pause," or "persevere."

When their experiments indicate they are on the right track, teams maintain their current course (persevere). If they discover they are slightly off course or are building the wrong thing, or if they find a better solution or way to deliver it, they adjust their solution and direction based upon their learning (pivot). When they determine they are building something nobody will want, nobody will use, or nobody will be compelled to switch from an existing alternative for, they stop (pause). This simple, but critical, decision framework is lean entrepreneurship's North Star, and is key to its success.

CHAPTER 4   LEAN ENTREPRENEURSHIP AND WHY IT MATTERS

Confirming Desirability, Feasibility, and Viability

Experiments to confirm a solution is desirable, feasible, and viable are executed in stages. In the seed stages, intrapreneurs focus their experiments on the desirability of their idea. Seed 1 experiments explore things such as whether anybody actually *has* the problem the team plans to create a solution for, and whether the problem is painful enough that people would switch from an existing alternative and/or pay for a solution (e.g., with cash, data, ad consumption). In the public sector, that "payment" usually takes the form of investment or funding, though sometimes it may involve an actual customer or beneficiary payment or user fee.

Seed 2 experiments are focused on whether customers or beneficiaries would likely *adopt* a proposed solution. (In *Lean Entrepreneurship*, we referred to Seed 2 as the "If you build it, will they come" stage.)

In the series stages, intrapreneurs focus their activities on feasibility and viability, while keeping an eye on desirability and maintaining a maniacal customer or beneficiary focus. Series A focuses primarily on feasibility, as teams build their minimum viable product. They are, essentially, answering the question "can this be built?" They also begin to measure the solution's traction, answering the question, "now we've built it, did they come?" Though intrapreneurs keep their eye on desirability, feasibility, and viability throughout the remainder of their journey, Series B and C focus more on ensuring the output of their efforts is a viable and sustainable solution to a confirmed, compelling problem.

Finally, a key tenet of lean entrepreneurship is that the level of investment in an idea must be commensurate with its traction. Investment is only increased when customers, beneficiaries, and/or adoption data prove doing so is warranted.

There are many important nuances to how a lean entrepreneurship initiative might be deployed. What I have covered thus far should provide sufficient context for now. In Chapter 7 I will dive more deeply into the details of a lean entrepreneurship approach and the options available to practitioners.

Words Matter

You may be wondering why I have been periodically emphasizing the importance of language. The following anecdote may help illustrate why language can matter a lot when building an approach to innovation.

I participated in an innovation panel during a conference at the University of Washington in late 2019. Following the session, someone from a major government organization approached me and said, "But we're the Government! We can't move fast and break things! Things have to keep working!" I was initially confused. During the panel, I had not used the phrase, "move fast and break things." But as they spoke, it became clear that the word "innovation" and the phrase "break things" were tightly linked in their mind. In response to their statement, I asked, "What if I asked you to learn fast and iterate? Could you do that?" Their answer, "Yes, of course, we could do that."

First and foremost, **lean entrepreneurship is not about *breaking* things. It is about *learning*.** The lean entrepreneurship approach is much better characterized by the slogan:

> **LEARN FAST AND ITERATE!**

Similar conversations with others helped me to realize that the seed and series stage names did not resonate with many people in the public service. In some cases, use of those terms alone might prevent a lean entrepreneurship approach from being considered. As a result, you'll see in Chapter 7 that I have included alternative, descriptive names for lean entrepreneurship's stages. (Thank you to the public servants who helped me develop them.)

Some people still prefer the seed and series stage names. If those resonate with you, and do not have any negative connotations or implications in your organization, you can, and should, use them. When we built the accelerator referenced in *Lean Entrepreneurship*, speaking to executives in *their* language was one crucial element of our success. Use of the seed and series labels resonated very well with our senior executive team, especially our C-level team (e.g., CEO, CTO, CMO, CRO) and our Board of Directors. It helped them to more rapidly understand what we were trying to achieve and our approach to mitigating risk.

2. Lean Entrepreneurship Principles

The lean entrepreneurship approach is guided by several key principles. These include:

- **Maniacal customer or beneficiary focus** from the time an idea is proposed and throughout its entire life, never losing sight of the objective of solving a real problem and making someone's life better as a result

- **Small, incremental investments** that increase commensurate with a solution's traction and *only* ramp up significantly when a team has evidence they are building something people actually want, can use, and will abandon their existing alternatives for

- **Lean experimentation and iteration**, delivering the greatest amount of learning by running the smallest possible experiments using the fewest possible resources

- **Learning fast and pivoting quickly**, using the learning from each experiment as input to subsequent experiments, building an overall body of knowledge, and making data-based decisions and adjustments to any and every aspect of an hypothesis

- **Lean evaluation and disciplined governance** that keep teams focused on building things people want and increase their probability of success while reducing cost and waste

Lean Governance Is *Not* an Oxymoron

People often look at me with confusion when I use the term "lean governance." I agree, it looks like an oxymoron. Fans of lean and agile methods might ask, "how can governance, which is frequently characterized by heavy oversight and process pageantry, be lean?" In contrast, people with governance experience who are responsible for managing risk might have the impression that "lean" means ungoverned, undisciplined, and risky. Nothing could be further from the truth.

The dirty little secret about lean governance is that it is usually more frequent, more robust, more responsible, and far more disciplined than traditional governance methods such as waterfall project management or quarterly business reviews. Lean governance's advantages arise from several key characteristics, including:

- **Absence of heavy governance pageantry:** There are no meetings for the sake of meetings, time is valued, and waste is removed from ceremonies, all of which drive efficiencies without compromising results.

- **Governance information that is a by-product of the work:** Whenever possible, information and artifacts required for governance is captured as a natural outcome of a team's work, without the need to perform work or create material that is *only* used for governance.

- **Focus on activities and measures that will advance the idea:** Wherever possible, governance activities help validate the idea, facilitate solution delivery, and help bring the idea to life.

- **Predictable cadence:** The presence of a rhythm of work, often referred to as a team's "heartbeat," removes ambiguity in expectations for all participants and drives an unspoken sense of accountability.

- **Transparent self-discipline:** Teams practice self-discipline and openly commit to next steps, experiments, and hypotheses, all of which they share transparently; providing visibility to others without disrupting their own work or flow, while eliminating the need for more frequent checkpoints and meetings.

The philosophy is simple, "no governance for the sake of governance."

It is not usually possible to capture *everything* needed for governance as a work by-product, but it might surprise you how much governance-only activity can be removed. Capturing information as a work by-product enables teams to provide governance-related updates at a frequency that is usually higher than traditional approaches (e.g., monthly vs. quarterly), but which requires less of their time to prepare (sometimes no time), less time to communicate (sometimes as little as 10 to 15 minutes for a routine monthly update), and does not disrupt their creative flow.

That **increased frequency** delivers what might be the greatest advantage of lean governance, and a lean approach overall. It **enables teams to inspect and adapt before problems become too large, or before they veer too far off course**. To explain that further I would like to share some experience from a different passion of mine, wilderness navigation.

CHAPTER 4 LEAN ENTREPRENEURSHIP AND WHY IT MATTERS

3. The Benefits of a Lean Approach

I am often asked, "so, why lean?" How is a lean approach better, and how can it help ensure people stay on the right path and avoid building things nobody wants? To explain, I find it helpful to leverage something that might be a bit more familiar to some of you, or at least a little more relatable.

Figure 4-4. *The author single pass portaging during a 12-day trek in Algonquin park*

I used to train people in wilderness navigation, and in the use of paper maps and magnetic compasses. (You're probably wondering whether I kept my meal plans on stone tablets.)

Personal GPS devices did exist, and I did use them. But I taught with a magnetic compass because a magnetic compass's battery never runs out. I used paper topographical maps because they also require no power source, and they can give a navigator a much better feel for terrain

93

prior to visiting a location than many displays. They let a navigator get "the big picture" ahead of time, and enable them to better visualize their upcoming journey and potential hazards.

"*Does One Degree Matter?*"

Participants in my training sessions would often be off by a degree or two when practicing taking compass bearings for the first time. When corrected, they would frequently ask, "does one degree of difference really matter?" or "what if you're only off by one degree?" This question brings to light one of the key advantages of a lean approach.

But first, what do *you* think? Does one degree matter? In the spirit of lean entrepreneurship, let's run an experiment.

Suppose you and a friend or colleague were standing at one end of a football or soccer field, at the center of one goal line, and facing the opposite goal. At that point you would be approximately 100 meters (approximately 109.36 yards) from the opposing goal. If you both walked 100 meters toward the opposite goal, but with a one degree variance in your bearing toward that goal (e.g., one person walks on a 270 degree bearing while the other takes a 271 degree bearing) you would be roughly 1.75 meters (approximately 5 feet 9 inches) apart when you completed your walk. Would that matter?

It might. Though it may not.

I am not avoiding the question. There simply is not enough data to answer it conclusively yet. For example, if you were simply walking to the end of a field it probably would not matter. Though if you arrived at a fork in a road or pathway, it might impact which path you chose. If you were navigating in a swamp, on a hillside, or in some other hazardous area, 1.75 meters might make a very important difference. But let's extend our experiment and make it a bit more realistic.

Small Errors Are Compounded Over Time and Become Large Errors

If you were to walk at approximately five kilometers per hour (just over three miles per hour) for 24 hours, you and your companion would become approximately 87 meters further apart each hour you walked. At the end of your journey, you would be roughly two kilometers (just under 1.3 miles) apart.

To further illustrate, someone navigating that same distance, headed northeast to visit Canada's Parliament buildings in Ottawa, in the Province of Ontario, who is just *one* degree off course, might end their journey at École Saint-Rédempter in the Province of Québec (Figure 4-5). They would find themselves in a different province with major geographic barriers, such as fast-moving rivers and rapids, between them and their intended destination. That same errant traveler in Washington, D.C. might end up in Arlington Cemetery when looking for the Lincoln Memorial, or behind the Smithsonian Air and Space Museum when looking for the White House.

CHAPTER 4   LEAN ENTREPRENEURSHIP AND WHY IT MATTERS

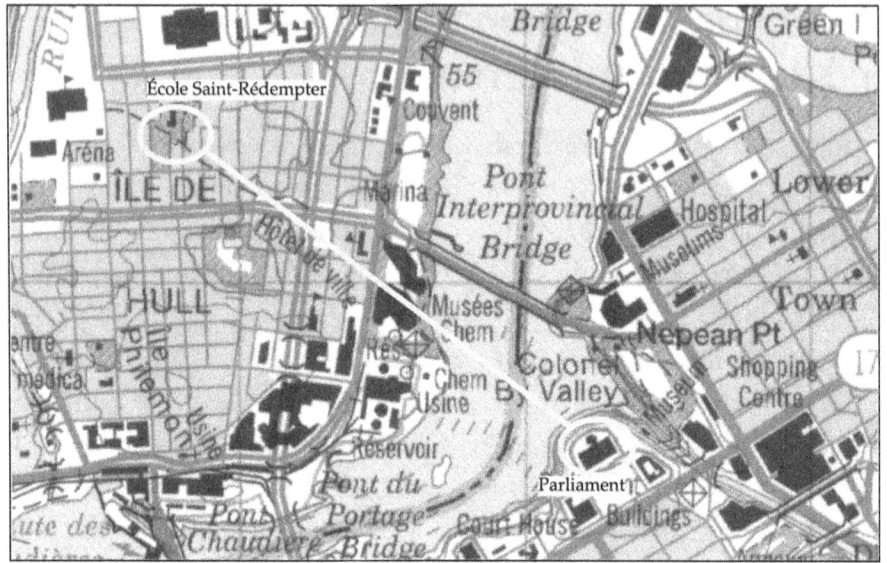

Figure 4-5. *When navigating, small errors are compounded over time and become large errors*[1]

As our example demonstrates, over time small errors can compound and become large errors. That compounding can bring added complexity and "wilderness navigation debt." For example, without the bridges which are present in Figure 4-5, our travelers might have to journey much further than their two kilometer deficit in order to reach their final destination. They might have to circumnavigate some of those obstacles or, in the worst case, even travel back to, or near to, their point of origin.

---

[1] Map Source: Government of Canada, Natural Resources Canada: https://natural-resources.canada.ca/science-and-data/science-and-research/earth-sciences/geography/topographic-information/10785

Given that example, and given that people regularly make mistakes, sometimes have faulty equipment or maps, or get tired… it begs the rhetorical questions "Why weren't all explorers or wilderness enthusiasts lost forever?" and "How did they ever find their way to their destinations?" This is where lean thinking comes in.

People often speak about lean approaches as if they are, at their heart, revolutionary. Like they are brand new, modern concepts. They are not. All great contemporary lean work is derivative.

As long as people have been deliberately navigating – for hundreds, perhaps thousands of years – they have been using lean thinking. Let me illustrate why I believe that to be true by answering the rhetorical question, "Why weren't wilderness navigators all lost forever?" The answer is that we *always* apply a lean strategy when navigating in the wilderness. Here's how.

Prior to our departure we answer specific questions such as:

Do I know and understand my objective?

Do I know where I am going and why I am going there?

Do I have a plan for the journey?

Have I plotted what I believe to be the best route?

Have I considered potential hazards along the way and how I will deal with them?

How will I know if what I am doing is taking me to my objective?

Have I taken note of the landmarks I expect to see?

Have I planned for circumnavigation of hazards, and how will I know I am back on course?

CHAPTER 4 LEAN ENTREPRENEURSHIP AND WHY IT MATTERS

While traveling, we **periodically** ask questions like:

Do I know where I am?

Which landmarks do I see now? Which have I passed? Can I see the objective?

Am I still progressing toward the objective?

Have I encountered the landmarks I expected to see, when I expected to see them?

Should we still be headed there?

Is the original objective still desirable? Do we still need to go there?

Is there a better objective?

Is there something preventing me from reaching the objective? (e.g., a forest fire)

Is a path to that objective still feasible?

Do I need to address a problem or a need before continuing to the objective? (e.g., Do I have adequate food and water?)

Do I need to divert from my current course to address that need or problem?

Is the original objective still viable?

Is it still there?

Are there hazards that would cause me to change my objective (pivot)? (e.g., Are there bears? Is it flooded? Is it on fire?)

These questions are asked by wilderness navigators, often subconsciously, from the beginning of their adventure until their journey is complete and everyone in their party has arrived safely at their destination.

Since the questions are asked periodically throughout the entire journey, the impact of any error is much less than it would otherwise be. For example, in our fictitious 24-hour journey, imagine if our navigator noticed they were on the wrong side of a landmark after the first 100 meters and course corrected. The impact of that initial error would be minimal (approximately two to three steps). Certainly much less than the effort required to adjust for it 24 hours later and two kilometers off course.

Bringing New Ideas to Life Through Lean Navigation

You may already see where this is going. The lean approach to bringing new, innovative ideas to life is, more or less, the same as our approach to wilderness navigation. Let's review how we bring new ideas to life using a similar structure.

Before we begin *building* something, we ask questions such as:

Do I know my objective?

What problem are we trying to solve? For whom?

Do I have a plan?

What is my hypothesis? How will I know if I have achieved it?

Which experiment(s) will I run (next)?

What action might I take based upon the result of the experiment(s)?

How will I know if what I am doing is taking me to the objective?

What outcomes do I expect from my experiments?

What are my objectives and key results?

How will I measure my progress or learning?

What action will I take if those measures are what I expect? What if they are higher? What if they are lower?

While we are validating our hypotheses and business models, and building our solution, we ask questions such as:

Do I know where I am now?

Have I successfully completed the experiments I planned?

What do my measures and key results tell me?

Am I still progressing toward the objective?

What are the results of my experiments?

Do the results confirm my hypotheses?

Am I on target with my objectives and key results?

Do I need to adjust any aspect of my business model or experimentation (pivot)?

Should we still be headed there?

Have our experiments confirmed that our objective is the right objective?

Have our customers or beneficiaries confirmed (e.g., through experiments, interviews…) that our solution would solve a painful problem and that they would adopt it?

Have we learned anything that suggests the current objective is not desirable, feasible, or viable, or that suggests there is a better solution?

The question, "should we still be headed there?" is extremely important. It can be easy to forget to ask it, both when navigating, and in the practice of lean innovation. Most of us do not like it when we are forced to acknowledge that we might be on the wrong path. Such an acknowledgement might mean the onset of a heavy workload to execute a pivot or, sadly, admitting that an idea is not desirable, viable, *and* feasible, and that it should not be pursued.

Lean Innovation Reduces Risk and Waste

A lean approach to bringing new ideas to life minimizes the impact of any error and ensures we stay on a path toward building something viable that people will actually use. Its inherent transparency and rapid iteration and adaptation also creates the conditions for a lean approach to governance that is less taxing for senior executives, and easier for them to understand. For risk-focused executives, the rapid iterations and lean experiments lessen the impact of any missteps and provide a transparent strategy for risk mitigation. Let's look at how that is different from traditional approaches.

4. Avoiding Wasteful Committed Bets

One of the best ways to appreciate the advantages of lean entrepreneurship is to contrast it with traditional approaches to new idea incubation. For example, consider a scenario where a new idea is conceived at an event where an organization's employees gather, such as a conference, large organizational meeting, or kick-off. Perhaps someone presents an idea

CHAPTER 4 LEAN ENTREPRENEURSHIP AND WHY IT MATTERS

to their colleagues during a brainstorming session, or while a group is enjoying a break. The idea gets traction with the group, and eventually someone says something like, "I have some surplus funding. I'll fund that."

What happens next? Someone builds a team to bring the idea to life. Sometimes that team rapidly becomes 20, 30, or even 40 people. Then they "go away" and start building.

On their own, they build for 12 or 18 months, sometimes up to 24 months. When they have finished building their solution everyone gets back together for a demonstration. Often a very awkward conversation follows. The three most common types of awkward response I encounter might be characterized as follows:

1. "That's not what we talked about."

2. "It's very nice, and it's well built. And if we had it a year ago (or nine months ago...) I think it would have been extremely useful. But its time has sort of come and gone. It's yesterday's solution."

3. "Well... It's an elegant technical solution, and the user experience is great. And if you *gave* it to me I would probably use it. But I just can't see spending money on it."

Any of these outcomes is tragic. All are avoidable.

In the first case, the team missed the target completely. This might seem impossible, but it is far more common than you may think. Countless times I have seen a group and their sponsors and stakeholders truly believe they were aligned when, sadly, they were using the same words to describe vastly different things. Since the team building the solution "went dark" and did not maintain a maniacal beneficiary or customer focus, they did not receive the feedback that would have enabled them to course correct early on and deliver something people wanted. They had no idea they were building the wrong thing.

It gets worse. Statements like the first one often come from more senior executives, so missing the target in this way can put careers in serious jeopardy. At the very least, it will normally result in a high level of unhealthy stress for all involved, and it is likely to damage the personal reputation of one or more of the solution's builders.

In the second case, by not maintaining customer focus and learning fast and iterating, the team did not keep up with changing needs and built something nobody really wanted. Solution-problem fit was not sufficiently confirmed, and they did not pivot their idea based upon evolving circumstances.

In the third scenario, the innovators built an elegant solution that the customer wanted, but it was not compelling enough to make them switch from an existing alternative. I have seen this happen a lot as well. In one case, a startup I was working with had built a very compelling solution in the DevOps space. Potential customers liked it a lot, and it was often *the customer* who requested a follow-up meeting after becoming aware of it. Great, right?! They created a solution that was being pulled. A salesperson's dream.

Something very interesting happened in their follow-up meetings with prospective customers. In almost every case, the customer indicated that they truly liked the solution and that it solved a nagging problem for them. But! It was always "second in priority," or "next on the customer's list." It was never the most important thing. The problem that the solution solved was costly. Customers had been forced to direct their most skilled people to address it with workarounds and home-grown solutions. But the startup was never able to compel the customer to switch from their existing alternatives and workarounds to the team's offering.

CHAPTER 4 LEAN ENTREPRENEURSHIP AND WHY IT MATTERS

So Much Waste!

Once people finally discover that a committed bet will not drive sufficient value, it is usually shut down (Figure 4-6), with nothing to show for the expense and effort directed toward it. The act of shutting down a committed bet can, itself, be costly. In *Lean Entrepreneurship*, we shared a "Committed Bet True Story" where the shutdown cost alone was US$2.7 million.

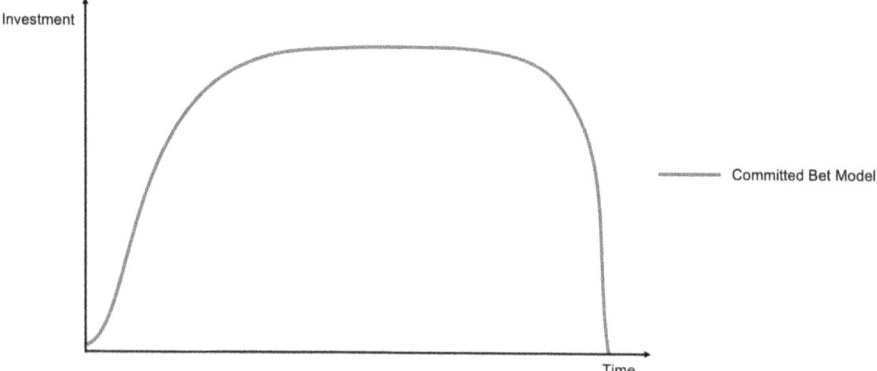

Figure 4-6. *The committed bet model of innovation*

Not all committed bets fail. Sometimes they can be given "innovation CPR" to set them on a path to delivering something that people will want (Figure 4-7). When that happens, delivery of the solution is often way behind schedule, and the team is over budget. The resulting pressure and time constraints can drive compromises that ultimately bring forth a solution that is much less compelling and delivers less value than it should have. This can make the solution more vulnerable to fast followers, who will not have the baggage and technical debt of a revived committed bet.

CHAPTER 4 LEAN ENTREPRENEURSHIP AND WHY IT MATTERS

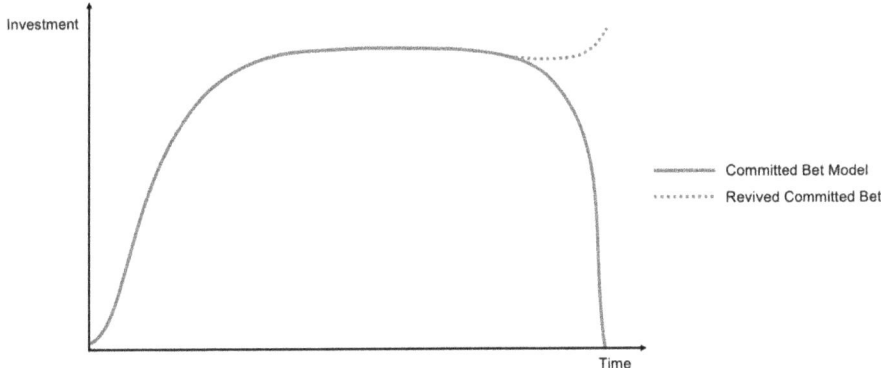

Figure 4-7. *Revived committed bet*

If you contrast the committed bet model with the lean entrepreneurship approach described earlier, lean entrepreneurship's benefits become obvious. Figure 4-8 illustrates the minimum amount of waste in any committed bet, even a revived one, versus a lean entrepreneurship approach.

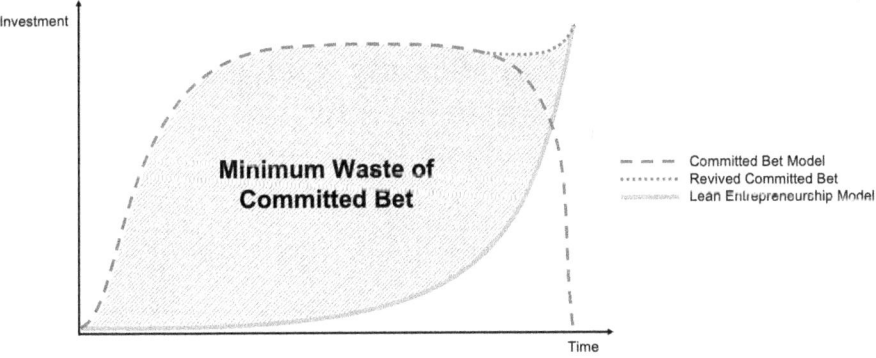

Figure 4-8. *The lean entrepreneurship approach versus the committed bet model*

105

It is worth repeating that in the many cases when a committed bet is shut down, *all* investment and time is wasted. Furthermore, revival of a committed bet most often results in extending the time required to deliver the solution, design and development compromises, addition of technical debt, and incurring additional expenses and resource requirements.

5. Leveraging the Lean Advantage

By now the impact of the lean advantage might be obvious. But there's more. A lean entrepreneurship approach can deliver significant waste reduction, even in cases where ideas are not viable and are shut down early (Figure 4-9).

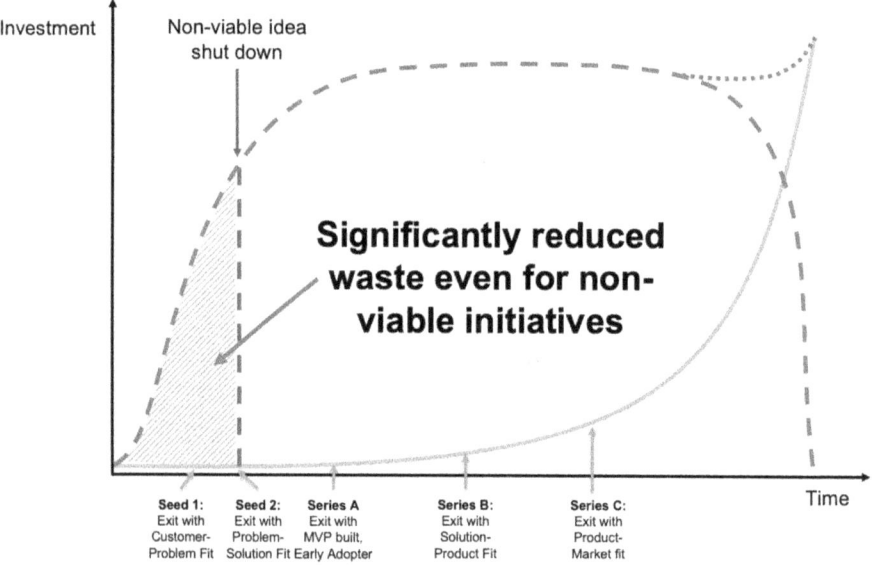

Figure 4-9. Lean entrepreneurship reduces waste, even when ideas are shut down early

CHAPTER 4 LEAN ENTREPRENEURSHIP AND WHY IT MATTERS

In many cases, the impact might be even greater than that illustrated in Figure 4-9. Due to their rapid, lean experiments and continuous adaptation, lean entrepreneurship practitioners are more likely to discover an idea is not viable in less time than those using other, more traditional approaches. When that happens, the savings might be even more compelling, as illustrated in Figure 4-10.

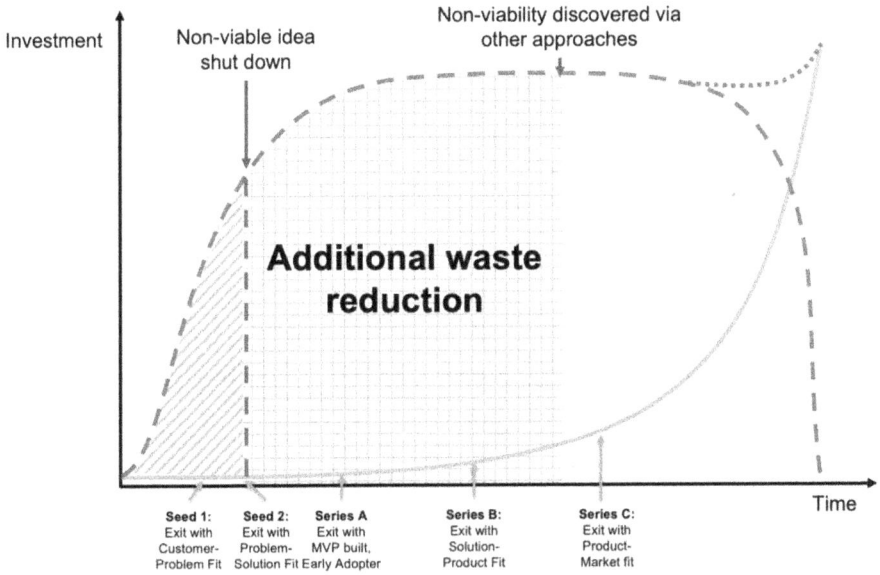

Figure 4-10. *A lean approach can lead to earlier discovery of non-desirable, non-feasible, or non-viable ideas, resulting in even greater waste reduction. (Illustrative)*

CHAPTER 4 LEAN ENTREPRENEURSHIP AND WHY IT MATTERS

Let's Get Started!

That's it! By now you should have a basic understanding of the key challenges to innovating in an established organization, and you should be familiar enough with the lean entrepreneurship approach to begin preparing for your initiative. In Part 2, I will describe how to begin your preparations, starting with one of the *most critical* steps, an assessment.[2]

---

[2] If you would like additional information regarding the topics covered thus far, or if you are interested in how and why the lean entrepreneurship approach was developed, the rationale behind it, or the journey that led to its creation, those topics are covered in much more depth in *Lean Entrepreneurship: Innovation in the Modern Enterprise*.

PART II

Preparation

CHAPTER 5

Assessing the Current State

Part 2 explored some of the key reasons established organizations fail to bring new and innovative ideas to life, why programs and initiatives created to address those pitfalls break down, and how a lean entrepreneurship approach addresses both. With that as a backdrop we can begin to discuss the steps required to design and develop your own initiative. The first of those is a lightweight assessment. In this chapter I will explain how to design a simple, lightweight assessment, and why it is valuable (Figure 5-1). The chapter that follows will provide guidance on conducting assessment interviews and capturing the learning they provide.

CHAPTER 5   ASSESSING THE CURRENT STATE

> **In this Chapter**
>
> Before you begin:
> 1. What is an assessment
> 2. Benefits of an assessment
>
> Performing the assessment:
> 3. Begin with goals
> 4. Design with a purpose (optional)
> 5. Leverage knowledge bases
> 6. Plan and estimate time requirements
> 7. Create an interview guide

Figure 5-1. What's in this chapter

You're *Almost* Ready

Since you have already had a preview of the lean entrepreneurship approach, you may be tempted to begin assembling a team, jumping ahead to the design step, and creating and deploying elements of your own initiative. There is nothing wrong with beginning preparations, setting preliminary objectives, and sketching a hypothesis for your approach at this point. However, embarking on a final design and beginning a "production" deployment armed only with generic information and untested hypotheses might spell a quick, and potentially painful, end to your initiative. Or worse, a long and painful end.

While most successful lean entrepreneurship initiatives are similar at a high level, each has its own nuances. Those nuances matter. A lot. Furthermore, additional information is required in order for you to correctly make several key decisions, such as the kind of initiative you should build (e.g., a toolkit, a framework, an incubator-accelerator), which of your organization's specific problems it will be designed to address, and which outcomes it will be expected to deliver. In addition, you need to be certain you understand sponsor, participant, and stakeholder needs and expectations. Your program must be aligned with and address those needs and expectations, *and* your sponsors and stakeholders must be aware it does.

It's Not Time-Intensive

In my experience, the best way to achieve the understanding and knowledge required to design a successful initiative of this nature is to perform a brief assessment. I am not referring to a lengthy one- or two-year, or even six-month study that might involve engaging a large consulting firm and spending hundreds of thousands of dollars or more. Those might provide deep insight, but **a brief, informal exercise that consists of two-to-three person-weeks of effort over a two-to-six-week period (likely four weeks) should be all you need** to gain the insight you require to begin building a successful initiative.

It is also worth noting that if you take *too* long to perform an assessment, the information you gather might be outdated by the time you put it to use. An organization's strategy, markets, and objectives will evolve. Its leadership may change. Team membership and composition may change. Some of the problems you discover may have been addressed by the time you act, and some may be worse. And new issues and challenges may have arisen. So, it is important to obtain a contemporaneous understanding of the current state, team members, obstacles, and opportunities at the outset.

CHAPTER 5　ASSESSING THE CURRENT STATE

Don't Skip This Step!

If you skip the assessment, at best you will likely find yourself wasting time and energy performing stressful damage control exercises and rebuilding all, or part, of your initiative once it is operational. At worst, your initiative may be shut down. I've seen that happen more than once because of things like misalignment with stakeholder needs or sponsor expectations, or even something as simple as a vocabulary mismatch. A brief assessment can help ensure your initiative is properly targeted, and alert the initiative's team of potential pitfalls and traps far enough in advance for them to be addressed proactively.

The payoff for an assessment will usually far outweigh the minor effort required to perform it.

1. What Is an Assessment?

If you consult a dictionary, you will likely find an assessment described somewhat like, "the evaluation or estimation of the nature, quality, or ability of someone or something." That's not a bad place to begin, and there may be more power in those words than may be initially obvious.

First, that definition mentions nature, quality, and ability. All three are important in our context. We need to understand the nature of the organization, how it accomplishes things, how it consumes information, how it communicates, and how initiatives and endeavors succeed within its boundaries. We need to understand the quality of current and past initiatives, and the skills and resources available to them. We need to understand the ability of the team driving the initiative to achieve it, the abilities and capabilities of any person or team who has attempted to drive similar initiatives in the past, the abilities of teams that have tried to bring new ideas to life in the past whether they were part of a similar initiative or not, and whether or not those past ideas succeeded. That is just the beginning. So, an assessment must take a broad view within a specific context.

As the previous paragraph might suggest, an assessment should create a good understanding of both the past and the current state. That understanding will help us to see into the future somewhat. It will enable us to determine what we are capable of now, and what objectives we might achieve with our current team and resources. It will help identify gaps that might exist, and what skills or resources might be required to fill those gaps.

That leaves two key words in the definition: evaluation, and estimation. You likely expected the former. The words "assessment" and "evaluation" might be synonymous to some. However, the word "estimation" is critically important. There will likely be cases where some of the information you receive will be incomplete or estimated at its source. That is OK. We need to accept that we may not discover every detail and nuance. We do not require perfect information. It may not exist and, if it does, the time, effort, and cost required to obtain it will likely far outweigh its value. So, with all of this in mind, let's expand upon that definition to remove ambiguity as we use the term in our context.

In our context, **a lean entrepreneurship assessment includes**:

- A 360-degree evaluation and estimation of the nature, quality, and ability of:
    - An organization's current and desired states related to bringing new ideas to life
    - The organization's related strengths, weaknesses, opportunities, and barriers (threats)
    - The alignment of key stakeholders, sponsors, and participants
    - An organization's readiness for adoption of the initiative

- The establishment of relationships, and a knowledge base that will help refine, develop, and achieve an initiative's objectives

- Development of initial messaging and communication that will help confirm and refine early hypotheses

- Development of an understanding of related or competing initiatives and opportunities for synergy

Now that we have a shared understanding of *what* this type of an assessment is, let's look at why we would bother to spend time performing one.

2. Benefits of an Assessment

You may be thinking, "But I know what kind of initiative I want to build, why waste time on an assessment?" Think of it this way. If you were bringing a new business idea or public sector program to life using a lean entrepreneurship or lean startup approach, you would begin by confirming whether you understand the problem and whether it is sufficiently painful that people would adopt a new solution to solve it. That is, you would achieve customer-problem fit or beneficiary-problem fit. Your initiative is in the same state at this point, and it possesses similar inherent risks. So, use the same type of approach to bring this new initiative to life as you would coach others to use when bringing their new program or business ideas to life.

Not all of the benefits of performing an assessment may be obvious. **Performing a brief assessment before you begin your final design and deployment efforts:**

- Exposes themes and priorities that will help focus your initiative

- Highlights changes in the landscape
- Prioritizes learning
- Drives vocabulary alignment necessary for transformation
- Identifies issues and opportunities
- Surfaces "pockets of excellence" which can improve the probability of success, increase speed, and drive early wins
- Discovers stories which drive more powerful communication and messaging
- Exposes bias in prior work and prior attempts
- Brings critical nuances to light
- Begins to prepare people for change (including you)
- Makes participants less likely to work at cross-purposes
- Helps participants become invested in the initiative's outcomes

While some of these benefits might be obvious or self-explanatory, some may not. I will expand briefly upon each to avoid ambiguity. Each explanation is written independently of the others so you can skip those you understand.

The remainder of this section expands briefly on each of the above-listed benefits. You can read those that interest you or skip ahead to the "Trust is essential" section.

An assessment exposes themes and priorities: Having discussions with a sufficiently diverse group will surface commonalities in challenges and needs. It will help you understand how those challenges are distributed, and which have the broadest impact. Understanding this will help you design your approach and to set priorities for its delivery.

An assessment highlights changes in the landscape: You may have based your initial design hypothesis on discussions or studies that were conducted months, or even years, ago. Leadership, teams, skills, markets, economic conditions, strengths, and weaknesses may have changed since that information was gathered. That is not to suggest older information will be useless. We leveraged information that was compiled a couple of years prior our project's commencement when building the Accelerator referenced in *Lean Entrepreneurship*. But we benefitted greatly from confirming which conditions still existed, and which had evolved or changed substantially.

An assessment prioritizes learning: The information discovered during an assessment will move you beyond hunches and hypotheses and deliver facts. It will provide data to confirm or refute hypotheses and theories and uncover new insights to help refine ideas or even shape new approaches. It will also help the team creating and deploying the initiative to develop a learning mindset.

Continuous learning and improvement are necessary for the delivery of a maximally effective initiative that drives long-lasting impact. A learning mindset will also be critical for teams who leverage your initiative to bring their new ideas to life. Establishing good learning habits early should accelerate your progress.

An assessment drives vocabulary alignment: Each organization has its own vocabulary. In larger organizations, individual teams, departments, or business units sometimes have their own unique way of using words. Using the proper words in their proper context can accelerate your initiative. Using the wrong ones can create friction, or – in the worst cases – even cause an initiative to be paused, reset, or shut down. (You might recall the anecdote from Chapter 4 where a member of a large government agency interpreted the word "innovation" as "break things.")

> There can also be important differences in the use of words across the private and public sectors. For example, I worked with one large private sector organization that used the word "program" to describe any internally facing initiative that had broad organizational impact. I later used that word with a large public sector team and it created conflict, tension, and confusion.

I learned they defined a program as a large, externally facing, executive and politically approved, and broadly deployed formal offering (e.g., unemployment insurance, government pension). So, when I used the term "innovation program" it was interpreted as a full, high budget, externally deployed, politically sensitive government offering, *not* an internal initiative that was focused on a specific team, as was intended.

> While there *can* be commonalities across groups (e.g., within and across the public sector, within and across the private sector), do not *assume* those commonalities exist. For example, I worked with one public sector team that referred to the people who consumed their services as "customers" or "clients." Other groups in the same government organization used terms like "beneficiaries" and, for them, use of terms like "customers" were off-putting. Even in simple cases like this, using the wrong terms can create tension or friction, or position you as an "outsider."

You'll often learn the idiosyncratic uses and trigger phrases by using them "incorrectly." Don't be embarrassed when that happens. You won't be the first, and people will understand and appreciate that you are making an effort to learn about their organization. Learning the vocabulary early is the key. Understanding the organization's vocabulary will help you better design your initiative's artifacts, communicate more effectively, and avoid negative triggers and traps.

CHAPTER 5   ASSESSING THE CURRENT STATE

An assessment identifies issues and opportunities: Discovery of issues, challenges, and opportunities – or issues and challenges that are also opportunities – is likely the most obvious of the benefits of performing an assessment. To address a problem, we must first understand it. If we believe we understand it, we need to confirm it exists.

This might also be the aspect of an assessment that is most fraught with peril. Unconscious bias can cause someone to unwittingly focus their assessment efforts on *confirming* their own existing beliefs and hypotheses, as opposed to learning with an open mind, listening, and following the facts wherever they may lead. If you are not surprised by something during your assessment, if you are not learning anything new, especially early on, you should take that as a sign of potential confirmation bias.

An assessment will surface "pockets of excellence": In every organization I have worked with, there have been groups and/or individuals who have faced some, or all, of the challenges the organization is attempting to overcome. In some cases, those people may have been able to overcome those challenges. In others, they may know what needs to be done, but are held back by conditions such those discussed in Chapters 2 and 3. In my experience, these people become fast allies. They "know what good looks like." They are often very passionate about bringing new ideas to life and have a very strong desire to make an initiative of this nature successful.

These people are a gift to your initiative. You can quickly leverage their experience to understand what may have worked for them, what did not, and any minefields or trap doors they encountered. They have likely thought of techniques, issues, and opportunities you may not have considered. People like this are often willing to help in some way, and they make great advisors, champions, and/or contributors.

Finding one or two people of this nature will, alone, make your assessment worthwhile. But they won't always be on your initial list of interviewees. I find people with this type of experience are often referred, informally, during assessment interviews with others. It's one of the reasons I always ask interview participants whether there is anyone else they believe I should speak with.

An assessment will discover stories: Every story is a gift. Throughout your assessment you will learn stories of past successes and failures, and current and future challenges and opportunities. More powerful than simple facts, stories deliver knowledge with context, detail, and emotion. They provide a springboard for discussion and empathizing. They drive understanding viscerally and communicate the value of action, the need for it, or the downside of its absence. They provide order that drives insight. Often captivating and entertaining, stories bring people together and can create bonds between them.

The stories you learn as you conduct your assessment will help you to better understand the organizational environment, the people, their roles and personalities, the opportunities you might leverage, and the challenges you will likely face. They will help you identify past errors and minefields you might encounter. They can also be leveraged to help communicate your initiative's vision and value.

An assessment can expose bias in prior work: During your assessment you should review any initiatives and research previously completed by the organization. Depending upon the organization's size and culture, you may find one or more of a wide variety of formats, ranging from formal memos, to email, to presentations, to white papers. I encounter a broad range of material, some of which was created as a formal assignment, and some of which was produced informally by passionate individuals or groups. It is all extremely useful. You might also find material regarding currently active systems to be of use during your preparation, even if the systems are unpopular or ineffective. But beware!

Often you will encounter information that was written with a political bias. That is, it may have been prepared in a very specific way in order to be acceptable in a specific organizational context, for consumption by a specific person or executive with a known or perceived bias, or to tell someone what they wanted to hear. Such information can be useful as long as that context is provided, and any bias is understood. An assessment can make you aware that such bias exists, and dramatically improve your interpretation of such material.

An assessment brings nuances to light: Even similar organizations, in similar sectors or lines of businesses, have differences. Large differences typically pose less of a threat to an initiative of this nature because they are easily detectable. Small, nuanced differences can be imperceptible from outside a group, and can matter a lot. Sometimes something as simple as using the wrong word with a specific group or stakeholder can result in misaligned expectations, friction, delay, or even the demise of an initiative.

A small nuance in a group's needs, opportunities, or strengths, can require small but critical adjustments to the approaches, toolsets, or even nomenclature required for an initiative's success. Learning about an organization's important nuances early can increase an initiative's delivery speed and reduce friction and risk. If you thought, "we have that problem" as you read one or more of the challenges enumerated in Part 1, it is important that you confirm those issues still exist, and understand the nuances of how they are manifested in your organization.

An assessment will begin to prepare people for change (including you): The commencement of your assessment will begin to signal to people that change may be, or is, coming. Many, perhaps most, people are initially uncomfortable with change; and even those who embrace change would prefer not to be surprised by its arrival.

An assessment provides an opportunity to begin building the relationships necessary for an initiative's success. You will be able to ease participants into the change and, through their own contributions, they will begin to embrace it. Perhaps most importantly, participants will begin to see their ideas and concerns reflected in the initiative's design and communications as you incorporate their input. They will see themselves as part of the change.

During the assessment you will also begin to develop and refine the initiative's sense of urgency, and recruit participants, visionaries, and champions. Selling your idea to participants should *not* be the primary goal of your assessment, but it does provide you with an opportunity to begin to introduce them to the potential landscape of your solution. It also enables you to learn participants' potential concerns.

The assessment will allow participants to "ease into" the change in a safe space. In this low-pressure, one-to-one format, they will be able to voice potential concerns and objectives they may otherwise keep to themselves. You may not always have time to address those concerns during the assessment interview. That's better than OK. It will give you a reason to engage with them later.

An assessment will make participants less likely to work at cross-purposes: I once worked with a group who developed and sold systems that managed very large, complex, real-time environments. Given the high-stakes nature of their customers' environments, their potential customers almost always insisted on some sort of trial or pilot before they would agree to purchase those systems. This group learned there was value in charging prospects for every pilot (i.e., pre-purchase, on-premises trial). The reason may surprise you.

Quite often, their potential customer would assign someone with a "Protector" personality type to lead the pilot. In *The Innovative CIO*,[1] I explained how "Protectors" believe it is their mission to protect the organization from all things that might bring harm to it. To accomplish this, those protectors would direct all their intellect, effort, and energy to attempting to *break* the things they were testing. Their goal was to see whether they could cause the pilot to fail.

---

[1] Andy Mann, George Watt, and Peter Matthews, 2013. *The Innovative CIO: How IT Leaders Can Drive Business Transformation*, New York, NY, Apress Media, *Chapter 2: Stories from the Trenches*

Intentionally breaking things is easy. Ironically, success is almost always guaranteed. As such, a protector can almost always find a way to make virtually anything fail; even if they sometimes do so via an edge case that could never happen in a real-world context. A protector's focus on failure added a lot of friction, frustration, and cost to a sale.

Eventually, the sales team learned that by charging a nominal fee – something that would not require lengthy approval – they changed the potential customer's mindset from looking for ways to make the solution fail, to looking for ways to make it succeed. The difference was jaw-dropping. It dramatically increased the probability customers would purchase their solution. It also reduced customer acquisition costs even though each paid pilot cost the organization more than the potential customer was charged.

An assessment helps participants become invested in the initiative's outcomes: Participants you interview will be actively helping create your initiative. They will see their input reflected in the design, communication, and deployment of it. The information you capture during the assessment will provide you with an opportunity to demonstrate you were truly listening by including topics and keywords participants will recognize as theirs in the material that describes the initiative. This will help them to become vested in its success.

Trust Is Essential

A successful assessment is built upon a foundation of trust. If you're not sincere about the simple things, you won't earn the trust required for discussion of high-stakes issues with absolute candor. But, if you come to the assessment with the success of your participants as your true objective, conduct yourself transparently, and demonstrate you are a good custodian of the participants' trust, you will be amazed at what people will share with you. Every one of those golden nuggets will dramatically increase your probability of delivering a successful, high-value, high-impact initiative.

In many cases, the assessment will be the first opportunity for the assessor, who is often the leader of the team which will deliver the initiative, to meet the stakeholders and vice versa. Your first impression will be lasting. Thus, sincerity and trustworthiness are table-stakes for anyone planning to perform an assessment. If you are not genuinely interested in the people, and their challenges and opportunities, this is probably not the right assignment for you. You might find yourself unhappy and disinterested, and your participants will sense that immediately.

Assessments Deliver

The preceding list shared some of the benefits I experience when performing an initial assessment, but it's not exhaustive. Assessments always bring positive surprises to me in the form of learning. They always result in a better initiative and, perhaps more importantly, better relationships with team members, stakeholders, and potential participants. They always drive better alignment, enriched by empathy. And they demonstrate that the person performing the assessment genuinely cares about the people who will be affected by the initiative, their challenges, and their outcomes.

Hopefully it is clear that there is much more benefit from performing a simple assessment than might be initially obvious. There is almost no better way to learn the landscape quickly. I urge you to get out of the context of your immediate team, and the potential unconscious bias that may be present, and begin your initiative by conducting some type of assessment. As X-Box co-founder and former CA Technologies CTO, Otto Berkes used to urge our Accelerator team, "Get out of (your) echo chamber!" How can you do that? Let's go through it step-by-step.

3. Begin with Goals

Suggesting that you begin preparing your assessment by setting objectives might strike you as beyond obvious, but it is important enough to warrant a mention. You should consider two types of goals at the outset.

First, **you should have objectives for your initiative**. At this stage, you should **think of those as hypotheses for its objectives**. After all, the point of your assessment is to learn, to confirm, or refute your current hypotheses regarding challenges and objectives, and to discover things you did not know or had not considered which might lead to new or updated objectives and hypotheses.

Second, **you should have goals for the assessment**. Since the assessment is a near-term activity, its goals will likely be much simpler and more tangible. But that does not make them any less important. Before you begin your research activities or designing your interviews, you need to ask yourself what you hope to learn from them.

As you design and conduct your interviews – and build your initiative – you should, as Silicon Valley technology forecaster and Stanford University Adjunct Professor Paul Saffo has suggested, have "strong opinions, weakly held." That is, you must question your own beliefs mercilessly and try to prove them to be incorrect. Let this be a guiding principle as you design, prepare, and complete your assessment.

Though the goals you set may be somewhat different each time you perform an assessment, there are several that will almost always be relevant. The following goals can be used as food for thought as you develop and refine your own:

- Identify the key challenges, issues, and impediments to bringing new ideas to life

- Identify and/or confirm the problem(s) to be solved

- Identify themes and commonalities and their significance and impact

- Identify and understand priorities at all levels
- Identify potential detractors and champions
- Learn about any current and past initiatives, and whether and why they were successful or unsuccessful
- Understand the outcomes participants and stakeholders hope to achieve
- Understand the value the participants expect
- Identify the "what's in it for me" (the "win") for each stakeholder or participant group
- Understand the time frames within which each participant or stakeholder expects to achieve their desired outcomes
- Confirm the type of initiative that will most likely address the problem at hand (e.g., toolkit, framework, approach, incubator...)
- Confirm the type(s) of new ideas that will be brought to life via your initiative (e.g., breakthrough, adjacent, projects, programs...)
- Identify any potential obstacles or friction to the delivery of the initiative
- Identify any potential accelerators
- Begin change management activities
- Gather data and evidence that will help with the transformation (change) activities
- Gather material that will support a stronger case for the initiative

- Test and refine early messaging
- Introduce yourself to influencers, stakeholders, and participants
- Establish new relationships and build trust

During the assessment, some sponsors, stakeholders, or participants may seek your guidance regarding the outcomes or value they should expect from the initiative, or request help with goal recommendations. To prepare for those discussions, you must compose an initial set of objectives for the initiative. Doing so will help you drive productive conversations and enable you to provide the guidance they may seek. But keep in mind that the goals you develop for the initiative are, at this point, hypotheses; and be careful not to over-influence other people's thinking.

You may have noticed that some of the goals above are related directly to soliciting information (e.g., identify key challenges), and others are more directed toward organizational transformation (e.g., establish relationships and build trust). The latter may not lead directly to questions in your assessment interviews, but they are equally important.

The assessment will be your first contact with many of the people with whom, or for whom, you will be building the initiative. As such, **the assessment is as much an opportunity to begin building relationships and trust as it is an information-gathering exercise**. It is also important to be mindful of the fact that you will be representing your primary contact and their team as you conduct the assessment. They will be risking some of their reputation by bringing you to the participants. This will likely be your first chance to visibly demonstrate that trust is well-founded.

Leverage Your Primary Contact's Knowledge

As you prepare, your primary contact will likely be able to provide you with guidance regarding the likes, dislikes, norms, and interests of each, and all, participants; and they can help you to be aware of sensitive or incendiary topics. This will help you to respect those norms and be adequately prepared for any "hot" topics you decide to explore. Your contact will also be aware of organizational, group, and team norms. This knowledge will be invaluable as you prepare, set goals, and conduct the assessment.

Even if you were part of the organization prior to the outset of this endeavor, your primary contact may have valuable insight that can help you better understand the assessment's participants, speak their language, and not embarrass yourself or those you represent. The last item is critically important. Take note of organizational norms and "dos and don'ts." As the saying goes, "you never get a second chance to make a first impression."

Don't Feel Overwhelmed

This might feel like a mammoth task. It should not be. You should not have to spend an enormous amount of time on the goals. And don't waste time creating a formal presentation on them. (If you are an external consultant, you may not be able to avoid that.) Writing them down, while not strictly necessary, usually helps. However, this step should be more about having conversations with your primary contact and/or stakeholder and building the proper mindset for the preparation of the assessment. The real learning begins during your secondary research and assessment interviews. Let's look at those next.

4. Design with a Purpose (Optional)

Now that you have some basic goals in mind, you should be ready to design your assessment. If you feel you are not, or would like to confirm that you can communicate the goals of your assessment succinctly, you might want to consider writing a purpose statement.

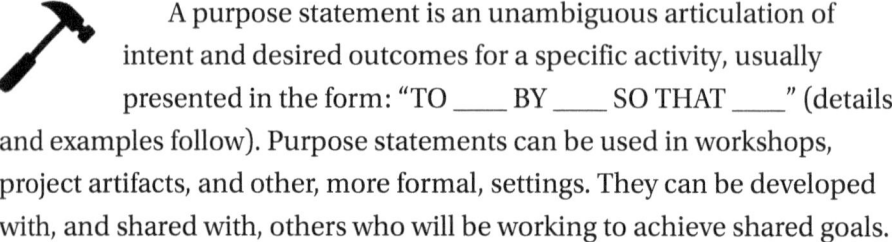

A purpose statement is an unambiguous articulation of intent and desired outcomes for a specific activity, usually presented in the form: "TO ____ BY ____ SO THAT ____" (details and examples follow). Purpose statements can be used in workshops, project artifacts, and other, more formal, settings. They can be developed with, and shared with, others who will be working to achieve shared goals.

This use case is much less formal in nature. The intent of a purpose statement for an assessment is simply to summarize and articulate one tactical goal in a simple format which you can keep top of mind as you design and execute your assessment.

This purpose statement will usually be for your consumption only, and you might never share it with anyone else. In addition to facilitating the coalescence of your own thoughts, a purpose statement will also provide you with a sound bite you can use when someone asks what you are doing. A purpose statement should also help you formulate the introduction section in your interview guide.

A purpose statement is structured as follows:

Purpose

TO: *A clear, concise statement of* **what** *the activity will accomplish (goal).*

BY: *A clear statement of* **how** *the goal will be achieved.*

SO THAT: *A statement describing* **why achieving the goal is important,** *and that adds context that will help frame the work and drive a more valuable outcome.*

For example, a simple purpose statement for an assessment might read as follows:

CHAPTER 5 ASSESSING THE CURRENT STATE

Purpose

TO: *Identify organizational strengths, weaknesses, barriers, and opportunities related to bringing new ideas to life, provide findings that will enable the design and deployment of a breakthrough idea incubator-accelerator, and begin organizational transformation and change management activities.*

BY: *Researching past successes and failures, understanding current and competing initiatives, interviewing key stakeholders, potential beneficiaries, and domain experts, and creating a summary of findings and recommendations.*

SO THAT: *We can design and deploy an initiative that delivers <solutions, products, programs, software...> that will ensure Fictitious Org remains relevant and financially viable five years from now and beyond, and that will overcome the perception – set by our competitors <detractors...> – that we are an old, stagnant organization that cannot deliver new, relevant solutions.*

Note This is a very generic example. Your purpose statement will likely be more specific, and may contain references to specific teams, organizations, or objectives. Regardless, it should be brief and easily internalized, simple to remember, and easily recalled when needed.

The importance of the "SO THAT" cannot be understated. It is the reason you are doing this. It is the thing that will most interest stakeholders, and that will capture the attention of people outside your organization (e.g., beneficiaries who want to know how your solution will benefit them; customers, who may be concerned about your long-term viability or how modern your solutions are). It is your initiative's "why." Interest in your "why" will drive interest in your "BY" (your "how"), which can drive traction for your initiative.

A purpose statement might not be necessary in every case. It is simply a tool that might help you consolidate your thinking and process your learning. If you have difficulty providing succinct answers to basic questions about your initiative, creating a purpose statement might be a good way to develop them. It captures your "why" in a sentence or two. It is important to have a crisp, compelling answer to questions you will likely get from every senior executive you encounter such as, "Why are you here?" or "Why should I care?" The questions are not always worded so abruptly, but that is often what those asking them are thinking.

It will not likely be necessary to broadly share your assessment's purpose statement in the form above. I don't think I have ever had to. Though you may find yourself paraphrasing it frequently. However, if you are a consultant, you may have no choice but to share it more broadly, or you may even have to develop and share a more formal research question.

5. Leverage Existing Knowledge Bases

Interviews are the heart of an assessment, but I believe it is always best to begin with a review of what is already known. This primarily consists of secondary research (learning from things others have created). This is as straightforward as it appears:

CHAPTER 5   ASSESSING THE CURRENT STATE

1. Find as much information as you can related to current and past initiatives (e.g., studies, white papers, PowerPoint presentations, videos, executive summaries, after action reports).

2. Look for information from initiatives that appear similar to what your current hypotheses lead you to believe you might create, and anything that might be somewhat related to your purpose (e.g., you may be building an incubator and find helpful information from past efforts related to an innovation contest or hackathon).

3. Examine information related to currently active initiatives, programs, and tools (e.g., project management frameworks, current approval processes), and get color regarding their effectiveness, popularity, and whether there were mismatched expectations or unmet needs.

    - Find out what people like and dislike about them.
    - Investigate the value they deliver and the value people in the organization believe they deliver, and note any differences and gaps.

4. Analyze both past success *and* failure and determine why things failed or succeeded (e.g., timing, personalities, team, leadership, participants, skill requirements, vocabulary mismatch, funding, wrong solution, training, sabotage).

5. Consider the differences between past and current conditions.

6. Question how things might be different now, and what may have changed.

    - Something that failed in the past may succeed in the future, so what would be different this time?

    - Something that worked in the past may not work in the future.

7. Determine which currently available processes, programs, and/or frameworks, if any, your initiative will have to coexist with, adhere to, or work with as a supplier (provide input to) or consumer (accept output from).

Performing this simple form of secondary research will provide you with information that will help you design, deploy, and communicate your new initiative, and it almost always helps with early formulation of an organizational transformation and change management strategy. The reason I like to perform **secondary research** *prior* to conducting interviews is that it **helps me to identify areas to further explore** (research often brings forth as many questions as it answers), **and helps me generate questions for the interviews.** It provides context that enables me to understand the answers participants provide in interviews and elsewhere, and provides a foundation that will help me understand conversations between others that I might witness opportunistically.

Good secondary research will usually put me on an equal footing with most of the people I encounter. It gives me background that enables me to have informed conversations. It makes me a better listener. An informed listener. And **at this stage it's *all* about listening and learning.**

Where to Find Secondary Research Information

You will likely easily find many sources of research information as you begin your project. If you were already a member of the organization for whom the initiative is being created, you may already know several locations where you are likely to find it (e.g., the location of shared drives, team Wiki pages, or SharePoint archives). If you were not, or if you do not have access to those (as is normally the case when I help an organization), you will need to ask someone whether they can share the information with you.

My primary contacts often provide most of the research information I use. But they never provide all of it. Other sources often provide some of the most insightful information, or reveal the last piece of a puzzle that helps me to put everything I have learned together. **Ask everyone you meet if they are aware of any information that might be helpful**. And when a participant mentions an initiative or process you were unaware of during an interview, always ask them how you might learn more about it.

Once I have been working with a team for a while, it is not uncommon for people to proactively offer to share information or documentation. Sometimes even people I have not met learn of my work and volunteer it. I usually gain some of the most valuable and unexpected insights in any engagement from these proactive sources.

Finally, sometimes documents and presentations I receive refer to other documents or processes. In some cases, they contain direct links which I can follow on my own. In other cases, I have to search for them or ask someone to help me obtain them.

Unscientifically, I would estimate that approximately 60% to 70% of the secondary research material I receive usually comes from my primary contact, 20% to 30% comes from conversations with others, and 10% comes from references within other documents. But don't let those numbers fool you. The value of each of those sources is usually equal, despite those differences in volume. The most valuable discoveries can come from any of them. I encourage you to explore them all.

6. Plan and Estimate Time Requirements

Many factors can influence the duration of your assessment. **Under normal circumstances, you should be able to complete one in four-to-six weeks.** With perfect conditions, it is *possible* to complete one in as little as two weeks. I recommend against that in all but the most exceptional circumstances; especially if you have never performed an assessment like this.

Completion of an assessment in two weeks or less will likely require a Herculean effort and perfect alignment of schedules. Allocating this amount of time for the assessment will also create risk of missing deadlines for subsequent tasks, and place the quality of your interviews and/or the assessment's synthesis and findings at risk.

The exception to the four-to-six-week guideline might be people who have management consulting, or similar, experience. People with such experience are often able to perform this type of assessment using muscle memory alone. I have been fortunate to work with many of them, and I have always been impressed by their amazing ability to rapidly design this type of research, execute it efficiently, and synthesize and present the findings in creative and compelling ways.

I recommend scheduling *at least* four weeks from the start of your assessment through to its completion, and six weeks if you have the time. I believe you will find the additional two weeks extremely valuable if you have never performed this type of assessment, since it will give you additional time to learn and deal with setbacks.

An **assessment schedule** typically looks something like this:

```
Week 1: Preparation; secondary research;
interview guide creation; interview scheduling
```

```
Week 2: Interviews; continue/complete
secondary research; note enrichment;
preliminary synthesis
```

Week 3: Interviews; complete secondary research; note enrichment; preliminary synthesis

Week 4: Final synthesis; preparation and delivery of findings

As with other examples, this framework is intended to be a guideline and not a directive. You may need to adjust it, and some things in the schedule will likely move. For example, at least one interview is likely to slip into the final week. That happens frequently. When it does, reschedule it as early in the final week as possible so you will have the maximum amount of time to synthesize it and respond to anything that might require further investigation. You can also use any gaps interview scheduling creates to begin work which is scheduled later.

I recommend you try not to schedule any interviews in week 1. If you must interview someone in week 1, try to schedule it as late as possible in the week. You must also ensure you have your interview guide ready before the first interview, even if it is a draft.

Finally, **I strongly recommend against scheduling senior executives or high-stakes stakeholders early**, if you can avoid it. It's better to have some experience and some initial insight ahead of those discussions.

Tip Strategy teams, people teams (HR), marketing teams, groups that conduct primary user research, and people with management consulting experience often have advanced skills in this area and may be able to provide guidance, direction, and/or assistance with your assessment.

If you engage someone outside your project for assistance with the assessment (e.g., a consultant), I strongly recommend you be present during the interviews. You may have important context necessary for interpreting responses that the person helping you does not possess.

CHAPTER 5 ASSESSING THE CURRENT STATE

Furthermore, if you are not present, you will not be able to ask follow-on questions based upon your experience and what you have already learned. Reading findings secondhand, in a synthesized form, will lack the richness of detail that might otherwise lead to important insight.

Finally, if you are not present during the interview, you will not be able to build relationships or begin the "soft" organizational transformation and change management activities. That would be a tremendous loss of value, and potentially a missed opportunity to accelerate the development of trust and the progress of your initiative. This aspect of the assessment is every bit as valuable as the insight you will gain from the interviews.

7. Create an Interview Guide

Our time with people whom we interview is extremely limited. It is critical that we respect our participants' time and make the most of it. The well-known saying, "failing to prepare is preparing to fail" definitely applies in the context of assessment interviews. Having an interview guide:

- Defines the flow and structure of the conversation
- Ensures you focus on the most important information
- Helps you stay on track, or regain focus if distracted
- Ensures you respect the participant's time
- Prepares you for ad-hoc changes in a participant's schedule
- Helps you prepare for diversions and exploration of new material
- Provides a plan for making changes during an interview

- Keeps you productive, focused, and on track when you are tired or are having a bad day
- Increases the interviewer's self-confidence which will, in turn, increase the participant's confidence in the interviewer and drive better outcomes

The structure and the specific questions you ask during your interviews will depend upon your circumstances, your objectives for the interview (what you want to learn and what you hope to accomplish in addition to learning), and the problem(s) you are planning to solve. While I can neither predict the specific questions you might wish to ask, nor the specific areas you will want to explore, I can share a structure that should provide a good foundation. I will also share some sample questions that might help during your brainstorming and preparation.

The examples that follow are intended to provide a foundation that will help you develop your own interview structure, guides, and questions. They include elements that you *may* include in your assessments but are not intended to be presented as elements that *must* be included in your own assessments. Some of these elements might apply, some might inspire derivative ideas, and some may be irrelevant in your circumstance. You might also include sections and/or questions that are not included in these examples.

Structure

Some people like to develop a structure and then create questions that align with each of its sections. Others like to write questions and then organize them into a structure. Both styles work. In my experience, the process often involves several iterations with changes to both the questions and the structure. What is most important is to ensure that the questions and structure address all of your assessment's objectives and gathers the information you require in order to begin designing and building your initiative.

Though there are always differences in the questions and nuances in the structure, at a high level my structure always consists of three major parts:

1. Opening
2. Discovery
3. Closing

Opening

The purpose of the opening is for the interviewer and the participant to get to know one-another (at least a little), to ensure the participant is aligned on the context and purpose of the interview, and to begin to build trust. It is also an opportunity to get the participant "warmed up" with a few simple questions that should not require a lot of deep thinking.

I usually include two steps in my opening. First, "gathering time" provides the participant with an opportunity to reset themselves from the task or meeting they may have just left. People are often scheduled very tightly and may be joining the interview immediately following a fast-paced, high-stakes discussion or activity. This will give them a minute or two where the stakes are not high, and the pressure and cognitive load is low, that will enable them to take a breath and reset their rhythm. This first section also enables the participant and interviewer to get to know one-another if they have not already met, or to reconnect; and provides an opportunity for the interviewer to thank the participant for their time.

This section of the interview is almost always very pleasant, so you may be tempted to prolong it or, more likely, you may lose track of time. Keep in mind that you typically have only 30, 45, or 60 minutes for the entire interview. This section should take two or three minutes at most. That may not appear to be enough time. In my experience, it is plenty. But you may need to adjust the time of this, or any, section in order to follow a lead or explore something that was offered in the introduction (insight often begins quickly), or to not be rude. There is an element of artistry in an interview of this nature, and you may be required to apply it very early on.

I use the second part of the opening to provide an introduction of the interview's purpose and to set any necessary context. We must be certain the participant understands the purpose of the conversation and that they have the proper frame of reference as they respond to questions and offer their insight. This not only ensures you are interpreting responses in the same context they are offered, but also reduces the risk you will have to reframe your questions, revisit portions of the interview part way through it, or discard early responses.

In the introduction, I like to include information about the current state, present the opportunity and a vision for what we are trying to achieve with the new initiative, and introduce the format of the interview. This ensures the participant knows exactly what we will be doing, exactly why we are doing it, and the specific purpose for which the information they share will be used. I believe this step is important even if the participant is already aware of this information. In such cases, it not only serves as a checkpoint to confirm the participant's understanding, but it also demonstrates that interviewer is being transparent.

Transparency and anonymity are paramount. Let participants know that the information they share will be captured anonymously, that it will be aggregated with other feedback to further disguise the source, and that the source of any information will not be shared with anyone.

At this point, I also let them know that the information they share will be captured anonymously, that it will be aggregated with other feedback to further disguise the source, and that the source of any information will not be shared with anyone. I stress that we are trying to capture the true state of things, unpolished, regardless of whether they are good or bad. We need a frank understanding of the current state in order to improve conditions, or to leverage strengths and elements that are already working.

At this time, I also obtain, or confirm, formal informed consent, if necessary. This is typically not necessary for the type of assessments I perform, though it is always worthwhile to verify with your sponsor or primary contact whether formal consent is required. Transparency is a key element of trust, and we want to ensure people understand what we are doing, why we are doing it, what will happen to the information they provide, whether it will be shared and, if it will, in what format.

Keeping in mind that our interview time is limited, I typically cover each of these items in one sentence or less. Thus, the entire opening section typically takes four to five minutes in total. Sometimes less if the participant is time constrained. In some cases, I might add a minute or two to learn a bit more about a person and their role if I have not learned enough about them prior to the interview.

Discovery

The discovery section is the heart of the assessment interview. As mentioned earlier, what you include in this section will vary based upon your objectives and learning needs. Since I cannot know what those are for each of you, I will suggest a few high-level areas that I find are frequently worth exploring in this type of assessment. I will also include a more detailed list of potential questions in the Toolkit section of this book which you can use as inspiration as you develop your own questions.

The major topic areas I like to explore during discovery are:

- **The current state**
  - Currently used methods, approaches, and methodologies
  - What is going well, what is working
  - What is not going well, what is not working
  - Needs, challenges, and conflicts
- **What has worked well in the past**
  - What went well, and why
  - What failed, and why
  - Whether success or failure was experienced at an individual, team, department, and/or organizational level
  - Trap doors and pitfalls that were discovered
- **Opportunities for improvement**
  - Gaps in skills, funding, resources, people...
  - Challenges
  - Needs
  - Clarify whether each opportunity for improvement is experienced at an individual, team, department, and/or organizational level
- **Future vision**
  - What does success look like
  - What would participants do if there were no constraints

CHAPTER 5   ASSESSING THE CURRENT STATE

- **Value**
    - What value the participant hopes or expects the initiative will achieve

Questions related to each of these areas will vary greatly, depending upon what I have already learned, what I learn during each interview, and my objectives. There are also a few, specific questions that I almost always include in every assessment interview I conduct. These questions generate interesting, actionable insight from multiple participants every time I conduct assessment interviews:

- **If you could get everyone doing one thing consistently, what would that be?**
    - Elicits positive behavior that, applied consistently, will have a substantial positive impact
    - Often helps identify pockets of excellence in execution and/or expertise
- **If you could change one thing – but only one thing – what would that one thing be?**
    - Helps highlight priorities
    - Surfaces positive or negative conditions
- **As you think about your mission, what keeps you up at night?**
    - Surfaces the highest priority item
    - Aids prioritization, planning, and messaging preparation

- **What is your greatest challenge?**
  - Often surfaces cross-team or cross-organization challenges and conflicts
  - Can expose key design requirements
  - Can offer insight into participant motivation
- **Is there anything you need that you don't have now?**
  - Can surface immediately actionable needs and drive short-term wins
  - Can identify obstacles that require immediate, or near-term, attention
- **Is there anything you would like to ask me about?**
  - Demonstrates openness
  - May surface exploration targets that were not yet identified
- **Is there anything you expected me to ask you about that I have not?**
  - Identifies missed areas, gaps, and blind spots
  - Many participants answer "no"
  - The few participants per assessment who have an answer usually provide amazing insight
- **Would it be OK if I follow up with you?**
  - Establishes permission for further discussion and exploration
  - Potentially creates the opportunity for a deeper working relationship

- **Is there anyone else you think I should speak with?**
  - Identifies stakeholders and influencers you may have missed
  - Identifies potential new sources of knowledge, subject matter experts, champions and/or detractors
  - Can identify people or teams which might be insulted or feel slighted if overlooked
  - May help avoid political infighting

I do not usually ask *every one* of these questions in each assessment, but I always include many of them. They often generate some of the most useful insights. **I almost always reserve the last four questions for closing.** Those questions are direct and do not typically take the participant much time to answer.

Closing

In the closing, I like to wind down the interview and make sure the participant is once again comfortable and relaxed. I make it clear we are wrapping up, and take care of any logistical items that might remain. It is at this point that I ask one or more of the last three questions from the preceding list:

- Is there anything you expected me to ask that I did not?
- Would it be OK if I follow-up with you, if necessary?
- Is there anyone else I should speak with?

Even though they are simple questions, asking them during closing often solicits some of the most insightful information. Perhaps it is because the participant is more relaxed at this point (it's over and it wasn't that bad). Regardless, the result is often a fascinating and unexpected conversation about topics that were not discussed earlier, and that open new lines of research.

Go Deep

I like my interview guides to include more questions than I could possibly ask in the time allotted. Having more questions than I need gives me the flexibility to explore different areas or levels of detail with each participant based upon what I learn during their interview. It also gives me something to turn to if I reach a dead end in a specific line of questioning because a participant does not have knowledge in the area or is uncomfortable discussing it.

Creating these questions helps me better acclimatize to the area under study as well. Generating detailed questions forces me to consider the topic carefully, deeply, and broadly. It also forces me to be self-reflexive and to understand how *my* experiences and biases might impact my interactions with participants and my interpretations of their responses.

Prioritize

Once you have completed your initial list of questions and grouped them into themes or sections, I believe it is important to organize them in order of their priority; especially if you have decided to generate more questions than you can use in the time allotted. This will ensure you get to the most important items first. If you are running out of time, or if your participant's schedule has changed, you'll know what to focus on in the time you have left.

I leave a few blank lines between each question while prioritizing and organizing. This lets me use the interview guide to capture participant responses during the interviews. I simply copy the guide, update it with any questions or notes specific to the participant, adjust the timings, and update the landmarks as necessary. I will discuss landmarks and timing next.

Set Landmarks

Once I have completed the first draft of the interview guide, I like to establish landmarks (easily spotted guideposts) throughout. I usually begin by placing timing landmarks throughout the guide. I will start with the major section headers and add the time I believe should be spent on each section in parenthesis next to the section title. This helps me to understand whether there is enough time to cover everything I have selected for a specific interview. If I believe I do not, I can start adjusting timings, trimming questions, or rearranging or reprioritizing questions or sections.

Once I have added the section time estimates, I look at the details in each section and decide which questions I want to ensure I cover in each. This is usually a simple exercise since I have already prioritized each of the questions in each section. I add a landmark that indicates I should move on if I have exceeded a specific amount of time in each section. For example, if I have ten questions in a section I have allocated ten minutes to, and I have determined I must ask the first three questions, I will put a landmark between questions three and four that tells me to move to the next section if more than ten minutes have passed.

Depending upon where the interviews lead me, I may not always adhere to my own landmarks. Regardless, I find that using this technique ensures I am always aware of where I am in the interview and how much time I have left. This lets me assess the value and cost of deviating, without interrupting the flow of the interview. Though I initially state these time and progress landmarks in terms of minutes of duration or elapsed interview minutes, you will see in the next section that I augment those with an actual time of day as each interview is scheduled.

I also include other landmark instructions such as whether I feel a section is optional or might be skipped for some, or all, participants.

Prior to each interview I make a copy of the interview guide and update the landmarks to: include specific times of day; highlight areas I should focus on with that participant; note areas or questions I might potentially skip; and indicate sections I feel are optional.

Interview Guide Template: Putting It All Together

 Once you put it all together, you will have an interview guide structured something like this partial example (landmarks and notes are shown in parenthesis and angle brackets):

ORGANIZATION NAME – INITIATIVE NAME – INTERVIEW GUIDE

02 January 2028
Structure (45 min)

1. Gathering and personal introductions (3 min)
2. Introduction and context (2 min)
3. Current approach (10 min)
4. What's going well (10 min)
5. Opportunities for improvement (10 min)
6. Future vision (10 min)
7. Value expectations (10 min)
8. Closing (5 min)

CHAPTER 5   ASSESSING THE CURRENT STATE

Introduction and Context (2 min)

- Introduction line 1
- Introduction line 2
- ...
- Last line of introduction

<Pause here for comments and confirmation>

Current Approach (10 min)

Explore current methods, methodologies, and approaches

(*Opening statement to introduce the section and add context, if necessary.*)

- First question of the section
- Second question
- Third question

<MOVE TO NEXT SECTION IF PAST 10 MIN>

- Fourth question
- ...
- Last question of the section

What's going well (10 min)

Introductory statement and context

- First question of the section
- ...

[Remainder of the interview guide...]

CHAPTER 5　ASSESSING THE CURRENT STATE

Note The partial sample above is intended only to illustrate the basic structure of the interview guide. A more detailed example is included in the Toolkit.

You may have noticed a discrepancy in the preceding example. The structure section states the interview duration will be 45 minutes in total. However, if you add all of the time estimates in each section you will see that they add up to a total of 60 minutes. This discrepancy was included to illustrate a state you will commonly find yourself in as you develop your interview guide. You may have a tendency to include more discussion than can fit into your targeted time.

When that happens, you have two options: (1) expand the duration; (2) reduce the number of questions. Depending upon the nature and role of the participants, you may have the option of increasing the time – if you have not already scheduled it. (Another reason it is a good idea to create your interview guide as early as possible.) I strongly recommend against interviews longer than 60 minutes. The exception might be your primary contact, or someone who is becoming a passionate champion. Even in those cases you will likely have the option of meeting with them more than once, and may want to consider staying within the scheduled time allotment.

Even if you set your target interview duration at 60 minutes, some participants may not be able to give you that much time. That is often the case for more senior people, for whom 30 minutes would be a more than generous contribution. You will need to focus your questions more tightly for them, and prioritize capturing knowledge they may uniquely possess. Note those in your interview guide when preparing for their interview.

Once your first interview is complete, trimming or consolidating your questions when needed should be much easier than was starting with a blank page. Preparing the guide will also help you to refine your focus and ensure your priorities are set properly. As you update the guide, I recommend placing any questions you trim at the end of each section in priority order, or at the end of the guide. Those questions may become useful if you want to explore a specific area more deeply with a specific participant, or if you have exhausted a topic and are looking for other areas to investigate in subsequent interviews. I recommend you leave a landmark ahead of trimmed questions to remind you to skip them under normal circumstances.

Learn Fast and Iterate

The bottom line: expect to iterate. Don't beat yourself up if you don't hit all your timing targets on the first attempt. If you do, you will have a lot of bruises. I don't think I have ever seen anyone hit all of them. Learn fast and iterate for the win!

Now that your interview guide is ready, the next chapter will guide you through preparing for, rehearsing, and conducting, your assessment interviews to make them as productive and insightful as possible.

CHAPTER 6

Conducting Assessment Interviews

Now that you have performed some initial research, structured and designed your interview, and prepared an interview guide, you should be ready to conduct assessment interviews. This chapter will help you to prepare for, and conduct, assessment interviews, and synthesize and communicate what you learn (Figure 6-1).

In this Chapter

Interview preparation:
1. Select interview participants
2. Prepare for the interviews

Conducting interviews:
3. Conduct the interviews
4. Review and cleanse the data
5. Update stakeholders (don't "go dark")

Synthesis and preparation of findings:
6. Prepare the findings
7. Finalize the findings

Figure 6-1. *What's in this chapter*

G. Watt, *The Lean Entrepreneurship Playbook*,
https://doi.org/10.1007/979-8-8688-0122-8_6

CHAPTER 6   CONDUCTING ASSESSMENT INTERVIEWS

1. Select Interview Participants

Now that you have objectives and a plan, it is time to decide whom to interview. The good news is that this is never as challenging as it appears. In fact, it is often the easiest part of the assessment. Since it is obvious that I cannot tell you specifically whom to interview during *your* assessments, I will share a few guidelines beginning with the answer to one of the most common questions I receive.

"How Many People Should I Interview?"

 I was the newest member of the corporate strategy team. Prior to joining them I had mostly conducted quantitative analyses, where more data is better. In preparation for my first open-ended *qualitative* analysis I had targeted dozens of interview participants, maybe 20 to 30. Way too many. My manager – who had a lot of qualitative analysis experience – suggested my plan would require substantially more effort than necessary and challenged me to trim the list. Significantly.

This guidance prompted me to be much more mindful of the goals of my interviews. What type of information and insight was I looking for? Who would have it? Which people might have similar insight and opinions? Which people would have different experiences and insight? Where might I look for a counterintuitive point of view? Which people might be supporters? Which might be detractors?

As I reviewed my list, I discovered two key errors:

1. **Over-representation:** There were groups of people with virtually the same experience and expertise.

2. **Insufficient diversity:** Key experience or constituencies were not represented.

CHAPTER 6   CONDUCTING ASSESSMENT INTERVIEWS

Number two was a surprise, but predictable in hindsight. With no limit on the number of participants, I did not have to think about composition. This led both to over- and under-representation. Ironically, more participants had produced a less diverse group. I would have expended three times the effort and added four-to-six weeks to the timeline for a poorer outcome. The additional data might have also been overwhelming, increasing the chance something important would be missed.

The impact of this simple exercise was profound, and it led to another question.

"When Should I Stop Interviewing?"

I asked my mentor, "When should I stop interviewing?" His answer: "**When you stop learning.**" I did not fully appreciate that simple answer until the last few interviews I conducted. I realized I had discovered much less new information during each. In the last couple of interviews I received additional color, but I did not really learn anything new. **I had conducted 15 interviews. I had stopped learning at around interview 12.**

With each subsequent analysis, I found I almost always stopped learning new things by interview 12, and often by interview 9 or 10. That is not to say I did not learn *any* new things after 10 or 12 interviews, but the amount and value of the new learning after that was rarely commensurate with the effort required to obtain it.

155

CHAPTER 6 CONDUCTING ASSESSMENT INTERVIEWS

Twelve to Fifteen Interviews Should Be Enough

Years later, I learned of scientific research that supports that estimate. Qualitative researchers refer to the point where new data or input delivers little to no change in the knowledge, information, or themes that are being revealed as "saturation." Some studies of saturation have concluded that 10-12 or 12[1] interviews should be sufficient for this kind of analysis.

With that as context, **approximately 12 interviews should be enough** for you to achieve saturation. **I suggest a more cautious 12 to 15 if you are new to this type of research**. Two or three additional interviews will not require a lot of additional effort, and you can always stop interviewing earlier if you stop learning. I almost always achieve saturation at or before interview number 12, but there is more to consider.

The number is less important than the composition of the interviews. Diversity is key, and you must ensure that the landscape of expertise and those impacted is sufficiently represented. **The quality of the information is also much more important than the quantity.**

Sometimes More Is Necessary

There may be political reasons to expand your list. For example, you may wish to ensure a person or group will not feel insulted if excluded, or you may want to interview a potential champion. You might also decide to interview someone in support of the other goals of your interviews such as beginning to build relationships and beginning to prepare people for the coming change.

Don't go overboard on including people for these secondary reasons. There is usually an opportunity to satisfy both primary and secondary objectives with a small sample size by identifying people who both

---

[1] Greg Guest, Arwen Bunce, and Laura Johnson, "How Many Interviews Are Enough? An Experiment with Data Saturation and Variability," February 2006, https://journals.sagepub.com/doi/10.1177/1525822X05279903

have the information you need and satisfy those secondary objectives. Nevertheless, there may be times when you must keep interviewing past your point of saturation, or include someone who possesses information you have already received, in order to achieve your secondary goals or avoid insulting someone. Embrace those opportunities. You will meet someone new, and you will always learn something.

Seek Experience

Another thing to consider is that there is almost always someone in the organization who has "been there." Someone with a positive attitude who has either participated in or witnessed previous attempts at initiatives like yours, or perhaps more targeted solutions, and who knows what worked, what did not, and why. They will know if a solution simply did not work, or if it should have worked but was stopped for political reasons. They can often help you anticipate potential objections and understand what might resonate with key stakeholders.

Include at least one of these people in your assessment if you can. Don't worry if you do not find them in the initial assessment. You will likely encounter them as you socialize the initiative later. When you do, be sure to obtain as much knowledge from them as you can. It's never too late to learn, inspect, and adapt.

Be Open and Transparent

Once your interviews are under way, you may receive some unsolicited volunteer participants. This can present both opportunities and challenges. People with valuable experience or information might volunteer to be interviewed. But you may also find you have more volunteers than you can reasonably include. When that happens, be transparent about your schedule to ensure the people you cannot interview do not feel insulted, slighted, or intentionally excluded. They will generally understand you have finite capacity and cannot interview everyone.

Beware of Bias

You may find you achieve saturation at ten interviews. That can happen, especially with a topic like this, which is often is well-known and broadly understood across an organization. If you feel you are saturated any earlier than that you should ask yourself whether your participant group is diverse enough. Be careful not to mistake a poorly selected participant group for saturation, and as you conduct interviews periodically (e.g., every three to five interviews), ask yourself whether your sample is sufficiently diverse.

Diversity Over Quantity

I recommend you begin with a target of 12 participants and expand if you sense you need to. You can also add participants based upon what you learn from other participants (more on this later in this chapter) or as you sense potential gaps in your coverage. Focus on quality and diversity. Identify people who will speak openly and candidly, who will deliver the unvarnished truth, and who will share what they believe to be good *and* bad news.

Try to find people who are seen to be, or have been, successful innovating and bringing new ideas to life, and those who have seen similar initiatives fail. Find optimists and skeptics. If you can, find someone new to the organization (who may be unconstrained by organizational folklore wisdom), and others who have been around for a long time. And don't forget to include sponsors, key stakeholders, and/or people who might be candidates for participation in the initiative you build.

Additional Considerations

If you are already part of the organization for whom you will create the initiative, you likely already know your target participants. You may know some personally, and others by reputation. I am usually new to organizations I work with, so my greatest source of ideas is almost always my primary contact. They can usually come up with an initial list in minutes.

When obtaining advice from others regarding whom to interview, make sure to ask *why* they recommended each candidate. This will help you understand whether you have a sufficiently diverse group that will enable you capture the range of perspectives you require.

Keep in mind that you may need to get permission to interview one or more of the people you select as participants, either as a courtesy or due to organizational norms or policies. Not doing so when you should may result in damage to your reputation (or your sponsor's), loss of trust, or worse. If you are not part of the organization you will almost certainly need one of its members to introduce you to participants and/or to obtain the appropriate permissions when necessary.

Finalizing the Participant List

There are several reasons you might have to adjust your participant list after you have "finalized" it. For example, you may encounter someone with key experience or a perspective not yet covered, or someone may back out or develop an unresolvable conflict. There may even be cases where candidates simply do not want to participate. That should not be cause for concern. It is a normal part of this type of exercise and there are likely others who can fill any gaps.

There may be positive surprises. You may find that people you were having difficulty recruiting become willing participants after you have interviewed a few others and begin to demonstrate that you are

CHAPTER 6 CONDUCTING ASSESSMENT INTERVIEWS

trustworthy and worth speaking to. You can also consider using a proxy for someone whom you are unable to recruit. For example, we once interviewed a CTO as proxy for other C-level executives and the Board of Directors because they were able to provide the broad perspectives of both of those groups.

As should be clear by now, there is a lot of work and thinking to be done before you begin your interviews. We're almost there, but there is one more thing that must be done before interviews can begin.

Choosing Your First Interview Participant

I strongly recommend that your first interview be with someone with whom you are comfortable, who is comfortable with you, and with whom you have an existing relationship (even if it is a new one). Find someone who will be open and candid, and upon whom you can count for direct, honest feedback. For me, this is almost always my primary contact. They understand my mission and are usually a legitimate interview candidate. Since they are normally the person within the organization tasked with the success of the mission, they also understand its objectives and have a stake in its success.

When I conduct the first interview, I try to arrange an additional 15 to 30 minutes at the end for feedback on the interview itself. I like to obtain the participant's evaluation of the interview's tone, flow, timing, and completeness. When we convene, I first conduct the interview as if it were any other interview. I end it formally, and *then* ask the "friendly" participant for feedback on the interview itself. Did it cover the right topics? Were there gaps? Did I fall into any traps? How was my energy, tone, performance?

Prior to the interview I let the participant know I will be asking for this type of feedback. I also ask them to write their observations down during the interview, and not deliver them in real-time, so evaluation of the interview will not disrupt our feel for the flow and timing of the interview itself.

If you are unable to find a friendly participant with whom you can do this, you could perform a dry run with someone who is not a participant provided doing so would not breach confidentiality or other agreements or expectations.

I recommend you find people who support, and are passionate about, the initiative as your first one or two interview participants, even if you cannot find someone who will give you feedback about the interview itself. **Do not start with high-stakes participants, such as senior executives or board members, or others who may not have patience if you encounter challenges. Conduct interviews with those participants at or near the end** of your schedule when you will have more experience, will have evolved your questions and focus, and will be much more comfortable with the material and flow.

Leave Time for Adjustment

Allocate time between the first and second interviews in case you need to adjust the interview guide or reset in some other way. You will almost certainly want to adjust some of the questions, landmarks, question optionality, timing, and/or the flow. This should not require an inordinate amount of time. But try to avoid scheduling the first two interviews within an hour or two of each other. For example, if you schedule the first interview at 3 PM one day, perhaps schedule the second interview the following day.

2. Prepare for the Interviews

The greatest risk to your interview schedule will be your interview participants' calendars. Scheduling meetings is challenging, especially in larger organizations. Scheduling someone's time in less than a week can be nearly impossible.

CHAPTER 6   CONDUCTING ASSESSMENT INTERVIEWS

Scheduling Interviews

Begin scheduling the interviews as early as you can, and demonstrate respect for interview participants as follows:

1. Learn each participant's time zone.
2. Learn the organization's norms for scheduling meetings.
3. Avoid scheduling interviews during participant lunch and break times.
4. Never schedule interviews during upcoming holidays.
5. Never schedule interviews before the normal start, or after the normal end, of the participant's work day.
6. Take the business cycle into consideration and avoid busy periods like quarter end.
7. Avoid hectic times like first thing Monday or late Friday.
8. Avoid scheduling meetings immediately adjacent to other meetings.

Of course, none of the items in this list will be an issue if they are the participant's preference.

I find using a tool like Microsoft Bookings or Calendly is the simplest way to schedule interviews. It lets the participants select the time and day that is most convenient for them without your direct involvement. You can include a link to the tool in your introductory note and provide the participants with a one- or two-week period within which to schedule their session. This puts them in control and demonstrates your respect for their convenience. Using a tool like this also:

- Increases scheduling speed
- Eliminates annoying multi-round email exchanges
- Provides immediate confirmation
- Eliminates double bookings
- Ensures the right amount of time is reserved
- Can make scheduling more pleasant and professional through customization
- Can ensure adequate preparation and review time between interviews through scheduling rules

If you use a scheduling tool, **I recommend creating a rule that puts at least 15 to 30 minutes of unscheduled time between interviews**. You will need time to reset mentally and to prepare for each interview, to adjust for last minute participant schedule changes, or to enrich your notes (more on this later). Be careful not to add too much time automatically as it can make scheduling difficult for participants.

Pay attention to the organization's scheduling norms when configuring your tool. Those might be different for different teams. And you should be prepared for some participants to ask you to manually resolve conflicts. Scheduling norms are almost always different for senior executives. For example, you may have to schedule less time (e.g., 30 minutes vs. 60 minutes), or you may need to contact a senior executive's assistant (as opposed to contacting them directly).

You may find some people have a strong disdain for scheduling tools. The less friction you can create while scheduling, the better, so you may have to manually schedule their time.

Most scheduling tools will consider all appointments in your calendar, not only those the tool added, so make sure you have placeholders in your calendar for all of your professional and personal commitments; and don't forget to schedule transit time for appointments when appropriate.

Finally, **be sure to include time for interview preparation prior to each interview**. This can be done a day or two in advance, so it should not normally put a strain on your schedule. However, beware that **preparing for your first interview may take a lot of time**. You should rehearse every possible question and answer. This can take at least an hour or two, and you may need to do it more than once before you are comfortable. Once your first interview is complete, schedule time to reflect upon it, process any feedback you may have received, refine your guide, and rehearse.

Subsequent interviews should require much less preparation, and each interview should require less preparation than the one before it. However, there is almost always some uniqueness to each interview (e.g., the questions you ask, the level of depth you explore on a specific topic), so resist the urge to become complacent and not prepare. That urge can be especially strong during the last half of the interviews, as the interviewer becomes comfortable with the material and with leading the conversations.

Rehearse

Rehearsal is one of the most essential elements of an assessment interview. I recommend beginning by playing both the interviewer and participant roles. Start a timer and run through the entire interview, beginning with your introduction. I suggest you speak the interviewer questions, comments, and introductions aloud. Sometimes just saying the words aloud (as opposed to reading them in silence) will make you aware of awkward wording, bad tone, awkward flow, or even that you are on the wrong track. Think about how a participant might respond, and about what your response to that might be.

Practice every section of the interview. Whether or not you speak an anticipated answer aloud, at least think about the kinds of answers you might receive and leave sufficient pauses for them. This will help you to gauge timing. Reading the questions and thinking about potential answers might also lead you to discover something you missed, gaps in your flow, inappropriate, redundant, or unnecessary questions, or awkward wording.

Try to anticipate a diversion or two, and how you might bring the conversation back on track if that happens. Most participants are not upset when an interviewer keeps them on track. Proactively mentioning that time is limited, and that you may have to switch topics abruptly, during your opening is usually all that is required to avoid any potential bad feelings that might otherwise result from your doing so.

Once you have completed your dry run, update your interview guide to adjust, add, or remove questions, and update your landmarks and timings. Depending upon how smoothly your dry run went, you might want to run through the exercise one or more additional times. Some people find recording their rehearsal with a video conferencing tool helps. Once you are comfortable, you'll be ready for your first interview. But you should also make sure you have sufficient background information.

Learn About the Organization and the People

Learn as much as possible about the organization, its mission, challenges, and current conditions prior to the first interview. I find my primary contact usually has a wealth of useful information and historical context. On rare occasions when they do not, I ask them to refer me to others. I also gather information informally when in meetings or conversations, even those unrelated to the initiative. I listen to everyone I can, pay attention to conversations and sidebars when they occur, and consult open source material such as the organization's public web site.

CHAPTER 6   CONDUCTING ASSESSMENT INTERVIEWS

Most organizations, especially larger ones, have documentation about current and past efforts and processes. Some of that might be in the form of "official" process documents, perhaps stored on a corporate Wiki or SharePoint server. Some material may be in the form of pitch material, proposals, and presentations used in the past, or even notes or opinion papers. I try to consume as much of that as I can before the first interview. This helps me to establish context, refine questions, and identify areas to further explore during the interviews. It also helps me understand the organization's jargon, acronyms, and its unique interpretation of words. This type of background information will also help immensely if you need to design your initiative to interact with – or at least not conflict with – existing processes and norms.

Prior to interviews, I ask my primary contact or colleagues about anything I discovered but do not understand. I also try to learn as much about the *people* I will be interviewing as I can. Where do they fit in the organization? What are their roles and responsibilities? How do they fit within the initiative? Are there any "land mine" topics that should either be avoided or at least approached gently. Are there hot-button issues for them? What are they passionate about? What are they focused on? Have they recently written any articles or blog posts? Were they related to the initiative?

This may appear to be a lot, but it usually isn't. At this stage, the objective is to learn *enough* about the people and the organization to have sufficient context in the interview, and to inform yourself about areas you may wish to focus each interview on. A simple conversation with your contacts (which normally happens as they recommend people as interview candidates), a quick review of participants' *public* social media (e.g., LinkedIn posts), and a brief search for publications should be enough. Some of your participants may have been authors to the internal documents mentioned earlier in this section, and those might also provide insight into their interests and areas of expertise.

You may not always be able to perform even this basic level of research prior to an interview, or you may not be able to find any information prior to the session when you do. That is fine. The goal is to make your best *reasonable* effort to prepare for the interview so you can make the most of your participant's time.

Preparation ahead of an interview always drives value for me. Participants will notice and appreciate your effort, and that you have a genuine interest in them and in their success.

Have an Initial Hypothesis

You will likely have an initial hypothesis regarding some of your initiative's major objectives and how you might achieve them by the time interviews begin. Great. I recommend capturing those, though not sharing them broadly. You don't want to give people a false impression that you've already decided what the solution is, nor that your assessments are pure theater. You might test some of them with your primary contact, perhaps through questioning. But you still have a lot of listening and learning to do, and those hypotheses might change substantially.

Check Your Bias

Once you get to this point, you should spend some time thinking about what, if any, bias you may have developed. Some additional introspection prior to your interviews, however small, will be worthwhile. It is incredibly easy to drive bias into an interview and not realize it is happening. Your interview guide should help mitigate that risk, so review it and scan for leading questions and other areas that might introduce bias or unintentionally close an area of exploration.

CHAPTER 6   CONDUCTING ASSESSMENT INTERVIEWS

Be Well Rested

Be well rested each day you have interviews. Conducting a dozen interviews over a one-to-two-week period can be exhausting. Each interview requires hyper-focus. Your brain will be fully engaged as you listen intensely, note responses, adjust the flow, and make notes regarding new questions or areas to explore.

Preparation will lighten your cognitive load. Knowing everything you might ask, having more questions than you have time, and knowing what to skip and what you absolutely need to get to are absolute requirements. The good news is that these should all be in your interview guide. The interview guide will be your best friend on days when you are not well rested or have been distracted by a challenge or crisis. A good interview guide can make you function like you are having a great day even on days when you are functioning at less than 100% of your capacity.

Prepare Your Environment

Before you begin your interview, ensure your environment is prepared, tested, and ready. In face-to-face interviews, that may mean setting the meeting room up to be inviting, throwing trash away, getting your interview guide, notes, laptop, and/or notepad ready, and/or setting up a recording device. If you are fortunate enough to have a partner, ensure you both understand each other's role (e.g., which person will ask questions, which person will take notes, exceptions, protocol).

If you are conducting the interview remotely, this is your final opportunity to make sure your video conference environment is ready. Preventable disruptions steal time from your interview and may leave participants with a bad impression of you. Your interviews mark the commencement of your transformation initiatives in earnest, so this first impression will matter a lot. You don't want to waste participant's time while you troubleshoot or recover from something preventable.

CHAPTER 6   CONDUCTING ASSESSMENT INTERVIEWS

Incidentally, I like doing assessment interviews remotely. Though I cannot see the full range of participant body language I would in person, remote interviews have other advantages. They are usually simpler to schedule and do not involve travel expense or disruption. The physical environment is often easier to control (e.g., finding a quiet space), and it is easier to take notes without distraction since the participant cannot see me type. In addition, most people created environments that enable them to easily work remotely during the COVID-19 pandemic, and remote conversations of this nature are now more acceptable and commonplace.

I always make a checklist of things to verify or prepare prior to an online interview. Most of these are very simple and do not take much time. Therefore, they are also easy to forget. Here are a few of the items I include in my preparation checklist, with some additional context as necessary:

Video Assessment Interview Checklist

- **Make sure the camera is connected, set, and tested.**
    - I prefer an external camera, as it provides more flexibility for angles, framing, and positioning.
- **Make sure you are well framed and centered.**
    - Avoid strange angles – people will be distracted if you are a giant eyeball or nose.
    - Ensure your head is not cut off (high or low).
    - Frame yourself with space on all four sides in case the video conference software crops part of your image.
- **Ensure lighting is good.**
    - Make sure you are not backlit.
    - Three well-placed light sources will usually be enough to address lighting issues.

- **Look behind you!** (Clear your frame.)
  - Know what is in frame behind you when you broadcast.
  - Ensure your work area looks tidy, clean, and professional.
  - Ensure there is no confidential or personal information in view.
  - Ensure there is nothing distracting behind you.
  - Do this every time you are about to begin a session!
- **Make sure the proper mic is connected, selected, and tested.**
  - I find an external mic better than most built-in mics, and less apt to capture typing noises.
  - Beware that some mechanical keyboards can be distractingly loud, and position of the keyboard relative to the mic may matter.
- **Ensure the network is properly configured.**
  - Use a wired connection, if possible.
  - If you have been switching between wired and wireless networks, it may be a good idea to reboot your machine with the connection type you plan to use (e.g., wired) active, as I have found some video conferencing software can fail or perform poorly otherwise (I usually do this the evening before an interview, or early in the morning, in case there are problems).

- **Reboot the modem your Internet provider supplied** (when working from home).
  - This *can* improve performance in *some* cases (your situation may differ).
  - I usually do this the evening before an interview, or early in the morning, in case there are problems.
- **Have a backup Internet connection, if possible.**
  - For example, I have tested that the hotspot capability on my mobile phone is good enough for some types of video conferences, and set it up prior to online sessions so I can switch quickly, if necessary.
- **Ensure others know an interview is being conducted** (especially when working from home).
  - This will prevent people from walking in on your interview or disrupting it with loud or distracting noises.
  - I use an "on air" light outside my office in case people who are unaware of the scheduled interview visit unexpectedly.
  - Don't panic if someone does come in, just use a calm, professional tone to let them know you are conducting an interview.
- **Ensure keyboard, mouse, and other peripheral batteries are fully charged.**

- **Have a second laptop or desktop available, if possible.**
  - I prepare a second machine and launch the video conferencing software, but do not join the session.
- **Turn off or pause backups, automatic updates, anti-virus scans, and maintenance activities during the interview.**
  - If your machine's maintenance is scheduled by a corporate administrator, it might be a good idea to check for and apply, pending maintenance the day prior to the interview.
- **Shut down unnecessary applications.**
  - They may be distracting.
  - They may cause performance issues, depending upon your system.
  - Hiding your browser's tabs or favorites may also be appropriate, depending upon what you may share.
- **Open applications that will, or may, be used during the interview, and have material ready.**
  - For example, if you are going to show an illustration, have it ready to share.
  - Ensure you have tested sharing them using the video conference application and configuration you will use during the interview.
- **Configure your desktop or laptop workspace to maintain eye contact** (additional detail follows).
- **Turn off or extend system time-out periods as needed.**

- This will prevent disruptions.
- This will also remove the distraction caused by the need for you to keep tapping a display or hitting a key to keep the system from going to sleep.

• **Silence messages, notifications, email alerts, and pop-ups for the duration of the interview.**

- They can be distracting.
- They can be embarrassing (your friends and colleagues may not know you are sharing).
- I have seen some very embarrassing, and extremely not suitable for work, messages and spam email notifications pop up while people were sharing slides or illustrations.
- Share specific applications, not your desktop or workspace.

• **Dress professionally, even if you are working from home.**

If you have not used the configuration you plan to use during an interview, or if you plan to make changes to it, I strongly recommend testing it by joining yourself in a practice session at least a day or two in advance. Even better, ask a colleague if they can meet with you for two or three minutes. Another video conference participant's experience may not always look or sound like what you expect. I also recommend testing in this way when switching video conferencing software. Some of these systems make their own changes to your video or audio (e.g., reframing the video), so it is always best to verify what will happen and what, if anything, you need to do to adjust for it.

Finally, there is no need to panic if something unexpected happens. I find people are usually very understanding. Everyone you will interview has probably been in a similar position, and they will likely be especially patient if you've done everything possible to mitigate easily anticipated risks. The likelihood you will need to deal with an unexpected interruption will be minimal if you have adequately prepared.

Eyes Forward for Better Participant Experience

Nothing can poison an interview faster than giving a participant the impression you're not paying attention. It can happen in an instant. Something as simple as looking at your interview guide or notes can lead a participant to believe you are looking at your phone or checking email instead of focusing on their responses. I have learned that configuring my workspace so I maintain eye contact lets me avoid these potentially catastrophic misunderstandings.

When I perform assessment interviews, I typically have two applications active: the video conference software (e.g., Teams, WebEx, Zoom…), and a note-taking application (e.g., Word, Pages, Notes…). **Placing my note-taking application at the top of my workspace, directly under my camera, helps me maintain eye contact with participants and keeps me looking toward them as I check my interview guide and make notes** (I take notes directly in a copy of the interview guide). It ensures I do not appear to be distracted or disinterested when checking the guide, as might be the case if I had to look away from the camera to do so. Having the note taking app in that position also casts another direct light source upon the interviewer.

I also place the video conferencing application's window at the top of the screen, slightly to the right of the note taking application, so when I look at it I am also looking toward the camera (Figure 6-2). Regardless of the horizontal placement of your note-taking and video conference applications, I recommend you keep them at the top of your display, near your camera.

CHAPTER 6 CONDUCTING ASSESSMENT INTERVIEWS

***Figure* 6-2.** *Placing the interview guide and participant video immediately below your camera ensures you do not appear to be looking away, disinterested, or looking at something unrelated to the interview*

3. Conduct the Interviews

I enjoy meeting people and learning from them, so I like conducting assessment interviews a lot. Through them I have met many remarkably nice and incredibly intelligent people – most of whom I would never have met otherwise. I sometimes wish the conversations could continue for hours. But they cannot, and we must be deliberate about time management as we interview people.

CHAPTER 6   CONDUCTING ASSESSMENT INTERVIEWS

Respect Participants' Time

Respect for others' time is always important, and it is paramount during assessment interviews. The time will pass much more quickly than you might imagine, even in an interview of 60 minutes or longer. Rehearsing, understanding your interview plan, understanding your priorities, and planning what you will do if a section is running long or if time is cut short, is of the utmost importance. That should all be captured in the notes and landmarks in your interview guide, which should be in front of you throughout the interview.

Be Early

Respect for a participants' time begins with you being early for the interview. I prepare my environment well in advance. For in-person interviews, I arrive at least a half hour early. For video conference interviews, I set a reminder 15 minutes prior to the interview to provide time for final preparations. I start video conferences five minutes before the scheduled time, and never less than two minutes early.

Being prepared and on-time will be your first opportunity to demonstrate your respect for a participant. Being early will also give you an opportunity to reset yourself mentally and physically, and to get into an appropriate emotional state. It will enable you to break free from the stress of what happened earlier in the day and to be present for the participant. The more hectic the day, the more time you might wish to give yourself to reset.

End on Time

Finally, **stop at or before the scheduled end time**. Participants will appreciate your respect for their time, and they will be more likely to accept subsequent meeting requests from you if you start, stay, and stop on time. On rare occasions a participant may ask for additional time because they want to share additional information, further explore something, or even ask you for advice. Extending a session is OK, but make sure the participant has agreed to it, set a new end time, and end on or before that new end time.

During the Interview

I find it best to conduct interviews in accordance with each interviewer's personal style and preferences. I prefer a semi-structured style. That is, I use the interview guide as a foundation for the interview, but I do not constrain myself with it. To **make the interview a conversation and not an examination** I do not share the guide with participants, or talk about it.

While there are usually some questions I ask all participants, not every participant is asked the same questions. I use the flow of the interview and my knowledge of the participant's role and background to gauge areas of participant knowledge and interest. I always skip some (usually many) of the prepared questions, and I formulate new ones during each interview based on what I learn therein.

In addition, I often find I take what qualitative researchers might call a "pedagogical" interview stance. That is, during interviews, participants frequently ask me to share related viewpoints, experiences, or expertise they believe I have. I find this presents an excellent opportunity empathize, offer emotional support, help the participants, and/or build trust and rapport. It can turn an interview into a more meaningful conversation. Therefore, I am always happy to respond, while being careful to keep my responses brief and relevant. I also do my best to ensure I do not introduce bias via my responses.

I find this pedagogical style to be very compatible with my personality and style, but you may find that a different approach better aligns with yours. That is fine. Your authenticity and comfort are, in my opinion, more important than adopting any specific interview style.

CHAPTER 6   CONDUCTING ASSESSMENT INTERVIEWS

As you conduct each interview, keep these things in mind:

Tips for conducting interviews

1. **Bring High, Positive Energy!**

    - Be your authentic self, but dial your positivity up as high as you authentically can.

    - Both the participant's and interviewer's energy levels will fall throughout the interview, so it is important to start high.

    - Put bad days in your desk drawer before an interview begins, (unfortunately) they will be there when it's over.

2. **Confirm the participant is still available for the scheduled period.**

    - Sometimes participants develop schedule conflicts after they have confirmed their availability.

    - It is best to know that your 60-minute interview has become 30 minutes before you ask your first question, so you can adjust priorities or reschedule it.

3. **Let participants know you will be taking notes, and how you will do that.**

    - Never record audio or video without prior informed consent.

    - When typing notes, I ask participants to let me know if my typing is bothering them (I use an external mic positioned away from the keyboard to prevent that from happening, but I always ask).

4. **Have a crisp personal bio and elevator pitch ready.**

    - Participants sometimes ask an interviewer to share a little personal information, or ask about the initiative, so be prepared to answer those questions in a simple sentence or two.

5. **Listen.**

    - Use active listening techniques.

    - Ask probing questions based upon participant responses.

    - Don't rush through your interview guide and accept all answers at face value; listen to the participant's answers and, when appropriate, explore those more deeply (Don't just say, "OK" and move to the next question).

    - Your guide should contain notes on how to stay on time if you follow an unforeseen path.

    - Participants frequently answer questions before they are asked, so don't ask questions they have already answered when you encounter them in your guide.

6. **Your interview guide is *only* a guide.**

    - Don't be subservient to it, phrase your questions in a manner consistent with the conversation, then go where the conversation leads (as long as it's a relevant place).

- Tailor your priorities based upon the participant's role, experience, and knowledge (e.g., practitioner vs. senior executive).
- Focus on information you can only obtain through an interview.
- Don't feel the need to dive deeply into well-explored areas with every participant; use that time to cover new ground.
- Leverage your preparation, and the guide, to ensure the most critical information is captured.

7. **Pay attention to the participant's body language.**
   - Listen with your eyes.
   - A change in body language can let you know there is more to an answer than the words that were spoken, and catching that can help you to identify areas to probe.
   - It may help you detect when a participant is giving you an answer they believe they are "supposed" to give versus telling you how they really feel.
   - Watch for reactions to your questions and style, observe how you are being perceived.
   - This is more challenging in video interviews, but not impossible.

8. **An assessment interview is a conversation.**
   - Be present, welcoming, warm, and engaged, and don't be cold and clinical.
   - Rehearse, and try not to dryly read questions.

CHAPTER 6 CONDUCTING ASSESSMENT INTERVIEWS

9. **It's *not* about you** (the interviewer).
   - Keep your comments brief, though not rude, even in pedagogical style interviews.
   - When asked a complex question, provide a brief response and offer to follow up.

10. **It *is* about you** (the interviewer).
    - This will likely be the first time many participants will meet you, and first impressions matter.
    - Be authentic.
    - Bring your best self.

11. **Save controversial or challenging questions until late in the interview, or near its end.**
    - It gives the participant a chance to get "warmed up" and into a good mindset.
    - It gives the interviewer an opportunity to build trust and rapport before challenging a participant.
    - It reduces the risk of moving the conversation off course or poisoning the interview.
    - Carefully framing the question and acknowledging its controversial nature can help (e.g., "I realize this is a bit of a sensitive area, but I would really like your insight...").
    - You will not likely have overly controversial questions in this type of interview, but keep this in mind since some questions might be more sensitive or challenging than others.

CHAPTER 6   CONDUCTING ASSESSMENT INTERVIEWS

12. **Take note of new learning and knowledge gaps, and follow up.**

    - Capture information regarding new topics, political conditions, technology, techniques, and anything you learn, whether or not you see a direct connection to your initiative.

    - Note when a participant mentions a process, group, or technology that you are unaware of, and make an action item to learn more about it following the interview.

    - Ask participants where you might learn more about a topic when appropriate.

    - To economize time, keep a follow-up list and ask questions at the end of the interview, or in a follow-up note.

    - Closing these gaps will often help with subsequent interviews, communication planning, and designing your initiative.

Taking Notes

That you take notes during an assessment interview is essential. How you take notes is a matter of personal style. I like to open an editable copy of the interview guide and place it just below my camera, as explained earlier (Figure 6-2). Using the guide this way:

- Enables me to check my notes while looking toward the participant
- Makes it easier for me to stay on track
- Ensures I always have the proper context when reviewing participant responses
- Helps me to keep track of time and landmarks
- Enables me to better focus on the conversation
- Helps me take note of potential adjustments for future interviews
- Allows me to do all of the above without flipping between documents

I tend to take verbose notes, capturing much of what each participant says, so this approach has been extremely valuable to me.

Prior to each interview, I customize the interview guide for the specific participant. I highlight questions I want to focus on, those I may want to skip, and adjust the time I plan to spend on topics as necessary. I often add specific clock times to landmark times. For example, I might update a note from "skip to the next session if past 15 minutes" to add "(10:15)" for an interview that begins at 10:00.

Following each interview I adjust my interview guide in preparation for subsequent sessions. If you notice you are not making any changes to your interview guide as your interviews progress, it may be worthwhile to pause and consider the reason. For example, you may not be listening well enough, or you may not be noting areas for improvement of the interview. It may also indicate something positive, such as you are approaching saturation, or that you have found high-value questions and topics.

CHAPTER 6   CONDUCTING ASSESSMENT INTERVIEWS

What's Noteworthy?

I usually record the following types of information during assessment interviews:

- Participant responses to questions and other remarks (of course)
- Noteworthy quotes
- Participant body language
- Participant tone of voice
- Trap doors and triggers
- Sensitive topics
- Additional color, context, or explanation (not specifically stated by the participant)
- My own thoughts and emerging learning and hypotheses
- Items to learn about and things requiring follow-up

The bulk of my interview notes always consists of participant responses. I tend only to note body language or tone of voice in rare cases such as when there is dissonance with a stated response, when it helps with interpretation, or to capture the participant's strength of conviction. Sometimes what is unspoken can be more powerful than what has been said.

When capturing additional context, observations, personal thoughts, and hypotheses, make sure you can distinguish them from participant responses. I use what you might think of as a markup language to make sure I don't put words into my participants' mouths. For example, if capturing a personal thought while recording a response I begin it with "THOUGHT:" I do the same for a "HYPOTHESIS" or items I need to

"LEARN" more about. When I am in a hurry, I just put angle brackets (<>) around the observation to make it stand out. Doing this ensures my own thoughts and biases are not attributed to a participant. These tags are especially important and helpful when I read notes days or weeks after an interview.

If you decide to use your own shorthand, it might be a good idea to keep a legend of your symbols and abbreviations; especially the first time you do it.

Thank the Participants!

Each participant you interview will have their own priorities, and many things competing for their time. Please do not forget to thank them for their time and contribution. I am always genuinely grateful to those who take time they could have used to advance their own objectives and priorities to help me achieve my goals. I usually briefly thank the participant for making time for the interview at the opening of each interview. At the end of the interview I thank them more specifically for their contribution and reference specific elements of our conversation that were helpful or insightful.

Ethics Matter

Trust is the engine that powers a good assessment. Ethics are that engine's fuel. During the assessment you will be asking people to be unambiguously and thoroughly candid. You will be asking them to share good, bad, and sometimes embarrassing experiences. To tell you the unvarnished truth. When they do, you have an absolute obligation to honor the trust they place in you.

This type of relationship requires that both parties unambiguously understand the parameters within which the conversation will take place. In the brief introduction to the interview, I always reconfirm those parameters. This usually includes a few, simple rules I follow such as:

1. The interview will be completely confidential.
2. I will capture the participant's input anonymously.
3. I will share the information in aggregate with feedback from other participants to further anonymize it.
4. Sources of information will not be shared with anyone.

If you plan to use automatic transcription, tell participants who will have access to the transcript (that should only be you), how long you will keep the audio or video, and when you will delete it. You should also inform them once recordings or transcripts have been deleted.

I don't share sources with anyone, even my primary contact. If I ever feel it might be helpful or necessary to share an attributed quote or source, I ask the source whether they approve, and only share it if they agree. Otherwise, everything remains anonymized.

You should also let your sponsor and/or main contact know how you will treat assessment data so their expectations are properly set. I have never had a sponsor object to anonymity, nor has anyone ever asked me to divulge a source.

Pseudonyms

I mentioned that I do not use participant names or attributed quotes in reports or artifacts unless the participant has given their explicit permission. (It is rarely required.) To further ensure anonymity, and that sources are not mistakenly divulged, I use pseudonyms in my notes. That

CHAPTER 6   CONDUCTING ASSESSMENT INTERVIEWS

is, in transcripts and interview notes I use either a fictitious name, or something like "Participant 1," as opposed to recording the participant's actual name. This ensures my notes will not expose their source even if someone somehow encounters them.

Use of pseudonyms may be especially important for assessments performed in the public sector. Many public sector organizations are subject to access to information requests (e.g., FOIA,[2] ATIP[3]), wherein there is a remote possibility someone might make a request that places your notes in scope. If that happened, keeping actual names in the notes would expose the participant's name and their thoughts. Even though I tend not to capture information that would be embarrassing in my interview notes, I am confident some people would prefer not to have the information exposed regardless. Putting pseudonyms in the notes removes that concern. Archiving and deleting recordings as a matter of practice also helps.

Though my notes and reports have never been subject to a freedom of information request, it is always worth keeping things like this in mind as you make promises to your participants.

Back Up Your Data

Compiling an assessment's raw data (e.g., interview notes) requires a lot of effort. Losing some or all of it would be catastrophic. It will be difficult, if not impossible, to reproduce, and will likely never have the acuity of the original work. Even losing a single set of notes can mean the loss of important discoveries and hours of work. So, as the saying goes, "save early, save often!"

---

[2] Additional information regarding the United States of America's Freedom of Information Act may be found at this web site: www.foia.gov

[3] Additional information regarding Canada's Access to Information and Privacy may be found at this web site: https://atip-aiprp.apps.gc.ca/atip/welcome.do

I recommend a "3-2-1" style backup strategy. That is, have at least three copies, on at least two different storage media, with at least one copy off-site. While some people count the original copy as one of the three copies, I tend to make at least two backup copies at my office and keep one additional copy remotely on a service such as OneDrive, Google Drive, or Box. I also keep at least one copy isolated and offline (air gapped). Sometimes that is a third local copy. As I often explain tongue-in-cheek, "it's not paranoia if everyone *is* out to get you."

If you plan to use a cloud service to back up data related to a public sector project you may need to make sure that the regulations, legislation, and policy related to the kind of material you are gathering permit you to do so. This kind of project does not usually involve highly confidential or classified material, and I have not yet encountered a case where this type of remote backup was not permitted. However, bespoke workshops you might conduct that may not be directly part of the assessment may be subject to restrictions. Your primary contact will usually know how this information should be treated. If they do not, they will likely know where to find that out. If you are unsure whether you can use such a service, ask.

Enjoy the Experience!

If you have conducted assessments of this nature before, this should all be familiar to you. If you have not, and you are feeling apprehensive or awkward, that is completely normal. You will get more comfortable with each interview you conduct. Your understanding of participants will evolve, and you will better know what to ask, where to dig deeper, what to focus on, and what you can skip. Your last interview will be complete before you realize it. Perhaps, like me, you might even come to enjoy the opportunity interviews provide for you to meet, and learn from, new, interesting people.

4. Review and Cleanse the Data

Reviewing notes days or weeks after an interview can sometimes be challenging. I take a lot of notes during interviews, so I use abbreviations. Occasionally I make a typing error, and autocorrect and autocomplete functions can sometimes result in unintended changes. The risk of missing or misinterpreting something a participant says while correcting errors is too great, so I rarely do so during an interview. To compensate for this, I always schedule some time closely following each interview to clean up my notes.

During the review, I:

1. Correct errors, misspellings, and bad auto-corrections
2. Expand abbreviations
3. Elaborate on shorthand notes
4. Expand sentences to make them readable and understandable to anyone
5. Enrich the notes by adding thoughts or comments I did not capture during the interview that I recall, or realize are important, during the review itself
6. Record observations that I may have formed through the interview, but which may not be directly related to what the participant said
7. Capture emerging themes, hypotheses, and observations formed during the interview that may or may not be based directly on participant statements, noting the latter separately to avoid confusion
8. Put the notes in a state where I, or anyone reading them for the first time, could understand them without additional context or assistance

9. Ensure all action and follow-up items are recorded and scheduled

10. Update the interview guide

    - Consider what went well, and what might have been better

    - Recall the participant's reaction to my questions and demeanor

    - Consider whether I received the information I was seeking and, if not, how to adjust the interview to get it

    - Evaluate whether I received information or insight I was not expecting, and whether I need to confirm it with subsequent participants

    - Consider whether new avenues of exploration are required, and whether they should be explored with all, or a subset, of participants

These steps ensure I can fully recall and understand what I learned up to two to four weeks later as I finalize the findings.

Be Deliberate, Make Time

Scheduling quiet time to review and clean up interview notes delivers benefits beyond its obvious administrative hygiene. **This post-interview review gives me an opportunity to think more calmly and clearly about what I learned, and helps me capture new learning and hypotheses that I may not have noted while the interview was in session. It often results in some of the greatest moments of discovery.**

I suggest scheduling an amount of time equal to the interview duration (e.g., schedule a 60-minute review following a 60-minute interview) as you begin. But the amount of time you require for each review may vary.

I find **this retrospective exercise delivers the best results when it is performed as soon after the interview as possible**. **I recommend scheduling time immediately following the interview for a note review**. If that is not possible, try to find a time as close to the interview as is practical, and try to avoid having too many interviews occur between note reviews or conducting the review after a day or more has passed.

Automatic Transcription

I recommend you review your notes this way even if you use automatic transcription services. Those services are very good now, even the ones that are built into the video conference applications. But they still miss things and make mistakes, and they won't include your observations. Some of those observations may be equally, or more, important than some of the things the participant said.

I tend not to rely on automatic transcription services for a couple of reasons. Foremost, they capture too much. They often transcribe every vocalization made, every half-sentence, every time the participant starts down an irrelevant thought path and switches to another. Sometimes there is so much irrelevant data that it can take forever to figure out what is important. Thus, reviewing a transcription can take much more time than reviewing my own notes. Newer AI-based transcription tools may address some of those annoyances, but be aware of their limitations.

Where I do find transcripts useful is in cases where I am taking notes and miss something a participant said. In those cases I capture the time in my notes so I can review that specific portion of the transcript with the benefit of the context of my notes. Transcripts can also be helpful when I am trying to decipher shorthand or autocorrected items in my notes.

Taking notes helps me to stay focused on the conversation and process what the participant is communicating, so I take notes even when a transcription is available.

Finally, I tend not to use transcription services as I find participants are more candid and forthcoming without them. This works for me since I take very detailed notes. I admit this is a personal style choice. People have become much more comfortable with live transcription services, and other interviewers use them quite effectively. However, **the one unbreakable rule regarding transcripts is that they should never be recorded without the participant's prior informed consent**. I believe doing so would be unethical and, at the very least, would likely be considered a breach of the participant's trust.

These initiatives are nothing without trust and ethical conduct. If you use a transcription service, remember to be clear about how the transcripts will be retained, who will have access, and whether and when they will be destroyed.

5. Update Stakeholders (Don't "Go Dark")

You will likely communicate with your sponsor and/or primary contact frequently prior to the commencement of your interviews. Once the interviews begin, the increased level of activity and focus required to prepare for, conduct, and follow up on the interviews may result in your ignoring them. This can happen unintentionally or insidiously. It can even be rationalized very simply. "I'm heads-down doing the work now. I don't need any input from my sponsor/contact. I won't have any real information for them until I'm done, so I don't want to bother them unnecessarily. I'm doing them a favor." Don't fall for it!

I have learned that people sometimes get more apprehensive and upset when they don't know what is happening than they do when they know something is not going well. They often assume the worst. Your interviews can span a period of two-to-six weeks. A communication gap of this magnitude can result in unwarranted and unnecessary damage control exercises, so don't "go dark." Be deliberate about providing regular updates to your primary contact or stakeholder, even when the updates are minor.

Stakeholder Conversations Are Always Valuable

Contrary to the logic above, you will always have something of interest to report to your stakeholders. For example:

- Early on you can report the status of your preparation or interview guide, and vet the participant list.

- Once you start recruiting participants you can share who has accepted, whom has yet to respond, and anyone who has declined.

- You can engage their assistance finding replacement participants or introducing you to someone you have been having difficulty contacting.

- As you conduct the interviews you can report your progress (e.g., how many are complete, how many remain) and you can discuss interesting themes that are beginning to emerge (noting they are subject to change).

All these actions *involve* your primary contact or stakeholder in a key aspect of the initiative.

I usually set up a weekly conversation with my primary contact or stakeholder for the entire duration of an engagement. The topics we cover vary greatly from stage to stage, but each of us almost always has something of value to share with the other. During the assessment period these conversations are often brief, but they are always valuable. On rare occasions, where neither of us has anything substantial to share, we cancel the meeting. But even the cancellation involves a brief email conversation. As a result, I never "go dark," even during the weeks we do not meet.

6. Prepare the Findings

This style of qualitative research has surfaced exciting and sometimes unintuitive discoveries every time I have conducted it. It can expose what people are actually doing, as opposed to what they say they are doing, or what they want to appear to be doing. Each of those insights are useful, and the differences between them can be unexpected and enlightening. Done well, an assessment can deliver insight into the performance and culture of an organization that even its own members may not have. That all comes together in the assessment's findings.

As you set out to prepare your findings think about your target audience. In many assessments, the objective might be to create an "informal" report for a primary audience of two to four key contacts and stakeholders closely involved in the project. After all, the primary objective of the assessment is to inform the initiative's design, change management (transformation), and communication activities. While this provides opportunities for efficiency, keep in mind that the findings may eventually land on anyone's desk. It is almost always the case that data or excerpts are extracted for use in reports or, more frequently, presentations created by others in the organization. **Design your report so that it can be read and understood by someone who did not participate in the assessment.**

I find a progressive disclosure style report works well. That is, I provide a PDF that contains at least three levels of detail. Though the specific content usually varies based upon the assessment's learning and focus, the findings normally include the following major sections:

1. **Introduction:** A one-page summary that provides the context of the assessment, including what was done (the assessment's basic parameters), the structure of the findings, and how to use the findings (e.g., what to read if you want an overview, what to read if you need detail)
2. **Executive summary:** A one-page summary of the top discoveries, conclusions, and recommendations; usually consisting of one bullet for each major theme
3. **Summary of findings (themes):** The highest level of detail of each finding, usually consisting of one page of additional detail for each bullet in the executive summary (each major theme)
4. **Detailed findings:** The detailed findings and evidence that led to the conclusions which were expressed as the major themes, normally consisting of one or more pages of detail related to each bullet in the summary of findings
5. **Appendix:** Additional detail, helpful artifacts, and/or answers to key questions (top ten lists)

The detailed findings section is normally very long and is sometimes placed in an appendix. Most readers will only refer to the detailed findings to clarify their understanding of a specific conclusion or to satisfy their curiosity about what was discovered in an area of personal interest. To make the connection between summary and detail easier, and drive readability and understanding, the page titles of the summary of findings section are consistent with the bullet they are connected to in the executive summary. In the detailed findings, the page titles correspond to bullets in the summary of findings (Figure 6-3). Though page titles may be expanded for readability and context, they are always easily associated with the corresponding bullet in the section above them.

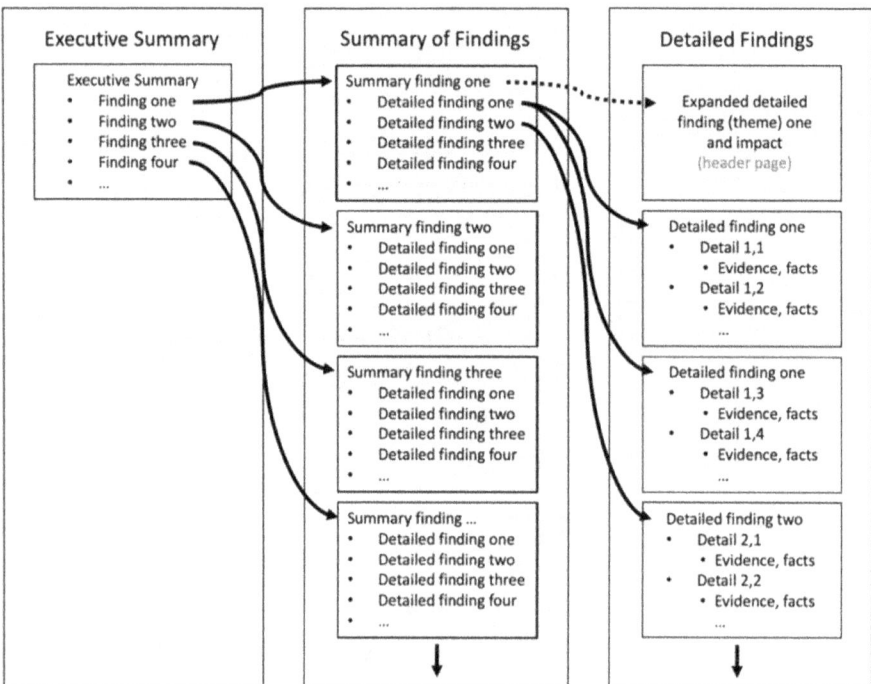

Figure 6-3. *Findings in progressive disclosure form (illustrative). Details are grouped to produce findings, findings are grouped to produce summary findings (themes), themes are grouped to produce the executive summary.*

I sometimes include a section on answers to key questions which I have asked all (or most) participants in the appendix. That section provides an anonymized list of answers to specific questions mentioned earlier such as, "If you could get everybody doing one thing consistently, what would that be?" or "If you could change only one thing, what would you change?" These questions often lead to easily consumable insight, which is sometimes immediately actionable. I include these only if they offer such insight, and only include the questions which offer such insight.

Begin at the End

One of the ironies of producing findings in this style is that they are prepared in the opposite order to which they are presented. The interviewer must begin by assembling the detailed findings. Themes emerge as interview notes are processed, and findings are placed into detail sections and grouped by theme. The detailed findings and themes will be constantly changing throughout this period of synthesis and preparation. Once all of the interview and other input has been processed and added to the details, several iterative reviews will be required in order to refine and clarify the emergent themes.

Review, Reduce, Repeat

Another irony that emerges at this stage is that the interviewer's initial fear they will not discover enough usually turns to a concern they have discovered too much. Thus, once the findings and themes begin to make sense, another iteration or two will likely be required to reduce the size and complexity of the findings. Once the detailed findings are complete, they are condensed into summary findings. This usually involves another series of iterations of both the summary and detailed findings. Condensing the findings in this way can also expose new discoveries or findings, or surface a need to combine or split findings or themes that had already been included.

Schedule "Quiet Time" for Preparation

As you may have guessed, this period of synthesis takes a lot of effort. It can take several days, or even a week or more, to synthesize, condense, and present the findings for even a 10-to-12-participant assessment. It requires focus and concentration, and is best done without interruption. Be sure to reserve time in your calendar for synthesis and preparation of findings well in advance. It is better to block more time than you need and release it, than to be trying to focus on this brain-heavy exercise following a full day of work.

Why Progressive Disclosure?

To be clear, you can present your findings in any format you are comfortable with. I prefer progressive disclosure because it:

- Communicates the key findings powerfully in an easy-to-understand form
- Backs conclusions up with detailed facts
- Is lightweight and easy to read
- Takes much less time to prepare than alternatives
- Eliminates the waste work required to create more formal reports

Formal reports can require as much editing and formatting work as they do synthesis. What's worse, in my experience almost nobody reads them. Most people have too much to read. The last thing they want is another "heavy" report, so the style itself can be a turn-off.

The progressive disclosure format can be created in a slideware application (e.g., PowerPoint or Keynote), and leverages bullet form and concise statements that enable comprehension of the high-level findings in a few minutes. Concise wording also reduces the potential for ambiguity or misinterpretation. While referencing detailed information and artifacts is rarely necessary, they are available, if needed.

I will stress again that the format and the style you use are less important than whether it clearly communicates what you learned from the assessment. **If you choose to use a more traditional format, ensure it has a brief and powerful executive summary.**

Don't Wait, Iterate!

You do not need to wait until the end of the last interview to begin your analysis and theme development. While some people might find it advantageous to wait until all the results are available before they begin synthesis, there are advantages in performing some along the way. For example, if you do not begin until after your last interview, by the time you get to final synthesis, you might forget about a developing theme you sensed early on.

Beginning to compile findings early may be helpful. It may even reduce the time between the last interview and the delivery of the first full draft. However, review the entirety of your assessment notes during final synthesis, regardless of whether you have done some interim review. As well, be careful not to introduce bias into subsequent interviews based upon your learning and hypotheses if you synthesize during the interview period.

Themes and Discovery

If you have never performed an assessment, you may be surprised at how much you can learn in such a short period of time through focus, active listening, and retrospective review. As your interviews progress you will start to discover similarities, differences, and affinities in participant responses. While it is impossible for me to know specifically what themes you will discover in each of your assessments, here are a few I commonly find:

Themes to explore during an assessment

- **Problems**
    - What problem(s) does the organization hope to address with your initiative? Does it (do they) actually exist? Is it (are they) painful enough people would act to solve them?
    - What is the impact of the problems the organization (team…) faces? What threats do they pose?
    - Are there adjacent or non-adjacent problems or organizational dysfunction that might impact the initiative?
    - What are the primary concerns of people, teams, and/or the organization? What "keeps them up at night"?
    - What external threats and risks is the organization dealing with?

- **Expectations and aspirations**
    - What outcomes do people want the initiative to deliver?
    - What value do people expect from the initiative? How will it be measured?
    - What are the differences in expectations across people, different roles, different departments, different regions? Are they in conflict?

- **Organizational values**
  - What does the organization value?
  - What do employees value?
  - Are the organization and employee values different? How? Are there conflicts?
  - Are the values interpreted differently across teams, departments, by managers...?
  - What is the organization's attitude toward new idea incubation or innovation?
  - What is *really* happening?
  - What is rewarded?

- **Performance and execution**
  - Are there synergistic individual or team strengths, or pockets of excellence? Where?
  - Are there obstacles or impediments to execution? How prevalent are they?
  - What do people believe they are doing? What are they actually doing?
  - Is there consistently good execution in specific areas?
  - Is there consistently poor execution in specific areas?
  - Are there potential champions?

- Is there anyone who would want your new initiative to fail? Why?
- What, if anything, is holding the people, teams, groups, or organization back?

- **People**
  - Does the current team have the skills required for the initiative?
  - Can the current team acquire skills to fill any gaps? How quickly?
  - Are there required skills which cannot be acquired in a reasonable time frame?
  - How is morale?
  - What, if any, conflict exists between people, teams, departments, leaders, or leadership teams?
  - Is there healthy or unhealthy competition between people or groups?

- **Opportunities**
  - What are the opportunities for early wins that could help build momentum and credibility?
  - Are new ideas currently incubating somewhere which could seed your initiative?
  - Are other people or teams attempting to address similar issues? Could they become partners?
  - Are there compatible initiatives and incentives which could be leveraged? (e.g., HR programs or focus)

- Are there emerging organizational goals or core values which might be leveraged?
- Are there people with experience in similar initiatives or in bringing new ideas to life?

- **How frequently was each theme, fact, or example mentioned?**

  - Were there commonalities across those who mentioned it? (position, role, location...)
  - Were there differences?
  - Which themes are strong? Which are weak? Which weak ones should be further explored?

You may not find evidence related to everything in this list, and you will almost certainly find things that were not listed in it. Think of the list as food for thought as you prepare and perform your own assessments. It may also help you notice things once your interviews begin. It can be easy to miss the importance of something a participant said, so thinking through these, and other, themes during synthesis may help you discover something you may have otherwise missed.

This may seem like a lot to think about but, in my experience, it is simpler to perform an assessment than to describe one in detail. Each assessment is, as you might expect, different. Each assessment will also be much more like others than you might anticipate.

7. Finalize the Findings

Once synthesis is complete and the first full draft of your findings is ready, I recommend an informal review with your primary contact and/or key team members before releasing it more broadly. Sometimes just saying things aloud to others can help identify unclear statements, missing context, or important details which may have been omitted.

CHAPTER 6   CONDUCTING ASSESSMENT INTERVIEWS

Input from others who know both the objective of your work and the organization's current situation and culture can be invaluable. Your contact can, of course, give you feedback on the overall presentation of the materials and how it is likely to be received. They can also help you to identify areas where key points may be misunderstood due to the organization's unique vocabulary, and terms and statements that might cause someone to stop your initiative in its tracks. (I've seen major initiatives paused because a specific word was, or was not, used.) Your contact can give you feedback regarding the preferred styles of the organization, and can help you identify incendiary terms or references that you may be unaware of or may need to approach with additional subtlety.

Additional Considerations

Here are a few additional things to consider as you design and conduct your assessments, and prepare and synthesize your findings:

- Your assessment captures a point in time, so keep sensing, inspecting, and adapting as you design, build, deploy, and operate your initiative.

- Assessments can be daunting the first time you perform them, but you will get better at them, and you will become more comfortable as you complete each one (rehearsing, and starting with a couple of friendly faces will help a lot).

- Sometimes assessments are as much artistry as they are science, so listen carefully, bring a high level of positive energy, and do not be reluctant to explore unanticipated topics during your conversations.

- Ask for help if you need it (and if you don't), there are likely people in your organization or network with a

CHAPTER 6 CONDUCTING ASSESSMENT INTERVIEWS

lot of experience with assessments and qualitative research (e.g., strategy, marketing, HR, management consulting...).

- Know the specific information you *must* elicit from each participant, and the questions you *must* ask, and be sure to get to those in each interview.

- Keep a list of people you recruited (with some additional context such as why they were chosen), the people who declined, and people you decided not to recruit; it may be helpful later, especially if you need additional feedback or perspective (make sure doing so will not violate organizational policies or privacy regulations or norms).

- Keep a legend of which people correspond to which anonymized interview pseudonyms in a secure location, at least until the final draft of your findings is complete (e.g., in case you need clarification from one of them).

- You can *begin* some of the activities covered in subsequent chapters of this book as you conduct your interviews (e.g., begin updating objectives, preparing communication material, and/or preparing inputs for a final design), and there will likely be downtime during the assessment which may present an opportunity for those things to be done.

- When synthesizing your findings, remember to consider what you learned from conversations and workshops that happened outside the formal interviews, though also be aware of potential bias they might introduce, and be sure to respect confidentiality when referencing them.

CHAPTER 6   CONDUCTING ASSESSMENT INTERVIEWS

Become a Member of the Team

I find the more interaction I have with a team, the better I understand their challenges and opportunities, and the better I can interpret what I learn from an assessment. For example, my clients are almost always aware I can design and facilitate workshops that enable people to collaborate to solve difficult problems. As a result, they sometimes ask if I can help design and/or run a workshop that is not directly related to the engagement or assessment. I always say "yes" to reasonable requests of this nature, if I have time.

The primary reason I do this is that I always like to deliver more value than my customers expect, and this is a great opportunity to give something back. In addition, I have come to learn that working with people outside the context of my primary assignment can have a highly positive impact on any engagement. As I work with people, I learn a lot about their norms, work culture, challenges, strengths, skills, personality, and sense of humor. I learn what they consider to be good and bad. I learn their collaboration skills and styles, and other things that I would not have otherwise had insight into, and which are of great importance in my primary assignment. Most importantly, I get to know people, and they get to know me.

Working on a *small*, unrelated item or two provides an amazing opportunity to build relationships and trust, will visibly demonstrate your motivation, and provides an opportunity to give a little back to the people who were kind enough to trust you and bring you into their organization and work lives.

This type of opportunity may also exist if you are not a consultant but work in a large organization. There are always groups looking for help, to fill a skill gap, or to get a "neutral party" to facilitate some activity or workshop. Most large organizations also have voluntary cross-organization initiatives that require volunteers. I have participated in many of these because I believed in their value, but always felt I received more value from them than I contributed.

What's Next?

Now that your research has concluded, you have gathered knowledge from existing research and documentation, and you have completed your assessment interviews and related discussions and/or workshops, you should have what you need to begin designing your initiative and planning its deployment and operation. As you will see in the next chapter, that begins with revisiting and finalizing your objectives to ensure they take into consideration what you learned from those activities.

CHAPTER 7

Designing Your Approach

Following the assessment, you should possess a wealth of information from at least three major sources:

1. **Stakeholder, primary contact, and fact-finding (and other) conversations**
   (e.g., charter conversations, workshops, brainstorming, ongoing discussions)

2. **Secondary research**

   a. Internal
      (e.g., presentations, white papers, process documentation, memos)

   b. External
      (e.g., books, articles)

3. **Primary research**
   (i.e., information discovered during the assessment)

This chapter describes how to leverage this information to design your initiative, and discusses how the choices you make may impact how you should engage others in the organization (Figure 7-1).

CHAPTER 7 DESIGNING YOUR APPROACH

> **In this Chapter**
>
> Designing your initiative:
>
> 1. Decide what you are building
> 2. Be deliberate about inputs and outputs
> 3. Select the initiative's structure
> 4. Prepare a detailed design
> 5. Engage cross-organizational teams

Figure 7-1. What's in this chapter

1. Decide What You Are Building

Lean entrepreneurship approaches, tools, and techniques can be leveraged in a variety of ways. The three archetypes I most commonly encounter are (Figure 7-2):

1. **Toolkit:** A collection of resources, tools, templates, artifacts, and/or software made available with little, or no, training, support, or guidance.

2. **Framework or approach:** A collection of guidelines regarding the steps required to bring new ideas to life (e.g., as outlined later in sections 3 and 4), usually accompanied by a toolkit.

3. **Initiative, service, or program:** Participants are guided by advisors and a framework, supported by mentors, infrastructure, and a support person or

team, and leverage a toolkit and, usually, additional resources such as hardware and/or software, workspace or test labs, funding, training, sales assistance, and/or access to potential customers.

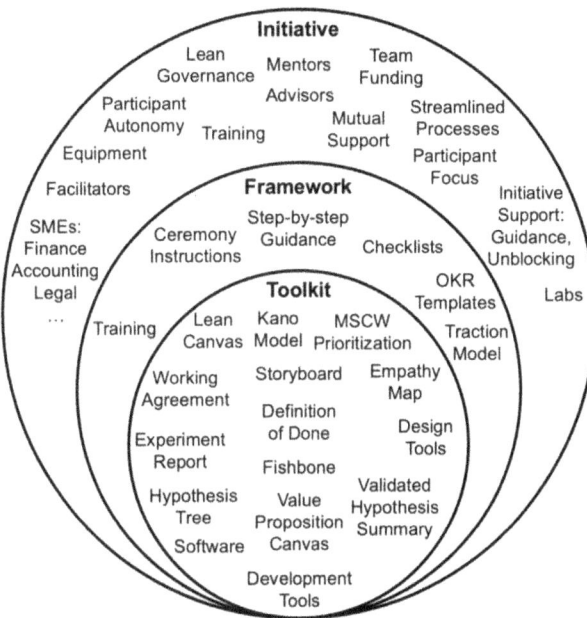

Figure 7-2. *Initiatives, frameworks, and toolkits. Items shown in each archetype are illustrative, not exhaustive. Not all frameworks provide toolkits.*

The volume and type of activity required to deliver each archetype differs greatly, and each has its advantages. Tables 7-1, 7-2, and 7-3 summarize some of the key differences between the three archetypes.

CHAPTER 7   DESIGNING YOUR APPROACH

Table 7-1. Characteristics of a toolkit (illustrative)

Toolkit

- Inexpensive: Many tools are inexpensive or freely available
- Low effort: Identify and share tools, acquire licenses as necessary
- Rapid delivery: First version can be delivered in less than one month
- Staff: One person short-term or part-time for creation; periodic maintenance and update
- Self-service: People use it at their convenience
- Maintenance (Low): Periodically review and update the toolkit (part-time)
- Effective for self-starters and teams who know how to bring new ideas to life

- No guidance regarding how to execute new idea delivery
- No coaching or support
- No resources (e.g., hardware, training, people) to help bring the idea to life
- Ideas can be lost, or participant burn-out can occur, if innovators cannot work on ideas during the workday
- Can be confusing for people without experience bringing new ideas to life
- Can be under-utilized if not actively promoted
- Usefulness can decrease if not properly maintained

Table 7-2. *Characteristics of a framework (illustrative)*

Framework

• Inexpensive: Many frameworks are available at low or no cost (books, web)	• No coaching or support
	• No resources (e.g., hardware, training, people) to help bring the idea to life
• Low-to-medium effort: Identify a suitable framework and modify it if necessary	• Ideas can be lost, or participant burn-out can occur, if innovators cannot work on ideas during the workday
• Rapid delivery: Ready in as little as one quarter or less	• Without advisors or mentors, people without experience bringing new ideas to life may not be able to overcome obstacles they encounter
• Staff: One person short-term to lead cross-functional evaluation, selection, customization, initial deployment, and fine tuning	
	• Can be under-utilized if not actively promoted
• Self-service: People use it at their convenience	• Usefulness can decrease if not properly maintained
• Maintenance (Medium): Obtain feedback from users, fine-tune the framework	• When mandatory, there is risk the governing body will surround the framework with heavy processes
• Step-by-step guidance helps new innovators	• May require fine-tuning or customization
• Can help drive an innovation culture or mindset	
• Use can be optional or mandatory	

CHAPTER 7 DESIGNING YOUR APPROACH

Table 7-3. *Characteristics of an initiative (illustrative)*

Initiative	
<ul><li>Rapid delivery: Can be built in stages</li><li>Staff (scalable): Ranges from one part-time person for small initiatives to larger teams for comprehensive initiatives (details in Chapter 10)</li><li>Full service: Initiative team guides participants through the steps required to bring new ideas to life and removes obstacles to their progress</li><li>Maintenance (continuous): Retrospectives, continuous learning, and improvement</li><li>Active guidance, mentoring, and resources ensure new ideas have the best chance to succeed</li><li>Full-time participants stay focused, avoid burnout</li><li>Provides the resources necessary for success</li><li>Drives an innovation culture or mindset</li><li>Can work in synergy with other initiatives</li></ul>	<ul><li>More expensive than toolkits or frameworks</li><li>High effort to fully deploy (e.g., perform the activities in chapters 5–13)</li><li>Usually requires continuous staffing commensurate with the initiative's size</li><li>Value can drift if teams do not practice continuous learning and improvement (more in Chapter 13)</li><li>Larger investment can drive unrealistic stakeholder expectations for rapid returns</li><li>Risk of delayed delivery, drift, or failure to launch when the initiative is not its owner's highest priority</li></ul>

Frameworks have much more of an impact on the day-to-day lives of practitioners than toolkits, especially when they are mandated. They often require fine-tuning once implemented, so closing the project that created them too early can leave practitioners with an ineffective, inefficient, or counterproductive set of guidelines. It can make them miserable. With the wrong ownership, mandatory frameworks and approaches can themselves become as despised as the heavy processes they may have been intended to replace.

Decision 1: Toolkit, Framework, or Initiative?

At this point, you should understand whether you are setting out to create a toolkit, framework, or initiative. Data from the three previously discussed sources should provide evidence that supports your choice. Even though you can change or evolve your decision, **it is critical to make a deliberate choice** at this stage so you will know which activities to focus on, and so you can properly set sponsor, stakeholder, and participant expectations.

If you choose to build an initiative, it can be built in stages. For example, you might lack sufficient funding or support to build a full initiative at the outset. If that is the case, you can begin by creating a toolkit, evolve that into a framework, and then leverage that work to create a full initiative once you have sufficient momentum and support.

This book will guide you through developing a full initiative that includes both a framework and toolkit. It will give you enough information to tackle any of the three. It includes several framework archetypes and information to help you select and customize the one that is best for you. It also includes a sample Toolkit, which you can utilize or use as inspiration while building your own. The Toolkit includes several artifacts that are also useful in the creation and deployment of a framework.

CHAPTER 7   DESIGNING YOUR APPROACH

2. Be Deliberate About Inputs and Outputs

Once people have decided to implement an approach or initiative like lean entrepreneurship, they can be tempted to begin their design activities by focusing on the details of each phase (e.g., "Seed 1," "Seed 2"). In fact, some just begin executing the initiative's early stages (e.g., conduct pitch ceremonies, begin Seed 1 incubation activities, conduct 3P reviews…). As someone who is very passionate about this, I can certainly empathize with them. However, two critical decisions must be made before you do either to ensure your initiative addresses your organization's specific needs and expectations, and achieves its maximum effectiveness (Figure 7-3).

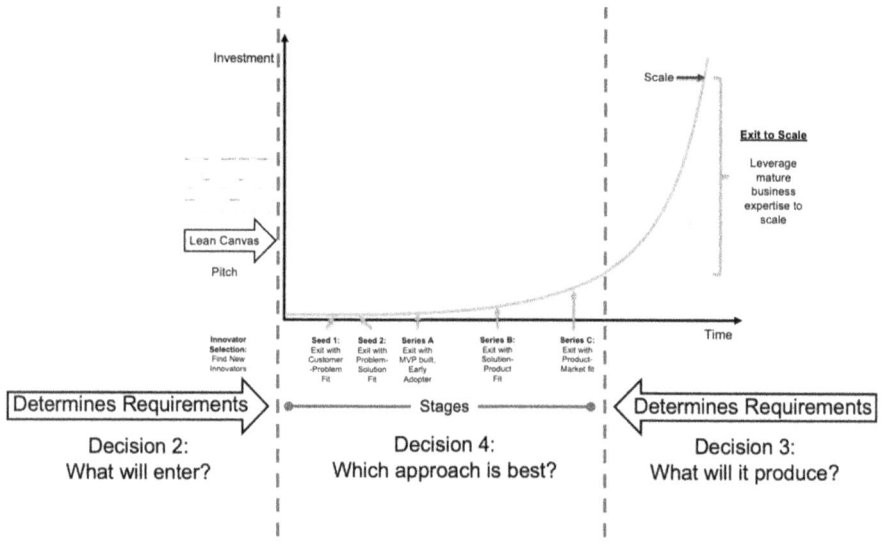

Figure 7-3. *Primary design decisions 2–4: (2) What will enter the initiative? (3) What will the initiative produce? (4) Which approach is best? Decisions 2 and 3 drive Decision 4 and define the requirements of each stage*

The type and maturity of ideas your initiative accepts will impact the types of activities it should, or must, include. Furthermore, what happens during each stage of your approach will determine what exits the initiative.

CHAPTER 7 DESIGNING YOUR APPROACH

Therefore, you must decide what the initiative will accept (Decision 2) and the initiative's desired outcomes and outputs (Decision 3) *before* your approach is selected and fine-tuned (Decision 4).

Figure 7-4 is an image of a whiteboard I used while preparing for a workshop during which we defined an early lean entrepreneurship-style incubator–accelerator. All three decisions are represented in this early, high-level diagram. The top horizontal section (purple and red), which runs from "Idea" through "Selection," deals with questions and thoughts related to what happens before an idea enters the accelerator (Decision 2). The horizontal section in the middle of the board (blue and green), running from "Early Incubation" to "Scale," includes questions and decisions related to what happens during incubation (the stages, Decision 4), and the small area on the right of the center section (black and orange) discusses the exit (the output, Decision 3).

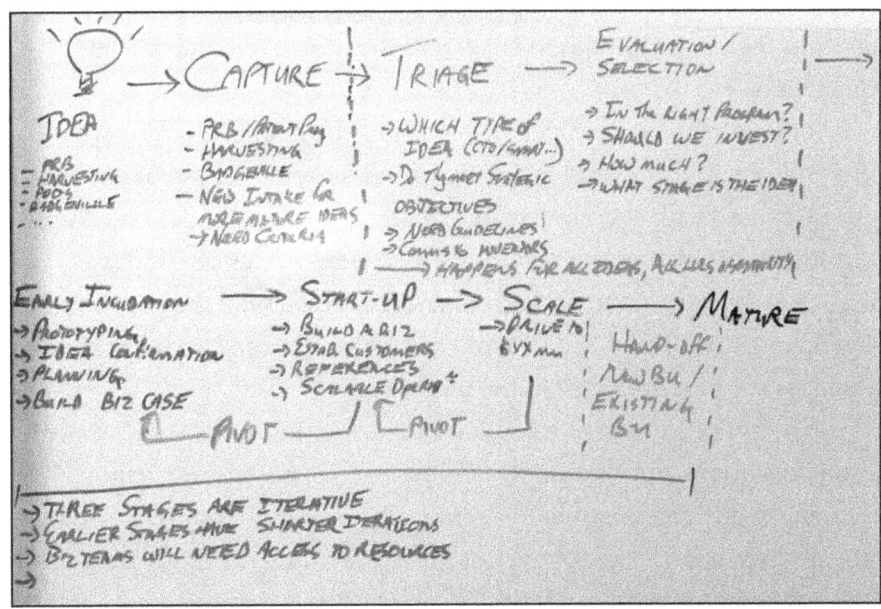

Figure 7-4. Photo of a whiteboard used in preparation for an early incubator–accelerator design workshop

CHAPTER 7   DESIGNING YOUR APPROACH

Now that you have an idea of the overall landscape, let's further consider each of these key decisions.

Decision 2: What Will Enter the Initiative?

"Ideas come from everywhere!" It's a phrase most of us have heard before, and likely more than once. It is frequently found in inspirational posts and on posters and promotional material for innovation programs and contests. Fortunately, in my experience it is true. Great ideas come from a multitude of sources. The accuracy of this statement also foreshadows one of the greatest challenges that will face anyone starting an initiative like this.

There is often a pent-up demand when innovation or new idea incubation initiatives are launched. If this demand is not anticipated and managed, it can lead potential participants, sponsors, stakeholders, and people in their social circles to have unrealistic, or even unachievable expectations.

Prior to launch, it is critical that decisions be made regarding which ideas will be supported and how they will be selected. These parameters must be shared with everyone to ensure the right ideas find their way to the initiative. They must be communicated clearly to ensure ideas are being selected fairly, to make certain people understand they are being adjudicated objectively, and to avoid mismatched expectations that might cause loss of interest or trust in the initiative.

You might be thinking, "easy, we want to capture every idea." Many people start there, but I would bet you have at least *some* restrictions. For example, if you are a member of a public sector safety organization or a software-as-a-service company, you probably would not incubate ideas related to a new ice-cream flavor? There are always parameters within which you will wish to operate. It may be best to set those parameters even more tightly early in the initiative's life so you can identify any flaws in the approach and inspect, adapt, improve, and prepare the initiative's team for scale before broadening the initiative's scope.

Consider the following as you decide what to bring into your initiative, and what to exclude:

- **What kinds of ideas will you accept?**
    - Breakthrough ideas?
    - Ideas adjacent to the existing business or mission?
    - Disruptive ideas?
        - Disruptive to the organization's existing business or services?
            - All of them? Specific ones?
    - Internal technology ideas?
    - External program offerings?
- **Will the initiative focus on a specific type of service or technology?**
    - For example: Will it be an AI focused initiative that will accept only AI related ideas? Blockchain focused? Cybersecurity focused? Either AI or cybersecurity focused? Only cybersecurity ideas that involve AI?
- **Will ideas be limited to those involving only services? Hardware? Software? Programs?**
- **How mature must an idea be?**
    - A well-considered idea and a lean canvas?
    - A set of wireframes or storyboards?

- An interactive prototype (e.g., design tool mock-up)?
- A functioning prototype?
- A suspected customer or beneficiary problem?
- A confirmed customer or beneficiary problem?

- **What combination(s) of the preceding parameters will be applied?**
  - For example: Will the initiative accept ideas only for disruptive technology related to existing businesses or services?

- **Will ideas be accepted from every geographic region?**
  - Will the initiative be available to specific regions and/or offices?
    - Which ones?

- **Will ideas be accepted from every business unit or department?**
  - Will the initiative be limited to specific groups within the organization?
    - Specific departments, specific business units?
    - Specific job functions or disciplines (e.g., engineering, software engineering, product management)?

- **Will ideas be accepted from outside the organization?**
  - From the general public?
  - From partners?

CHAPTER 7 DESIGNING YOUR APPROACH

- From existing customers?
- From prospective customers?
- From academic institutions?
- **If you accept external ideas, will the people who generated them participate in bringing them to life? If so, how?**
  - As advisors?
  - As active partners?
  - As new employees of the organization?
  - As contractors?
  - As interns?
- **Where and how will ideas be captured?**
  - In the course of completing everyday work?
    - Who will capture them?
    - How?
  - Through initiatives that generate, capture, or surface new ideas? How?
    - Internal innovation competitions?
    - External innovation competitions?
    - Hackathons?
    - Patent review boards?
    - Invention harvesting exercises?
    - Internal think tanks?

221

CHAPTER 7 DESIGNING YOUR APPROACH

- Internal or external conferences or meetups?
- Idea/innovation/patent pods (groups that gather to brainstorm)?
- Patent harvesting sessions?
- Internal crowdsourcing systems?
- Product Management teams?
- Cross-functional organizations?
- Academic partnerships?
- Technology partnerships?
- Business partnerships?

- **Are there other initiatives that foster or promote new idea generation or incubation which could be leveraged?**
- **Is there a record of past ideas that were not pursued that might be mined?**
  - Ideas rejected by existing departments or business units?
  - Old roadmaps?
  - Brainstorming sessions or idea pods?
- **Is there a record of past failed ideas that might serve as inspiration?**
  - Would any of those ideas be worth revisiting?

- **How will ideas be captured?**
  - Will they be mined from other sources by the initiative's team?
  - Will potential sources be informed and instructed how to submit ideas?
  - Will there be a way for people to submit ideas for consideration?
    - How? (e.g., internal web site)
    - Who can submit ideas?
      - Anyone?
      - Any job function?
      - Any geographic region or office?
- **How will ideas be selected?**
  - What criteria will be used?
  - Who will evaluate the ideas?
  - Who will determine if ideas are ready to be evaluated?
  - Will specific people be able to assign ideas to the initiative without a pitch?
    - For example, an executive with a validated strategic need

- Will hackathon or innovation competition winners be offered entry as a reward?
    - At whose discretion?
    - What happens if no winners meet the initiative's objectives?
    - How will people be informed of the decision to bring an idea into the initiative or not?
- **What will happen to good ideas that are not well suited to the initiative?**
    - For example, a new feature for an existing product or service, an HR service

These decisions will have a profound impact on your initiative. For example, limiting selection to a specific technology or region will likely simplify idea capture and triage. Accepting less mature ideas might result in longer incubation times, more pivots, and/a lower exit percentage.

The answers to these questions determine which ideas are captured, how they are captured, and how they will enter your initiative. This can be represented in the left side of your initiative's overview diagram (Figure 7-5).

CHAPTER 7   DESIGNING YOUR APPROACH

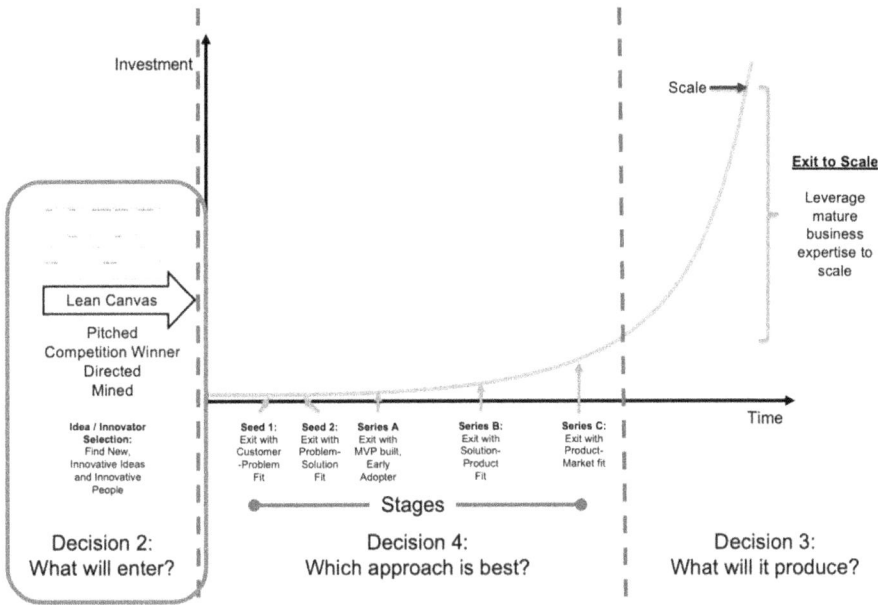

Figure 7-5. *Illustrative initiative overview diagram with additional specificity regarding how ideas are selected*

Though you need to be deliberate about, and clearly communicate, what will enter your initiative and how it will be selected, those decisions are not locked in for eternity. **You can deliberately begin with a narrow scope in the short- or mid-term and expand it as your initiative matures.** For example, you might begin by restricting participation to a specific team, job function, technology, or geography, and broaden participation over time.

It is important to clearly communicate the rationale for any such restrictions, why the specific restrictions were selected (e.g., existing facilities, budget restrictions, laws, policies…), and when eligibility will be expanded, if that is known. You can change or ease these restrictions at any time. Make sure to clearly communicate those changes when they occur,

CHAPTER 7   DESIGNING YOUR APPROACH

and make known any rationale for the changes, if possible. **Openness and transparency are key to building trust in the initiative, and the initiative will not likely succeed without trust.**

Now that you have made deliberate decisions about what will enter your initiative, it's time to do the same for what will exit.

Decision 3: What Will Exit the Initiative?

You may have noticed that Figure 7-4 does not explore many alternatives for what will exit the initiative it was created for. That should not be interpreted as meaning the decision is any less important than the selection of inputs, which covers roughly one third of that image. It simply belies the fact that the team working on the initiative had already spent time deciding what would exit.

The exits we defined for that initiative included new products which would exit to existing business teams that already sold similar offerings, and new products that were unique or substantial enough to become a new line of business. The team later determined that their initiative might also exit embedded technologies that would be included in, or support, one or more product offerings, but which would not be sold as products themselves. One such incubation exited as a back-end analytics engine that was embedded in several products.

The outputs you choose will impact the stages required during incubation, and what must happen during the final stage when an incubated idea is transitioning to exit the initiative. At this point, you should be considering questions such as:

- **What type(s) of things will exit?**
  - Services?
  - Programs?
  - Products?

226

- Internal tools or systems?
- Projects?
- A combination of those?

- **How mature will items be when they exit?**
  - Complete, functioning, and operational or for-sale?
  - As fully deployed public sector programs?
  - Ready for inclusion in a program roll-out or project?
  - Ready for deployment within the construct of an internal project?
  - Proven and ready for production?
  - Proven and ready for refactoring or fine-tuning prior to production?

- **Which people or groups will be the recipients of the exited items?**
  - Who will operate and support the technology once it is deployed in a program?
  - Who will drive a production roll-out of the IT project, and service and support the technology once it is in production?
  - Who will sell it (if appropriate)?
  - Who will support it?
  - Who will maintain and update it?

- **What pre-exit activities are required to prepare recipients for transition?**
    - How early will recipients need to be involved?
    - What will their role be during each stage of incubation?
        - Advisory?
        - Active participant?
        - Operational?
    - What training will they require?
    - What, if any, post-transition support will be required or provided?
- **Which activities are required to prepare the exiting items for their exit?**
    - Which turnover activities might be required?
    - Will any re-platforming be required?
        - How will it be planned?
        - Who will be responsible?
    - Will rebranding or renaming be required?
    - What approvals will be required? By whom?
    - Are any turnover activities, approvals, or certifications required to comply with policy, regulation, or legislation?
        - These are often required for public sector incubations.

- **How will people know when an item is ready to exit?**
- **How will people know when an item has exited?**
- **What, if any, post-exit follow-up will be performed by the initiative's team?**
  - When?
  - How frequently?

What, if any, post-exit measurement will be performed by the initiative's team?

- To whom will it be reported?
- What action will be taken based upon those measurements?
  - If they are higher than expected?
  - If they are lower than expected?
  - If they are as expected?

Now that you have decided what will enter your initiative and what will exit, you are ready to select a basic structure.

3. Select the Initiative's Structure

Since you have completed the research required to understand the organization's problems, needs, and desires, and you have used the knowledge you gained during your research to make explicit choices regarding what will enter your initiative and what will exit, you are ready to make choices about how you will create the conditions for repeatable innovation and new idea incubation. Let's consider two basic archetypes for the approach, beginning with the one introduced in Chapter 4.

CHAPTER 7   DESIGNING YOUR APPROACH

Structure 1: Seed-Series

The original lean entrepreneurship structure consisted of two phases with a total of five stages (Figure 7-6). Let's look at each element of the structure in a bit more detail.

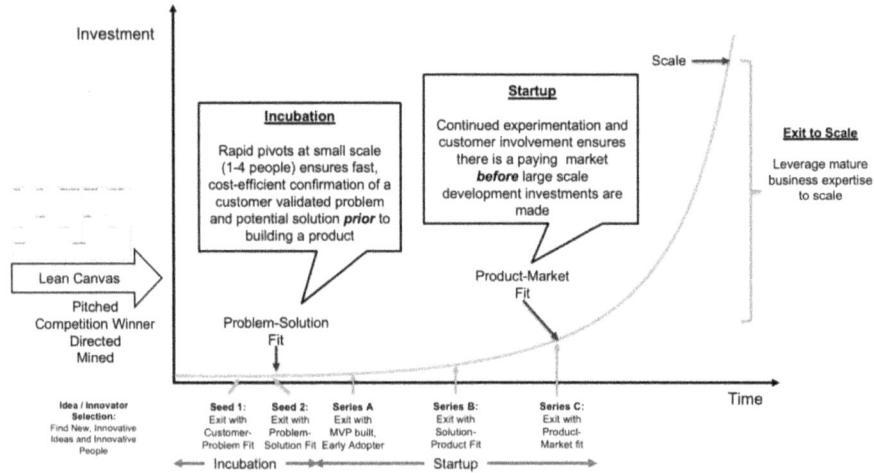

Figure 7-6. *The original lean entrepreneurship "Seed-Series" structure, shown with five stages*

The **Incubation phase** is designed to bring an idea from conception to problem–solution fit. It focuses on ensuring the solution addresses a problem that is worth solving, and that is painful enough that customers, beneficiaries, or program sponsors would act, commit resources, and/or pay to solve it. Solution hypotheses are also developed and confirmed as being desirable during this phase. Teams usually consist of one or two people at the commencement of the incubation phase, and do not typically grow beyond two to four people.

The Incubation phase includes two stages, as summarized in Table 7-4.

Table 7-4. *Illustrative Incubation phase activities*

Seed 1 (Customer–Problem Fit)	Seed 2 (Problem–Solution Fit)
• Validate the problem is real, understood by the incubating team, and painful enough people would switch from existing alternatives • Exit with customer–problem fit	• Design or more potential solutions • Prototype or wire-frame, but not build, a solution • Confirm people would adopt the solution • Begin building the MVT • Exit with problem–solution fit

Teams begin the **Startup phase** by assembling their minimum viable team (MVT) and building their minimum viable product (MVP). They build, learn fast, and iterate until they have traction and acquire early adopters. They maintain maniacal customer focus and prioritize continuous learning and improvement until they reach product–market fit. Once they achieve (in some cases "approach") product–market fit, the business created by the incubating team is "acquired" by an existing business unit, becomes its own business unit, or is sold or spun-off externally.

The Startup phase includes three stages, as summarized in Table 7-5.

CHAPTER 7   DESIGNING YOUR APPROACH

Table 7-5. *Illustrative Startup phase activities*

Series A (MVP, Early Adopter)	Series B (Solution–Product Fit)	Series C (Exit)
• Build the MVT • Build an MVP • Confirm feasibility • Obtain early adopters • Obtain earlyvangelists • Validate the business model • Exit with solution traction and evidence the business model works	• Increase demand • Demonstrate solution scalability • Demonstrate business model viability, scalability • Demonstrate customer satisfaction, retention • Create an exit strategy • Exit with evidence of viability and scalability, and an identified business acquirer	• Prepare for transition to the acquirer • Improve: business model fundamentals; growth; customer satisfaction; retention • Complete: due diligence; Series B commitments to acquiring team • Exit with completed acquisition, usually near product–market fit

Note   Additional detail regarding the specific types of activities that are typically performed in each stage of each structure is available in the Toolkit.

Additional information regarding the model, the rationale for this structure and how it evolved can be found in Chapters 3 and 4 of *Lean Entrepreneurship*.

The Need for a New Structure

The Seed-Series structure worked extremely well, but there were cases where it fell short. For example, some solutions require a combination of software *and* hardware. They might involve assistive devices, sensors, physical security, audio, or video. The equipment might be located in a business or government office, a public area like a shopping mall, or even outdoors.

When they do not perform well, globally deployed services of this nature can be time-consuming, expensive, and very challenging to unwind. There may even be legal reasons a "bad" service cannot simply be shut down. In addition, hardware and software used in production applications is often extremely expensive. Imagine rolling out a minimum viable product at a cost of millions, tens of millions, or even hundreds of millions of dollars and learning it is not suited to task. Or learning only after it is publicly available that it violates a law or regulation.

To mitigate those risks, teams need an operational low-fidelity prototype that is beyond a simple wireframe or mock-up, but less than a production-ready MVP. In some cases, the prototypes must be tested in the field to help teams determine whether employee-facing or public-facing deployments could even work, to watch the flow of people through the solution and the user experience, and to help discover any potential violations of regulations, legislation, or policies. Deploying a production-ready pilot for something of this nature could be prohibitively expensive, especially if hardware or specialized equipment is required; but doing nothing is too risky.

Using a low-fidelity prototype, teams assemble an *apparently* functional version of the solution from low quality components which might cost tens of dollars, versus production components which might cost hundreds or thousands of times as much. They can mock-up back-end services, stub out functions that are not required for their experiments, and even perform some functions manually behind the scenes ("Wizard of Oz" style).

CHAPTER 7   DESIGNING YOUR APPROACH

The Explore-Experiment-Transition (public sector) and Incubate-Startup-Accelerate (private sector) structures were developed to address these needs and mitigate these risks.

Structure 2: Explore–Experiment–Transition (Public Sector)

The Explore-Experiment-Transition model comprises three phases and six stages (Figure 7-7).

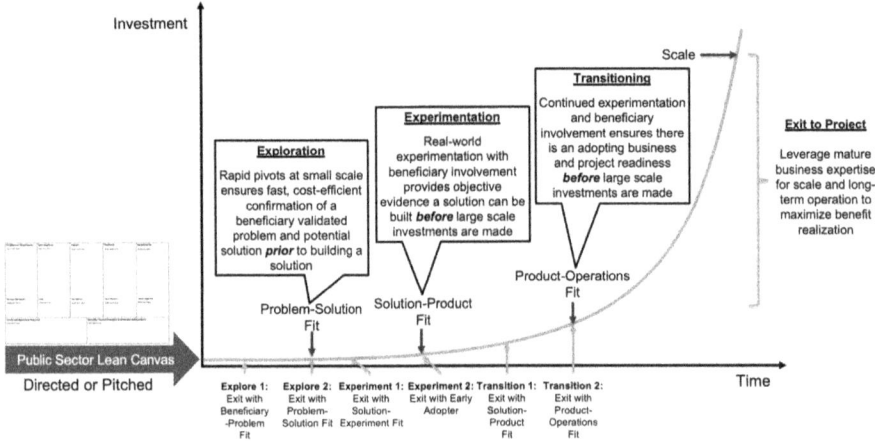

Figure 7-7. The Explore-Experiment-Transition model

The **Explore phase is** designed to **prove an idea is desirable**, develop the business model, and bring it from conception to problem-solution fit. It focuses on ensuring the solution addresses a problem that is worth solving, and that is painful enough that beneficiaries or program sponsors would take action, commit resources, and/or allocate funding to solve it. Solution hypotheses are also developed, and validated by beneficiaries during this phase. Teams are usually small at the commencement of the

CHAPTER 7   DESIGNING YOUR APPROACH

incubation phase, and do not typically grow beyond two to four people, though they might be larger depending upon the problem being solved. Others outside the team may provide some necessary services or expertise.

The Explore phase includes two stages, as shown in Table 7-6.

Table 7-6. *Illustrative Explore phase activities*

Explore 1 (Beneficiary–Problem Fit)	Explore 2 (Problem–Solution Fit)
• Validate the problem or need is real, understood by the incubating team, and worth solving for beneficiaries, users, or sponsors • Exit with beneficiary–problem fit	• Design one or more potential solutions • Prototype or wire-frame, but not build, a solution • Confirm people would adopt the solution • Begin building the MVT • Exit with problem–solution fit, initial low-fidelity test plan

During the **Experiment** phase, teams perform real-world experiments with users and/or beneficiaries to **provide evidence that a solution is feasible** *before* large scale investments are made. They confirm their proposed solutions will likely drive sufficient value or benefit, and that user and beneficiary experiences are good. They also confirm that the operational model is sound, that the solution can operate with, or alongside, existing solutions, and that the architecture is sound and likely to be scalable.

The Experiment phase includes two stages, as shown in Table 7-7.

CHAPTER 7   DESIGNING YOUR APPROACH

Table 7-7. Illustrative Experiment phase activities

Experiment 1 (Solution–Experiment Fit)	Experiment 2 (MVP, Early Adopter)
<ul><li>Iterate production-like experiments with low-fidelity prototypes</li><li>Use low-cost components</li><li>Technology and process de-risking</li><li>Address security, privacy, policy, regulatory, legal concerns</li><li>Exit with solution definition, MVP architecture</li></ul>	<ul><li>Demonstrate the solution addresses the problem or opportunity</li><li>Prove the solution drives sufficient value</li><li>Demonstrate good beneficiary and/or user experience</li><li>Demonstrate the solution functions in an operational context</li><li>Validate the architecture is sound and scalable</li><li>Exit with early adopter solution deployment</li></ul>

During the **Transition** phase, teams actively involve beneficiaries and/or users in continued experiments to **ensure the solution is viable and ready to be deployed in a production environment.** They also confirm a business or department is willing, and will be able, to adopt the solution, and that the teams which will receive the solution are adequately prepared to do so. Large scale investments are not made until those conditions are met. Teams, and their solutions, exit this stage when they have adequately proven desirability, feasibility, and viability, and the solution is turned over to the receiving adopter(s).

The Transition phase consists of two stages, as shown in Table 7-8.

CHAPTER 7 DESIGNING YOUR APPROACH

Table 7-8. Illustrative Transition phase activities

Transition 1 (Solution–Product Fit)	Transition 2 (Product–Operations Fit)
• Begin transition of solution to recipient adopters • Increase adoption • Demonstrate continuing value • Prove the solution is supportable in production • Confirm solution scalability • Begin transfer of leadership to the receiving team • Exit with proof of increasing demand, refined production-readiness, production adoption agreement, approved transition plan	• Address technical debt • Finalize production readiness • Transition solution to production or deployment • Embed with a project or program (if necessary) • Wind down incubating team • Transfer of personnel (if required) • Exit with solution turnover, knowledge capture and sharing, redistribution of incubation resources and equipment, incubating team reassignment

Structure 3: Incubate–Startup–Accelerate (Private Sector)

Though the Explore–Experiment–Transition structure is well suited to private sector requirements, some changes are needed to adjust for the delivery of a commercial product or service, and to achieve product–market fit versus product–operations fit. Combining the structure, detailed elements, and terminology of the Seed-Series and the Explore–Experiment–Transition structures results in a better private sector model (Figure 7-8).

CHAPTER 7 DESIGNING YOUR APPROACH

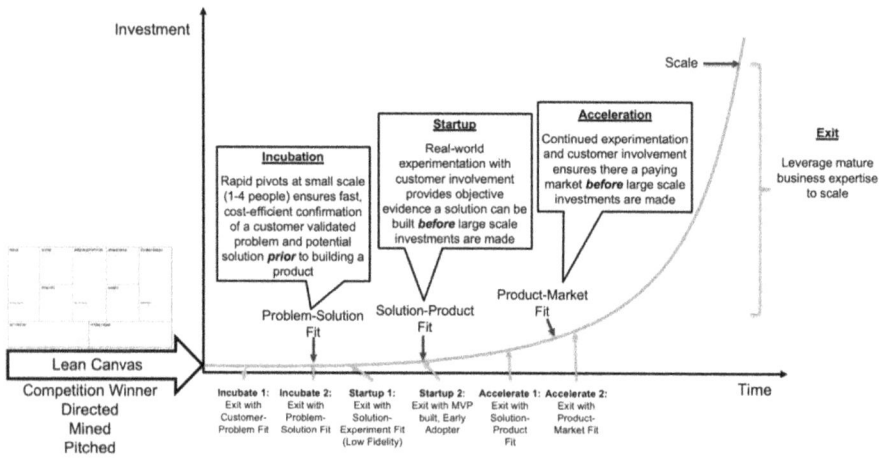

Figure 7-8. Incubate–Startup–Accelerate model

Note Detailed descriptions of the Incubate–Startup–Accelerate model stages are available in the Toolkit.

Alignment with Desirability–Feasibility–Viability

The Explore-Experiment-Transition and Incubate-Startup-Accelerate models more prominently expose alignment with desirability, feasibility, and viability (Figure 7-9), better surfacing and communicating the rationale for each stage, and making the purpose of incubation activities more obvious and easier to understand.

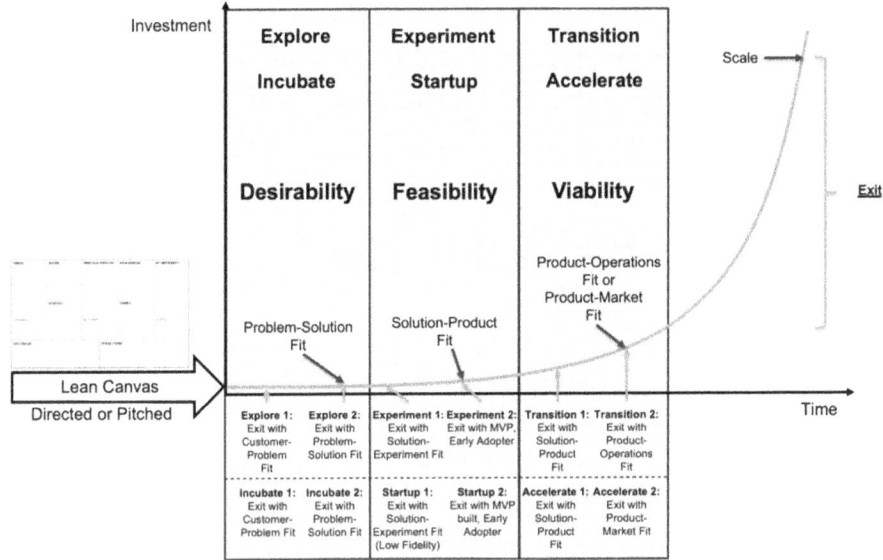

Figure 7-9. *Explore–Experiment–Transition and Incubate–Startup–Accelerate alignment with the lean startup principles of desirability, feasibility, and viability*

Decision 4: Select a Structure

Now it's time to combine the knowledge you gained during the assessment with the decisions you made about inputs and outputs and select a structure. One of the basic structures discussed in this chapter will likely suit your needs, but you may wish to fine-tune it to better suit your organization's unique requirements and culture. This might entail adding or removing stages as you design it, or as your initiative evolves.

Do not be concerned if you cannot think of any need to fine-tune your structure at this point. Often no changes are necessary early on. Fine-tuning the structure and its elements usually happens during the remainder of the design process, during the design workshops, and even throughout the life of an initiative once it is operational. Neither should you be concerned if your changes feel cosmetic. As previously mentioned, simple changes such as modification of terminology can make a big difference in adoption, speed of deployment, and/or the impact of an initiative.

4. Prepare a Detailed Design

Each stage depicted in the structure diagrams in this chapter represents a significant amount of activity required to deliver specific value and drive specific outcomes. To develop a deployable, operable, value-driving initiative requires that you move beyond concepts and basic structures to the specific details for each stage. This additional detail will help guide teams to focus on the activities and outcomes that matter most at the stage they are in, and help align expectations between incubating teams, the governance team, the team operating the initiative, and sponsors, stakeholders, and participants.

The basic design of each stage must include:

1. **A one page overview** that describes the stage in detail, lists illustrative activities that are expected to occur, outlines the desired outcomes, and presents the high-level governance characteristics of the stage

2. **A detailed checklist** that incubating teams can use as guidance to ensure they are focused on what matters most at that stage, and that can be used to set expectations properly for governance teams or sponsors to ensure they focus on providing the right advice and assistance for the stage

3. **A summary of ceremonies** (e.g., 3P review, pitch ceremony) that might be conducted at each stage, with guidance regarding the basics of conducting those ceremonies

4. **Tools and artifacts** that might help simplify or accelerate the work of each incubating team as they complete the stage

The intent of the material enumerated above is to shepherd incubating teams and their support resources, not to constrain them. It is intended to provide a guidepost, not to be an absolute directive. Some of the included checklist items, tools, ceremonies, or artifacts might not be applicable or helpful to some teams. In other cases, teams may need to add new items. The material for each stage should be a resource to incubating teams, not a tax. **The intent of a lean approach to innovation and new idea incubation is to focus time and energy on delivering a new solution, not to add overhead.**

To help you better understand what you will be designing, let's look at an example of each of these using the Explore 1 stage of the Explore–Experiment–Transition model.

Note A detailed copy of each stage overview for all three structures, stage checklists, sample tools and artifacts, and step-by-step guides to the ceremonies are included in the Toolkit. These resources will jumpstart your initiative and provide food for thought as you fine-tune your design.

CHAPTER 7   DESIGNING YOUR APPROACH

Stage Overview

The stage overview (Figure 7-10) is a single page that summarizes the following characteristics for a single stage of an initiative:

1. The stage's objectives
2. The estimated duration of the stage
3. Key questions the stage will address
4. Outcomes expected upon completion of the stage
5. An illustrative list of activities and outputs for the stage
6. A statement of ownership for the stage's day-to-day work
7. An overview of the governance appropriate for the stage

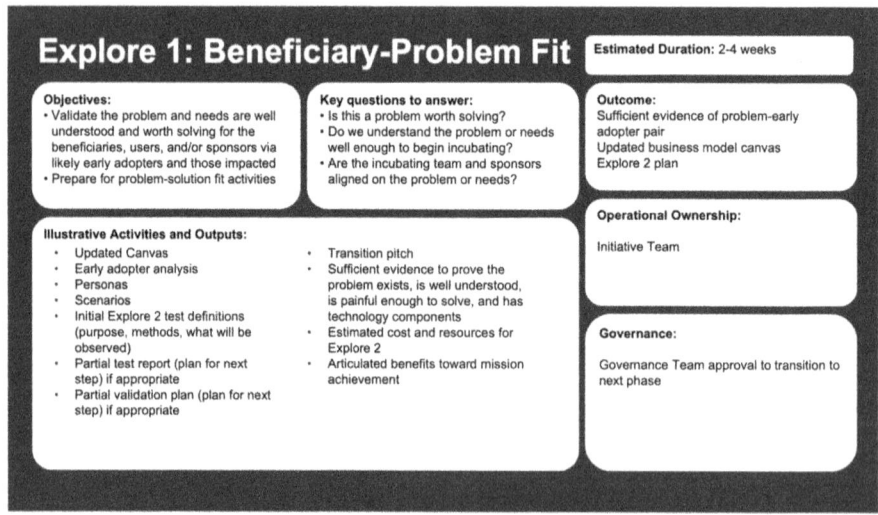

Figure 7-10. Sample stage overview (Explore 1)

242

CHAPTER 7   DESIGNING YOUR APPROACH

The stage overview provides a simple tool teams can use to refresh their understanding of what is to be accomplished in a specific stage and the *types* of activities to expect. It can be used to align teams and their sponsors, set governance team and executive expectations, and help people develop a more detailed understanding of the initiative.

Detailed Stage Checklists

As you might expect, detailed stage checklists (Figure 7-11) are lists of activities and milestones, each of which should help teams successfully achieve the stage's objectives. These activities are meant to be illustrative and not directive and will likely need to be fine-tuned for each initiative, and each incubating team. That is, some items in your checklists may not be applicable to specific incubation projects and should be ignored by the incubating team.

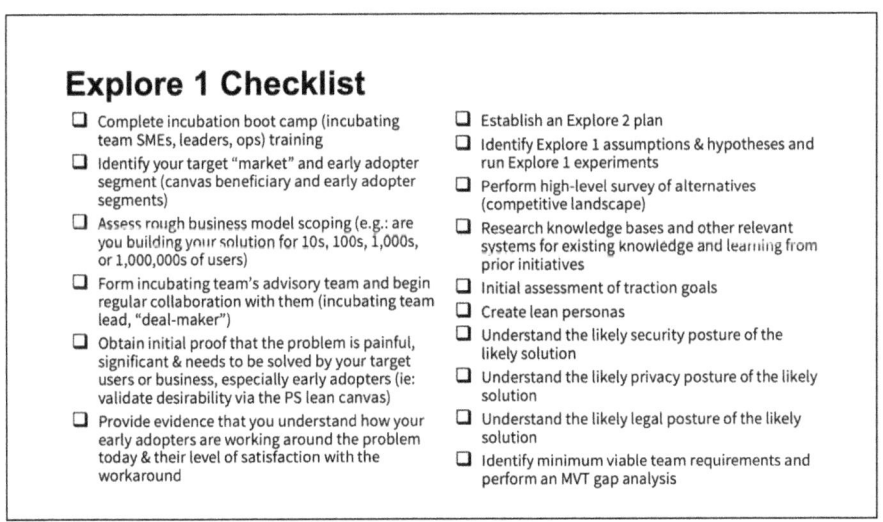

Figure 7-11. Sample stage checklist (Explore 1)

Removing checklist items should always be a deliberate choice and explicitly communicated to avoid errors and mismatched expectations. Teams may also need to add new items to better accommodate their unique needs. Items added to incubation-specific checklists by an incubating team should be considered for inclusion in the initiative's checklist templates since they may be helpful to subsequent incubating teams.

In addition to a checklist for each stage, the following checklists should be included in your design:

1. **Incubation Entry Checklist:** Ensures the team which will be performing the incubation work is prepared to begin

2. **Initiative Team Entry Checklist:** Ensures the team responsible for the initiative assembles the resources and logistics required to enable the incubating team to begin their work

3. **Pause Checklist:** Ensures smooth conclusion of an incubation regardless of the stage at which it is paused or shut down, and that technology and learning are preserved regardless of the disposition of the solution (i.e., even if it was shutdown prior to exit)

Note Each of these checklists is included in the Toolkit.

Ceremonies

Ceremonies are gatherings of people targeted at accomplishing a specific objective such as selection of ideas for entry into an initiative (i.e., pitch ceremony), advancing an incubating idea (i.e., 3P review), or fostering continuous learning and improvement (i.e., retrospectives). Lean ceremonies should be designed to advance the initiative and/or specific incubating ideas as far as possible while minimizing effort, resource consumption, and time requirements. They can be conducted in-person or remotely (e.g., via Teams, Zoom, or WebEx).

Supporting material for each stage of the initiative should include a summary of the ceremonies that are likely to be useful during the stage so participants can easily identify those which may help them achieve their objectives. While most ceremonies should not be mandatory and should be selected by participants based upon their unique needs, there will likely be a small number of anchor ceremonies which will be used by all of an initiative's participants. Figure 7-12 provides both an example of a ceremony summary and of the three ceremonies which normally serve as anchor ceremonies for initiatives of this nature.

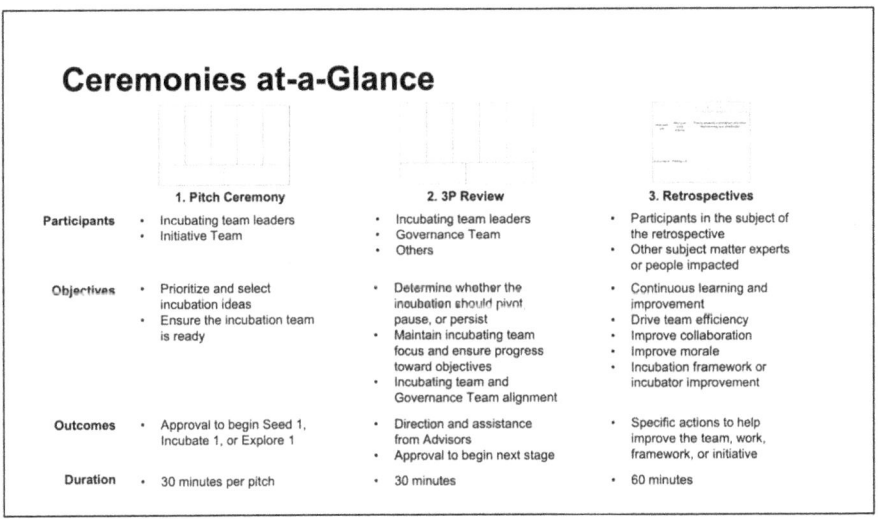

Figure 7-12. Sample ceremony summary depicting anchor summaries (Explore 1)

CHAPTER 7   DESIGNING YOUR APPROACH

A ceremony summary alone will not be sufficient for people who have not facilitated or participated in such a ceremony. Therefore, it is also important to provide additional detailed guidance for each ceremony. Providing teams with facilitation or coaching as they begin may also be helpful, depending upon their experience facilitating events like these.

Note The Toolkit contains summaries and step-by-step instructions for many commonly used ceremonies. With two exceptions (Pitch Ceremony, 3P Review), these ceremonies can be, and are often, used in a wide variety of situations unrelated to innovation or incubation initiatives, and may be of use outside your initiative.

Tools and Artifacts

Every incubating team will employ tools, techniques, and artifacts to achieve their objectives. While you may not be able to predict every tool and artifact that an incubating team might need or use, and you may not be able to anticipate the creation of new tools, you can give them a running start by providing them with tools, artifacts, and techniques that others have used to successfully achieve similar objectives. You can also help them by letting them know which tools might be useful during the stage they are currently executing (e.g., Explore 1, Seed 1).

Figure 7-13 shows an example of one way you can help teams to easily identify tools which may be useful. In addition to the summary, you should provide a library of as many of the tools as you can (e.g., via a Wiki, SharePoint, OneDrive, or Google Drive), while also respecting copyrights and licenses where applicable. For convenience, you can provide external links to licensed or protected items or references to the organization's software delivery catalog when appropriate. You should also make it possible for teams to add tools to the

CHAPTER 7   DESIGNING YOUR APPROACH

library as they are discovered. Including a way for people to comment on the purpose for which they used a tool and why they found it to be useful might also be very helpful.

Artifact	Description	Ceremony	Collab	Explore 1	Explore 2	Experiment 1	Experiment 2	Transition 1	Transition 2
Public Sector Lean Canvas	Capture, communicate, and de-risk a business model		Y	★	✓	✓	✓	✓	✓
Lean Canvas	Capture, communicate, and de-risk a business model		Y	★	✓	✓	✓	✓	✓
Classic Retrospective	Drives continuous learning and improvement	Retro	Y	★	✓	✓	✓	✓	✓
Wind in our Sails Retrospective	Drives continuous learning and improvement	Sails	Y	★	✓	✓	✓	✓	✓
Hypothesis Tree	Determine experiments and data required			★	✓	✓	✓	✓	

Figure 7-13. *Sample tool and artifact summary (partial)*

The example in Figure 7-13 provides the following information about each tool or artifact:

- **Artifact:** The common name(s) of the tool or artifact.

- **Description:** A brief description of the purpose for which the tool is commonly used and, optionally, comments from teams who have found it useful (alternatively, comments might be added in a separate column).

- **Ceremony:** The label, index, or name of the ceremony or ceremonies that will help teams use the tool or complete the artifact.

- **Collab:** Whether there is a pre-defined template in the organization's collaboration tool (e.g., Mural, Miro, Figma).

- **Explore 1 – Transition 2:** A check mark in a cell in a stage's column indicates the tool may be useful during the stage, a star indicates the earliest stage during which the tool or artifact is likely to be introduced.

CHAPTER 7   DESIGNING YOUR APPROACH

> **Note**   This book's Toolkit contains many commonly used tools and artifacts, and several ceremonies that can assist with their utilization.

Design Workshops

The Toolkit in this book contains detailed stage overviews that describe each stage's objectives, key questions to answer, outcomes, and activities and outputs. These were included to help accelerate your design and deployment, and to serve as inspiration as you develop and fine-tune your initiative. I recommend using that material to prime your design, and that you also perform one or more design workshops to customize the approach to meet your organization's unique needs and adjust for its culture.

You can use any style of workshop you are comfortable with to work through the details of your initiative. Here is an approach that I find helpful.

Step 1: Capture Learning in an Initial Model

Once I have completed the assessment, I set up a wall or a collaboration tool as shown in Figure 7-14. I use what I have learned to complete the information in the "Objective," "Key Question to Answer," "Outcome," and "Activities and Output" areas for each stage. Once those areas have been populated, I think through the "Cost + Risk," "Governance," and "Operational Ownership" sections. At this point, references to cost are directional as opposed to specific. Specificity will be added later. Should you choose to use this format you can use the stage overviews in the Toolkit either as inspiration for, or to pre-populate, your wall.

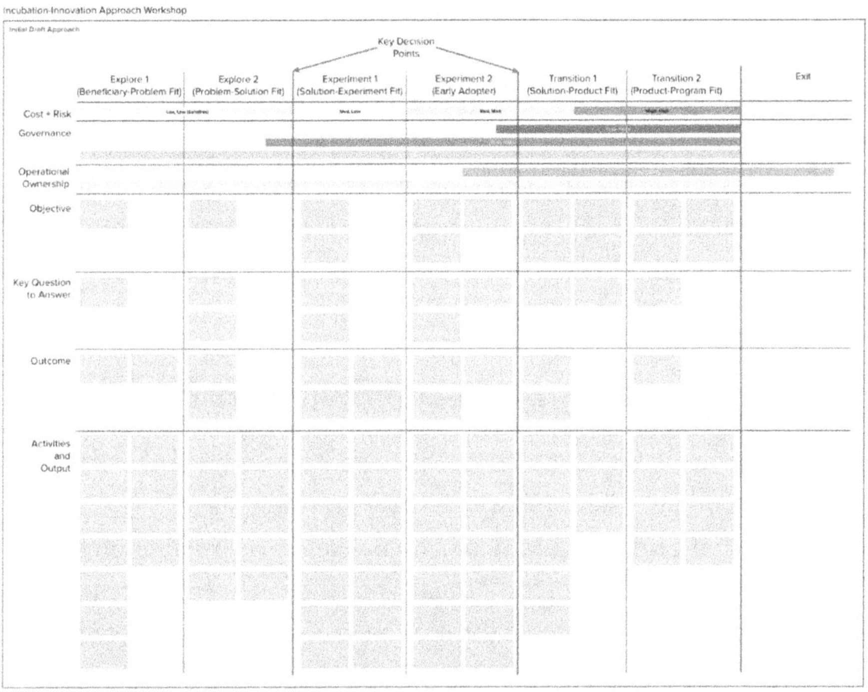

CHAPTER 7 DESIGNING YOUR APPROACH

Figure 7-14. Illustrative detailed design workshop layout

This exercise usually requires several iterations. Once complete, it delivers a very robust initial model. Having everything on a single virtual or physical wall makes it easy to spot missing information, areas which are lightly populated and may require attention, and inconsistencies across the stages. This "wall" is also suitable for a wide variety of workshop styles.

I like to first perform this exercise with a very small group and work through the initial design before involving even a moderately sized team. Sometimes I will run an early iteration or two with only myself and my primary contact or the person who is responsible for deploying the initiative. This is often because there usually aren't many others involved that early in the initiative's life. If others are ready and willing to participate, I might involve a group of three or four.

In preparation for the workshop I often create an initial model design on my own and populate it with what I learned in the assessment, including multiple alternatives for some of the areas. I iterate through this several times, and then bring it to the small group for the initial workshop. Sometimes I will pre-populate the wall with my thoughts as a primer, but on other occasions, I will bring the information in the form of notes and let the team begin with a blank wall, or prepare pre-completed sticky notes which I can use during brainstorming exercises.

Step 2. Expand the Details and Refine the Model

Once the initial model has been constructed, I like to conduct a second workshop so we can dive into each stage in additional detail, and with additional focus. I set up a virtual or physical wall with an area for each of the stages in advance of the workshop (Figure 7-15). Participants work through each of the stages in detail, usually in the following order:

1. Objective
2. Key Question to Answer
3. Outcome
4. Activities and Output
5. Ownership (Governance, Operational, or other as appropriate)

CHAPTER 7   DESIGNING YOUR APPROACH

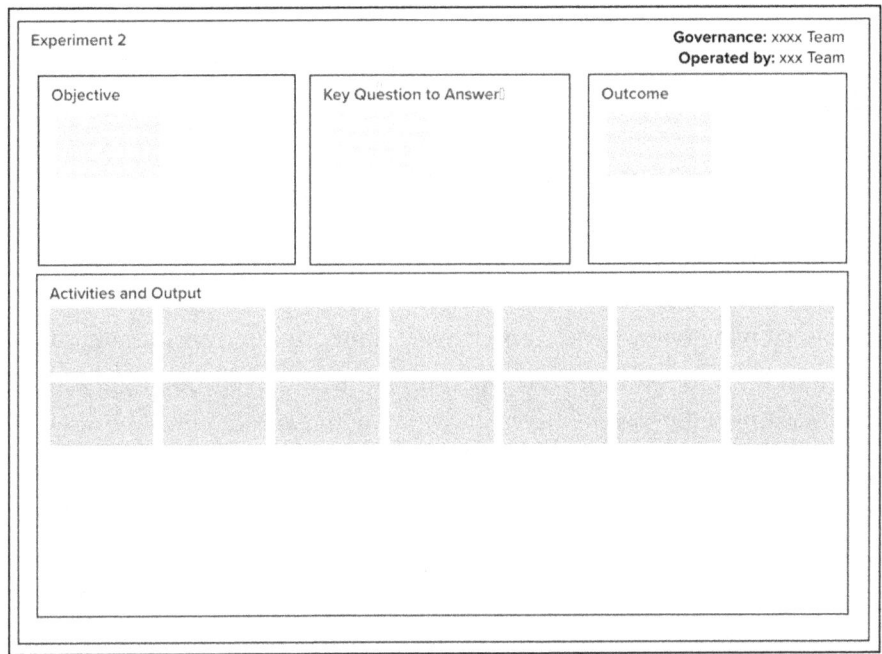

Figure 7-15. Sample single stage detail workshop wall layout

Workshop participants should also consider whether the stage names are appropriate. My experience is that a review of the names is best done after all the stage detail has been worked out.

If you performed the exercise described in Step 1, you can either pre-populate some of the stage detail information before the brainstorming exercise or you can add it following an initial brainstorm. I find the former to be the better alternative, but the better option for you will depend on the group attending the workshop, what was captured in the initial model, and your facilitation style.

This step may appear to be redundant to those who have already created an initial model. My experience is that it adds a lot of value, helps capture errors and omissions in the initial model, surfaces inconsistencies, and drives an additional level of acuity. The additional acuity enables the initiative's team to anticipate resource requirements, especially those related to activities. It also enables the incorporation of information or insight that has been received since the initial model's creation.

Step 3. Socialize and Fine-Tune the Model

Once you have a model that you are comfortable with and are confident will address the organization's needs, it will be worthwhile to run a workshop style review with a larger group. I recommend including the people who will be running and operating the initiative. You might also include representatives of other interested or stakeholder groups, or even champions, mentors, or people who have experience bringing new ideas to life in established organizations. Keep the group small. I recommend four to eight people, and no more than ten.

This workshop should be simple, straightforward, and should only take a couple of hours. Certainly no more than a half day.

I recommend the facilitator place a completed version of the details for each stage (e.g., Figure 7-15) on a wall ahead of the workshop's commencement. During the review the facilitator should briefly review the initiative's objectives and current state, and ensure participants understand the workshop's mission. Then the facilitator should guide the group to each completed stage overview. The facilitator, or a designee, will describe the stage and what each element means. The group will then discuss the stage and recommend any additions, changes, or deletions to the stage material, including suggestions for changes in wording or positioning. I like to post the stage checklists (Figure 7-11) for input and review during this workshop as well.

Once the group has completed each stage, they can turn their attention to "big picture" items such as naming, terminology, and vocabulary. You might even learn during one of these steps that you need to adjust your basic structure (e.g., move from Seed-Series to Explore–Experiment–Transition, add a stage...).

CHAPTER 7   DESIGNING YOUR APPROACH

I strongly recommend conducting this review workshop as it:

1. Helps fine-tune and harden the model
2. Socializes the details to a broader group
3. Demonstrates the level of detail and rigor in the initiative
4. Engages a broader group in the creative process and definition of the model
5. Drives better understanding and fosters broader buy-in

Be Roughly Right, Not Precisely Wrong

The objective of these exercises is to get the best initial model definition possible. There is always a risk of over-engineering this type of exercise or workshop. They should be lightweight and focused. Steps 2 and 3 should take less than a half day each, and Step 1 should take a day or less, most of which is sifting through data and thinking. Step one may require a few iterations, so set aside a few days for it.

Regardless of how well you define your model, some inspection and adaptation will almost certainly be required. Avoid the temptation to over-engineer it and strive for perfection. Beware of the risk of spending too much time, at too deep a level of detail at this stage. Ironically, an over-engineered model has the potential to be a less effective model.

5. Engage Cross-Organizational Teams

As mentioned earlier, successfully incubated ideas that exit an incubator typically fall into one of the following categories:

1. Products
2. Programs
3. Projects

The type of support required throughout each incubation, and the type of experts and mentors that might best benefit the incubating teams, are slightly different in each case. Transition activities required to exit the idea from the initiative, and the type of team that receives the solution when it exits, will also be different for each. Therefore, you must be deliberate about the type(s) of exits your initiative will support, since each type will impact the detailed design and checklists for each stage of your model.

For example, if your initiative will exit products, you may need to involve the broader organization's sales or marketing teams prior to exit to ensure they are ready to promote, sell, and support the product. If the initiative will exit public sector programs, you may need to involve a program management team, bureaucratic field representatives or leaders, or even political staff. If you exit internal projects or technologies, you may need to involve project managers and IT operations and support staff. The time at which each group is engaged, and their level of activity, will also differ in each case.

The Impact of the Different Archetypes

Each category you support requires explicit acknowledgement and representation in your model's details. Thus, you may need to design one set of objectives, activities, and checklists for each type of exit the initiative will support. Though the differences between exit types are important, those designs will be more similar than dissimilar. If you plan to produce more than one type of exit, you can start with one design – perhaps the one you are most comfortable with – and then use that as the basis for the others.

To help you better understand the implications of each, let's look at three simple, illustrative archetypes (Figures 7-16, 7-17, 7-18).

CHAPTER 7 DESIGNING YOUR APPROACH

Note The following figures provide an illustrative description of how differences in types of exiting solutions might impact an initiative's structure. While each diagram provides an archetypical depiction of a specific scenario, your specific requirements may vary. Careful consideration of which groups to highlight in your environment, and what might be required of each person or team therein, is necessary.

Figure 7-16 is an illustrative depiction of how some teams which are not directly involved with the incubation of a specific, new, for-sale private sector product or service might interact with its incubating team. You will notice several teams are listed vertically on the left in the bottom portion of the figure. To the right of each team name you will notice an object that stretches below and horizontally across one or more of the stages of the initiative. The leftmost at point at which the horizontal object begins marks the point in an incubation where that team would typically engage with the incubating team. The height of the bar at any point indicates an approximation of *how* involved they will be, as well as their expected level of time and resource commitment at that point.

CHAPTER 7   DESIGNING YOUR APPROACH

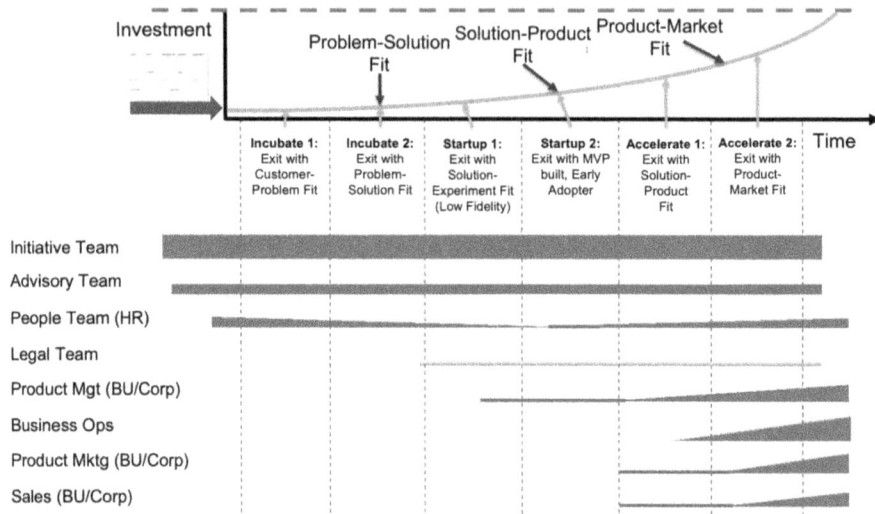

Figure 7-16. *Illustrative private sector product exit structure*

For example, you will notice the horizontal bar to the right of the "Initiative Team" label in Figure 7-16 begins below the pitch stage and continues throughout the entire width of the incubation structure. That indicates that the team operating and driving the initiative begins working with incubating teams from the moment they enter the initiative through to the time of their exit. The fact that the bar is fully shaded for its entire length indicates that the Incubation Team is fully engaged, with a high level of effort expected from them. That is to be expected, since it is their primary job function. In contrast, the Marketing Team ("Product Mktg (BU/Corp)") engages minimally at the Accelerate 1 stage and ramps up to a substantial level during the Accelerate 2 stage.

Figure 7-17 shows a similar example for an initiative that supports public sector program incubation. You will notice that this structure involves different teams such as privacy and program management.

256

CHAPTER 7 DESIGNING YOUR APPROACH

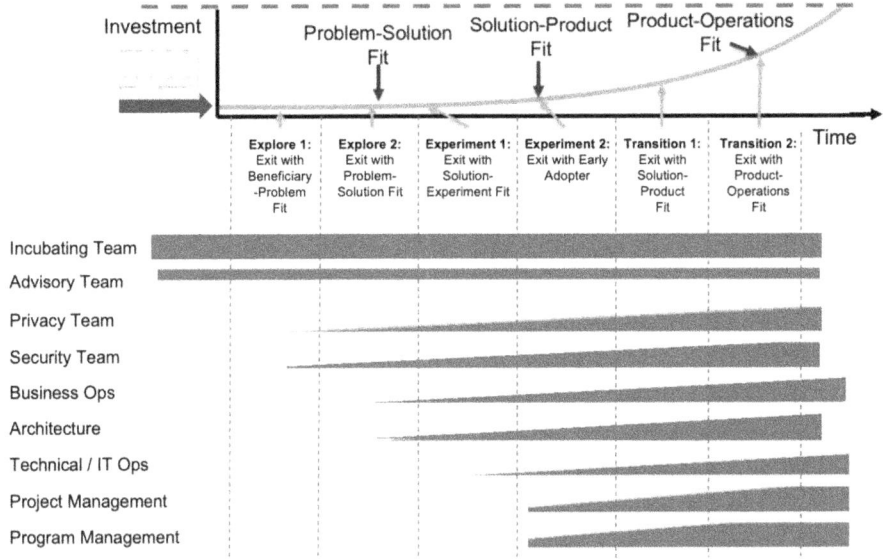

***Figure 7-17.** Illustrative public sector program exit structure*

Finally, Figure 7-18 shows a similar example for an initiative that supports project incubation.

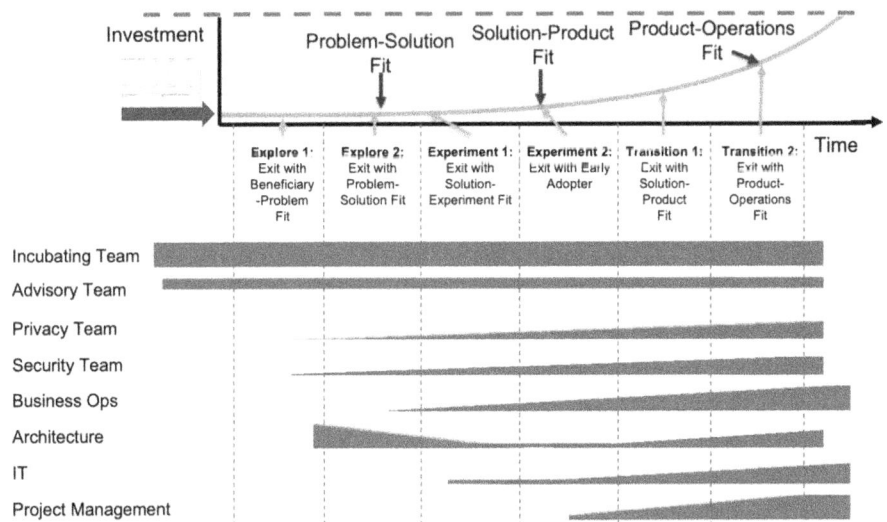

***Figure 7-18.** Illustrative public sector internal project exit structure*

257

CHAPTER 7   DESIGNING YOUR APPROACH

Nuances Matter

The primary reason I included these illustrations is to help you to understand that each scenario has its own nuances, and that those nuances have an impact. For example, in the public sector program scenario, the Security Team may become involved during the Explore 2 stage because a security assessment or approval is mandatory before they can proceed with a live customer test during the Experiment 1 stage. That security assessment and approval should be part of your Explore 2 checklist, and the security assessment should be captured as an Explore 2 activity.

While this type of illustration is not precise, it can be very useful in helping set sponsor and cross-team expectations. It can also be useful for vetting your stage checklists and ensuring you are preparing people involved in the initiative in advance of their engagement. Furthermore, if you notice something *material* on your checklist that is not depicted in the diagram, it may indicate you have not yet engaged a team you should be working with. Such a discovery may also indicate one or more checklists need to be updated.

The Impact of Portfolio of Initiatives

Though the focus of this book is the type of initiative that creates the conditions for repeatable innovation and new idea incubation in established organizations, there are many other types of initiatives that foster and support innovation and idea generation and incubation across short-, mid-, and long-term time horizons. While this book will not address those other types in detail, it is worth introducing some of them, as they can have an impact on an initiative like the one you will be designing.

CHAPTER 7 DESIGNING YOUR APPROACH

The presence of additional initiatives usually has a very positive impact. For example, the presence of something like an applied research program might result in a broader selection of well-tested breakthrough technologies and ideas that are ready for incubation. But there can even be benefits if the other programs have no direct connection to your initiative. The momentum they create can facilitate sponsor acquisition and executive support for your initiative. The community that might form as a result of their existence may also serve as a support structure for your initiative and, possibly, a source of mentors and champions.

The types of initiatives you might encounter, or even create, include:

- InnerSource programs[1]
- Incubator-accelerators
- Applied research teams
- Scientific research teams
- Academic partnerships
- Patent support programs
- Idea/innovation/patent meetups or pods
- Customer advisory groups
- Databases or information stores of lessons learned from successful and failed projects
- Communities of practice
- Publication programs
- Hackathons
- Idea or innovation competitions

---

[1] Additional information regarding InnerSource programs may be found at: https://innersourcecommons.org

- Skunkworks projects (sanctioned or unsanctioned)
- Meetups
- Open source and open standards groups
- Internal or external think tanks

The more of these you have access to, the more potential benefit you might gain. For example, consider the following scenario:

1. Someone in a scientific research team develops a new artificial intelligence (AI) engine. Since this engine was not designed to be used broadly or commercially, it consists of a collection of scripts and algorithms that might be beyond the understanding of some, or may simply require too much effort for someone in a product development team to consider using.

2. An applied research team picks up the scientific research team's work and creates a working prototype of a simple application. That application is not commercially robust, nor does it solve any compelling problem, though it does serve to easily demonstrate the AI's capabilities. In addition, the applied research team wrapped the engine in APIs that enable any developer to use it easily.

3. An innovative employee identifies a painful, compelling problem and realizes they can use the AI engine to solve it. They pitch the problem to the incubator–accelerator.

CHAPTER 7 DESIGNING YOUR APPROACH

4. The innovative employee enters the incubator-accelerator and brings a new product to life leveraging the AI engine and the applied research team's APIs.

5. A product team from one of the company's business units "acquires" the product from the incubator-accelerator.

Each initiative has the potential to feed, or leverage, any of the others. As in our example, a team in an incubator accelerator might be incubating an idea that was inspired by a scientific or applied research activity, idea competition, or hackathon. The incubating team might also consume InnerSource components, generate ideas for the research teams, create patentable solutions or ideas that feed a patent program, or contribute core technologies to a knowledge base or InnerSource program. Each initiative can drive an enormous amount of value on its own, but an ecosystem of this nature has the potential to generate substantially higher value than any of the components in isolation.

If you are fortunate enough to have access to an ecosystem like this, consider how it might interact with each stage of your design. Most mid- to large-sized organizations have programs like these, so make sure to inquire about them during your assessment. You might also find some "unofficial" programs of a less formal style that have been started by groups of employees.

Many of these initiatives do not require a lot of effort or investment, so consider whether starting any would be of value to the organization.

CHAPTER 7   DESIGNING YOUR APPROACH

Additional Considerations

Here are a few additional things to consider as you complete your design:

- Learn fast and iterate: Don't let perfection be the enemy of progress, build in small batches, measure, and inspect and adapt.

- Be a resource, not a tax: Focus on the participants, not the process, and if something does not add value for them, don't do it.

- Keep it simple, keep it lean: Resources, tools, artifacts, and checklists should help drive the most possible learning by applying the least possible amount of effort and resources.

- Welcome and encourage participants' feedback, good and bad, thank them, and adjust based upon what you learn.

- Once you have an initial design, critique it, and run exercises or workshops to identify blind spots, gaps, or aspects that might be heavier than necessary.

- Simulate a few hypothetical ideas running through your incubator to test your initial design (e.g., conduct a table read of different potential scenarios) prior to deployment.

- Include stakeholder, executive, and assessment participant language, and organizational vocabulary in the initiative's material to link it to their input and demonstrate their input matters.

CHAPTER 7   DESIGNING YOUR APPROACH

- Be deliberate, clear, and transparent about what the initiative will and will not do, and what may follow (e.g., it will serve one region for the first six months and others will follow).

- Don't over-commit early on: Make sure the initiative is feasible, and that the initiative's team can deliver what is promised.

Investment or Funding, What's in a Name?

If you read *Lean Entrepreneurship*, you may have noticed that model's Y-axis' label was changed from "Funding" to "Investment" in the overview diagrams in this book (e.g., in Figure 7-7). I discovered that certain public sector teams preferred the term "Investment," that the term "Funding" did not resonate with some, and that some teams even had a negative reaction when the term "Funding" was used. Since the term "Investment" was generally understood and accepted by the public sector teams I worked with, I began using it more broadly. Since then, it has been my experience that the term "Investment" also resonates with private sector teams.

The specific term you use to communicate the key lean entrepreneurship concept that investment (or funding) scales commensurate with the level of traction and success of the solution is less important than the fact that whichever term you use is well understood by, and resonates with, the people with whom you are working. In some cases, a change in terminology can make a remarkable difference, so it is always worthwhile to verify that key elements of your initial messaging and design are understood and are not being received negatively. Whether "funding," "investment," or something else, use the term that will be best understood in your organization.

CHAPTER 7   DESIGNING YOUR APPROACH

Public Sector Lean Canvas

You may have noticed that some figures reference the "Public Sector Lean Canvas." Though there are many similarities between business model requirements for the private and public sectors, there are key differences which are not addressed in the Lean Canvas. The Public Sector Lean Canvas, developed by Tony Mungham, addresses these important nuances. There are other alternatives that may also better suit public sector needs such as The Public Policy Lean Canvas[2] or the Strategizer Mission Model Canvas.[3] If you find none of these canvases meets all of your needs, there are plenty of derivatives to choose from freely available on the Internet (most through Creative Commons licensing), or you can create your own. If you do, please share it with others, as Ash Maurya, Tony Mungham, Dave Moskovitz, and Alex Osterwalder have done.

It's Time for Action

Now that you have a design, it's time to do something about it. But what? What are the next steps? Who will take them? Why do they matter? What value will they drive? How will we know if we are achieving our goals? Those questions will be answered when you finalize your objectives. As you may have guessed, that is the topic of the next chapter.

---

[2] Additional information regarding The Public Policy Lean Canvas can be found at: https://leanpolicy.org

[3] Additional information regarding The Mission Model Canvas can be found at: www.strategyzer.com/library/the-mission-model-canvas-an-adapted-business-model-canvas-for-mission-driven-organizations

CHAPTER 8

Finalizing Objectives

You have completed your assessment and design, and finally have the information you need to start creating and deploying your initiative. The initiative should be gaining momentum as your targets become clearer, and people may have begun to rally in support of it. It can be tempting to rush in and start building, but what happens if you build the wrong thing? Or you build the right thing (or *a* right thing), but it's not what people expected? It is time to set, or reset, your initiative's objectives to make sure that does not happen (Figure 8-1).

In this Chapter

Getting ready:
1. Be deliberate, be intentional
2. Objectives and Key Results (OKRs)
3. Setting objectives with OKRs

Finalizing objectives:

4. Set your initiative's objectives
5. Establish ownership
6. Establish a heartbeat (cadence)
7. Obtain alignment and buy-in

Figure 8-1. *What's in this chapter*

G. Watt, *The Lean Entrepreneurship Playbook*,
https://doi.org/10.1007/979-8-8688-0122-8_8

CHAPTER 8 FINALIZING OBJECTIVES

1. Be Deliberate, Be Intentional

Good strategy is about making unambiguous, *deliberate* choices about what will, *and will not*, be done. Clear objectives ensure everyone involved is focused on the actions required to execute that strategy. Setting, resetting, or confirming those objectives upon completion of the assessment and design:

1. Enables you to create objectives with greater acuity and specificity, and to get to details which would not have been understood earlier
2. Ensures the objectives have been updated based upon learning during the assessment
3. Enables adjustment to goals and targets to accommodate key design choices
4. Provides an opportunity to revise the language of objectives to reflect the language of stakeholders and executives, respect organizational vocabulary, and be better understood
5. Provides an opportunity to confirm stakeholders and executives understand your next steps and path forward, and to set their expectations regarding exactly what will be created, and how the team will know it is making positive progress

The first three of these ensure you are building the right thing. The fourth lets people know you have been listening and demonstrates alignment. The fifth may be the most important.

Confirm Alignment

Resetting or reconfirming objectives provides an opportunity for you to make a new "contract" with your sponsors and stakeholders and ensure they are aligned with, and support, the direction you have set and the path you have chosen to get there. It also enables you to identify and address any misalignment.

Some alignment adjustments might be resolved through a conversation, with no changes required to the initiative's objectives. In some cases, the required adjustment might be as simple as adjusting language in your objectives so they are better understood. In other cases, you may need to rethink and rewrite your objectives.

Consider yourself fortunate if you learn you were out of alignment. Being unknowingly misaligned is very risky. It can result in a team spending a calendar quarter, perhaps more, building something that does not meet sponsor expectations. Even if the team built the *right* thing, the entire initiative can be in jeopardy when there is misalignment.

Be Unambiguous

As with good strategy, good objective setting is about making deliberate choices and being intentional both about what you will do, and what you will not do. **Clarity, communication, and confirmation is critical.** If you decide not to include something you know one or more stakeholders are looking for, don't let them assume it *will* be included. Be clear and be proactive. Consider having a discussion with those affected before you publish your objectives. If something will be included, but at a later stage, let them know about that as well, and share your rationale.

I emphasize communication and alignment at all levels because I have seen initiatives fail solely due to misalignment or mismatched expectations. If you are not clear and explicit about your objectives for the creation of the initiative, people will make their own assumptions.

The misalignments that result can also cause a loss of trust, not only in the initiative but also in the initiative's team and their ability to deliver, and in you.

Pause for Introspection

This is also a good time to pause for some brief introspection. Give some final consideration to any bias you or your team may have introduced or fallen victim to. Consider how you may have impacted the research, and how you may, will, or can influence the outcomes and next steps. Not all bias is bad. But unchecked, unconscious bias is always risky. Spend a few minutes and ensure you have openly considered everything you have learned.

2. Objectives and Key Results (OKRs)

How you set and track your objectives is less important than the fact that you do set, confirm, and track them. There are a wide variety of successful methodologies for managing objectives. I have used many of them to successfully deliver large and complex projects. I currently prefer Objectives and Key Results (OKRs), but you can adopt any system that works for you and that you are comfortable with.

What Are OKRs?

OKRs are an outcome-focused approach for setting and tracking measurable goals. They were first introduced by Andy Grove at Intel in the 1970s, and were more broadly introduced to the technology industry decades later by John Doerr – who had worked with Grove at Intel – while he was working at venture capital firm Kleiner Perkins. Since then, they have become broadly popular across the technology, and other, industries.

CHAPTER 8 FINALIZING OBJECTIVES

I find the OKR approach to be very similar in spirit to, and very compatible with, lean philosophies. I prefer OKRs over other approaches to goal setting because OKRs:

- Are lightweight and simple to create, maintain, and update
- Are easy to understand and communicate
- Drive focus
- Support transparency and objective evaluation
- Drive alignment within and across teams
- Drive engagement and connection to organizational mission and goals
- Promote visionary thinking and innovation
- Help teams to grow by providing a safe environment for stretch objectives
- Support rapid iteration, feedback, flow, and continuous learning and improvement
- Promote and foster a lean approach and build lean, nimble habits

I find OKRs drive more specificity in outcomes with less effort than other approaches. With other approaches I often found I was spending as much time updating and maintaining the objectives management systems as actually performing work on the objectives themselves. Sometimes more. I find OKRs require minimal additional work, drive meaningful focus on outcomes, and support truly objective measurement. Furthermore, good OKRs provide ongoing feedback regarding whether the actions taken by a team are truly driving their desired outcomes.

CHAPTER 8 FINALIZING OBJECTIVES

How OKRs Work

Individuals or teams using OKRs typically set three to five objectives, each with three to five key results, depending upon what they are working on, their team size, and their overall scope. I like to keep the number to no more than three objectives with up to five key results each for initiatives of this nature, especially for quarterly OKRs.

In the OKR model, an **objective** is something that is to be achieved by a person, team, or organization (e.g., "Win the XPRIZE to help end destructive wildfires"). Objectives should be significant, concrete, action-oriented, inspirational, and aspirational. Objectives are qualitative statements, and well-written objectives describe their desired impact.

A **key result** is a specific benchmark that can be used to monitor *how* the objective will be achieved (e.g., "Reduce model evaluation time from 10 minutes to 30 seconds by June 30th"; "Increase the fire detection area per agent from 1,000 square kilometers to 10,000 square kilometers by December 31st"; "Publish initial findings by March 31st"). I also like to think of key results as things that will let you know whether the actions you are taking are actually helping you make progress toward achievement of the objective. Where **objectives are *qualitative*, key results are *quantitative***, and should be measurable, specific, and time bound. While some key results should challenge the team, or even be a little scary, they should be achievable.

3. Setting Objectives with OKRs

To provide you with a bit more context, let's look at a simple example of a quarterly OKR that a fictitious team building an incubator–accelerator initiative might set early on (Figure 8-2).

January – March 20xx

Objective: Launch the incubator to prime the growth engine and build momentum
Key Results:
1. Prime the incubator with 2 new incubations (moving from 3 to 5 active incubations)
2. Deploy a pitch registration and intake site and process by January 15th
3. Conduct "road show" and training in 5 largest development centers by January 31st
4. Create ceremonies required for pitch and Explore/Incubation stages by February 15th
5. Accept 15 pitches and conduct 15 pitch ceremonies by March 31st

Figure 8-2. *Illustrative quarterly OKR for early stage activities*

In this scenario:

1. The initiative team is ready to launch.

2. They believe that five incubating ideas will create the momentum they need and sufficiently increase the probability one or more ideas will advance to a successful exit.

3. Three ideas that were incubating elsewhere in the organization have already been selected for entry, so two additional ideas will be selected.

4. The team believes they need to view at least 12 pitches to find two ideas, so they have decided to accept 15 pitches to increase the odds they will find two they like by the end of the quarter.

5. To increase the probability of finding 15 pitches, the team plans to host an event in the five locations with the largest concentrations of people most likely to have pent up ideas that are ready, or nearly ready, to pitch.

6. Though challenging, the team believes that they can prepare an event and visit all locations in one month (by January 31st).

7. The team does not want to lose any momentum following the road show, so they want to have a site ready to accept pitch requests before the first event (by January 15th).

8. Finally, the initiative's owners want the ceremonies necessary to enable incubating teams to begin their journeys ready by February 15th so they can start as soon as possible after they are selected.

An OKR tells the story of your journey to victory. I like to test OKRs by reading them backwards. To do so I would read the OKR in our example as follows: "If we accept 15 pitches, create the ceremonies required for pitches and early-stage activities, conduct a road show in the five largest centers, make a pitch registration and intake site available, and accept two new ideas, we will have successfully launched the incubator and primed it for success." I can then ask myself if those are truly the actions required in order to meet the objective.

In addition, as the team executes, they will be able to tell whether the actions they are taking are actually moving them toward achieving the objective. If no pitch registrations have been received by February 28th, the team will know they have a risk, that the actions they took did not drive the result they expected (i.e., no pitch requests were received), and that they need to adapt and act. The key result gives enough specificity that they should be able to determine the action they must take (i.e., actively recruit pitches).

OKRs can easily be cascaded to teams or individuals. For example, scheduling the road show events could be a key result included in a specific person or team's own OKRs. In fact, the OKR in Figure 8-2 may have itself been cascaded from an OKR set at a higher level in the organization, perhaps related to bringing new ideas to life, fostering innovation, ensuring the organizations' long-term viability, or even proving an incubator works and that it would address broader organizational objectives.

Three OKR Horizons

The example in Figure 8-2 shows one simple quarterly OKR. I like to think of OKRs on at least two time horizons, and often three. Usually through team workshops, I begin with a **three-to-five-year OKRs**, or at least a statement of the true north for the initiative(s) for which we are responsible. These OKRs are usually broad and aspirational, though unachievable in the short- to mid-term. They are useful in strategy discussions, but they are usually too high level and vague to execute meaningfully against daily.

Using the three-to-five-year OKRs, if I have them, and company and/or team strategy as a guideline, we workshop **12- to 18-month OKRs**. These essentially answer the question, "what will we do in the next year or eighteen months to make that vision real." This time frame is near enough that the KRs can be meaningful and specific.

From there, we create **quarterly OKRs**, usually for one fiscal year at a time. Those are the OKRs we execute on daily. We review those regularly, sometimes weekly, depending on the team's cadence. The larger the gap between reviews, the higher the risk there will be insufficient time to respond to discoveries, so I recommend reviewing them weekly or every two weeks, and no less than monthly. Though monthly reviews can be more risky than desirable in certain circumstances; especially early in the life of an initiative before the working team has established a cadence and momentum.

4. Set Your Initiative's Objectives

During your design, you made several key decisions such as what your inputs and outputs would be, what kind of ideas you would accept, from whom you would accept them, and how mature they need to be to be considered. Those decisions will shape your specific objectives. There are so many possible combinations that it is not possible for me to predict specifically what your objectives or OKRs will, or should, be. Here are a few things to consider as you set them:

- **What is the mission of your initiative?**
    - To drive long-term longevity?
    - To drive leadership in new markets?
    - To discover and/or validate new sources of revenue?
    - To provide more cost-effective services to citizens?
    - To prove an incubator–accelerator functions and drives value?
- **What is the initiative's true north?**
    - What overarching theme will guide your decision-making?
- **What problem does the initiative solve?**

- **How does your initiative align with organization and/or department or business unit strategy?**
  - What actions are required as a result?
  - How, if at all, will alignment be tracked and reflected in the objectives?
- **Is the initiative part of a larger initiative or objective?**
  - How do they align?
  - What role does your initiative play in the larger objective?
  - Does the larger initiative have objectives (e.g., OKRs) which can, or should, be cascaded to your initiative?
- **Are there secondary missions or objectives?**
  - Employee development?
  - Creating an innovative culture or mindset?
  - Developing good habits for creativity or innovation?
  - Improving operational hygiene?
- **How will you accomplish those objectives?**
  - What key results will achieve the objectives?
- **What are your potential participants', sponsors', and stakeholders' expectations?**
  - What progress do they need to see to understand you are on the right track?
  - How can you communicate your targets and progress to them in a way that will both advance the initiative and help them to understand where things are and how they are going?

CHAPTER 8   FINALIZING OBJECTIVES

- **When does the initiative need to show results?**
  - What kind of results?
  - Validated learning for incubating ideas?
  - Incubating ideas evolving through the stages?
  - Positive press?
  - Political interest?
  - New prototypes?
  - Customer interest?
  - Beneficiary interest?
  - Products in test with customers?
  - Solutions released to new government projects?
  - Active government programs that include exited solutions?
  - Ideas exited as products?
- **How can you demonstrate those results were achieved?**
- **What is your budget?**
  - What can you reasonably achieve with that budget?
  - What is the most optimistic estimate of what can be achieved?
  - What is the most pessimistic estimate of what can be achieved?
  - How can you rationalize the optimistic and pessimistic estimates in your objectives and key results?

- **How large is the initiative's team?**
  - Are they all employees now, or will some require hiring?
  - What skills do they have?
  - When can they begin working on the initiative?
  - Will they be available full-time or part-time?
  - What can they reasonably achieve?
  - Will they require training?
    - What training? When?
- **Are there other initiatives with which your initiative must work?**
  - As a consumer?
  - As a provider?
  - In a complementary fashion?
- **What cross-organizational participation will be required?**
  - Will you need help from the People (HR) team, Engineering, Training, Procurement, Legal?
  - This may result in specific cross-team objectives and/or key results.
- **What is the primary milestone you need to achieve at this point in your initiative's life?**

- **How soon will teams be actively incubating within the initiative?**
  - Have teams been selected for entry into the initiative?
  - Has a protocol for selecting teams for entry been designed and agreed upon?
- **Are there actively incubating teams that might, or will, be brought into the initiative?**
  - How mature are the incubations?
  - What style of incubation are they using (e.g., lean, waterfall, committed bet...)?
- **What kind of support will teams that first enter the initiative require?**
- **At which stage of incubation will the incubating teams be when they enter?**
  - Are the artifacts and/or ceremonies that will be required by the initial entrants ready?
  - When must artifacts and/or ceremonies be ready?
  - Do any artifacts or resources currently exist than can be leveraged or used?
  - Does everyone agree with the stage of maturity assessed for each newly selected team?
  - How can we assess whether that is their actual stage of maturity?
    - (Hint: Use the checklists in the Toolkit)

- **Has a facilitator for each ceremony been selected?**
  - When will they be ready to begin?
  - Do they require training or coaching?
- **Has the advisory team (a.k.a. "Angel Team") been selected?**
  - Have they been recruited?
  - Have they agreed to participate?
  - Have their managers agreed to their participation (if appropriate)?
  - Is the material they require available? When will they need it?
  - Has a cadence been set for their ceremonies and events?
- **Which, if any, advisors will be required?**
  - When will they be needed?
  - Have they been recruited?
  - Have they agreed to participate?
  - Have their managers agreed to their participation (if appropriate)?
- **What, if any, is your targeted idea mix?**
  - For example, 70% aligned with existing business strategy, 20% adjacent, 10% moonshots
- **What potential early wins can you leverage?**
  - What do executives, stakeholders, sponsors, and potential participants value?

- **What is the least acceptable amount of progress?**
  - How could it be achieved with the least possible effort in the shortest possible time?
- **How will you communicate news and progress?**
  - To whom?
  - How frequently?
  - In what format?
  - Self-service dashboards?
  - In-person updates?
- **Are there potential collateral benefits of your initiative?**
  - For example, creating a positive brand image, educating people, promoting career growth, building good habits, improving operational hygiene
  - How can they be leveraged?
  - How can their benefit be promoted?
  - Are specific actions required to leverage them?
- **Have you included continuous learning and improvement in your objectives?**
- **Who will be responsible for each objective and each key result?**

5. Establish Ownership

Each key result and each objective must have an unambiguous, named owner, and someone needs to be accountable for the initiative overall. I realize how obvious this appears, but ambiguous ownership can cause these initiatives to fall short of expectations, or even fail.

Ownership should always be explicit and never assumed. Even when the person whose scope would normally result in ownership of a specific key result is "obvious to everyone", that conclusion is sometimes not obvious to the assumed owner. In other cases, the assumed owner may be overloaded, or they may not want to voluntarily take responsibility for the key result for some other reason. So, it goes unowned.

Serious setbacks can occur when people make assumptions about who will be responsible for a specific key result. To avoid such setbacks, delays, and missed targets, **there must be explicit agreement from all involved regarding who will own each key result, who will follow up on its progress, and how progress will be shared with others in the team**.

The Initiative Must Be Its Owner's Top Priority

In addition, the overall initiative must itself have an owner. This needs either to be the owner's full-time assignment, or it needs to be unambiguously their highest priority. Without an accountable owner for whom the initiative is their most important assignment, key work items will never be "at the top of someone's list." Those items will languish until they become a crisis.

If *you* are driving an initiative, *you* own anything that is not explicitly assigned to someone else.

A single, full-time owner is good, but not mandatory for success. A good team of people with this as their highest priority assignment, but not their only assignment, can execute an initiative like this quite successfully.

Finally, while it is possible for one person to run a large initiative on their own early on, or for short periods, that is not likely sustainable over the long term.

External Ownership

As someone who has both owned an initiative like this while an employee of the organization it supported, and been an external consultant, I strongly believe that these initiatives are better off when owned by employees of the organization they will serve. That is not to state that consultants cannot add a lot of value to an initiative, or even drive one on behalf of its owner. I simply find that managers and executives often take internally owned initiatives more seriously, or at least handle them with higher priority. By their very nature, managers and executives will have to pay more attention to internally owned initiatives. They will be invested in the success of their people, and the performance of internal initiatives will often impact their own objectives and reputation more directly.

Managers and executives can sometimes be less committed to externally owned initiatives than those which directly impact their own personal equity. This bias is not always conscious, and can manifest itself in subtle ways such as postponing meetings, not attending meetings and updates where their input is required, not completing actions they commit to, or deprioritizing actions they are responsible for. This can result in costly delays or failure to achieve one or more key results.

Internal Ownership Advantages

Internal owners will usually have a few key advantages over external owners. The organizational knowledge and network an employee possesses will almost always be greater than that of a consultant, usually exponentially greater.[1] The employee will be immersed in the organization all the time. They will be exposed to opportunistic circumstances that occur during a normal workday, or during organizational events. They will have more opportunities to make chance encounters that can advance the initiative.

I am not stating that an initiative like this can *never* be externally owned. Externally owned initiatives can be successful, especially for experienced consultants. However, give some serious thought to having an employee – and their executive if they are not one – be the ultimate owner of the initiative, even if you engage a consultant (or are one). If you do plan to have an external owner for the initiative, beware that you and/or they *may* have to put additional time into stakeholder management, project managing, and assisting managers, directors, or other executives. (If you are an experienced consultant, this should be a familiar state.)

6. Establish a Heartbeat (Cadence)

Have you ever been to a live music show where one or more of the musicians in a band were playing slightly out of sync, or where the audience was clapping slightly off the beat? Even though it can sometimes be barely perceptible, it is always uncomfortable when people are working at diffcrent rhythms. It can be even more uncomfortable – or damaging – when people contributing to an initiative are not in sync.

Everyone has a lot to do. We have individual professional commitments, team commitments, personal commitments, family events, mandatory training... at times the list feels infinite. We need to continuously prioritize, adjust, and prioritize again. Then the demands and objectives change.

---

[1] There *are* circumstances within which a consultant or external party might be on par with an employee, such as when they were formerly an employee of the organization, or when they were embedded in the organization as a full-time contractor for a long period of time.

CHAPTER 8 FINALIZING OBJECTIVES

With so much changing it can be easy to forget to do something, or to do it in a timely fashion. As a result we develop our own cadence of work. Our own professional rhythm. Work can suffer, and conflict can occur when our rhythm does not align with our colleagues' drumbeat. I'm sure you've seen it happen.

Working together can become *even more* challenging when working across teams. This is especially the case when one team needs input from the other and the teams have different schedules and priorities. For example, one team developing a product might miss their delivery date because a component supplied by a different team was not ready when expected, or because their sprints were not aligned.

When this happens milestones are missed, people are disappointed or seriously negatively impacted, and trust between people and/or teams is eroded or lost. This results in inefficiencies and dysfunction that reach far beyond the scope of our discussion. If you look at Figure 8-3 it's easy to see why.

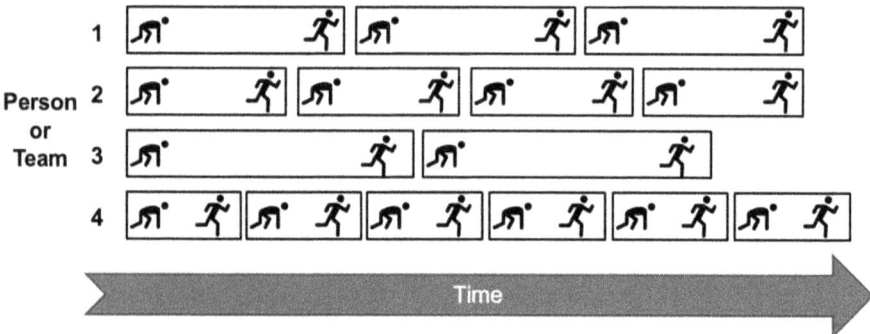

Figure 8-3. Illustrative example of people or teams working at different cadences

CHAPTER 8 FINALIZING OBJECTIVES

Figure 8-3 shows a simplified depiction of four people, or four teams, working at different cadences. In this scenario, there are no times at which the cadence of all of the people align, and some of the people never align with others. This results in inefficient workflow and, usually, unaligned assumptions and expectations between the individuals and teams involved.

If you contrast that with Figure 8-4, you can see that everyone's cadence is aligned. This enables the entire team to play to the same tempo and time signature and perform like an orchestra. Without being reminded, every team member knows when others expect things to be delivered and when key events will occur.

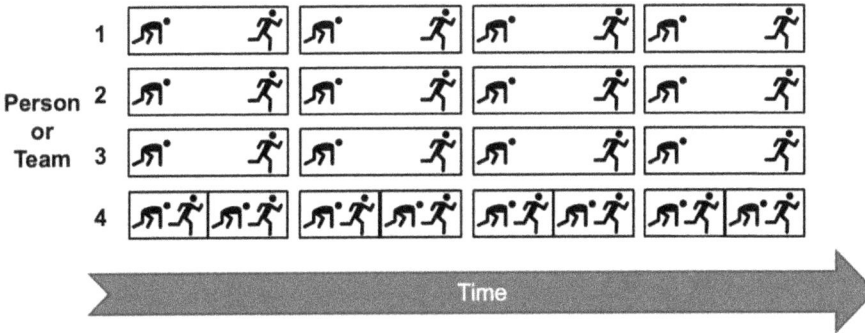

Figure 8-4. *Illustrative example of a team working at a common cadence*

Set a Deliberate Cadence

Cadence may develop naturally in a small team, but I prefer to be deliberate about it. This example might help you understand why.

When I was the Vice President responsible for a large portfolio of projects at a multibillion-dollar technology company, I was required to present a brief, weekly update to senior management. Even though the update focused only on anomalies and events in all but one week per quarter, I needed to understand every key detail about

285

each project to provide that update. I also needed to be prepared for rare, detailed exploration of any of the projects at the request of any of the executives.

As part of my weekly preparation, I asked each project director to make sure their dashboards were updated with any relevant information by the end of each Thursday. That ensured I had timely information for the updates. But something else interesting happened as a result.

Each Thursday, an *enormous* amount of key work was completed, a very large number of key milestones were met, and many deliverables were delivered. Why? Project directors would spot things that had been forgotten, neglected, or deprioritized while verifying their dashboards were up-to-date. Not wanting to let anyone down, they would structure the work to ensure they met their key milestones and deliverables that day, or as soon as possible afterward. And *always* ahead of my Monday update.

We had, unintentionally, established a weekly cadence. And it gave us swing. The swing was contagious, and others adopted our approach.

Weekly Rhythm

I prefer a weekly cadence for the team creating the initiative, especially in the early stages when there tends to be a flurry of activity and change. I prefer a Monday–Friday cadence. I start the week with a very brief commitment of which *key actions* each person will take that week to advance the objective(s). I end the week with a team acknowledgement of everything that was accomplished.

The Monday–Friday cadence results in ending each week on a high note, and significantly reduces the probability work will spill into a weekend.

Don't Set Monday Deadlines!

Incidentally, **I recommend people *never* set deadlines for Mondays**, especially Monday mornings. Monday deadlines frequently result in people working over a weekend. I am sure there are many reasons this happens. For example, I have witnessed many cases where, early in a week, people with a "next Monday" deadline felt they had more time than they actually did. As a result they often accepted additional ad hoc tasks. That put them behind, and they worked the weekend to catch up and meet their commitments. I also have seen people *unnecessarily* set deadlines on Friday, for the following Monday. (I am not referring to legitimate, unpredictable emergencies.) Please don't do that. It's abusive, though it's often unintentional.

7. Obtain Alignment and Buy-in

Once you have set your objectives, it is critical they be confirmed with your sponsor(s) to ensure you are aligned and their expectations are set properly. In addition to aligning expectations, conversations regarding objectives at this stage help your sponsors understand the initiative in greater detail, demonstrate the progress you and the initiative's team have made, and help develop or strengthen a sense of shared ownership in the initiative and its potential outcomes. It can improve your relationship with the sponsor and help them develop a sense of belonging. It can strengthen their feelings of being a part of the initiative and invested in its success.

The closer your sponsor is to the initiative, the more involved they are, the closer they feel they are connected to it, the better. An invested sponsor can often help you to advance the initiative. They can explain the initiative and its state to others in your absence, and they can alert you when they hear something that may require proactive damage control. If you

CHAPTER 8 FINALIZING OBJECTIVES

authentically earn their trust, they might even take a stand for you in your absence, or create time and space you may need to address any critical, potentially damaging, events.

There is, of course, an obvious and practical side to this. You and your sponsor need to agree how the initiative's progress will be measured. To unambiguously agree upon how they will know if the actions the initiative's team is taking are working, and how you will know when it is time for adjustment. These measures (often key results) must be unambiguous, objective, and agreed upon.

Broader Alignment

Alignment with others outside your immediate sponsor(s) and primary contact(s) will surely be required. This alignment will not necessarily be linked directly to your goals or OKRs. But there are usually influencers in an organization who could either help or damage the initiative, or even create the conditions that put it in jeopardy of being shut down. Each of these influencers will have different interests and motivation, and each may require different action. A brief stakeholder analysis at this point can be game changing.

Figure 8-5 shows an example of a simple worksheet that can be used to perform a simple stakeholder analysis exercise. (Additional information regarding stakeholder analysis is provided in the Toolkit.)

Name	Strongly Opposed	Somewhat Resistant	Neutral	Somewhat In Favor	Strongly Supportive	Rationale
Tina Sponsor					CR	The reason
Omar Executive		C ⟶ C		R		Another reason
Marta Detractor	C			R		More reasons
Goodwin Standing			CR			Other reasons
Greta Position			R	C		More Reasons

Figure 8-5. Simple stakeholder analysis

You, or better still the initiative's team, can use a simple worksheet such as this to identify key stakeholders, champions, and detractors, their current state with regard to the initiative, the state you need them to be in, and the reason you believe they are in their current state. Working through an exercise like this will help you to understand where you must take action to improve a stakeholder's position, and where you might need to take action to maintain their current position.

For example, if you look at the row for "Marta Detractor," you will see that her current state, marked with a "C," is that she is strongly opposed to the initiative. An "R" in the "Somewhat In Favor" column indicates we believe she must be at least moderately supportive of the initiative to ensure its success. The distance between Marta's current and desired states indicates we have a lot of work to do to improve Marta's support of the initiative. In contrast, we need Greta Position to be neutral or better, and she is already somewhat in favor of the initiative.

This approach can also be used to track the evolution of stakeholder sentiment over time. For example, if you look at "Omar Executive's" row, you will see their opinion has recently moved from somewhat resistant to the initiative to neutral. We need Omar to be somewhat in favor, but this is positive progress.

Relationships can be complex in transformation initiatives. Using a simple, methodical approach such as this can ensure you do not miss key stakeholders, and that you are aware of both positive and negative movement of stakeholder opinions and support.

There are other ways to perform stakeholder analysis which will enable you to ensure you are aligned with key influencers, and you can use any with which you are comfortable. But use *something*. A very simple exercise like this, which can take as little as an hour, can be invaluable in ensuring you keep stakeholders top of mind as you build and deploy your initiative. Periodic review will ensure you do not forget about key stakeholders and their opinions and remain aware of the direction in which their sentiment is trending.

CHAPTER 8 FINALIZING OBJECTIVES

What's Next?

Once you have mapped the current and desired states for key stakeholders, you can develop a strategy for addressing gaps, adjust objectives and/or key results, if necessary, and develop a communication plan to help advance your initiative. Good communication throughout the life of your initiative is key, and it is critical at this stage. I will expand on that in the next chapter.

CHAPTER 9

Communicating

I have been responsible for field engineering, pre-sales technicians, and research and development "SWAT" teams several times throughout my career. While in those positions, highly stressed customers would sometimes contact me because they believed an important task had not been completed – or their systems were malfunctioning – when, in fact, those tasks or repairs were delivered long before our conversation. In those cases, not only did the sometimes Herculean effort of a team member go without the accolades it may have deserved, that team member was often lambasted by a customer or a member of our organization who was unaware their work was finished.

The many weeks, months, and hours you spend on an initiative could end up being meaningless if you are not communicating effectively, even if your initiative is delivering value beyond expectations. Without good communication people will not know what to expect, and they won't know it is there when you deliver it. Without good communication people may lose interest in your initiative, or you may not even gain their interest to begin with. And without good communication your initiative might not be able to recruit people to incubate ideas, or it might fall victim to rumors or nefarious attacks. This chapter discusses how good communication can help reduce the risk these things will happen to your initiative (Figure 9-1).

CHAPTER 9   COMMUNICATING

> **In this Chapter**
>
> 1. Broaden your communication scope
> 2. Refine your communication needs
> 3. Get help
> 4. Communicate proactively
> 5. Communicate to preempt threats

Figure 9-1. What's in this chapter

1. Broaden Your Communication Scope

The positioning of this chapter is not a statement that communication should *begin* at this point in the life of an initiative. Some form of communication will have been happening concurrently with the activities discussed in the preceding chapters. Communication is positioned here because at this point you need to broaden the scope of your interaction and involve others more actively as you build, deploy, and operate your initiative. It is time to evolve from what may have been largely lightweight, informal styles of communication to a broader variety of formats suitable to that broader audience. Fortunately, you will also have a much richer level of detail to communicate, with much more acuity for every element.

CHAPTER 9 COMMUNICATING

Don't Go Dark, Be Deliberate

This is typically an exciting point in the evolution of an initiative. The team has clarity, a plan, and buy-in. Unfortunately, that clarity and excitement can lead people to execute "with their heads down," ignoring the world outside their team. Please do not fall into this trap.

It is important to be deliberate about communication, and it does not have to take an inordinate amount of time. In fact, if it *is* taking an inordinate amount of time you may be overthinking things, and you may wish to get a fresh perspective from someone outside your team. A good way to begin is by thinking about the many different reasons you may need to communicate such as:

- **Promotion:** Building interest in your initiative; maintaining excitement and momentum; communicating events; inspiring confidence in the initiative; sharing the value of incubating solutions

- **Celebration:** Sharing team milestones, celebrating customer wins; recognizing and rewarding individual achievements; celebrating successful pitches; generating excitement

- **Recruitment:** Finding new intrapreneurs, mentors, advisors, champions, and sponsors, and getting them excited

- **Status:** Demonstrating the initiative's progress and value; showing incubating team progress

- **Stakeholder Management:** Demonstrating progress; maintaining interest; highlighting value delivery; preemptive and reactive damage control; perception management

- **Feedback:** Soliciting input from participants, stakeholders, sponsors, and others
- **Learning:** Sharing lessons learned, tools, tips, and resources

It should be clear that the landscape is quite broad. Don't worry. You won't be doing all of these at once, and you may not do some at all. The type, volume, and frequency of communication you require will depend upon several factors such as the nature and size of the initiative, the nature and size of the organization, and organizational culture and norms. It will also depend on your audience, which might include:

- **Initiative insiders:** Current or potential sponsors, stakeholders, or participants; initiative team, advisory team, and governance team members; mentors; advisors; champions
- **Senior Executives:** C-suite (e.g., CEO, CMO, CTO, COO); board of directors; senior executives and leaders; key influencers
- **Employee groups:** Specific departments or business units; people in specific roles; potential intrapreneurs; champions; detractors; the entire organization
- **External groups:** The organization's customers or potential customers; an incubating idea's customers or potential customers; press or media; analysts; investors; the general public

The form, format, or media used for each message will also vary depending on the content and purpose of the message and its intended recipient. The range will typically include:

- Informal messages via messaging apps (e.g., SMS, Slack, Teams)

- Formal or informal email messages
- Formal presentations
- Written briefs
- Team, departmental, business unit, domain, or organizational newsletters
- Dashboards
- Knowledge bases (e.g., Wiki, SharePoint)
- Team, departmental, business unit, or organization-wide town hall meetings or fireside chats
- Keynote presentations in internal or external conferences
- Videos
- Podcasts
- Informal conversations

2. Refine Your Communication Needs

The breadth of options may feel intimidating. Fortunately, not everything will be necessary, some will only be necessary periodically, many do not require a lot of effort, and some can be automated. An intentional review of what you need to communicate, to whom you need to communicate it, and when and/or with what frequency they need to receive it can help ensure you focus on what matters most while reducing the risk you will miss something important. A simple communication plan workshop is one relatively easy way to get started.

CHAPTER 9   COMMUNICATING

Figure 9-2 shows an example of a simple worksheet that can be used to help a team think through its initiative's communication needs.

Audience	Objectives	Message	Format	Date	Frequency	Location	Owner

Figure 9-2. *Simple communication plan worksheet*

A team can leverage this worksheet in a simple one-to-two-hour workshop to:

1. Brainstorm the different constituents they must communicate with (audience)

2. Brainstorm which messages each needs to receive and why (objectives, message)

3. Decide how each communication would best be delivered (format, location)

4. Determine when the message will be delivered and whether communication will require regular updates (date, frequency)

5. Assign an owner and a delivery date (owner)

If you prepared a stakeholder analysis (as described in the previous chapter), it can be used to prime this exercise.

There are many ways to prepare a simple communication plan. You can use any tool you or your team is comfortable with. *That* you think through your communication needs is more important than *how* you do so.

A Structure for Informal Communication

Your needs will include a combination of formal and informal communication. Your informal communication needs may be as simple as ensuring key stakeholders and influencers have regular informal updates from a member of the initiative's team. Nevertheless, these informal channels are as important as the more formal forms of communication. Sometimes more important. Such informal communication *typically* requires much less preparation and can often be thought of as relationship management.

 You can track your informal communication needs together with more formal requirements, or separately using the format shown in Figure 9-2, or a simpler format such as the one shown in Figure 9-3.

Relationship	Owner	Objectives	Frequency

Figure 9-3. *Informal communication, or relationship management, worksheet*

This informal communication can often be accomplished opportunistically during routine work functions. The worksheet in Figure 9-3 is intended to be more of an aide-memoire or memory jogger than a tool which is actively tracked and managed. It is something that individuals might look at periodically to ensure they have been keeping in touch with key contacts. Over time, this artifact will likely fall out of use and become obsolete for your team.

CHAPTER 9   COMMUNICATING

The primary purpose of an informal communication exercise like this is to ensure every stakeholder need is addressed, every stakeholder relationship is managed and has a primary owner, and everyone in the team is aware of who that owner is. It is also important to note that the assignment of an owner or primary contact to a person does not imply others in the team cannot or should not speak with that person. Relationship ownership is simply a recognition that at least one person on the team will ensure a stakeholder's needs are met.

You Won't Need a Massive Team

When you take all of this into account, it may seem like you will need a massive communications team. You won't. The purpose of this chapter is to ensure you deliberately consider communication needs at this point, and to make you aware of some of the most common methods and targets so you can select the ones you need at any point in your initiative. You will not be doing all of this at once, and it won't all be at the same frequency.

It has been my experience that most communication needs can be captured in the normal course of work, automated or semi-automated (e.g., via dashboards), or satisfied through informal means (e.g., an informal conversation with a stakeholder over lunch or a break). Be deliberate about capturing as much information as possible "in process." Avoid assigning additional work related to generating data whenever you can by capturing information generated by a team's day-to-day work.

Leverage Existing Channels

Take advantage of existing communication channels such as regularly scheduled group, department, business unit, or organization-wide video updates, newsletters, town halls, or fireside chats to reduce your own communication workload. For example, while responsible for a large accelerator, I found the CTO's Fireside Chats to be one of the most effective

CHAPTER 9 COMMUNICATING

ways to deliver information to a broad internal audience. They were well attended, the format made preparation minimal, and they allowed for an informal question-and-answer period.

I also leveraged other existing forums and channels to communicate effectively while minimizing effort and cost. An added benefit of leveraging those other mediums was that they provided me with access to people who were more skilled at communication than I was (e.g., the business unit or corporate level communications people who created, edited, and managed those channels). Which brings me to my next suggestion.

3. Get Help

Do not assume you have to do all of this on your own. If you are leveraging other groups' communication vehicles, you may receive some assistance automatically, as those groups edit, format, proofread, and copyedit their entire publication or event. They may take care of scheduling, preparation, formatting, and production. I was always grateful for the assistance of these other teams. I was able to learn from them, and became better at creating material each time they edited mine.

If you do not have a lot of experience with more formal communication, I also recommend you ask for assistance when you are creating communication material on your own. There are normally many great communicators in most mid-to-large-sized organizations. The larger the organization, the more numerous they usually are. You may be able to find someone to provide coaching or advice, or perhaps even help you to prepare your material. Also consider bringing someone with these skills into your advisory team. Concentrations of these skills can be found in teams such as:

- Corporate or Product Marketing
- Corporate, Department, or Business Unit Communications

CHAPTER 9   COMMUNICATING

- Product Management
- Public Relations
- Analyst Relations
- Education
- People (Human Resources)
- Investor Relations
- Corporate Strategy

4. Communicate Proactively

As with any new initiative, especially one that is transformational in nature, proactive communication with stakeholders, sponsors, partners, and beneficiaries is critical.

Early on you will need to ensure senior leaders, sponsors, and stakeholders have a clear understanding of the objectives, characteristics, and milestones of your initiative. As the initiative's team begins to deliver, it is important to proactively communicate progress at *every* level - even the highest level. When I was responsible for an incubator-accelerator at a publicly traded technology company, I prepared an extremely brief but comprehensive update for the board of directors every time they met. It was typically about a single page, but included highlights and headlights for the initiative overall, *and* for each of the incubating teams.

Clearly State Your Intentions

People associate a very broad range of activities and services with innovation and new idea incubation initiatives. If you do not tell them explicitly what your initiative entails, they will make assumptions. If they make the wrong assumptions – and some almost certainly will – it can be very costly to you or your initiative. People may expect things you have no plans to deliver. They may believe you plan to restrict their ability to innovate. Or they may even think you are making a political play to take over something they are responsible for. I have encountered all of those. The risks are truly too many to enumerate completely here, so it is critical that you be proactive, transparent, and explicit about what you plan to do and, in some cases, what you will *not* do.

For example, one of the key risks we had to manage in one internal accelerator was a perception that our intention was to make our initiative the only place innovation would be permitted. That was never a goal, and it would be a terrible strategy. We needed to get out in front of the rumor that our initiative meant "innovation only happens here," which had begun to spread before we even started delivering anything.

In addition to that, we wanted to ensure people interested in bringing their ideas to us understood the kind of ideas we were looking for, and we needed them to know how ideas were being adjudicated. Our interest was primarily in breakthrough ideas. The types of ideas the existing organizations (the business units and product lines) were not structured to support because the ideas were too nascent, too novel, or too risky. In fact, we created the initiative because we knew the business units would not and/or could not incubate those ideas.

Figure 9-4 shows one of the simple graphics we used to communicate these things.

CHAPTER 9 COMMUNICATING

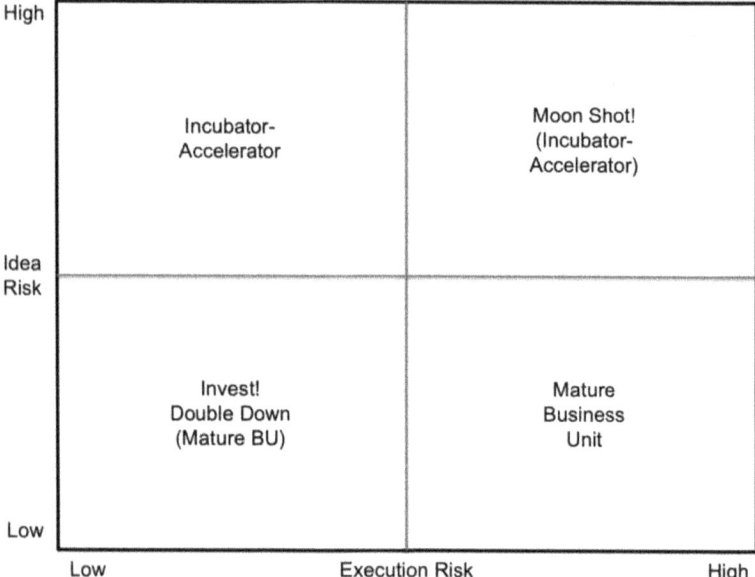

Figure 9-4. How one accelerator communicated where ideas were best incubated

You can see we made it clear that innovation would still happen everywhere, and that we were looking for breakthrough ideas where the risk of the *idea* itself was high. That was our initiative's strength.

We needed people to understand we were not "coming for" mature business units' innovation, or their budget. Furthermore, we clearly communicated we were willing to help any mature business unit that wanted to foster other types of innovation. We helped those teams to establish their *own* initiatives, distinct from our accelerator.

In addition, the diagram in Figure 9-4 proactively helped us explain why we might not accept an idea, or why we might redirect it to a mature business unit.

 The graphic helped one team a lot, but when working with a different team, we found it fell short. To address the new team's needs and styles we adapted it as shown in Figure 9-5 to more

CHAPTER 9 COMMUNICATING

explicitly show that the purpose of their incubator–accelerator was to remove risk *from the idea* and ensure participants were building things that were desirable, feasible, and viable.

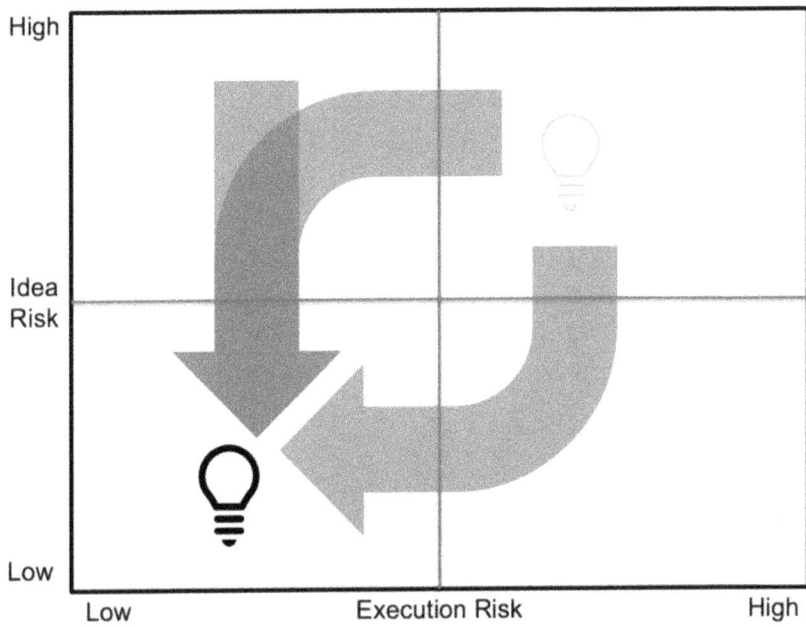

Figure 9-5. *The lean entrepreneurship approach removes risk from bringing new ideas to life*

Inspect and Adapt the Messaging

Messaging does not always resonate the first time it is delivered, and it can lose its impact or effectiveness over time. Like bringing new ideas to life, communicating with constituents is often an iterative process. Before I created the diagram shown in Figure 9-4, I, and others, made many less effective attempts at depicting the initiative's position. You will see in Figure 9-6 that even small adjustments to Figure 9-5 were required to help clarify our message in one case.

CHAPTER 9   COMMUNICATING

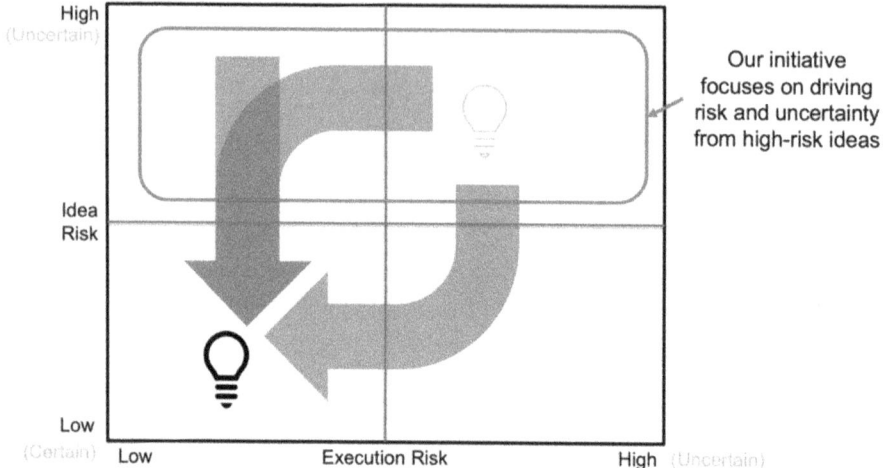

Figure 9-6. Lean innovation is designed to remove risk and uncertainty

We proactively communicated to our varied audiences in many different ways, and inspected and adapted numerous times afterward. This included informally communicating and testing candidate messaging in one-to-one conversations or in small gatherings, and stating things more explicitly via forums such as "frequently asked questions" (FAQ) posts. However, some of the simplest graphics were incredibly effective.

Set Expectations for Long-Term Gains

It can take a relatively long time to take a brand new idea from concept to functioning solution, and even longer to get it to the point where it is delivering significant value (e.g., driving citizen or beneficiary benefits or private sector revenue). Your communication strategy will need to prepare key stakeholders and sponsors for those longer-term results. If you read Part 2 of this book, that may seem obvious. What may be less obvious is that you may need to regularly remind them what they agreed to.

For example, if your private sector initiative is accepting nascent ideas, stakeholders may need to be periodically reminded not to expect revenue in the early months of incubation while a team is working through customer-problem and problem-solution fit. That has almost always been an expectation in my experience.

Realistic expectations need to be set clearly early and reinforced on a regular cadence. Setting a cadence can be tricky because you do not want to annoy your audience, but you don't want their expectations to drift either. You will need to stay attuned to your stakeholders' sentiment.

 For example, we experienced a challenge like this related to an initiative that an organization's C-level team (e.g., CEO, CMO, CFO, COO...) was very interested in, and excited about. When they approved the initiative, they accepted that it was targeted at very nascent ideas and, therefore, it would be a long while before incubating teams would generate meaningful revenue (e.g., millions or tens of millions of dollars). Everyone was aligned at the outset, but we learned their expectations would drift over time. The addition of new people to the executive team or their inner circle could also cause expectations to drift, and the drift could be infectious.

 We created a value migration model, like the example in Figure 9-7, to address this. The value migration model provided an illustration of how the value produced by the initiative would evolve over time. For example, though the primary reason the initiative was created was to generate new, meaningful businesses, you can see from Figure 9-7 that the anticipated value from revenue was almost zero in the first year, and it was not anticipated to grow meaningfully until the third and fourth years.

CHAPTER 9 COMMUNICATING

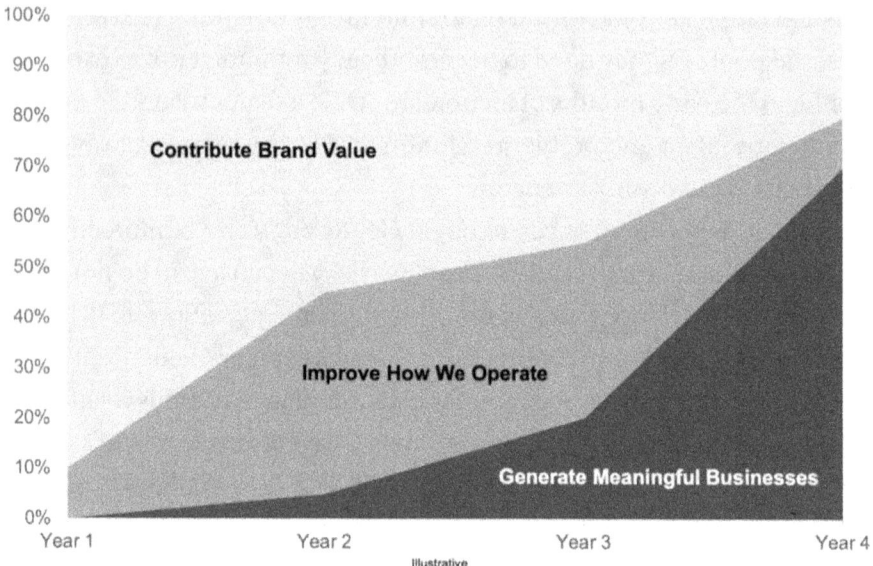

Figure **9-7.** *Illustrative example of a value migration model*

A second objective of the initiative was for it to influence the broader organization, drive an innovative culture, and improve overall technology operations. We anticipated it would take a year or so for that to have a real impact, and that, over time, the contribution of the initiative toward that would be less as the good habits driven by the program became embedded in the company culture.

Finally, we knew the initiative would show the world we were innovative, growing, and leading in new markets and technologies, and that would make a significant contribution to our brand. This would be the initiative's greatest value driver early on and would continue throughout its life. We also determined that the initiative would have less impact on the brand over time as customers, analysts, and others became more familiar with it. They would evolve to expect us to do these things.

This value migration model was very effective at aligning senior executive's expectations. It also helped us to remind them periodically what to expect, without being annoying, condescending, or patronizing.

We could periodically include it in material we sent to them, or use it in response to questions asking why revenue numbers were not large, or when we expected to see a significant revenue contribution from the initiative.

5. Communicate to Preempt Threats

You may have noticed the value migration model discussed in the previous section initially served as an alignment tool but was later used to preempt potential conflicts. It is much simpler and more pleasant to proactively address potential conflicts and threats than to have to perform "damage control" due to miscommunication or mismatched expectations. Imagine responding to a crisis resulting from a senior leader, C-level executive, or board member losing confidence in an initiative and declaring they feel it should be shuttered. I have seen that happen in a wide variety of projects and initiatives. It ages people.

It is important to consider proactively addressing potential threats to an initiative when creating its communication plan. Threats can occur for a variety of reasons. Most of the threats I witness can be attributed to miscommunication, misperception, or failure to set expectations. But there are many other potential threats. One of the most common sources of threats is people who feel threatened by the initiative.

Embrace Other Initiatives

People in other teams may be building their own innovation initiatives, and they may see your initiative as a threat. Your initiative should not pose a threat to other initiatives (or you're doing it wrong). Nevertheless, when this is unchecked, unhealthy competition can result.

Healthy competition can raise performance standards and morale for everyone. Unhealthy competition often results in widespread failure. Where resources and expertise may have otherwise been pooled and leveraged to the benefit of multiple initiatives, teams, departments, or business units, unhealthy competitors often work against one another. Making new things can be challenging, but breaking things is simple. When teams compete in this way, successful failure is almost guaranteed.

Unhealthy competition often arises when other teams believe your new program will take away their ability to innovate. When they believe that the arrival of your initiative means that innovation is only to be done there. This should never be the case. If it is, you need to inspect and adapt your program immediately.

To preempt this, make sure that your initiative is not implicitly or explicitly sending the message, "innovation only happens here." Explicitly communicate that your initiative is not the only place innovation will be permitted. If you are able to collaborate with others to help make their initiative better, make sure that is known; and make it easy for others to contact you.

You can even be explicit about what you can help with, and proactively help teams without being in their way. For example, I like to make an initiative's tools, artifacts, ceremonies, and resources broadly available for anyone who might benefit from them (e.g., by posting them on a shared site that can be accessed by anyone in the organization).

Be Transparent About Restrictions and Timing

There may be instances where you are not able to address all stakeholder needs, are not able to meet specific needs at an early stage, or have overcommitted and have to temporarily reduce your scope. For example, you may have to limit who can pitch an idea early in the life of an initiative, or limit the types of ideas that will be accepted, due to your team's capacity to accept pitches. Be transparent when those things happen, and get in front of them immediately. When you do, it is important to clearly communicate the rationale for your decisions, why the specific restrictions were selected (e.g., availability of facilities, budget restrictions, laws, policies…), and when eligibility will be expanded if that is known. **Openness and transparency are key to building trust.**

Be Aware of Innovation Killing Personalities

In *The Innovative CIO* I introduced several personality types that can stifle innovation or new idea incubation.[1] People with these personality traits can also impact an innovation or incubation initiative. Three key personalities to watch out for are:

1. **"The Perfectionist,"** who can dampen innovation and new idea incubation for themselves or others, miss opportunities by insisting ideas be perfect before they are shown to others, or bias toward "precisely wrong" over "roughly right"

2. **"The Innovative Authoritarian,"** who can dampen or prevent innovation due to their own experience, bias, and blind spots

3. **"The Protector,"** who will often seek out, and can kill, new ideas while intentionally trying to break things in the name of protecting the organization from harm

It is important to keep in mind that people who have these personality types are not always being intentionally obstructive. In many cases, their motivation is noble. That does not make their behavior any less

---

[1] Andy Mann, George Watt, and Peter Matthews. 2013. *The Innovative CIO: How IT Leaders Can Drive Business Transformation*, New York, NY, Apress Media, *Chapter 2: Stories from the Trenches*

harmful, but keep in mind their motivations are not always bad when proactively communicating with them. Getting in front of their concerns with understanding and humility is more likely to be fruitful than a head-on collision, but you may have to have more difficult conversations in some cases.

You will probably encounter at least one of these, or other similar, personalities as you deliver your initiative. If you have been in an organization for a while, you may already know who they are. Be prepared, because they are often able to exercise influence over the progress of an initiative, and they cannot be ignored.

Beware of Overoptimism

Good fortune can lead to unfortunate outcomes when it is not properly managed. For example, if you have constructed your initiative with the target of having one successful idea for every ten attempts, that does not mean that your first idea will be successful, the next nine will not, and the eleventh will be successful. Nor does it guarantee that ideas number ten and twenty will be hits. It will likely be more random. It might be ideas eighteen and nineteen that pay off. It usually doesn't take that long, but my point is that things may happen randomly.

But! What if you *are* fortunate and your first idea is rapid success? Unless your team is remarkably good at selecting ideas (and you will improve over time), the risk is that people will expect another quick hit. If that hit does not come when expected (and it likely will not), you may be faced with unhappy stakeholders and a damage control mission.

Things can go poorly when expectations are allowed to ramp up unchecked. It's a bit counter intuitive, but this needs to be managed proactively when it happens. I am not suggesting you forego celebrating the success. Quite the opposite. Celebrate it, but also remind stakeholders that this is very fortunate and, while the team will try to make *every* idea successful, that will not likely happen. Don't be concerned if you *do* have another success. Nobody will mind if you are more successful than you promise.

Prepare People for the "Chaos"

Innovation and new idea incubation are messy. They can begin with low fidelity mock-ups or prototypes that look chaotic and unimpressive. They can involve experiments that deliver counterintuitive results, pivots, and restarts. This is especially true for breakthrough or nascent ideas.

This rapid experimentation and iteration, inspection and adaptation, starting and restarting, is a normal aspect of bringing new ideas to life. When that is not communicated and understood it can look to an outsider as if things are disorganized, sloppy, and chaotic. As with other threats, you need to let people know how your initiative works, and how it will be measured and governed.

Hardening Against Reorganizations

Reorganizations happen, and when they do, *any* initiative can be at risk. While there is nothing that can be done to guarantee an initiative will not be shuttered, paused, or cut back during a reorganization, some things *can* be done to increase the odds it will survive.

Reorganizations are usually hectic, especially for those deciding what to move, what to keep, and what to discontinue. Time to make decisions is usually constrained. In my experience, the better an initiative and its value is understood *before* a reorganization or its planning begins, the better the odds it will survive the reorganization.

To be proactive about this threat, broaden your messaging. Make sure as many people as possible are aware of the initiative, the value it delivers, and its potential. Be sure to include:

- Key influencers across the organization
- Leaders who might be involved in planning a reorganization
- Leaders who are responsible for the initiative, and their executives

- Leaders of groups where the initiative might land in an upcoming reorganization
- People who might replace leaders currently responsible for the initiative
- Executives across the organization at the highest possible level

Broaden awareness horizontally and vertically. Building broad executive support and awareness is a good idea in general, but it can also help more directly when a reorganization occurs. I used to explain to the leaders of my team that, when a reorganization happens, you want your initiative(s) to be discussed as follows: "Next is <your initiative's name>. We don't need to discuss them. They are doing great work. Next is…"

Things happen quickly during reorganizations, so have your material and proof of value ready, leverage key influencers and everyone's network, and get in front of decision-makers quickly.

Additional Considerations

Here are a few additional things to consider as you are preparing your communication strategy and plan:

- **Speak with anyone who will listen:** Opportunistic discussions and presentations can accelerate initiatives, create new opportunities, and open doors.
- **Keep a finger on the pulse:** Get help from people who are in positions where they will become aware of needs, interests, and problems early (e.g., are in senior leadership meetings where they might become aware of concerns during casual conversations with their peers).

- **Always have your elevator pitch ready:** You never know whom you will encounter and what doors they might open or close for you (I used to routinely encounter board members at events, and in elevators at our headquarters).

- **Get your story in front of everyone you can:** This includes both formal and informal conversations, and making sure your data and value contributions are understood and easily available when you are not around (e.g., via dashboards, videos…).

- **Bias to transparency:** Get into the habit of asking "is there any reason we should not share this" instead of asking "should we share this" (the answer to the first question is almost always, "no").

- **Ensure stakeholders recognize themselves in your material:** When appropriate, include their ideas and their language in your material, or in your explanation of the material when presenting it.

- **Ask for confirmation:** Don't assume you are aligned, confirm alignment explicitly, and check in periodically.

- **Confirm the communication format and frequency are effective:** Ask people whether they are receiving the information they want and need, and whether they feel it is too infrequent, too frequent, or just right.

- **Get help:** Find communications professionals and/or talented communicators to help you, and leverage their delivery channels.

(This can be a game changer.)

- **Speak *their* language:** Communicate using terms that match your audience, don't expect them to adapt for you, especially if they are senior leaders or executives.

- **Use a lean canvas:** Creating a lean canvas for your initiative can help you craft, fine-tune, and communicate your messaging, and help you to de-risk the initiative.

- **Promote contributions:** Publicly recognize anyone who contributes to your initiative in a meaningful way, regardless of their team or position.

- **Attribute shamelessly:** Ensure people receive credit for good ideas the team adopted, even those adopted behind the scenes, never steal credit, and never let anyone take credit by omission (i.e., do not let them accept praise and credit for the work of others).

- **Overshare, especially early:** Finding the right communication frequency can be tricky, but over-communicating is usually better than under-communicating, or "going dark," especially early in the initiative's life when assumptions can be deadly.

- **Leverage existing channels:** Other groups will have already figured out what form, format, and frequency their audiences prefer; take advantage of their channels and the collateral assistance those channels might bring (e.g., editorial assistance).

- **Bad news travels fastest:** Proactively communicate changes, issues, and delays; it results in better service and builds and reinforces trust.

- **Informal communication matters:** Building and leveraging relationships and informal communication channels can, at times, be more valuable than formal channels.
- **Promote early wins:** Find the opportunity for early wins as you plan your initiative, and promote them broadly when they happen; though be careful not to over-hype.

Summary

Communication is important at all stages of initiatives like this, but it is extremely important as you begin building and deploying. You need to be clear about what the initiative will and will not do. Communication must be proactive, and the initiative's team should bias to transparency. Proactive communication must focus on alignment and status, and must also consider potential threats and help preempt them. Most importantly the initiative's team should always be checking in with key stakeholders, sponsors, and other constituents to ensure they are receiving the information they need at the frequency they require, and that they are not being overwhelmed with information or noise.

Communication must be deliberate throughout the life of the initiative. Specific communication needs will change, the volume of communication will change, and its focus will change, but the need for effective communication will be constant. A deliberate approach to communication will ensure you supply the right information to the right audience at the right time, and will enable your team to spend more time laying the foundation for your initiative – which is your next step, and the subject of the next chapter.

PART III

Build–Measure–Learn

CHAPTER 10

Laying the Foundation

You're ready! As Henry David Thoreau might have observed, you have built your castles in the air.[1] You've set goals, determined the specific needs and nuances of the organization, finalized and fine-tuned your initiative's initial design, finalized or updated your objectives, and set an initial plan for communicating and keeping things on track. Now you are ready to lay a foundation under those castles (Figure 10-1).

In this Chapter

Laying the foundation:

1. Form the Initiative Team
2. Form the Governance Team
3. Engage Advisors and Allies
4. Consider a Maker Team
5. Prepare a budget

Figure 10-1. *What's in this chapter*

[1] *"If you have built castles in the air, your work need not be lost; that is where they should be. Now put foundations under them."* Henry David Thoreau, 1817–1862

G. Watt, *The Lean Entrepreneurship Playbook*,
https://doi.org/10.1007/979-8-8688-0122-8_10

CHAPTER 10   LAYING THE FOUNDATION

Up to this point, you may have been doing much of the groundwork on your own. You now need to form the teams that will guide, build, launch, and operate your initiative:

1. **The Initiative Team:** The people who will build, deploy, and operate the initiative, and assist incubating teams

2. **The Governance Team(s):** The people who will set direction for the initiative, select ideas, and evaluate incubating teams' progress

3. **The Advisory Team:** People who will provide guidance and subject matter or domain expertise to participants, help guide the initiative through organizational processes and constraints, and help design new processes, if necessary

4. **Incubating Teams:** The participant-intrapreneurs bringing new ideas to life

5. **The Maker Team (Optional):** A person or group possessing specialized skills that participants may require early but are not likely to have

Figure 10-2 provides a summary of how each team fits within the overall initiative. In this chapter I will discuss all but the incubating teams, which I will discuss in Chapter 11.

CHAPTER 10   LAYING THE FOUNDATION

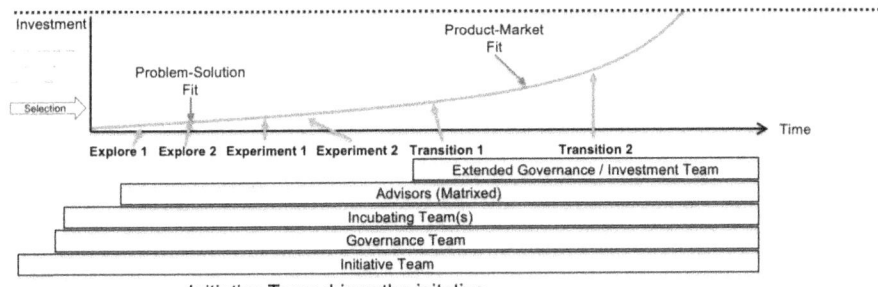

- Initiative Team drives the initative
    - First point of contact for aspiring intrapreneurs, establishes and maintains cadence
    - Creates program artifacts, measures, and OKRs/KPIs
    - Drives retrospectives and inspects and adapts the program
    - Unblocks incubating teams
    - May have some bench expertise (e.g.: business development, design, marketing)
- Governance Team provides end-to-end oversight
    - Evaluates pitches and selects ideas for entry
    - Conducts regular 3P (pivot, pause, or persist) reviews
    - Approves budget, objectives, and timelines at each investment round
    - Stage-specific checklists ensure focus on outcomes vs. output
    - Ensures teams remain customer-focused
    - Guides the overall direction of the inititive
- Extended Governance or Investment Team guides larger investments
    - Transition 1, Transition 2, and Exit
- Incubating Team brings ideas to life
    - Incubates idea through all stages (Entry to Exit)
    - (Optional) Ad hoc assistance from Maker Team
- Advisory Team provides matrixed direction and assistance from Entry to Exit

Figure 10-2.   Team roles (illustrative)

Not a Cast of Thousands

Don't let Figure 10-2 intimidate you. You won't likely need a large full-time staff, and you can start small (e.g., one full-time or part-time person) and grow as needed. As I will explain in this chapter, even fairly large initiatives can be run with just a few people.

CHAPTER 10   LAYING THE FOUNDATION

1. Form the Initiative Team

The Initiative Team is the initiative's anchor and is the first team that must be formed. The Initiative Team:

- Establishes and maintains a cadence for the Initiative and Governance teams
- Creates and maintains the initiative's artifacts, or leads their creation
- Sets the initiative's objectives and targets
- Defines, produces, and maintains the initiative's measures
- Is the first point of contact for the initiative
- Is the first point of contact for those who want to pitch ideas
- Recruits pitches
- Onboards incubating teams and guides them through the initiative
- Unblocks issues for incubating teams, the Governance Team, and the initiative overall
- Champions the initiative and communicates progress and value to stakeholders and executives, and outside the initiative's boundaries
- Coordinates with advisors and ensures they have the resources they require
- Coordinates and manages the initiative's events (e.g., training, summits, showcases)

- Leads retrospectives at all levels except incubating teams' internal retrospectives
- Provides facilitation and leadership for anchor ceremonies

It may appear you need a lot of people to accomplish everything listed above. That may be the case if your initiative gains momentum and supports multitude of incubating teams. However, the Initiative Team can be as small as a single person. For example, if you were the person who has performed most, or all of the activities in Part 3 – which would not be uncommon early in an initiative's life – you have essentially been a one-person Initiative Team.

The GEFN Advantage

When we built the initiative described in *Lean Entrepreneurship*, I was tasked with laying a foundation under its initial design. I was responsible for setting a cadence, creating the initial artifacts, creating presentation material for our Governance Team and champions, delivering presentations to other groups, and designing and facilitating our workshops and ceremonies. I was also responsible for a host of other unrelated programs, and scientific and applied research teams. But I spent most of my time working on the initiative. I would estimate my effort at the time to have been approximately one full-time person equivalent (FTE) per week (one 35-to-40-hour week), maybe more.

I held this responsibility for approximately four to six months. This happened primarily due to the timing of other team members' absences, but it was not untenable for a few reasons. First, I was not alone. The initiative had a *very* strong and active Governance Team, and we had identified and selected four teams to prime it. They were very patient and supportive, and I could count on them whenever I needed help. But the greatest relief may have come from "GEFN."

CHAPTER 10   LAYING THE FOUNDATION

As an "army of one," I quickly realized I would not be able to deliver the *entire* initiative at once. At each point in its evolution, I had to ask which ceremonies, artifacts, and resources were absolutely required, and which were not. I had to determine what the minimum valuable version of each would be, and when each would be needed. I had to repeatedly determine what would be "good enough for now" (GEFN). I learned that if I could anticipate the initiative's needs and deliver things slightly ahead of when they were necessary, I could "survive."

For example, I did not need any Series B or C artifacts or resources when we launched because we did not have any incubating ideas that were that far along. I did not need a Pitch ceremony until we were ready to take pitches. I did not need to work through the first 3P ceremony until we were ready to have one.

Once we set our OKRs, I knew exactly what I would need and exactly when I would need it. It was a sprint that required constant focus and discipline, but it wasn't awful.

If you've read *Lean Entrepreneurship*, you already know it ended well. We took advantage of the timing of an unrelated Senior Leadership Team meeting to take our first two pitches and soft launch the initiative over three months ahead of schedule. Again, thanks to a great team and the fact that we primed our initiative with four incubating teams.

A Lean Mindset

That experience taught me a few things. I learned **I did not have to build it all at once. I just had to stay a little ahead of the incubating teams and our planned activities.** Further leveraging the power of GEFN, I realized the things I created did not have to be in their final state. I could build the minimum required to support the current state of the initiative and the incubating teams. An MVP. Then, I could inspect and adapt what I built through retrospectives and feedback and improve things as the initiative evolved.

It seems obvious now, but that initial challenge necessitated a lean mindset. **I learned we could build our initiative using the same approach that we were espousing the incubating teams use to bring *their* ideas to life**.

How Many People?

The number of people your Initiative Team requires will depend entirely on your ultimate objective. It is possible that your Initiative Team might be one person, or have two or three part-time members. The skills and experience of the team members will be a determining factor. The more experienced the people, the more likely you will be able to use them part-time, and the fewer of them you will likely need.

The number and composition of the team is also likely to evolve over time. Early full-time participants might eventually become part-timers, new part-timers might join, and part-timers might become full-timers. I realize this seems a bit complex, so let me provide an example.

Following the soft launch of our initiative, activity began to ramp up and our needs changed. A very experienced program manager who returned from leave joined the Initiative Team part-time, which enabled me to reduce my participation to part-time. Together we worked on delivering resources, scheduling training, and managing the initiative's logistics. Combined, we spent at least the equivalent one full-time person working on the initiative.

Since we had primed the initiative with four teams, had accepted one additional team following our initial pitches, and intended to have approximately ten concurrently incubating teams at once, an Engineering and Senior Vice President (SVP) had been assigned to help and guide incubating teams full-time.

Finally, we added a senior program manager ("unblocker") to adapt mature processes which were too heavy for new idea incubation, address issues, and remove obstacles so incubating teams could focus on bringing their ideas to life.

If you add it all up, we had approximately three to three-and-one-half full-time equivalents for an initiative running five active incubations, and ramping up to ten:

- Two part-time people with senior program management skills creating, deploying, operating, and managing the initiative (1–1.5 FTE)
- A full-time senior software engineering leader mentoring and guiding incubating teams (1 FTE)
- A full-time senior program manager helping guide, train, and unblock teams (1 FTE)

Start Small and Evolve

The Initiative Team morphed and expanded as we evolved. In our first evolution, we moved from one full-time person to two part-time people, and later added two full-time people, as previously described. The four previously incubating teams were moved into the initiative's budget and reported to the SVP. This incremental growth enabled us to keep expenses low and increase investment as the initiative evolved and began to show value.

That structure worked very well for a long time. The Initiative Team levelled off at approximately 3.5 FTEs, consisting of three part-time senior program and project managers, a full-time master unblocker, and the SVP.

In your initiative you might, alternatively, have one person filling both the program management and technical leadership roles; depending upon the nature of your incubating ideas, the number of concurrently incubating ideas, and the skills and experience of the people available to lead your team.

You should also think about which "bench" expertise your initiative might benefit from as it evolves. For example, once we had ten teams running concurrently, we brought in a full-time designer to help the incubating teams. While no individual incubating team required, or could justify, their own full-time designer, ten active teams provided more than enough work for them.

Stay Small but Mighty

You can see that it is possible to drive a fairly large initiative with very few people. A small initiative might be able to succeed with a very experienced one-person Initiative Team. Though beware, the one-person team may need a lot of help early on.

A benefit of our replacing one full-time person with three part-time people was more diversity of thought and better flexibility in scheduling (we could cover for one-another). We could also leverage our individual strengths, and I believe we became more efficient and productive as a result.

The optimum team composition for you may vary. Think through the responsibilities of the team as set forward in the list at the beginning of this section, and make sure that your team (or person) has the skills and resources to deliver them. Prioritize outcomes and results and let the team structure fall from that. However, if you find your Initiative Team is larger than a mature incubating team, or the Governance Team, you might want to give some thought to whether it has grown too large.

Additional Considerations

Here are a few additional things you might consider as you develop your Initiative Team structure:

- Are you building a toolkit, framework, or approach?
- How quickly must the initiative be up and running?
- Will the initiative's leader be full-time or part-time?
- What is your budget?
- Will Initiative Team members be seconded from other groups, or will the initiative fund them?
- How many incubating teams do you intend to run concurrently?
- How many incubations will be active during the fiscal year? When will each join?
- What type of ideas do you intend to incubate?
- Will incubating teams require additional specialized support?
- Will incubating teams require resources or facilities that require specialized support, management, or maintenance? Are they currently available?
- Will incubating teams be moved to the initiative's structure and budget center, or remain within their budget of origin?

Each of these things may impact the number and type of Initiative Team members you require.

Who May Matter More Than How Many

Whom you select may matter more than how many people are on the team. The initiative needs to be driven by trustworthy people with a servant-leader mindset.

The Initiative Team's members must be trusted by the incubating teams, the Governance Team, and the mentors and advisors. The Initiative Team's members need the people on those other teams to be frank and candid with them, and they need to be deemed worthy of the unvarnished truth, good and bad. The Initiative Team needs to be able to drive any of those other teams or their members to action, and to motivate and lead people – even when the people they are leading far outrank them in the organizational hierarchy.

Characteristics of Good Initiative Team Candidates

Selection of the wrong people for any of these teams can create challenges and setbacks. Select the wrong people for this team and you'll never get your initiative off the ground. Look for:

- Humility
- Positive energy
- The ability to quickly build and demonstrate trust
- Experience leading or building programs or initiatives
- A track record of positive results
- The ability to self-manage and self-motivate
- Servant-leader mindset
- Strong written and verbal communication skills

- The ability to motivate others
- The ability to "manage upward"
- Strong facilitation skills
- The ability to listen, learn from mistakes (theirs and others), and adapt
- The ability to build and leverage a personal network

You won't necessarily find all of these attributes in all good candidates, but hopefully this list will help you to understand the kind of person who is most likely to be a successful Initiative Team member, capable of driving your initiative forward.

Initiative Team: The Bottom Line

Start small and scale up:

- Start with one experienced initiative owner.
- The more experienced the Initiative Team's members, the fewer you will need.
- External assistance with logistics and tactical items will extend a small, or one-person, team's capacity.
- As the initiative evolves, program managers with senior levels of experience may be able to share Initiative Team responsibilities while working on other things, but
  - Make sure each task and objective is clearly owned.
  - The overall initiative must have a single, accountable owner.
  - These tasks must be in each person's OKRs (MBOs...) as their highest priority.

- This will work best if they are all in the same part of the organization (e.g., report to the same executive, or report to the initiative's owner).
- Workloads will begin to crescendo when incubating teams begin to enter the initiative.
- Peak workload will depend upon the targeted number of incubating teams and, initially, the pent-up demand for pitches.
- Consider applying part-time or temporary assistance to discrete events such as summits, demo days, or conferences to avoid overloading the team.
- The Initiative Team should require no more than two-to-three full-time equivalents (FTE) for building and operating the initiative and unblocking incubating teams, even for a fairly large number of incubating teams.
  - One FTE or less may suffice for small initiatives at steady state.
- Consider whether you need to add a "technical mentor" like our SVP, Innovation (e.g., senior software engineer, process engineer...).
- Consider adding bench expertise (e.g., design) as your initiative grows to avoid overloading your Advisory Team or matrixed advisors.
  - In some cases, incubating teams may need to bring specific expertise (e.g., marketing) into their team as they evolve.

2. Form the Governance Team

The Governance Team provides direction and guidance for the initiative, and for incubating teams. They also act as champions for the initiative, and provide a cross-organizational conduit for information. The Governance Team:

- Helps set direction for the initiative
- Evaluates pitches and selects ideas to enter the initiative
- Conducts regular 3P (Pivot, Pause, Persevere) reviews for each incubating team
- Approves incubating team budgets, objectives, and timelines during the transition between each stage of incubation
- Mentors incubating teams and their team members
- Ensures incubating teams remain customer or beneficiary focused
- Leverages their network to assist the initiative, Initiative Team members, and incubating teams
- Champions and promotes the initiative
- Helps identify and recruit advisors for the Advisory Team, Governance Team, and Incubating Teams, and other initiative members and participants
- Focuses on outcomes versus output
- Leverages stage-specific checklists to ensure they are focused on the right things at each stage of incubation

- Leverages Advisory Teams to inform key decisions
- Is engaged part-time, and typically represents a cross-functional and cross-organizational constituency

Diversity Is Key

The Governance Team is a cross-organizational group of advisors and experts. As with any advisory team, the more diverse the team, the more successful it will be. Building a diverse team is also just the right thing to do. Consider diversity across as many parameters as you can, including, but not limited to, professional background (e.g., technical, leadership, management, business, startup vs. corporate, innovation…), gender, cross-organization representation, race, and personal network.

When I discuss this with people they often explain that building a diverse advisory team of this nature is difficult or "impossible." For example, when working with software development or SaaS organizations, a common initial response is there is no way they will be able to put enough women on their team. As justification they cite statistics about the number of women in software development overall, or in software development or engineering in their company (e.g., "Only 10% of our engineering workforce are women"). Don't fall for that. Work harder. Look further. Your advisory team will be ten or twelve people at most. You don't have to find that many.

Also keep in mind that you are looking for diversity in experience, and experience can move across disciplines. For example, we were fortunate to have a woman on one Governance Team who was a member of an organization's Corporate Strategy and Business Development group (e.g., intelligence and acquisitions). Though she was not then a member of the engineering organization, she also had extensive experience as a software engineering manager and senior leader. Expand your horizons, open your mind, and look more broadly.

CHAPTER 10   LAYING THE FOUNDATION

Caveat: Maintaining a Diverse Group

Building a diverse group *can* be a challenge. (That's not an excuse not to do it.) However, maintaining a diverse team can sometimes be more challenging.

For example, Governance Team members tend to be highly experienced high performers. As a result, they sometimes get promoted, usually to senior positions. The deluge of work required to acclimatize to a new senior position (e.g., SVP, EVP, Cxx, General Manager) can therefore result in a Governance Team member's resignation. When that happens, they (or their executive) will often appoint a replacement, and that can disrupt the team's balance.

For instance, I once worked with a Governance Team that had achieved balance between men and women. Given the organization's overall overrepresentation of men (I believe it was approximately 80%), this was a great accomplishment. One of the Governance Team's women was promoted to a very senior leadership role and had to step down to focus on their transition. They were kind enough to find a replacement from their organization. The person who was offered as a replacement was exceptional, and very good for the team… and a man. While this maintained the group's organizational and skills balance, it was a "minus two" for its diversity since one woman left and one man was added.

It created a challenge, but not an insurmountable one. It simply required deliberate action. We had several options, including requesting an alternative nominee, having a current team member step down or take an advisory role, or expanding the Governance Team. We expanded the team, since the initiative had been growing and the team was already looking to broaden its representation.

My apologies if this example seems overly simple. My intent is not to attempt to oversimplify this topic, or to suggest there is only one aspect of diversity. My point is only that diversity is important, and sometimes the diversity of a team can drift insidiously. Creating and maintaining a diverse team requires a deliberate approach, and diligent attention. It is always worthwhile, and it is always the right thing to do.

Build a Pipeline

One of the ways you can be proactive about diversity is through mentoring high-potential people who may not yet be ready to be fully fledged Governance Team members. These people can be invited to participate in Governance Team activities, and to learn from its members. But make no mistake, they can also be productive and active contributors.

I have seen great results when very few restrictions were put on such people. For example, in one team, high-potential participants were permitted, and strongly encouraged, to contribute opinions and data as equals, they attended all ceremonies and Governance Team-only meetings and deliberations and, at times, they led Governance Team sessions. But they were not given a vote during Pitch or 3P ceremonies, and they were not typically given time to ask questions during the ceremonies (due primarily to time constraints).

There were many benefits as a result:

- High-potential people were exposed to very successful, senior people and were able to learn from them, from how they interacted with others, and from how they interacted with one-another.

- High-potential people were given a chance to lead more senior people in a safe environment where they could learn and grow.

- The Governance Team was exposed to, and frequently benefited from, the knowledge and opinions of the high-potential people.

- It created a pipeline of potential new members for the Governance Team.

- It exposed the high-potential people to a group of senior people who were well-networked and in a position to help advance their career.

Whether or not the high-potential people went on to become members of the Governance Team, they developed valuable skills and exposure – to both the Governance Team and other senior executives – that would be of benefit to them regardless of where their career led them.

Lean Governance Is Lightweight, Responsible Governance

I have had many discussions with senior people whose response to the word "lean" was something akin to, "I don't want to live in the Wild West!" **It is a very common misconception that lean means "ungoverned." Nothing could be further from the truth.** The irony is, **done properly, lean governance should provide even better governance than heavier styles like waterfall**.

For example, in the lean entrepreneurship model, the Governance Team discusses progress and performance and mentors each early stage team monthly. Sometimes more frequently. This enables more rapid learning and adaptation and reduces waste by decreasing the maximum amount of time a team might spend going in the wrong direction. The same happens inside incubating teams on a more frequent basis, through experimentation and learning. But! They both spend the minimum amount of time on governance needed to keep things on track, *and* teams require a minimum of preparation. Why?

They key to successful lean governance is to apply the least amount of work to learn the most. **It's about capturing as much data and evidence as a by-product of the work as possible. No governance for the sake of governance, no work for the sake of work.**

Lean entrepreneurship teams run the smallest experiment possible, with the fewest resources possible, to learn as much as possible, and drive maximum value from every experiment. We apply the same philosophy to governance. Sure, not all additional work can be avoided. But teams do as little additional work as they can, and automate governance activities whenever possible. The result is better governance with less intrusion and less wasted work. Though it can take time to become accustomed to it.

Governance Is About People

It is worth noting that a significant aspect of the Governance Team's role is mentoring and nurturing people and teams. This can range from more subtle guidance, as might be given following a pitch or 3P review, to more active guidance when mentoring an incubating team leader. While the latter is usually optional, I have found it frequently happens organically (e.g., through offers of follow-up assistance during 3P reviews).

Many Governance Team members also offer to volunteer as an advisor for at least one incubating team. I believe it is best left to the discretion of the incubating team whether to accept the offer.

It should be clear that having patience and a coaching mindset is something to look for in Governance Team members. Let's review a few other things to consider.

CHAPTER 10   LAYING THE FOUNDATION

Characteristics of Good Governance Team Candidates

Ideally, Governance Team candidates will possess many of the following characteristics:

- Passion for the initiative, and for what they do
- An interest in bringing new ideas to life
- Depth of experience in their field and/or diversity of experience
- Leadership experience and a leadership mindset
- Respected in their domain
- Respected in the organization
- Can get directly to the point while being nurturing
- Patience
- Project positive energy (the group is small, bad energy will travel quickly)
- A broad professional network
- Some domain expertise relevant to the initiative's objectives
- A broad view of the organization and its impact
- Understands the organization's mission
- Knows how and where to get things done, and how to navigate the organization
- A track record of success

- Will contribute to discussions and participate in events (won't "phone it in")
- A team player
- Ability to coach or mentor people at all levels
- Candid, and speaks their mind
- Will become a willing champion for the initiative

This list should give you a feel for the type of person who is likely to succeed in this role and drive value for the initiative. It is important to note that not every good Governance Team candidate will possess *all* of these attributes. In addition, some of the attributes (e.g., "become a willing champion") may have to be earned.

Governance Team Time Requirements

The Governance Team's mission is to guide, not to "make," so their time commitment should not be onerous. Nevertheless, **be up front with Governance Team candidates regarding what you are asking them to commit to.** Having an advisor join the team and not show up will not likely be severely damaging to the initiative, but it *may* create delays and setbacks (e.g., failure to achieve a quorum for 3P reviews or pitch ceremonies).

Consider the following when calculating time requirements:

1. Estimate 30 minutes per month for each pitch (20 for the pitch, ten for deliberations) plus five to ten minutes between pitches.

2. Estimate 30 minutes per month for each incubating team's 3P review (some will be shorter, some will be longer) plus five to ten minutes between reviews.

CHAPTER 10   LAYING THE FOUNDATION

3. Estimate one hour for a monthly Governance Team meeting (usually scheduled immediately following the 3P review for the Governance Team's convenience).

4. Early in the life of the initiative, add time for team forming and, perhaps, review of the planned design, familiarization with ceremonies, and training, if necessary.

5. Estimate a one-time one-hour onboarding meeting for each new team member, to familiarize them with the initiative and how it works, and answer their questions (the inaugural Governance Team might do this as a group).

6. Estimate an additional 15 to 30 minutes following early ceremonies (e.g., 3P, Pitch) for a brief retrospective (this can be done during the monthly meeting once the initiative has momentum).

7. Allow some additional time during initial Pitch and 3P ceremonies, as the team acclimatizes and develops a rhythm, establishes their individual roles, and norms (e.g., add 30 minutes for early Pitch or 3P ceremonies, which may contain one-to-five pitches or team presentations).

8. Add an hour or two to the total early on, until you have a better idea of what your actual time requirements will be.

It looks like a lot, but it can be as little as one day per month for a team that has developed a rhythm and is overseeing five incubating teams. Table 10-1 shows a simple sample calculation.

340

Table 10-1. Illustrative Governance Team time requirement calculation

Task	Hours required
One Pitch Ceremony per month, up to four pitches + slack time (2–2.5 hours)	2.5
Five 3P reviews + slack time (2.5–3.5 hours)	3.5
Monthly meeting (1 hour)	1
Total time requirement per month (hours)	**7**

To be clear, **this one day estimate is for a five-team initiative that is performing well. Early on the requirement will likely be at least two days per month** as the team norms, works through issues, and perhaps drains a backlog of pitch demand by hosting multiple pitch events per month or extending scheduled events. **If we expand the model to ten incubating teams, an additional half day would be required at a minimum.**

There *are* ways to address the additional time requirements which will occur early in the initiative's life. For example, you may not need every Governance Team member at *every* meeting or ceremony. Stacking events can also help, as it eliminates redundant gathering time and can result in better focus (e.g., host eight pitches on the same half day). But be careful not to burn people out.

You might also want to allocate time for Governance Team summits throughout the year. I find a cadence of three per year to be ideal. Your ideal cadence may vary, and you may find your need for continuous learning and improvement to be less frequent as the initiative evolves.

CHAPTER 10   LAYING THE FOUNDATION

Governance Team: The Bottom Line

Start small and scale up:

- Start with a smaller Governance Team (e.g., 5–7 people).
- Select the founding Governance Team carefully:
    - People who are comfortable with ambiguity
    - People who will have patience for early issues, setbacks, and learning
    - People who can contribute to the direction of the Governance Team, and the initiative
    - People who can guide and evaluate early artifacts and approaches
    - People who will be passionate champions
- Add to the team as you discover gaps and opportunities.
- Be proactive and forthcoming about the commitment required.
- Schedule ceremonies up to a year in advance to develop a cadence (or at least for each fiscal year), and be mindful of holidays and organizational commitments.
- Be deliberate about diversity.
- If you plan to bring high-potential people into the team as mentees, wait until the team is performing well before doing so.

Extended Governance Teams (a.k.a. Investment Teams)

There are cases where your initiative might benefit from, or require, additional governance as an incubating team's exit approaches. For example, in the public sector, your initial Governance Team might include people at a Director Level. But to exit (launch in production, move to a receiving project…), you may need to involve more senior executives to assist with preparations, make necessary cross-organizational contact, or provide required approvals or budget authorization. This might necessitate engaging one or more Directors General (DG), or even someone higher in the organization.

Even when someone at a higher level has an interest in a specific incubating idea from its inception, their active participation will not likely be required until the idea had received sufficient traction and is highly likely to exit. This is likely to occur roughly at the time the idea is ready to move from the Experiment 2 stage to the Transition 1 stage. Rather than require the DGs to participate actively in the entire incubation, the Governance Team might be extended to add them during those crucial phases. Alternatively, they might be briefed as a separate Extended Governance Team.

The equivalent in the private sector occurs when an incubating solution is in the Series B or Startup 2 stage. At that point, senior executives (e.g., CEO, CMO) are more likely to want to understand where the solution is headed, how it is performing, and the impact it may have on current or future business. In addition, the incubating team will require assistance from these senior executives. For example, they will need the Chief Marketing Officer to engage their team to prepare to market the solution, and the Chief Revenue Officer will need to prepare the Sales Team to sell it.

The time requirement of these teams should be minimal, and will likely consist of a straightforward review of the status of the incubating solution and a few updates. It will essentially be a lightweight 3P review.

Minimal, Ad Hoc Time Requirement

Engagement of the Extended Governance Team will not occur frequently, since it only happens around the Transition 1, Accelerate 1, or Series B stages. Most of the time, no incubating teams will be at that stage. Unless you have a very large number of concurrently incubating teams, when an incubating team reaches that stage, it will likely be the only incubating team at that stage. Thus, the time requirement of this Extended Team will consist only of periodic reviews of successful incubations.

The Extended Team's time can be economized by aligning their reviews with other events. For example, the Extended Team for one private sector organization comprised C-level executives. Their reviews were scheduled by adding a brief agenda item to their regularly scheduled leadership team meetings.

It is important to emphasize that higher level executives *may* be interested in the more nascent ideas. This was the case with the team I referred to in the previous paragraph. To address this, we periodically scheduled a brief update to share information about the initiative, provide an update on what the initiative was incubating, showcase specific incubating solutions, and build and maintain interest and momentum.

By now you should have a good understanding of the team and governance structure. Let's look at what can be an initiative's force multiplier. It's unfair advantage. The Advisory Team.

3. Engage Advisors and Allies

When we set out to build the first lean entrepreneurship style incubator-accelerator, one of our primary objectives was to create an initiative that leveraged the benefits of both an independent startup (e.g., speed and agility) and a mature business (e.g., experience and resources). We hoped that we could deliver the benefits of both while minimizing – hopefully eliminating – the drawbacks of both. We believed that would deliver an unfair advantage to our startups (incubating teams) over those working independently. One of the first ways that paid off was our ability to make matrixed advisors available to our incubating businesses.

Early in the life of an idea, incubating teams encounter situations where they require, or would benefit greatly from, advice or assistance from people experienced in specific domains in which their team has little or no experience. For example, they may need legal advice regarding a contract a supplier has asked them to sign, or help structuring a contract or agreement. An independent startup would have to find and hire a lawyer. This would take time, funding, and resources away from bringing their idea to life. Some startups might not be able to afford the legal fees and may have to do things on their own or copy-and-paste agreements and licenses.

The incubating teams' needs were nowhere frequent enough to justify hiring their own lawyer. But when they needed assistance, it was important.

The infrequent nature of their needs presented an opportunity. As a large organization, we had an entire team of lawyers who specialized in the type of advice our incubating teams required. Our organization's Legal Team was happy to offer advice when needed. It did not take a lot of their time, it was in their area of specialty, and it did not require a lot of preparation or education; and they liked working on the new ideas.

The Advisory Team

This scenario played out in several other domains such as Marketing, Procurement, Accounting, Talent Management, Recruiting, and the People Team (HR). These advisors were a force multiplier for the incubating teams, and gave them a huge advantage over independent startups.

Once we had successfully developed those initial relationships, we set out to deliberately create a group of advisors that all teams could engage. We established a single point of contact in each domain (e.g., procurement, legal…). The volume and nature of requests for assistance was low enough that our primary contact often responded to most, or all, requests. When they could not, or chose not to, they served as a single conduit to their broader team.

Advisors Become Allies

We developed momentum. Advisors from one domain would mention what we were doing when they spoke with people working in other domains. When we approached new candidates they were often already aware of what we were trying to achieve, and what their time commitment would be. That made recruiting advisors in new domains easier. Some proactively found us on their own.

Our advisors became allies in more than one sense. Even though the Advisory Team was small, it covered a broad range of domains. This meant that the initiative had a champion in every one of the organization's leadership teams. They helped spread awareness of our initiative, explained it – and their role – to their team, addressed misconceptions, and made us aware of developments in their own team or domain (when appropriate). They also kept their most senior executives (e.g., Chief Legal Officer, Chief Marketing Officer) aware of the initiative's progress and value, and provided another channel of communication to them.

Caveat: Adding Bench Expertise

As we scaled the initiative up and added more incubating teams, we discovered that there were certain domains where we could keep advisors busy full-time. For example, none of the teams needed a full-time designer, but they all needed a heavily engaged designer periodically. All told, we could keep a designer busy full time.

We felt using a matrixed advisor full-time would be abusing our partnerships. It might even result in our matrixed partner working an inordinate number of hours per week just to keep up with their "day job."

It would be an abuse of our relationship, and likely would have ended some of them. When we recognized an advisor's workload was increasing, we discussed it openly with them and looked for the best way to address it, which was sometimes adding a full-time bench expert.

In some cases, the leaders of the matrixed advisor's team decided it best to assign someone to the initiative full-time, but leave that person in their group of origin. This had the added advantage of maintaining the two-way communication channel, and letting the advisor continue to grow with peers in their domain.

Be deliberate about managing the advisors and bench expertise. **Stay aware of the amount of time matrixed advisors are giving to the initiative. Check in periodically to ensure they are not overloaded or feeling abused. Have open discussions when those things happen.**

Advisors Can Prevent Consequential Errors

The benefits of a team like this may be far broader than is obvious. Domain experts will instinctively catch important nuances in operation or execution that an incubating team might miss.

One team I worked with wanted customers to acquire their solution via an online credit card transaction. At the time their broader organization did not accept business via online credit card transactions, so the team had to build the capability themselves. They built it successfully, but then almost fell through a potentially serious trapdoor.

They had built and tested their solution in a test environment and needed to test it in production, with a real transaction from a real credit card. They set out to use one of their own credit cards to test it. No issue, right. The money just went from the business back to the business. Wrong!

Had they put that revenue on their books they may have been committing fraud by booking revenue that did not exist. Fortunately, due to the presence of domain experts they did not have to find out how serious the consequences may have been.

Characteristics of Good Advisory Team Candidates

Ideally, Advisory Team candidates will possess many of the following characteristics:

- Expertise in a required domain
- Ability to make time to assist incubating teams or to engage their peers to do so
- Knowledge of how and where to get things done, and how to navigate the organization
- Respected in their domain
- Project positive energy
- Comfortable working with uncertainty or new teams
- Passion for the initiative, and for what they do
- An interest in bringing new things to life
- A team player
- Can become a willing champion for the initiative

The first two characteristics are the most important, and are mandatory.

Advisory Team Time Requirements

The time requirement for an advisor can vary broadly, depending on their area of expertise, the initiative's stage of development, the number of incubating teams, and the maturity of each incubating team. For many, it will consist of one to two 30- or 60-minute sessions per month, or addressing ad hoc issues or questions. I also like to invite the matrixed advisors to attend Pitch or 3P ceremonies (as observers). In some cases they might be invited to actively participate in a 3P review, either to assist an incubating team or to add context in their area of expertise.

An estimate of a half day per month would be a reasonable starting point. You will be better able to estimate these time requirements as you design your initiative, set objectives, identify gaps, and assess incubating team capabilities. There are also ways to minimize an advisor's time. For example, one of our advisors realized that running brief training sessions enabled them to reduce their total time requirement by coaching multiple teams simultaneously.

Advisory Team: The Bottom Line

When building the Advisory Team:

- Start small and bring advisors on as needed.
- Identify areas of obvious need (e.g., procurement, legal, people [HR]...).
- Identify domains where you might have to address challenges such as those discussed in Chapters 2 and 3 (e.g., find an alternative to a heavy or constraining process).
- Be easy to engage by advisors wishing to volunteer.

- Have only one primary advisor in each domain, even if multiple people are engaged.

- Engage with "The Phrase that Pays,"[2] "I need your help."

- Be careful not to overload advisors or abuse their kindness.

- Leverage advisors' network and communication channels as well as their domain expertise.

- Look for synergies and opportunities to economize advisors' time.

- Look for opportunities to broaden the impact of the initiative's new or modified processes by offering them to the broader organization whenever possible.

Incubation Team Advisors

Depending upon the types of problems your initiative targets, and the nature of your organization, your initiative might include another class of advisors. Like the advisors of an independent startup, their role will be to provide members of an incubating team with advice regarding their specific incubating idea. They may, for example, possess expertise in the domain being addressed by the incubating team, skill in the art of building solutions the way in which the team intends to build them (e.g., have built global SaaS solutions, have expertise in the application of biometric devices), have bureaucratic or business expertise, or some combination thereof. These advisory teams should be built by the leaders of each incubation, potentially with assistance from the Initiative Team and/or Governance Team.

---

[2] George Watt, and Howard Abrams. 2019. Lean Entrepreneurship: Innovation in the Modern Enterprise, New York, NY, Apress Media, Chapter 3: Lean Acceleration

Sometimes Initiative Team and/or Governance Team members become members of an incubating team's advisory group. When that happens be careful to ensure that their engagement with one team does not introduce bias into their Governance Team activities (e.g., 3P reviews). Initiative Team or Governance Team members should openly declare their potential bias when advocating on behalf of the teams they advise during initiative activities or ceremonies. In addition, Initiative Team and Governance Team members who join incubating teams as advisors should be careful not to favor that team over other incubating teams, and not to create a perception of favoritism.

Incubation Team Advisors' Time Requirements

The time commitment for each incubation team advisor is typically small. It is essentially a mentoring role, and can require as little as one or two 30-minute calls per month. Incubating teams should be up-front with advisors regarding how much time they believe they will need. They should be proactive about having conversations with their advisors if they believe they will require more time, and explain whether they will require the additional time once, periodically, or on an ongoing basis.

External Incubation Team Advisors

In cases where an incubating team is unable to find all the advisors they need within their organization's boundaries, you might consider allowing them to engage advisors who are not members of the organization. One incubating team I worked with engaged their legal team advisor to create an advisory agreement similar to those used by public accelerators that enabled them to engage external advisors. This protected the team, their idea, and the advisors.

Be deliberate. Check with your legal team if you are thinking of adding external advisors, and obtain any necessary approvals. The Governance Team should also discuss whether and when external advisors might be engaged before the need for them arises.

4. Consider a Maker Team

Early in an incubating team's life they might require specialized skills they do not possess. I am not referring to domain skills such as were described in the Advisory Team section. Rather, they might require what might be colloquially classified as "maker skills." For example, a team building a rough authentication kiosk prototype may lack the skills required to build a hardware mockup (e.g., soldering, fabricating).

If a skillset will be repeatedly required by a team it might make sense for them to hire someone to join their team full-time. For one-time requirements it might make sense to obtain outside help or bring in a contractor. However, if several teams will require those specialized skills or services periodically, it may make sense to create a Maker Team.

The potential range of maker skills is limitless, and might include some skills you may not have considered such as carpentry, electronics, chemistry, manufacturing process design, or scientific research.

Shared Maker Team

The Maker Team does not have to be part of the initiative. I once worked with an applied research group that had specialized skills which enabled them to create deployable components based on pure scientific research. This group was not part of the initiative, and performed work for any of the organization's teams.

Characteristics of Good Maker Team Candidates

Though their skills and experience will vary, look for the following characteristics in Maker Team candidates:

- Skilled in their domain, with at least a medium level of experience
- Good communicators
- A quick learner, able to understand the requirements of incubating teams
- Able to translate what people unfamiliar with the maker's domain state they need into requirements, and deliver based upon those requirements
- Optimistic and positive, and asks "how can we make it work" versus finding reasons something will not work
- Comfortable with the imperfection that may be required for a rapid prototype
- Safety conscious (when applicable)
- Capable of understanding how their prototype work or experimentation will be able to evolve into a deployable solution
- Able to help set the incubating team up for scale and success in a production context

Team Relationships

Figure 10-3 shows the major relationships that will exist between the initiative's teams once each has been established.

CHAPTER 10   LAYING THE FOUNDATION

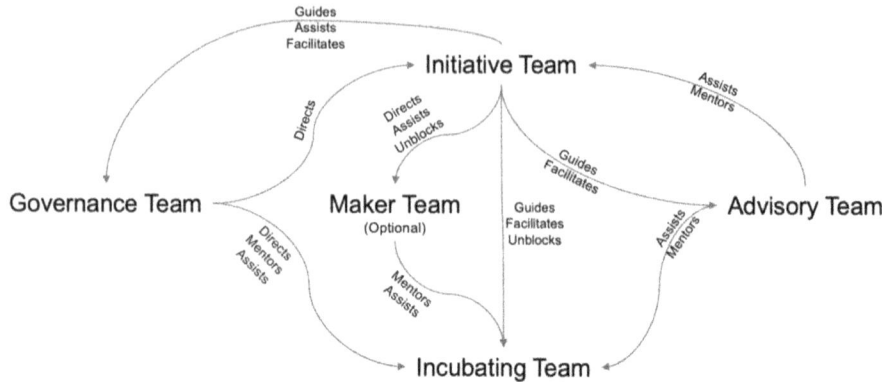

Figure 10-3. *Incubation team relationships (illustrative)*

You can see the teams interact in many interesting ways, with roles often changing situationally. It should also be noted that these teams are often logical constructs, with part-time or seconded members.

5. Prepare a Budget

Laying the foundation for an initiative usually involves preparation of a budget, though there can be exceptions. For example, teams creating a Toolkit or a Framework – where expenses are minimal – may not have sufficient direct expenses to warrant a separate budget.

Consider Expenses Across Major Categories, Groups, and Functions

There are many ways you can think through your budget requirements. One simple and intuitive approach is to begin by thinking about the major groups or functions that require funding, and then dive into each and

CHAPTER 10   LAYING THE FOUNDATION

ask what they will be doing, and what they will need in order to do it. For example, we can begin by considering the needs of the teams discussed in this chapter:

1. Initiative Team
2. Governance Team(s)
3. Advisory Team (matrixed)
4. Maker Team
5. Incubating Team(s)

Budgeting for these groups may not be as complex as you might anticipate. Though each team will have its own unique requirements, there will be many commonalities. You can begin by considering the following criteria for each, asking whether they apply, then asking whether the group has any additional needs not listed here:

- **Personnel**
    - How many people will be required?
    - Which job functions will they have, and at which level?
    - What is the average fully loaded cost of people in those positions?
        - Your People (HR) or Talent Acquisition team likely has estimates for the average cost of fully loaded employee for each position (e.g., Engineer, Senior Engineer…).
            - If they do not, it can be obtained from a variety of sources online.

355

- Will there be promotions?
  - Will those involve pay increases?
  - When in the year will they likely take place?
- What month will people join the team (onboarding ramp)?
- Are there any onboarding costs or allocations?

- **Overhead allocation**
  - Does the organization charge a fixed or variable amount for each employee?
    - There are often charges for office space, other physical space (e.g., labs, team rooms), stationery, IT support, subscriptions (e.g., Office 365, Slack).

- **Home office allowances**
  - Monthly or quarterly allowances for people who work from home
  - Office set-up funding for people beginning to work from home

- **Equipment**
  - Individual
    - Desktop and/or laptop computers, peripherals, whiteboards, safety equipment…
  - Team
    - Servers, team room equipment (whiteboards, furniture…), online subscriptions…

- Shared across the initiative
    - Hardware, software, collaboration tools, whiteboards, lab space, chemicals, supplies…
- **Training**
    - Open to all teams in the initiative
        - For example, in-house training sessions, exclusive online sessions
        - Usually budgeted by the Initiative Team
    - For each individual
        - For example, US$2500 allocation for one course per year, per quarter…
    - Don't forget to include travel expenses when required for training.
- **Travel**
    - What travel is anticipated for each individual?
        - Sometimes this can be estimated by role.
            - For example, every Engineer gets $2500 for training travel.
        - Often this must be considered on an individual basis.
            - For example, founders or team leaders will travel to Board Demo Days, summits, specific conferences.

- **Benefits**
  - Are there employee benefit allocations or costs?
    - For example, tuition reimbursement, bonus for patent submission, healthcare…
    - Are these allocated centrally or charged back to the budget to which each person is assigned?
- **Allowances**
  - Are there additional allowances that may require budgeting?
    - For example, car, lodging, relocation expenses
- **Recruiting**
  - Is there a charge to the budget for recruiting expenses?
  - Are recruiting expenses covered by another group?
    - Do they require advance notification of your potential needs for their budget?
- **Subscriptions**
  - Will regular payments be required for subscriptions?
    - Online subscriptions such as video conference software, office management software, or team communication software
      - These licenses are sometimes paid at an organization level and are sometimes charged back as overhead.
    - Incubating teams may have unique requirements.

- **Conferences**
  - As an attendee
  - As a presenter, panelist, or booth staff
- **Initiative-specific summits**
  - Gatherings of incubating team leaders and others to learn from experts and one-another, collaborate, and share tools, tips, and challenges
  - Which group will pay which expenses?
  - Where will overhead costs be budgeted?
    - Typically the Initiative Team would arrange and fund overhead items such as guest speakers or trainers, events and meals, or venue.
  - Where will individual travel costs be budgeted?
- **Demo days**
  - Travel and expenses related to presentations and updates to the Board of Directors, C-level Team, senior public servants (e.g., Directors General or ADMs), political leaders (e.g., Ministers, Committee Chairs, Secretaries), or other senior leaders
- **Bonuses**
  - Will there be discretionary or performance-based bonuses?
  - Will they require funding within the group for whom the budget is being created?
    - For example, some organizations fund bonuses centrally, some require allocations, some have headcount-based allocations.

- **Exit payouts or bonuses**
    - Will teams whose ideas exit successfully receive a payout or bonus plan?
        - How will it be structured?
        - Will it be paid in one payment, or over time?
        - When do you anticipate the first payout will be made?
- **Contracting**
    - Will incubating teams (or others) require specialist, or other, assistance or training?
- **Internally charged-back or cross-department charge-back services**
    - For example, privacy assessments, security assessments, penetration testing, architecture design or review…
- **Regulatory charges**
    - For example, license or certification fees, filing fees
- **Marketing and communication**
    - Will incubating teams have marketing or communications expenses?
    - Will the Initiative Team have communication expenses?
    - Will there be charge-backs from other groups?
- **Commissions**
    - Will commissions or payouts be made to internal or external sales personnel?

- **Royalties**
  - Will incubating teams be embedding technology that requires royalty payments?
  - Will incubating teams receive royalties? How will they be treated?
- **Taxes**
  - Will incubating teams have to collect and/or pay taxes? (e.g., sales taxes, VAT, HST, eco-fees)
- **Membership fees**
  - Are fees required for access to online resources, participation in conferences…?
  - Mandatory or optional professional association memberships

Team-Level Budget Considerations

The Initiative Team and incubating teams actively execute within the initiative's scope every day and will require the most investment. Depending upon their nature, Maker Teams might also require funding. Maker Teams are typically very small, but some may require very expensive equipment or supplies. The Governance and Advisory teams typically require no bespoke funding unrelated to their participation in initiative-sponsored events.

Using the basic expense considerations above as a guideline, we can consider each team's unique requirements:

- **The Initiative Team:** Carries all common expenses; may include budget for *all* the initiative's bonuses and payouts; may not need to budget for part-time or split-responsibility team members, but may be charged back (requires explicit confirmation); will likely have expenses in all categories except contracting, marketing, royalties, commissions, and taxes, but do not rule those out

- **The Incubating Teams:** Largest expenses will likely be personnel-related; may have unique equipment, training, contracting, and travel needs; will likely have expenses in all categories except use of common services or resources funded by the Initiative Team; funding requirements will increase as their idea matures and they advance to each new stage of incubation; each incubating team will require its own budget, and each will be unique

- **The Governance Team:** May not have any expenses to include in the budget; may require license seats or software, which would usually be included in the Initiative Team's budget; normally pay for travel from their own budgets (but not always); summits and events are normally budgeted by the Initiative Team; a budget for this team of volunteers is typically not required

- **The Advisory Team:** Normally matrixed from other organizations as part-time volunteers; a budget for this team is not usually necessary; any requirements are usually budgeted by the Initiative Team

- **Maker Team:** Will usually not include expenses in the demo days, marketing, commissions, royalties, and taxes categories; may require specialized equipment or physical lab space or maker facilities; budget items for maker teams are often included in the Initiative Team's budget, especially when the maker team is small; items required for bespoke work for specific incubating teams are normally included in the incubating team's budget (e.g., materials for a specific mockup or prototype)

Second Order Thinking

The information presented thus far should set you off to a solid start. But don't forget to perform some second order thinking regarding how the initiative will evolve. Think through what will happen in the next 12 to 18 months. Think through scenarios for each group and event. For example, ask yourself and your team questions like:

- **When will we launch the initiative?**
  - What will need to make ready prior to the launch?
  - What will need to be ready following the launch?
  - What equipment, space, resources be required? When?
- **How many people will we need on the Initiative Team at the outset?**
  - What skills are required?
  - Will we need to add people throughout the year?
  - When will we need them?
  - What kind of people?
  - Have they been identified?
  - Will we need to recruit them?
  - Will they be funded by existing teams (e.g., secondments, part-time allocation)?

- Will there be charge-back to our budget?
- Will they need training? Will they need to travel for it?

- **What actions will the Initiative Team take this fiscal year?**
    - For example, promotional "road show," pitch events, 3P reviews, summits...
    - What expenses might those actions entail?

- **When will we start looking for ideas?**
    - Who will be involved?
    - What are the associated costs?
    - Do we have all the equipment and facilities we require?

- **How many ideas might start incubating within the target fiscal year?**
    - When will each start incubating?
    - How large will each be?
    - How likely is it they will evolve?
    - How far will they be permitted to advance?
        - For example: Will we run a Skunkworks-style initiative, incubate only to Explore 2 or Seed 2, and exit the ideas to other teams?
    - What is the personnel onramp of each incubating team?
    - What kind of people will join the team? What does each cost?

- Will teams need specialized equipment?
- Will teams need training?
- Will the manager overseeing the entire initiative (e.g., SVP, Innovation) require specialized skills?
  - Can the person managing the initiative's design, deployment, and operation also manage and coach incubating teams?
- Which level and styles of coaching, training, or mentoring will teams require?
- **Will any teams advance far enough to qualify for bonuses or payouts?**
  - Which ones? When?
  - What are the likely payouts?
- **Will there be individual rewards?**
  - Always answer "yes" to this question.
  - What kind? (plaques, trips, cash, recognition...)
- **Are any necessary resources, teams, or individuals available at an organizational level or from a common services team?**
  - Is there a cost?
- **Will any teams or individuals need to attend conferences?**
  - Is there a cost?
  - Is there an organization-funded pass that can be used?

- Do other teams have booths?
  - Would they let incubating teams use them?
  - Would they expect the initiative to contribute funding?

Understand When Expenses Occur, and Forecast Monthly or Quarterly

As you budget, do your best to identify the month in which expenses are likely to occur. Understanding your initiative's financial ebbs and flows will help the organization's finance team prepare their top-level forecasts, and they may require visibility at a monthly or quarterly level. This can be critically important in some cases. For example, publicly owned companies can suffer severe negative consequences or embarrassment when unexpected expenses occur in a quarter and negatively impact forecasted performance. This may not be as critical when your initiative is small, but can be very important for larger initiatives with larger total expenses.

Unfair Advantage: Organizational Programs

The ability to leverage existing organizational programs and benefits is one of the greatest advantages initiative-led startups have over their "garage-based" counterparts. Initiative-led startups may have access to benefits such as:

- Discretionary bonus programs
- Funded cash, and other, awards
- Paid vacations

- (Parent organization) Stock options or restricted stock unit awards (with immediate value)
- Healthcare benefits
- Patent bonus awards
- Short-term and mid-term performance bonuses
- Tuition reimbursement
- Training allowances
- Parental leave
- Compassionate leave
- Vehicle allowances

Such benefits are often unavailable to independent startups or are cost-prohibitive. In mid-to-large-sized organizations they are typically available to all employees, including participants in initiatives like these, and often at no additional cost to the initiative (e.g., they are provided from a headquarters function or included in overhead charges). Even if there is an overhead charge, it is often substantially lower than would be available to a small startup. Leverage these, and other programs whenever possible.

Modeling Your Initiative

Once you begin bringing ideas into your initiative, there will be a lot of variables to consider when building your financial forecasts. These will be largely, if not entirely, related to:

- The number of incubating teams
- The progress and current state of each incubating team
- The expenses incurred by each team at their current stage

- Each incubating team's state at the beginning of the fiscal year
- Each incubating team's speed of advancement though the incubation stages
- The forecasted speed of incubating team advancement at each stage
- Forecasted expense increases or decreases upon transition to a new stage
- How quickly new ideas enter the initiative
- How new entries are sequenced and staggered

Modeling to this level of detail is not as onerous as it may appear. We provided a simple step-by-step approach in Chapter 7 of *Lean Entrepreneurship*.

Priming the Initiative

"Do we really want the first thing we do (in this initiative) to be asking for more money?"

That question was asked during the September 2015 workshop in Boulder, Colorado, where we defined what would become the first lean entrepreneurship accelerator. We had asked our C-level team and Board for, and received, a mandate to build an engine for organic innovation. It was the middle of a fiscal year, with approximately six months left under our active budget. That budget was created before we asked for, or were tasked with, creating what would become the accelerator; so no funding had been allocated for it.

The inaugural Initiative Team was already funded in the CTO's budget. We would just modify their objectives to designing, deploying, and operating the initiative. But what about the incubating teams? How could we fund those?

Fortunately, the answer was right in front of us. We had brought four teams which were already incubating their ideas under different schemes into the initiative, and the leaders of those teams were present at the workshop. Literally, sitting right in front of me.

We realized each team had been transferred to our organization along with their fiscal year's budget. After some deliberation, we discovered that once the teams began operating using a lean entrepreneurship approach, there would be substantial savings which could be redeployed to new ideas. This gave us all the funding we needed. In fact, we were able to allocate some surplus funding to endeavors outside the accelerator and still came in under budget that year.

Look for funded, currently incubating ideas to prime your initiative, especially if they have stalled, are taking longer than anticipated, or are heavily staffed. Doing this solved our budget puzzle, jumpstarted our initiative with four active incubating teams, and gave the incubating ideas a better chance to succeed.

Additional Considerations

Here are some additional things to consider as you lay your initiative's foundation:

- As a rule, start as small as is practical and grow only when you need to, but watch for overloaded people and burn-out.
- Be transparent, bias to transparency.
- Leverage benefits and programs from the broader organization whenever possible.
- Be forthcoming to volunteer teams and allies about anticipated time requirements and the contributions you expect them to make.

- A regular cadence is key to the success of every team.
- Leverage your Governance and Advisory teams for input and guidance while building and operating the initiative.
- Check-in regularly with volunteer teams and their members, make sure they are happy and energized, and ensure they do not feel they are being taken advantage of or are being abused.
- Be organized and professional, schedule events and ceremonies well in advance, give as much notice as is possible, always have an agenda, and if you get through the agenda before the allotted time has passed, end early.
- Be cognizant of the amount of time Advisory Team members are allocating to the initiative, and find additional volunteers to assist or hire bench expertise if they are being overtasked.
- Visit and update your Stakeholder Analysis regularly if you have one, especially early in the initiative's life.
- Apply good budget discipline at all levels, track and manage budgets regularly (at least every 2–4 weeks), and try to anticipate potential budget challenges.
- Have leaders of incubating teams manage their own budgets and include them in their 3P pre-ceremony reading package.
- Make budget management guidance and coaching available to incubating team leaders when necessary.

- Get help preparing and managing budgets from experts such as Finance Team members or department or business unit controllers; they know all of the most useful techniques, and will make sure you stay within accepted management practices.

- The more successful an incubating team is, the higher their costs will usually be; plan for each stage of incubation (e.g., Seed 1, Experiment 2) to cost more per month than previous stages.

- If you are not starting your initiative on day 1 of a fiscal year, be sure to account for that when planning for the next fiscal year (e.g., if you start your initiative in month seven of a fiscal year, your first fiscal year's budget will likely be less than half what you will need in the following fiscal year).

- Track the performance of each incubating team, their size and expenses at each stage of incubation, how long they spent in each stage, and the stage at which each exited the initiative; this will be extremely useful in the creation of cost and success models for future years.

Group Development

Each of your initiative's teams will be different. They will be composed of different types of people, formed for different purposes, and focused on different aspects of the initiative. Some will be full-time participants, some will be part-time team members, and some will be matrixed from other parts of the organization. Some may engage infrequently or on request, while others will engage on a regular cadence (e.g., a half day per month).

CHAPTER 10   LAYING THE FOUNDATION

Whatever their composition, a broad spectrum of fascinating things happen as a team begins to form. Sometimes teams form naturally, and quickly begin to perform at a high level. Sometimes things go off the rails rapidly and spectacularly. Other teams experience a combination of wins, false starts, and resets.

If you have spent any time on teams, I am sure none of this is surprising. But a little understanding of what is happening, and its potential root causes, can increase your odds of getting those teams to the required level of performance more quickly while avoiding much, or all, of the conflict and drama.

Tuckman's Stages of Group Development

As the person leading the initiative, the important task of managing the group dynamic and team formation will almost certainly be yours. I find the model created by former Ohio State University professor and Dennis Learning Center Founder, Dr. Bruce Tuckman to be an extremely valuable framework for assessing and mitigating team development risks. This, simple model identifies four stages of group development:[3]

1. **Forming:** The early stage of team development when the structure of the team is created; characterized by team members' uncertainty, discomfort, search for acceptance, and conflict avoidance

2. **Storming:** The stage at which the team begins to attempt to organize and develop processes and tasks; characterized by presentation of competing ideas and interests, interpersonal conflicts between team members, competition for leadership roles, and false starts and resets

---

[3] Dr. Tuckman later added a fifth stage, "Adjourning."

3. **Norming:** The stage at which the team begins to work together and develops new ways of working and interacting with one-another; characterized by agreement on how things are done, comfortable working and interpersonal relationships between team members, mutual respect, shared problem-solving and decision making, improved performance, and achievement of objectives

4. **Performing:** The stage at which the group has truly become a functioning (and not dysfunctional), highly productive team; characterized by well-understood member roles, the ability to organize itself as a whole or in smaller groups when needed, team members' understanding of one-another and what each member brings to the team, and good, or outstanding, interpersonal relationships

Different Stages Require Different Leadership

Each development stage requires different types and styles of leadership. For example, during forming you might need to add more structure and direction and provide time and opportunity for team members to get to know one-another. During storming, when team members are throwing ideas at one-another in a metaphorical snowball fight, you might need to focus on things like conflict avoidance and management, and consensus building. At the norming stage you might want to focus on solidifying and strengthening relationships, removing some of the structure, ensuring that team members all contribute, and making sure everyone is given an opportunity to provide input. Performing is the magical stage where your role might be more facilitative, as the team's engine begins to run on high-trust fuel.

It would be impossible to do Dr. Tuckman's model justice here. If you are interested in group dynamics there is a wealth of information regarding this model freely available on the Internet.

Different Teams Evolve Differently

It is important to understand that each team will evolve through different states such as those defined in Tuckman's Stages, and that your leadership style will need to evolve along with them. What's more, **each of the teams will go through all of these stages, and they will likely evolve at different times and at different speeds**. As a result, you may have teams in all of these stages at one time. Furthermore, each time you bring in a new Incubating Team, *they* will be starting from the beginning.

There will likely always be some disparity between the development stages of teams you are working with. It is important to recognize that each team is different, will have a different personality, and will evolve differently. You will need to shepherd every team through the early stages of development as quickly as possible, so be mindful not to assume they are all at the same stage and manage them the same way.

Though you may not be required to manage incubating teams directly, you will potentially be interacting with them in a formal or informal leadership role (e.g., as you lead a 3P review or serve as an advisor).

You Are Not Alone

You may not have to help teams evolve on your own. Once some teams are "performing" they may be able to help other teams evolve. For example, in one accelerator, once the Governance Team achieved a performing state they organically and instinctively began helping incubating teams (and others) to mature.

Summary

A deliberate approach to laying the foundation for your initiative is crucial, and details matter. Start small when building the Initiative, Governance, and Advisory teams. Begin by bringing in only the people you need. Build your initial teams with people who are patient, comfortable with ambiguity and the messy nature of initiatives like this, and who understand the potentially chaotic nature of the work required to deliver new, innovative ideas. Fill inaugural teams with people with positive energy who will find solutions when obstacles are encountered, as opposed to people who will simply complain about or malign things.

Remember that designing, deploying, and operating these initiatives is real work, and should be the highest priority assignment for the people in the Initiative Team. They will make or break the initiative.

Now that we have laid a solid foundation, we are ready to launch our initiative and find and nurture ideas. That means we will need to get outside our own office (physically or virtually) and engage people outside the initiative's teams. Chapter 11 discusses how.

CHAPTER 11

Launching the Initiative

Congratulations! You're here. You're ready. You have designed your initiative and set a long-term vision. You have assembled your *minimum viable* Initiative Team and Governance Team. You have begun spreading the word about your initiative and ramping up interest. Teams, observers, and champions are curious, excited, and perhaps even anxious. Potential participants want to pitch and start incubating, the Governance Team wants to select ideas, and people are beginning to expect progress and results.

It's time to get out of the office (physically or virtually), bring in some ideas, and prime your initiative's engine (Figure 11-1).

CHAPTER 11 LAUNCHING THE INITIATIVE

> **In this Chapter**
>
> Launching the Initiative:
>
> 1. Capture and select ideas
> 2. Onboard incubating teams (Entry)
> 3. Allocate Initiative Team time for removing obstacles (unblocking)
> 4. Use 3P reviews to assess and facilitate progress
> 5. Reward participants

Figure 11-1. *What's in this chapter*

As you build, remember that you do not have to do everything at once. Think about the activities that are approaching this month, quarter, and year; and those that are not. **Build what you need a little ahead of when you will need it.** For example, you will need a Pitch Ceremony right away but, unless you primed your initiative with a very mature solution, you most likely will not need your Transition 2 or Series C resources in the first year. Maybe not even in the second year.

Focus on the stages you need now, or will need soonest, build an MVP for each, experiment, inspect, and adapt. Just like you will be guiding the incubating teams in your initiative to do. Then focus on what your initiative's next set of near-term needs will be.

If all that sounds obvious, great! You are in the right mindset, and ready to act. **At this stage it is *all* about execution, communication, listening, inspecting, and adapting.**

Unless you plan to prime the initiative exclusively with actively incubating ideas, you will need a way to find and select new ideas early on. So, let's start there.

1. Capture and Select Ideas

Now it's time to have some fun. Capturing and selecting ideas can involve a lot of groundwork, but I find it to be one of the most enjoyable aspects of initiatives like this. I get to meet a lot of interesting people who have interesting and innovative ideas and watch them share their passion and intelligence. The Governance Team – I cannot help but think of it as an "Angel Team" at this point – engages pitch teams in thoughtful inquiry, and a number of candidates receive the opportunity to pursue their passion.

If you're lucky, you'll be amongst those who get to inform successful teams they, and their ideas, have been selected. You may also have to inform some teams they have not been selected, but I have found those conversations to be very pleasant, positive, and enjoyable opportunities to thank the teams and encourage their passion for innovation. It's all upside.

Ten Steps for Capturing Ideas

This stage's activities might be a bit time-consuming at the outset as you create the material you require, train your Governance Team, prepare the logistics, promote the initiative, and recruit ideas. But there is very little new material required, and the preparation work involved is largely logistical and social in nature.

To capture and select events, you will need to:

1. Design a Pitch Ceremony
2. Create the information and material candidates need to prepare for a pitch
3. Provide a mechanism for candidates to submit pitch requests
4. Promote the initiative and recruit participants
5. Accept and triage pitch candidates

6. Select and sequence candidates for pitches
7. Schedule pitch events
8. Direct and guide the Governance Team
9. Adjudicate the ideas via a Pitch Ceremony
10. Inform pitch teams whether or not their ideas were selected

There is some flexibility in the sequence in which you can execute these tasks, but there are some obvious dependencies. You cannot accept ideas until you produce the material pitch candidates require and provide a way for them to apply to pitch their idea. It would be best if you have that ready before you begin promoting and recruiting, so candidates can apply immediately, but you could also promote the initiative before those resources are ready and let candidates know when it will be available. You must design the Pitch ceremony before you train the Governance Team or host the Pitch ceremony. You must hold a Pitch ceremony before selecting ideas, and do both before informing teams of the outcome.

Several of these tasks are well-suited to be performed in parallel, or concurrently, by different people. Apart from respecting the obvious dependencies you can change the order in which you execute these steps to best suit your needs and resource availability. If you have no preference or constraints, executing the tasks in the order above should provide a path to a successful launch.

I will expand on each item in the order listed above.

Designing a Pitch Ceremony

The Pitch ceremony is one of two anchor ceremonies for initiatives of this nature. The primary purpose of the Pitch ceremony is to provide an efficient and consistent way for the Governance Team to review and select ideas for the initiative. In addition to finding ideas this ceremony enables the

Governance and Initiative Teams to determine whether both the pitch team and the idea are ready for incubation, to assess the team's composition (e.g., determine whether they will need assistance), and to identify any actions that may be required to prepare the team to begin their work.

A Pitch Event consists of one or more pitches, each of which takes approximately 30 to 45 minutes. The duration of a single pitch will depend upon the nature of the ideas being presented, the level of experience of the Governance Team and the ceremony's facilitator, and the size of the Governance Team (the larger the team, the more time you may need for questions). Ceremonies typically consist of ten minutes of uninterrupted pitch team presentation followed by ten minutes of questions from the Governance Team (or the team selecting ideas). Time is tightly scheduled, so the Governance Team should be the *only* people asking questions. The question time is followed by an in-camera adjudication by the Governance Team.

For lightweight initiatives and competitions this ceremony structure can be followed using an idea selection team that is not a fully functioning Governance Team. You might also use that approach as your idea selection MVP early in an initiative's life, before your Governance Team is fully operational.

As I explained in *Lean Entrepreneurship*, I prefer to let teams pitch in their own style as opposed to giving them a bespoke pitch deck format. It reduces team preparation time and lets the Governance Team get to know them better than if they were using a bespoke format. Ensuring teams are uninterrupted enables them to practice getting their idea across crisply and effectively in ten minutes, and adherence to the ten-minute time limit ensures teams are disciplined and focus on the most important aspects of their idea as they pitch.

I recommend using a lean canvas or lean public sector canvas to ensure ideas are complete and ready to pitch. Other, or custom, canvases might also be appropriate (e.g., I have used a custom Scientific Research Lean Canvas for Research Team pitches). I recommend making completion of a canvas the only mandatory artifact. Since teams are presenting in their own style I do not insist the canvas be included in the presentation portion of the ceremony. Governance Team members will be able to review it in advance of the ceremony and will be able to ask questions about it even when it is not included in the pitch presentation.

Note A Pitch Ceremony format has been provided in the Toolkit.

Creating the Information and Material Candidates Need to Prepare for Their Pitch

Our primary objective is to remove friction from idea submission, so candidates should not require a lot of material to prepare to pitch. They need to know how to apply, what kind of ideas the Governance Team is looking for, whether there are restrictions on candidate ideas, the format and protocols of a pitch ceremony, the format of their presentation (their own style), which artifacts are required and how to obtain them (the lean canvas, lean public sector canvas...), and what will happen after their pitch is complete.

The following material should be sufficient to get your initiative off the ground:

- An internal site to make the material easy to find and easy to obtain (e.g., SharePoint, Wiki...)

- A brief overview of the initiative explaining its overall benefits, the benefits to people who participate, and any restrictions on the types of ideas being sought after when applicable

- A downloadable, editable copy of the appropriate canvas (e.g., lean canvas, public sector canvas...)

- An overview of the Pitch Ceremony, including protocols and expectations of people in each role (e.g., The Governance Team will not speak during the pitch team's presentation…)

- Downloadable resources that might be helpful to pitch teams, or links to external resources (e.g., how to complete a lean canvas; articles or training sessions regarding how to effectively communicate an idea, recordings and/or artifacts from successful pitches)

- A Frequently Asked Questions (FAQ) article that addresses common questions, concerns, potential objections, and misconceptions

- A way to register their idea for consideration (e.g., a site where they can apply for a pitch event and upload their canvas for consideration)

- A way to contact one or more Initiative Team members if they have questions or need assistance

It should be clear that this is not an inordinate amount of material, and it should not require a lot of time to create. The material should be crisp, clear, and professional, but it does not need to be a perfect final product. Create an MVP and inspect and adapt it as you learn, and as your initiative evolves.

Providing a Mechanism for Candidates to Submit Pitch Requests

Since a key design principle of these initiatives is to remove friction from new idea incubation and innovation, it is important for the pitch application procedure to be as simple as possible. I like a three-step approach:

1. Submit your idea (i.e., upload your canvas to an internal site).

2. Pitch your idea in ten minutes.

3. Enter the initiative and start working on your idea (if you were selected).

Keep It Simple!

Regardless of the application method you choose, do whatever possible to ensure engaging the initiative, and the Initiative Team, is as simple and frictionless as it can be. I promote the procedure above as being "as easy as 1-2-3." It is simple to understand, conveys its frictionless nature, and is easy to remember. (It is also well suited to meme-based graphics.)

Promoting the Initiative and Recruiting Participants

None of your preparation or design will matter if nobody brings their ideas to you, so you must let your target participants know about the initiative and how to become part of it. Most of the material you need to accomplish this will have been created in the previous two steps. Now you need to package that information in a way it can be easily communicated, and decide which channels will most effectively deliver your message and will most likely reach your target candidates.

You may have several possible channels available to you. Some of the most effective I have used include:

- Town halls
- Fireside chats
- Traveling "road shows"
- Lunch and learn sessions

- Regularly scheduled department or business unit updates
- Off-site events
- Kick-off events
- Webinars
- Well-read newsletters

Leverage the Success of Others

Look for and leverage already successful channels. For example, the CEO's Town Hall was extremely well attended for one team I worked with. Just a few minutes in one of those generated a lot of interest and had global reach. The CTO's Fireside Chats were also well attended, very well liked, attracted the perfect mix of people, and were conducted in a format that was very well-suited for communicating this type of information. What made those even more attractive was that they were scheduled and organized outside the initiative. The Initiative Team did not need to take care of logistics, structure, or preparation (beyond their own speaking points). As a bonus, assistance from professional communication teams was often provided as part of those events.

I have also successfully leveraged other existing forums and channels such as already successful lunch and learn programs, regularly scheduled department or business unit updates, team kick-off events, and well-crafted, well-read newsletters (there are still a few of those). **Any time you can take advantage of an existing, proven channel you not only reduce your workload, you also increase your probability of success.**

In some cases an Initiative Team or their representatives physically travelled to locations where there were high concentrations of people likely to be good candidates for the initiative. Sometimes they did this on their own, but at times they were able leverage broader organization-wide initiatives (e.g., headquarters road shows). Those were always well-attended and provided an opportunity to socialize with attendees. They were also well appreciated by attendees and local leaders, especially in areas that did not receive a lot of visitors from "headquarters" or other shared functions.

What You Will Need

Apart from the logistics involved, you should not need to create too much for these events. For presentation-style events such as a road show, you will need an overview deck. Keep it lean and light, allow a lot of time for questions, and be sure your session answers the attendees' most important question, "What's in it for me?" If you are hosting the event on your own you will need to take care of logistics such as obtaining a venue (or setting up a webinar), providing refreshments and/or promotional material, and securing a speaker.

Town halls may require less effort. You may need to supply a speaker and presentation material. But if the host (e.g., the CEO for a CEO's Town Hall) will present your material, you might only be required to supply a few slides, graphics, or talking points for them. Don't let that fool you. Creating material for someone else always involves more effort than creating it for yourself, creating it for a major event often requires even more time, and creating a five-minute presentation is more difficult, and requires more time, than creating a 40-minute presentation.

Fireside chats might be the simplest channels. They often require only the preparation of a few notes, and perhaps some questions and/or answers for the host and/or panelists. They can be very effective due to their informal and interactive nature. Be sure the host or a guest has the information they need to answer any questions that might arise. Often hosts will request a "backup" person who stays in the wings or off camera but can be called upon to answer questions, if needed.

CHAPTER 11   LAUNCHING THE INITIATIVE

Accepting and Triaging Pitch Candidates

This step may be the simplest, but it can take a lot of time. It requires only that there be a mechanism and procedure for applying to pitch, and one or more people to review the applications. The amount of time required will depend on the number of applications received. The time requirement normally grows in a linear fashion. The more applications, the more time that will be needed to review them.

Reviewers are usually members of the Initiative Team who are familiar with the details and objectives of the initiative, and who can assess the quality of a lean canvas. **The objective of this review is NOT to judge the idea.** It is to ensure the lean canvas is complete (all boxes are filled in), that the contents are of high enough quality (e.g., the problem box contains a problem statement), and that the team likely has a good 360-degree understanding of their idea and will be able to sufficiently discuss it during their pitch.

The Initiative Team should not reject a pitch request because they do not like an idea. I like to structure this stage so the only reason the Initiative Team would not move an application to the next step is if the application material is incomplete (e.g., a canvas was not uploaded, the canvas has empty boxes).

There may be cases where an idea is outside the scope of your initiative and you want to reject a pitch request. I recommend never doing that without consulting the Governance Team. I would also recommend that the Governance Team consider letting the team pitch anyway. Things are not always as they seem, it only takes ten-to-twenty minutes (deliberation will be brief), you might realize the idea would be useful elsewhere in the organization, and you might sometimes be pleasantly surprised. Unless you are incredibly overloaded, take the pitch.

Note   A list of errors I commonly encounter when reviewing canvases is included in the Toolkit.

Optional Guidance

The Initiative Team might offer assistance to pitch candidates in some cases. For example, if, during their review, the Initiative Team notices areas where the canvas could be made stronger they might offer to have a brief discussion with the pitch team to give them advice regarding how it might be improved. I like to make that offer optional. I don't want to add friction to the process. The objective of the offer is simply to leverage the Initiative Team's experience reviewing canvases and observing pitches to increase the probability of a pitch team's success.

Selecting and Sequencing Pitches

Once the Initiative Team has determined that all application criteria have been met, the Initiative Team should sequence the pitch for a pitch event based upon the scheduling protocol described in the next section. There may be cases where the pitch needs to be put in a queue for later scheduling, such as when you have a deluge of ideas or a backlog, or when you are prioritizing a specific type of pitch (e.g., you have a competition or promotion where all pitches with an AI aspect will receive priority).

Scheduling Pitches

Scheduling time for a group meeting can be a logistical nightmare. It can be especially challenging if it involves senior people or executives such as those who will likely comprise your Governance Team. Thus, finding a time for the Pitch ceremony that is convenient for the pitch team and the Governance Teams might seem impossible. I have found that **setting a regular cadence for pitch events and scheduling the events as far in advance as possible dramatically simplifies pitch ceremony logistics**.

CHAPTER 11   LAUNCHING THE INITIATIVE

A simple protocol like this can make scheduling simple, even when busy senior executives and leaders are involved:

1. Work with the Governance Team to determine a day and time that would be best, and obtain agreement on the duration and cadence required (e.g., every third Thursday of the month from 1:00 PM to 3:00 PM; the first and third Friday from 9:00 AM to 10:30 AM).

2. Block time in the Governance Team and required Initiative Team members' calendars for the full fiscal year at least three months before the fiscal year begins (or the remainder of the fiscal year if you start mid-year).

3. Make the necessary adjustments to calendar entries that fall on holidays or conflict with organizational events (e.g., kick-off events, financial period peaks), and look for conflicts when changes are made to the organizational calendar.

4. Ask Governance Team members to indicate whether they can participate in an upcoming event using the calendar system's "accept," "decline," or "tentative" indicators as each event approaches (e.g., a week prior to the event or as they become aware of conflicts).

5. Pitch teams are assigned an open position in one of the future pitch events as they are selected.

6. A week ahead of the event, an assigned Initiative Team member verifies that there are pitch teams ready to pitch and that a quorum of Governance Team members has confirmed their attendance.

389

7. If there are pitches scheduled and a Governance Team quorum will be present, an Initiative Team member updates the appropriate instance of the calendar event with the detailed agenda and schedules a follow-up conversation with all scheduled pitch teams as close to the completion of the pitch event as possible.

8. The event is cancelled if no pitches are scheduled one week ahead of the event.

9. If there are pitches, but a Governance Team quorum has not confirmed their participation, the Initiative Team follows up to seek a quorum, and reschedules the event or moves the pitches to the next pitch event if they cannot secure one.

10. If there is a backlog of pitch requests, the Initiative Team might schedule additional pitch events upon agreement with the Governance Team.

11. The Initiative Team is responsible for providing a facilitator for pitch ceremonies and events, for ensuring all necessary logistics are managed and resources are available, and for the smooth operation of the event.

12. Someone from the Initiative Team and/or Governance Team is assigned to have a brief (usually ten-to-fifteen-minute) conversation with pitch teams, as soon after the pitch as possible, to inform teams whether or not their idea has been accepted and discuss next steps.

I have found this basic structure to be very effective. Logistics for your first couple of pitch events might be a bit more complex, since the Governance Team's calendars may not yet have adjusted to make time available for them. I have found such challenges normally disappear after a month or less, and the regular cadence usually keeps them from reappearing. Scheduling the pitches should require very little effort once the team develops a cadence.

Directing and Guiding the Governance Team

Lean entrepreneurship ceremonies are designed to drive the most possible progress and/or learning in the least amount of time. Once the structure of a ceremony is agreed upon, it is critical that everyone respect it so it can accomplish its intended objectives and start, stay, and stop on time.

Prior to conducting a pitch ceremony, the Governance Team needs to understand the purpose and structure of the ceremony and align on their roles and how it will be facilitated. For example, one of the most common reasons I have seen pitches that do not follow a structure like this go off the rails is that someone senior interrupts the pitch team's presentation, takes them down a rabbit hole, and they run out of time before they get their entire idea across. When that happens the pitch team usually ends up looking disorganized and unconfident to the senior people, and they leave feeling miserable and ashamed, concerned they may have irreparably damaged their reputation.

To address this, the pitch ceremony structure I recommend begins with a period of *uninterrupted* presentation time. This enables pitch teams to present in their own style, and to get their entire idea across before the Governance Team (or selection team) asks questions. The result is better for both. Pitch teams get their full idea across, Governance Teams develop and benefit from better questions, and no time is lost asking questions which would have been answered later in the presentation.

CHAPTER 11   LAUNCHING THE INITIATIVE

Some senior people may not be accustomed to not asking questions as they think of them. I am not suggesting they are rude, controlling, or privileged. I am simply suggesting that you may have to replace one habit, which would not be well suited to this ceremony, with another which will help drive a better result.

Changing habits of this type requires deliberate action and thought. It is highly likely someone will interrupt an early pitch, even if they have been introduced to the protocol. The pitch ceremony will be much more productive if the Governance Team understands the value of its structure in advance, and knows that if they interrupt, the facilitator will interject and remind them the time for questions will come later. I have found an advance warning also ensures that Governance Team members do not feel insulted when a facilitator intervenes. In fact, I am frequently thanked by them for intervening when I do so.

Make time before the first pitch event to ensure the Governance Team understands its structure and format, and their role. You might even want to have them join a private room five or ten minutes prior to your first event so you can remind them. In early events I also add a few minutes of hidden slack time to the agenda so I can remind everyone of the protocol for each step as we enter it (e.g., "We are ready for <*name(s)*> to share their idea with us. <Name>, you have ten minutes of uninterrupted time to..."). It takes less than a minute, and it's time well spent.

In addition to your ceremony's structure, here are a few suggestions for protocol items to review with the Governance Team:

- **Do not interject during the pitch team's presentation:** It sets a bad tone and interrupts the flow of the pitch; you will have time to ask questions immediately following the pitch.

- **Don't adjudicate during the ceremony:** It sets the wrong tone and takes time away from other's questions.

- **Avoid long preambles to questions:** Question time is ample but tightly scheduled; the shorter your preamble, the more time there will be for questions and answers.

- **Don't chase shiny objects:** Keep your questions focused on what you need to know to evaluate whether the idea should enter the initiative (facilitators beware, this happens a lot).

- **It's OK to compliment, but don't cheerlead:** Keep compliments brief (e.g., "thank you," "great presentation"), but be careful not to show your support for an idea during the question session; It consumes time unnecessarily, you may change your mind during adjudication, and we want to avoid the introduction of bias to other Governance Team members at this stage of evaluation.

Adjudicating Ideas via a Pitch Ceremony

The Pitch Ceremony usually follows the following basic format:

1. The pitch team presents their idea, uninterrupted.
2. The Governance Team, and only the Governance Team, asks questions.
3. The pitch team adjourns.
4. The Governance Team adjudicates the idea privately.

CHAPTER 11　LAUNCHING THE INITIATIVE

Following each pitch, Governance Team members, the facilitator, and sometimes other Initiative Team members move to a private room (or private virtual room) to decide whether the idea will be selected for entry. There are plenty of ways this can be done. When facilitating I like to begin by asking each of the Governance Team members whether they have any observations from the session they would like to share. Once everyone has weighed in I move the team to a fist of five vote (see the Toolkit for additional information on fist of five voting) to make the final decision.

There may be times when a facilitator wants to open the adjudication session with a fist of five vote to sense where the team is. There are pros and cons to this. For example, if the facilitator sensed during the question session that the team is obviously converging on a decision, this can save time. Over time, the facilitator may become very good at reading the Governance Team in this way. However, a potential downside is that the initial vote may bias the discussion. The fist of five structure is designed to generate discussion, so that is less of a risk, but it can still happen. The better choice might simply come down to the facilitator, their style, and the team's dynamic.

The structure I described has the Governance Team adjudicating each idea immediately following each pitch. Teams could alternatively hold several pitches consecutively and adjudicate them all in one session at the end. When done in that sequence there is risk that the Governance Team will forget about some of the things they learned during earlier pitches or conflate items from multiple pitches. While I have run successful pitch events this way, and you may have to do this at times to accommodate schedules, I recommend scheduling pitch adjudications as close to the pitches as possible.

Note　Additional information regarding the Pitch Ceremony can be found in the Toolkit.

Informing Pitch Teams Whether or Not Their Ideas Are Selected

As you might have guessed, during this step someone from the Governance Team has a 10-to-15-minute meeting with the pitch team (preferably a video meeting) and informs them of whether their idea was accepted. The purpose of this step is as much about demonstrating respect for the pitch teams, thanking them, and encouraging them to keep innovating, as it is about providing the update. Be specific about the reasons an idea was not selected and encourage the team to bring additional ideas your way. Tools like the grids in Figures 9-4, 9-5, and 9-6 can help objectively explain the rational for a decision when out of scope ideas are not selected.

There may be some cases where the Governance Team believes the pitch team has the root of a good idea, but they have not sufficiently developed it. When that happens be encouraging, offer specific information regarding what type of improvement is required, and encourage the pitch team to bring the idea back once they have further developed it.

There may also be cases where the idea falls outside the scope of the initiative. For example, it may be better suited to a mature department or business unit. When that happens, direct the team to the appropriate group, and introduce them to someone in that group who can help them.

One thing that surprised me when I was regularly evaluating pitches was how often we would receive a pitch that was, more or less, exactly like a pitch we had previously seen. In some cases the idea was the same as another we had already selected for entry into the initiative. What was interesting to me was that, in the cases I encountered, the people worked in different groups, in different regions, and they did not know one-another. They independently developed the same idea. If that happens to you, I recommend informing the pitch team that someone already pitched the idea and connect them with the other team. The two groups may be able to advance the idea together.

When ideas are selected, congratulate the pitch team, provide specific reasons why the idea was selected, and explain what the team's next steps are, and when they should expect them to happen. I also like to confirm an address where I can send welcome items. (I will expand on that later in this chapter.)

Priming the Pipeline

In addition to what has already been mentioned, there are several things that can be done to generate interest in, and a pipeline for, the initiative. These might include bringing in already incubating teams, running competitions, or prioritizing focus on a specific domain, problem, or technology.

Bringing in Existing Incubations

You may find groups in your organization who are already working on ideas outside the normal scope of their department or business unit. Bringing in already incubating ideas can accelerate progress, provide budget relief, and potentially drive early wins. It can get your engine moving quickly without the need to request new funding, and the initiative can increase the incubating team's probability of success by providing an environment that might be better suited to incubating nascent ideas. It should be a win-win situation.

Competitions

Competitions such as hackathons, idea competitions, or business model competitions can also be an effective way to create a pipeline, but they have been known to backfire. If you run these, be extremely clear and specific about what the winner will receive (e.g., an opportunity to pitch, entry into Seed 1 or Explore 1). If the award includes entry into the initiative, be specific about whether that is full or limited entry. Limited entry might consist of a finite and specific commitment such as one month to complete Seed 1 or Explore 1 with no guarantee the idea will move to the next stage even if the idea shows promise.

I recommend also clearly stating that there may be no winner if that is a possibility. You may find a lot of good ideas, none of which are in scope for the initiative. You might also find great ideas that the initiative's teams are not capable of helping to move forward. Your initiative will not benefit from either, so be forthcoming. Transparency and clarity will build trust in the initiative, and in your team.

Leverage existing channels

Many organizations regularly run competitions of this nature. If that is the case, see if you can leverage an already scheduled event. When we built the first lean entrepreneurship accelerator we learned of a hackathon that was already planned for a large engineering center. Its coordinators permitted us to add an optional business model aspect to it. None of the rules or awards of the hackathon were changed. Teams were permitted to optionally create a lean canvas and submit it along with their entry.

Submitted canvases were evaluated, and the winning team was offered the first pitch session in front of our very popular CTO and his team. It was a very positive experience, and it required nothing but a few minutes of the Initiative Team's time to review the models.

In addition to leveraging active competitions, reviewing the entrants and winners of recently completed competitions might be another way to find ideas worth pursuing.

Focusing on a Domain

There are times when a specific technology or domain (usually an emerging one) becomes of highly strategic value to an organization or group. One way to find new ideas in that domain, raise awareness amongst employees, communicate the strategic value of the domain, and get people thinking about it is to emphasize and prioritize it using existing programs and initiatives. In the context of an initiative like this, that may mean giving priority to any ideas in that domain (e.g., ideas related to AI are placed at the top of the pitch queue; special guests like the CEO or Chief Product Officer will join the Governance Team or selection team for ideas related to large language models).

This can be extremely effective if multiple initiatives are aligned. For example, one organization I worked with would periodically focus on a specific domain or technology for one month (e.g., "AI month"). Each initiative would offer an incentive for participants to focus on that domain. The incubator-accelerator would prioritize pitches, the patent review team would prioritize reviewing patents (for which there was also a cash award), and the publication team would prioritize publications. This required almost no additional effort by the initiative teams. Sometimes this emphasis was supplemented with additional events like idea competitions.

2. Onboard Incubating Teams (Entry)

Onboarding teams is one of the most exciting and enjoyable aspects of these initiatives. The Initiative Team has successfully launched the initiative, generated interest, and successfully found an idea. Win! The incubating team has successfully pitched their idea, has been selected, and are about to begin bringing their idea to life. Win! It's wins all around. Spirits are high. Now it's time to get to work.

The volume and variety of tasks necessary during this entry stage is broad, and a high execution speed is required. The volume and speed of required activities will also increase as the initiative matures and grows. Checklist execution is the best way to ensure all teams are ready, all necessary tasks are executed, teams focus on the tasks required for their current stage, and nothing is forgotten in any excitement or chaos that may develop. Checklists are also great tools for ensuring alignment between teams and sponsors. They are easy to consume, easy to understand, and errors or omissions tend to stand out. They are also useful during retrospectives.

You will need to have four checklists ready as teams prepare to enter the initiative and work on their ideas:

1. **Initiative Team Entry Checklist:** Ensures that the Initiative Team attends to the necessary logistics, prepares the resources necessary for successful onboarding of the incubating team, and positions the incubating team for success (tasks on this list are executed by the Initiative Team)

2. **Incubating Team Entry Checklist:** Ensures the team bringing the idea to life has everything they need and is ready to begin incubating their idea

3. **Explore 1, Seed 1, or Incubate 1 Checklist:** Ensures the incubating team is performing the right activities for that stage, keeps *everyone* focused on the right level of activities, and serves as a guidepost for the Governance Team when evaluating the incubating team's progress (i.e., during a 3P review)

4. **Pause Checklist:** Ensures a smooth conclusion to incubation activities at this (or any) stage, and ensures technology and learning are preserved even if ideas are shut down

A checklist will also be required for each subsequent stage (e.g., Explore 2 through Transition 2, Seed 2 through Series C). Remember that you can build your initiative incrementally, and you only need the checklists, tools, and artifacts that are required by currently or soon-to-be incubating teams.

CHAPTER 11   LAUNCHING THE INITIATIVE

> **Note**   Sample Entry checklists, a sample Pause Checklist, and sample checklists for each stage of incubation are provided in the Toolkit.

Eliminating Waste by "Testing Out"

The stage of maturity at which you capture ideas may vary widely. Some teams may have vetted their ideas with potential customers, users, or beneficiaries, some may have developed a working prototype, some may have an early adopter, and some may have none of those. Teams brought into the initiative that were incubating elsewhere may have *very* evolved solutions.

Making more mature teams go back to the very first step (e.g., Explore 1 or Seed 1) is likely to be wasteful and frustrating for the incubating team. However, blindly estimating their current position might also be a path to failure. Consider allowing teams to "test out" (to borrow a phrase from academia) of a stage to address this issue and avoid the potential waste resulting from repeated experiments and activities.

To test out of a stage, teams should provide evidence that they have satisfied all objectives of that stage. The checklists provide guidance regarding what those criteria should be. This evidence can be provided during the team's first 3P review.

I recommend not asking teams that believe they are in later stages to conduct several 3P reviews to test out. For example, a team that believes it has achieved Series A could bring evidence it has satisfied the objectives of the Seed 1 *and* Seed 2 stages to a single 3P review. A team that believes it has achieved Experiment 1 could bring Explore 1 *and* Explore 2 evidence. What is most important is that you ensure test outs are evidence based if you permit them in your initiative.

I have seen several teams successfully test out of early stages. One team I worked with moved to Seed 2 in one week. They had performed customer outreach before pitching and had achieved customer-problem fit. I have seen other cases where teams had achieved most of the objectives of the stage they wished to test out of, but were missing one or two key pieces of evidence. When that happened we decided whether to keep them in their current stage, or move them to the next stage with the condition they run the necessary experiments before their transition.

Allowing teams an opportunity to test out helps achieve the initiative's objective of being lean and minimizing waste and effort while ensuring solutions are properly vetted and important information or evidence is not missed.

Welcoming Incubating Teams

I believe these initiatives are as much about helping people grow as they are about bringing new ideas to life. The Initiative Team will be the first to greet new teams, will serve as their key point of contact for needs and issues that might arise, and will be their lifeline at times. Initiative Team members should ensure new incubating teams feel welcome, and that they are comfortable contacting – and being completely candid with – Initiative Team members.

I like to send successful pitch team members a couple of books the day I inform them of their success. I ask them to send a note informing me where I can send the information during the meeting where I share the results of their pitch. I typically send them a copy of Eric Ries' *The Lean Startup* and Ash Maurya's *Running Lean*. Those books provide excellent context and content that will help them throughout their journey. I find those books also place team members in the right mindset. Arrival of the books has been very well received, and you can send them along with any other welcome material you may have.

CHAPTER 11 LAUNCHING THE INITIATIVE

Typical onboarding activities include:

- A brief orientation conversation with the Initiative Team
- Provision of access to all initiative resources, checklists, and tools
- Provision of access to Founder FAQs and lists of advisors and key contacts
- Joining the initiative's message groups (e.g., a Slack or Teams channel for the initiative overall, one for Founders, one for Marketing or Sales tips and tricks)
- Development of a plan to withdraw incubating team members from their existing roles and commitments and transition them to the initiative without disrupting their current team's activities and plans
- Working with the People Team (HR) to transition to an incubation rotation plan if one exists (i.e., a formal leave from their old team with guaranteed return if their idea does not succeed)
- Reading *The Lean Startup* and *Running Lean*
- Brief onboarding training (also referred to as Bootstrap Training or Boot Camp)
- Optional self-evaluation to help them identify personal growth areas (see the Competency Model in the Toolkit)
- Identifying potential gaps in their Minimum Viable Team

- Observing other incubating teams' 3P reviews to get a feel for their rhythm and learn how to get the most from interactions with the Governance Team
- Beginning to build their initial staffing plan (with assistance from the Initiative Team)

Onboarding training will vary based upon what is being incubated and the needs and objectives of the initiative, but may include things like:

- An introduction to lean startup concepts
- Lean thinking and using the scientific method to conduct experiments (even non-technical ones)
- Design thinking
- Agile approaches
- Creating working agreements and definitions of done
- Building a foundation (e.g., business systems, backup, CI/CD pipeline, lab procedures, safety protocols...)
- Introduction to strategy and competitive analysis
- Lessons learned by others who have already been incubating their ideas through the initiative
- Creating their Explore 1 Incubate 1, or Seed 1 plan and budget
- How to leverage advisors and what to look for in team-specific advisors if they need them
- Where to find tools and resources that can help them at each stage (some tools of this nature have been provided in the Toolkit)

- How to leverage and customize electronic checklists or Kanban boards for each stage (e.g., which contain an instance of the stage's checklist)

The overarching theme should be frictionless entry. Teams should be focused on incubating their idea as quickly as possible. Any onboarding activity should facilitate or accelerate that. Facilitators of the onboarding training should also take advantage of opportunities for morale boosting and team building.

Note The Toolkit in Part 5 of this book contains checklists for all stages of incubation, and tools that may be useful to incubating teams or the Initiative Team.

Tools and Resources

I have included many tools that I have found to be useful in the Toolkit in Part 5 of this book. Though there are many tools within, if you flip though it quickly, you might immediately think of others you wish to add. You will find the same occurs once you make your own toolkit available.

Teams will encounter situations for which the initiative has not supplied a tool, and others where they prefer to use an alternative tool. Embrace both when they happen, and make it easy for teams to contribute tools they have found useful. You can also consider asking incubating team members to make others aware of tools they add via the message groups, informally, or during information exchanges or summits.

CHAPTER 11   LAUNCHING THE INITIATIVE

Developing Good Habits and Guiding Principles

A scientific study discovered that approximately 45% of everyday behavior tends to be habitual.[1] A key factor in the success of an incubating team is often whether they can break some of their old habits (which are not conducive to innovation and new idea incubation) and develop new, healthy habits and guiding principles. Your habits may vary, but consider the following:

- Maniacal customer or beneficiary focus
- Business model centricity
- Simplicity
- Small, incremental investments
- Evidence-based decisions
- Rapid experimentation and iteration, leveraging the smallest experiments possible for the greatest learning
- Continuous learning and improvement
- Lean evaluation and disciplined, lean governance
- Radical candor
- Transparency bias
- Valuing good habits and disciplined approaches over process and artifacts
- Trustworthiness and integrity
- Innovation mindset:

---

[1] David T. Neal, Wendy Wood, and Jeffrey M. Quinn. "Habits – A Repeat Performance" Duke University, 2006, https://dornsife.usc.edu/assets/sites/545/docs/Wendy_Wood_Research_Articles/Habits/Neal.Wood.Quinn.2006_Habits_a_repeat_performance.pdf

- Believing anything is possible until an experiment proves it is not possible
- Believing unexpected results in experiments are not failures, and often lead to the greatest discoveries

Consider the Impact of Cohorts

Many incubators and accelerators such as TechStars and Springboard Enterprises leverage cohorts to deliver outstanding value. They select groups of candidates and bring them all through their program at the same time. This can be an extremely successful, efficient, and effective way to help incubating teams to develop and grow, especially if they are all at the same stage of maturity and need the same kind of support.

Cohorts may be right for your initiative, though I usually opt not to use cohorts for an initiative such as this because:

- Having every idea at the same stage at the same time can create a budget crisis, as teams hit their peak financial requirements simultaneously.
    - Such a crisis might mean having to pause, slow, or exit an incubating team.
    - This risk is especially high as teams mature and each requires more investment.
    - Without cohorts the financial peaks of each team are dampened by the valleys of others.
- If placed in cohorts, all incubating teams would require the same resources and assistance at the same time, creating high peaks in demand for the Initiative Team and mentoring and advisory support.
    - This demand would likely increase as teams evolve.

- Placing the teams in cohorts might overburden the Governance Team, as incubating teams would hit key inflection points at or around the same time.
- Not using cohorts provides an opportunity for new incubating teams to learn from more experienced teams.
  - This helps better evolve the initiative and lessens Governance Team, Advisory Team, and Initiative Team workloads.
- Without cohorts the risk of concurrent pauses is reduced.
  - Concurrent pauses can create a challenge if you plan to help place incubating team members in new roles when an idea is paused or shut down, or if you have an incubation rotation scheme.
  - Each concurrent pause creates additional work for the Initiative Team and anyone assisting them, and results in more candidates vying for the same number of available positions.
- Great ideas can come from anywhere and at any time and, without cohorts, they can be captured immediately, incubating team passion and momentum can be leveraged, and the risk of losing ideas because intrapreneurs lose interest or take their idea somewhere else is reduced.
- This type of initiative's objectives are different.
  - The ideas that are incubated in these initiatives are normally much less mature than participants in programs like TechStars or Springboard Enterprises, and have different needs.

I have nothing against cohorts. I have brought a couple of teams that were selected in close proximity to one-another into an initiative at the same time. That's not really a true cohort in this sense, but we were able to take advantage of some efficiencies (e.g., running one onboarding training session for both) with limited risk because the number of teams was low and we had a mature, performing initiative with already incubating teams that were more mature.

The bottom line is that you should perform some second order thinking regarding the benefits and drawbacks of using, and not using, cohorts before you make your final decision. If you are starting your initiative with a small number of incubating teams, you will have plenty of time to learn what those impacts might be before you must decide, and you will have the benefit of watching its first few teams evolve.

3. Allocate Initiative Team Time for Removing Obstacles (Unblocking)

A key element of the role of the Initiative Team is to ensure incubating teams are spending as much time as possible working on their ideas, and as little time as possible doing anything else. Their goal is to reduce the friction of bringing new ideas to life.

Allocate a significant amount of time for unblocking teams in the initiative's early days. Pioneering incubating teams will encounter almost every obstacle that exists, and you probably won't be able to predict them all. Someone with good unblocking skills, great interpersonal communication ability, and a good knowledge of the organization and where to find help will be invaluable early on.

Teams should encounter fewer obstacles over time, and less time should be required for these activities as your initiative matures. Each incubating team will benefit from those who started earlier, encountering fewer obstacles than those who incubated before them. But there will always be obstacles. Preparing early incubating teams for these speedbumps will help them to better deal with obstacles when they are encountered. Having a single point of contact for unblocking assistance will let incubating teams focus on bringing their ideas to life.

4. Use 3P Reviews to Assess and Facilitate Progress

The 3P (Pivot, Pause, Persevere) Review ceremony drives the heartbeat of the initiative. Its cadence will affect all of the initiative's other cadences. It drives a healthy sense of urgency and aligns all the initiative's teams. The 3P review's purpose is to:

- Establish a working cadence for an incubating team and the Governance Team
- Ensure alignment of incubating teams and the Governance Team
- Enable an incubating team to request assistance with obstacles, resources, or needs
- Provide a forum for the Governance Team and incubating teams to evaluate progress and discuss whether an incubation should pause, pivot, or stay on its current course
- Provide a forum for the Governance Team and incubating teams to determine whether an incubation is ready to advance to the next stage
- Drive responsible, lightweight governance

The 3P review is the second, and final, anchor ceremony. Each incubating team will participate in regularly scheduled 3P reviews from its first stage of incubation until it exits the initiative. I recommend monthly 3P reviews for all teams, especially early in their life when stages may last from one-to-three months. This will ensure teams that are headed in the wrong direction do not waste too much time and effort on unproductive activities.

I have found a monthly cadence to be optimal even for more mature teams. There may be times when a mature incubating team does not have much to share in their scheduled 3P review. For example, a mature team building their MVP may need more than one month to make sufficient progress for a material update. Rather than move to an every-other-month or quarterly cadence, I have found it better to keep a monthly cadence and enable teams to request any of their 3P reviews be canceled when they are at this stage. This keeps the dialogue open and the cadence fresh.

I *can* envision, and have encountered, scenarios where an every-other-month or quarterly cadence would be acceptable and/or optimal. The optimal decision for your initiative's cadence will depend on the nature of the ideas you are incubating, the skills of the incubating teams, and the organization's culture.

3P Review Format

The format of 3P reviews is simple and flexible. Achieving the 3P objectives is what matters most. A typical 3P review consists of two portions:

1. An *uninterrupted* update from the incubating team
2. Questions from the Governance Team and open dialog

I typically recommend one of three forms:

1. **15–15:** Up to 15 minutes of uninterrupted presentation by the incubating team followed by up to 15 minutes of open dialogue and Q&A with the Governance Team (routine 3P)

2. **10–20:** Up to ten minutes of uninterrupted presentation by the incubating team followed by 10 to 20 minutes of open dialogue and Q&A from the Governance Team (quick form)

3. **30–30:** Up to 30 minutes of uninterrupted presentation by the incubating team followed by up to 30 minutes of open dialogue and Q&A from the Governance Team (transition request or major event)

A 3P review is analogous to stand-up meeting in the sense that it is designed to align teams in a lightweight fashion with a minimum amount of time and effort. In a 3P review the incubating team is essentially answering the questions:

1. What did they say they were going to do?
2. What did they do?
3. What did they learn?
4. What will they do next (as a result of what they learned)?
5. Is anything blocking them, or do they need any help?

A 15–15 review is the most commonly used format and is well suited to routine updates and events. A 10–20 review is often used by teams who are in a period of peak building (e.g., creating their MVP), but who do not want to cancel their review. Those often take less than 10 or 15 minutes in total. A 30–30 review is typically used for a special type of 3P review referred to as a "Transition Request 3P Review."

Note Additional information regarding 3P Review Ceremonies can be found in the Toolkit.

Transition Request 3P Reviews

Transition Request 3P Reviews are scheduled when an incubating team believes they have achieved all the objectives for their current stage of incubation and are ready for the next stage (e.g., they have completed Seed 1 and are ready for Seed 2). For the most part, a transition request follows the same format as all other 3P reviews. The difference is that the incubating team update includes a request that the Governance Team approve their transition to the next stage.

Incubating teams typically bring a lot of evidence to a Transition Request, so their updates are typically scheduled for 30 minutes. The Initiative Team will also add an additional 10 to 15 minutes to the end of the transition request for Governance Team adjudication. Incubating teams are informed of the Governance Team's decision immediately upon its completion.

In Camera Adjudication?

When I first ran 3P reviews, the Governance Teams would perform their adjudication in camera, in a virtual or physical room separate from the incubating team. Once the Governance Team completed their adjudication, they would rejoin the incubating team and share their decision. Eventually some of the incubating teams asked if they could join the adjudication so they would have a deeper understanding of the reason for an approval or a redirect.

The reason adjudication had been in camera initially was so Governance Team members could speak openly without being concerned they might unintentionally insult the incubating team or damage morale or relationships. With the benefit of experience, we assessed the risk of that happening to be low and let them join. It worked very well, helped strengthen the relationship between the incubating team and Governance Team, and, periodically, identified areas where the Governance Team had misunderstood something and resulted in a change in their decision or a conditional approval.

Depending upon its composition and personality, you may wish to consider having your Governance Team adjudicate early transition requests in camera. Once the Team has some experience, you can consider whether you would like to invite incubating teams to adjudications or make it optionally available for them. A strong facilitator can make an enormous difference in the temperature of the discussions and outcome of these ceremonies and is highly recommended.

Scheduling 3P Reviews

Initiative Teams face the same challenges scheduling 3P reviews as they do scheduling pitch events. As with pitch events, **I have found that setting a regular cadence for 3P Reviews and scheduling the events as far in advance as possible dramatically simplifies 3P review logistics.** Though the two are mostly alike, there are minor differences when scheduling 3P reviews.

CHAPTER 11   LAUNCHING THE INITIATIVE

A simple protocol like this can make scheduling 3P reviews simple, even though busy senior executives and leaders are almost always involved:

1. Group 3P reviews together into a 3P event, work with the Governance Team to determine a day and time that would be best, and obtain agreement on the duration and cadence required (e.g., every third Thursday of the month from 1:00 PM to 4:00 PM; the first and third Friday from 9:00 AM to 11:30 AM).

2. Block time in the Governance Team and required Initiative Team and incubating Team members' calendars for the full fiscal year at least three months before the fiscal year begins (or for the remainder of the fiscal year if you begin mid-year).

3. Make the necessary adjustments to calendar entries that fall on holidays or conflict with organizational events (e.g., kick-off events, financial period peaks), and look for conflicts when changes are made to the organizational calendar.

4. Ask Governance Team members to indicate whether they can participate using the calendar system's "accept," "decline," or "tentative" indicators as each event approaches (e.g., a week out or when their status changes).

5. Assign each incubating team a time in the agenda (3P review durations are variable, so the Initiative Team must create a new agenda every month).

6. Allow slack time in the agenda for transitions, include breaks, and consider the impact of different time zones (e.g., different break and lunch times).

CHAPTER 11   LAUNCHING THE INITIATIVE

7. A week ahead of the event. the assigned Initiative Team member finalizes the agenda (in coordination with the incubating teams) and ensures a quorum of Governance Team members have confirmed their attendance.

8. If a Governance Team quorum will be present, an Initiative Team member will update the appropriate instance of the calendar event with the detailed agenda.

9. Incubating teams post the material for their review to a 3P review site 48 hours before the review, but can update it up to the start time of their review.

10. If a Governance Team quorum has not confirmed their participation, the Initiative Team will follow up to seek a quorum or reschedule all or part of the event.

11. The Initiative Team is responsible for providing a facilitator for 3P reviews, for ensuring all necessary logistics are managed and resources are available, and for the smooth operation of the event.

12. The Initiative Team is responsible for follow-up items related to the initiative or the event, but the incubation team leads are responsible for following up on requests made to them by the Governance Team.

As with pitch events, logistics for your first couple of 3P events might be a bit more complex as the Governance Team's calendars may not yet have adjusted for the events. I have found such challenges normally disappear after a month or less, and the regular cadence keeps them from reappearing. Once the team develops a cadence the greatest amount of effort will be creating the final agenda.

415

CHAPTER 11 LAUNCHING THE INITIATIVE

Guiding the Governance Team

The Governance Team will likely require guidance and direction from the facilitator during early 3P reviews, and from time-to-time thereafter. Engage a strong facilitator who can keep things on track, help the Governance Team evolve, and foster good relationships between the incubating teams and the Governance Team. The facilitator must:

- Ensure the Governance Team understands the stage the incubating team under review is at, and that they ask questions and provide guidance appropriately (the Initiative-at-a-Glance sheets in the Toolkit can help with this)

- Facilitate a mentoring mindset, and ensure that the Governance Team is nurturing the incubating team's ingenuity as well as governing (most of the time it should feel like coaching, not like governance or judging)

- Help the Governance Team to guide, direct, and coach rather than criticize

- Keep crows (those who chase shiny objects not critical to the review) on track

- Coach the Governance Team away from seagull management (swooping in, criticizing, causing chaos, making a mess, and flying away) and facilitate a stop to it when it occurs

- Manage conflicts or potential conflicts between attendees

- Help the Governance Team to eliminate long preambles to questions when necessary

Keep It Light, Keep It Lean

You don't want to replace a heavy, unnecessary process like those described in Chapter 2 with a new heavy process. The purpose of lean entrepreneurship ceremonies is to facilitate the work necessary to deliver the initiative's desired outcomes, and to support incubating teams as needed. The tools and ceremonies should provide a cadence and move the work forward. They should be a resource, not a tax.

Anticipate a potential rough start as people get used to things. The purpose of this approach is to increase focus, reduce waste, lighten the load, nurture the incubating teams and their ideas, and build things people want. **Your experience should be much lighter once a rhythm is developed, teams begin to norm and perform, bad habits are shed, and waste work is identified. If the approach feels heavy, the atmosphere is uneasy, or the teams feel unproductive, something is out of tune. Run a quick retrospective and inspect and adapt.**

5. Reward Participants

As you launch your initiative, think about how you can reward participants in all five teams. How can you reward incubating team members for excellence in execution or advancing their ideas? How can you reward Initiative Team members' performance and effort? How can you show appreciation to the Governance Team, advisors, or people who help advance the initiative?

People like to be recognized, and there is a typically a broad range of available ways to do so in any mid-to-large-sized organization. Some come at a cost, while others cost nothing but time. Involve the Governance Team and select Advisory Team members as you brainstorm ideas for rewards. People in those groups tend to have a lot of experience with employee

CHAPTER 11   LAUNCHING THE INITIATIVE

recognition, and some may know of existing programs or resources your initiative can leverage (e.g., organization-wide recognition programs, executive-sponsored awards).

Consider a broad range of reward mechanisms such as:

- Plaques, trophies, and figures
- Paid time off
- Family dinners or trips
- Cash bonuses
- Stock options or restricted stock units (the parent organization's)
- Exit bonuses or equity equivalents (for the incubating idea)
- Verbal recognition at a town hall, fireside chat, or organizational event
- A call or thank you note from a senior executive or senior leader
- A meal or refreshment break with a senior leader, senior executive, or organizational celebrity
- Promotions or changes in title
- Entry into "high-potential" training or sought-after programs
- Approval and funding to attend a conference or event
- Upgraded personal equipment
- A transit pass or premium parking space

Cast a wide net and consider all options. Test your ideas with the various teams and groups who might be candidates for the awards should they be offered. Ensure the awards are meaningful, appropriate, and respect the organization and culture. Reward excellence, remembering that shutting down an idea because a team discovers it is not viable in the most efficient and effective way possible is not failure, it is excellence.

Final Considerations

Here are a few additional things to consider as you launch your initiative:

- You don't have to do everything at once; start small and stay a step ahead of incubating team and Governance Team needs.
- Schedule teams' initial 3P reviews as close to their entry as possible, but not in the first two weeks.
- When launching, resist the temptation to onboard too many ideas at once; Bring a small number in, get the engine running and the teams performing, and expand once you know your capacity.
- Take every opportunity to get your message in front of people, speak with everyone you can, and find a way to leverage every volunteer.
- Don't expect everything to be perfect at the outset.
- The Governance Team will become better at selecting and nurturing ideas over time; don't be discouraged by "false starts."

- Don't let the tools, ceremonies, or artifacts become the goal, they exist to advance incubating teams' ideas; run a retrospective immediately if you detect teams are focused more on an artifact than their idea.

- When in doubt, run an experiment; don't be afraid to try new things.

Summary

Cast a wide net when looking for new ideas. Leverage existing innovation competitions and programs to accelerate your launch. Be clear and transparent about the types of ideas you are looking for, and create a frictionless, seamless way to capture them.

Once teams and their ideas are selected, welcome them onboard and make sure they know that everyone – the Initiative Team, the Governance Team, and the advisors – wants them to succeed. They would not have been selected otherwise. Remove obstacles and friction from their paths and let them focus their energy on bringing their ideas to life. Use 3P reviews to shepherd each idea through its lifecycle and engage a strong facilitator to ensure the atmosphere is positive, pleasant, and upbeat while keeping all teams on track.

Don't forget to find ways to reward all participants. Leverage low-cost and no-cost means as well as rewards provided by the organization. But don't try to do everything on the first day (or month…). You don't have to.

Once you have done these things, you will have an active initiative. But how will you know whether it is working? I will discuss that in Chapter 12.

CHAPTER 12

Measuring Performance and Impact

Now you're having fun! You have put in the hard work, done your research, designed with nuance, and been executing against your OKRs or objectives. You have built a strong foundation for your initiative, launched it, built interest, and found ideas worth pursuing. As a teacher of mine used to say, now you can take a minute to reach over your own shoulder and pat yourself on the back.

But wait! It might *feel* good. Spirits are probably high, and you *think* things are going well. They may be. But how do you *know* whether the actions you and the initiative's teams and allies are taking are having the impact you desire? More importantly, how can you demonstrate the initiative's value and progress to stakeholders, leaders, and executives?

Harold Geenen cautioned that performance is reality. That is true only if you can objectively demonstrate the initiative's performance. If you cannot, *perception* can become your reality. If someone feels good about the initiative, for them it is performing well. If someone is concerned or feels things are chaotic or not performing well, that is *their* reality. The impact of bad perception is obvious. However, even an incorrect perception that

CHAPTER 12   MEASURING PERFORMANCE AND IMPACT

things are going well can be damaging to an initiative, as adjustments that should be made to ensure its long-term success go unaddressed.

The best way to address both types of misperception is to remove perception, feelings, and guesswork from the equation by providing objective evidence based on objective measurement of the things that matter most (Figure 12-1).

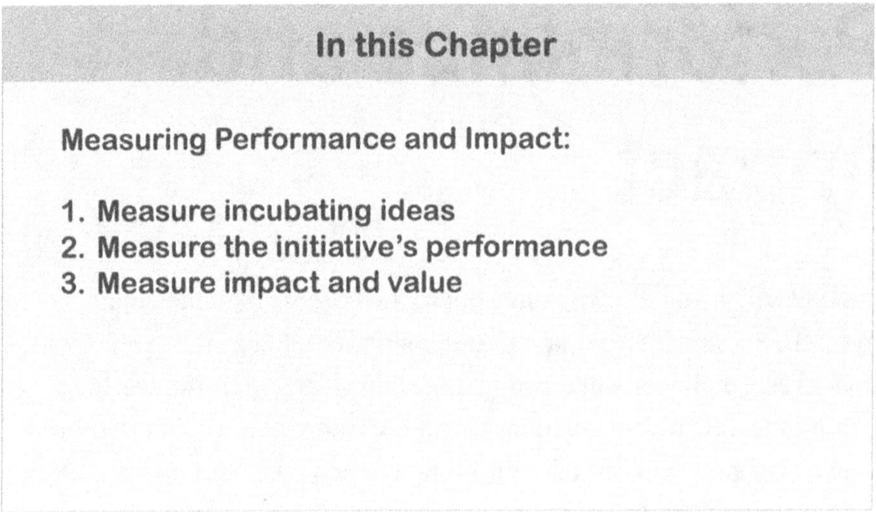

> **In this Chapter**
>
> Measuring Performance and Impact:
>
> 1. Measure incubating ideas
> 2. Measure the initiative's performance
> 3. Measure impact and value

Figure 12-1. *What's in this chapter*

Where Do I Begin? What Can I Measure?

As with many of the other things in these initiatives, getting started can be the hardest part. The objective of this chapter is to give you a head start by sharing a few examples and approaches that will help you understand how your initiative is performing, identify areas that may need attention – or things that are doing well that you might want to leverage – and help stakeholders and participants understand how things are going and where they might be able to help. Ironically, once you start identifying measures you may find it difficult to stop.

CHAPTER 12   MEASURING PERFORMANCE AND IMPACT

Two Measurement Classes

There are a lot of moving parts in initiatives like these. It can seem overwhelming, and if you consider everything at once it can be confusing. What's more, trying to measure everything the same way might make it even more confusing. Let's begin by simplifying the landscape by breaking things down.

A key principle of lean entrepreneurship and lean innovation is that each idea should advance – or not – based upon its own merit. Each incubating team is bringing their own, unique idea to life. Each team works on a stand-alone program or business and must be measured separately from the others. Finally, the measures that make sense for each incubating idea will be much different from those which best measure the initiative itself.

With that as context, the simplest way to begin simplifying things is by thinking of what you will measure in terms of two primary classes:

1. Each incubating idea, program, or business inside the initiative (the performance of each idea)
2. The initiative itself (the performance of the initiative overall)

I will introduce the former and expand upon the latter, which is the focus of this chapter.

1. Measure Incubating Ideas

One of the most common mistakes I see people make when measuring nascent ideas is the application of the same measures they use for mature programs, products, solutions, and initiatives. This results in evaluation of nascent ideas in the same way their mature counterparts are assessed. It is often characterized by the familiar refrain of, "what's your five-year

CHAPTER 12   MEASURING PERFORMANCE AND IMPACT

revenue projection?" asked well before a team has even confirmed their potential customer has a problem. As I discussed in Chapter 2 (and elsewhere), that can spell the rapid demise of a new idea. Sometimes that happens because the out-of-sync measurement and evaluation erroneously lead to the conclusion the solution should not exist, and *sometimes* it happens because of the resulting heated argument that develops between those bringing the idea to life and those evaluating it.

A Continuum of Measurement

One of the tricky things about measuring an incubating idea is a by-product of the fact that the idea itself is evolving and maturing as it incubates. What enters your initiative might be a nascent idea without confirmation that it would even solve a problem anyone cares about (or has), and nothing more. Just an idea. But what exits may be a mature program or business idea that, apart from its size, resembles the organization's other mature programs or ideas. Why does this matter?

The difference between a new idea as it enters your initiative and the evolved form it will have when it exits may be nearly identical to the difference between the nascent idea and the organization's mature businesses or programs. Since it would be a mistake to measure the latter two the same way, it should be obvious that we cannot use the same measurements for an idea throughout its entire evolution. We need to apply a continuum of measurements that are best suited to each stage of the idea's life.

I like to think of these differences in measurements in terms of three different levels of maturity. An incubating team with a nascent idea might begin by capturing the results of experiments as **validated learning** to measure the early potential of their solution and to confirm they are on the right path. As they develop an early solution they might evolve to the "**innovation metrics**" (i.e., acquisition; activation; retention; referral; revenue) to measure its progress and traction. (These are sometimes referred to as "pirate metrics" due to the mnemonic AARRR.) By the time the solution is ready to exit, **metrics that resemble those of the mature businesses or programs** might be more appropriate and useful.

These measurement styles will almost certainly coexist, and there will not likely be abrupt movement from one style of measurement to another. Thus, expect to use a continuum of measures as each solution evolves.

Measuring Validated Learning

Most people are familiar with the kinds of measurements a mature business or program might use. Mature business measurement is its own discipline, with a plethora of books and entire university curricula available for those who wish to learn more. In contrast, innovation metrics are a lightweight way to measure an early solution's performance and traction. Even if you have never heard them referred to by this term, you may already be familiar with them. The five innovation metrics are:

1. **Acquisition:** When someone who was unaware of a solution becomes aware of, and interested in, it

2. **Activation:** When an interested party takes action, tries the solution, and has their first moment of joy as a result

3. **Retention:** The rate at which activated users repeatedly engage with the solution

4. **Revenue:** A measure of each time someone pays for a solution and how much is paid

5. **Referral:** The frequency with which existing users drive acquisition of new ones

There are many books and resources that expand on measuring ideas using the innovation metrics. I am a fan of how Ash Maurya explains this as a "Customer Factory Model" in his book, *Running Lean*.

CHAPTER 12   MEASURING PERFORMANCE AND IMPACT

 The style of measurement which most often raises questions is validated learning. Simply put, **validated learning is knowledge acquired through the outcome of an experiment**. Figure 12-2 shows an example of a very simple method of summarizing validated learning from a series of experiments.

Question	Hypothesis	Result
Do *potential customers* have this problem?	At least 60% of *target customers* are looking to solve this problem?	**Validated** 23 of 30 interviewed (77%)
How are *potential customers* working around the problem?	>30% of *target customers* are using manual workaround #1	**Validated** 12 of 30 interviewed (40%)
	>25% of *target customers* are doing nothing	**Not Validated** 2 of 30 interviewed (7%)
	>30% of *target customers* are using workaround #2	**Not Validated** 4 of 30 interviewed (13%)
	<10% of *target customers* are using Excel™	**Not Validated** 14 of 30 interviewed (47%)
Will decreasing the AI model evaluation time result in increased use of the service?	Decreasing evaluation time to below 1 second will increase click-through by 20%	**Validated** Click-through increased from 30 users/hr to 45 users/hr (+50%)
Will simplifying the user interface reduce errors and result in fewer abandons?	Reducing prompt text by 50% will decrease abandons by 50%	**Not Validated** Abandons declined from 5/hr to 3/hr (-40%)

Figure 12-2. *Validated hypothesis summary (illustrative)*

Figure 12-2 summarizes seven experiments, each of which were constructed to test a hypothesis related to one of four key questions. For example, the first question was regarding whether customers even have the problem. The related falsifiable hypothesis was that 60% of target customers the team interviewed would confirm that they have the problem and are looking to solve it. You can see from the "Result" column that 22 of the 30 people the team interviewed confirmed they had the problem and were looking to solve it, representing 77% of all participants. This hypothesis is therefore considered validated because the result met or, in this case, exceeded the expectation. That is a simple example, but there is more to consider.

You should not interpret results that are "Not Validated" as a failed experiment. That term indicates only that the result was different than was expected. Unexpected results often lead to discoveries which are *more* exciting than initially hypothesized. A non-validated result may also indicate that a hypothesis was directionally correct, though specifically inaccurate. This may be insignificant when numbers are small (e.g., expected 3 of 5, observed 3 of 6). Furthermore, non-validated results may be sufficient to justify action (e.g., expected 75% to have a problem, 70% have the problem). In such cases you may even consider the hypothesis to have been validated, or validated with explanation.

If you were presenting these results as evidence to an advisor, sponsor, or in a 3P review, the summary in Figure 12-2 might be sufficient; provided you address both what you learned from the results, and what next steps the team will take as a result. Alternatively, you might add that context to your summary, as shown in Figure 12-3. The summaries in Figures 12-2 and 12-3 are very simple but *can* be used effectively.

Question	Hypothesis	Result	Learning / Conclusion	Next Steps

Figure 12-3. *Validated hypotheses summary with learning and next steps (illustrative)*

Each individual incubating team and their idea will be unique. Fortunately, there are many books that expand on how to measure incubating ideas. Two of my favorites are Ash Maurya's *Running Lean* and Alistair Croll and Benjamin Yoskovitz' *Lean Analytics*.

Note The Toolkit contains sample tools and artifacts that might be of use when measuring incubating teams or participating in 3P reviews.

---

2. Measure the Initiative's Performance

An initiative consists of a collection of incubating ideas, each of which are likely to be at different stages of evolution at a given time. For example, Figure 12-4 depicts an initiative and 12 ideas, each represented by a lightbulb. Starting from the left, you can see that there are four ideas ready to pitch, two ideas in the Explore 1 stage, one idea in Explore 2, two ideas in Experiment 1, one in Experiment 2, and one in Transition 1. (The arrows mark the completion of each stage of incubation.)

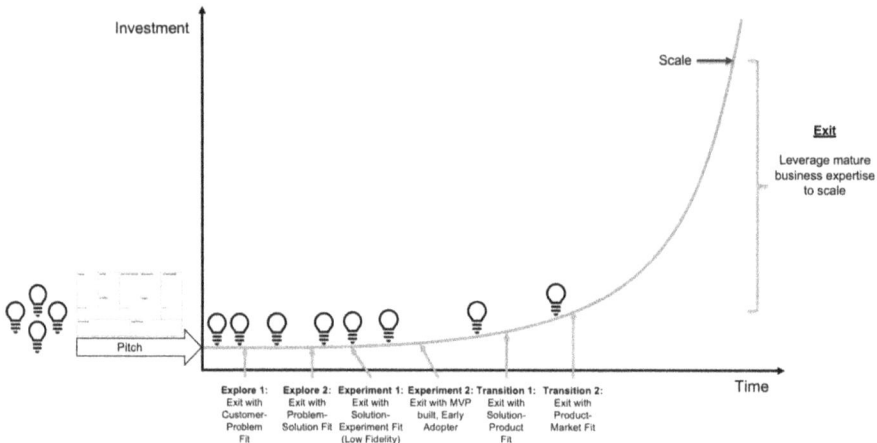

Figure 12-4. *An initiative with several incubating teams, each at a different stage of incubation*

Measuring Flow

An *initiative* achieves its primary objectives (e.g., delivering new product revenue; better serving citizens through innovative, new programs; maintaining organizational relevance) by helping individual ideas evolve through each of those stages of incubation. As such, **one of the most**

CHAPTER 12   MEASURING PERFORMANCE AND IMPACT

important indicators of whether an initiative is performing well is whether ideas are flowing through it at a reasonable pace. Whether the initiative's engine is running smoothly.

Not only is flow one of the initiative's most important measures, it is also one of the earliest available indicators. Flow can be measured from the moment the first pitch is accepted or the first idea begins incubating. To ensure there is no ambiguity, let's return to Figure 12-4 to illustrate what I mean when I use the term, flow.

Figure 12-4 tells a story, but it doesn't really tell much of a story. It shows there are several incubating solutions, and it shows that they are at different stages. While that is interesting, it does not demonstrate flow. It does not tell the reader *which* ideas are being incubated, nor does it communicate whether they are evolving, or whether they have pivoted back to a previous stage. Figure 12-5 begins to address this by breaking the ideas out a bit more and including a name and logo for each. You will also notice one idea has been selected for entry but has not yet entered the initiative ("Selected Idea").

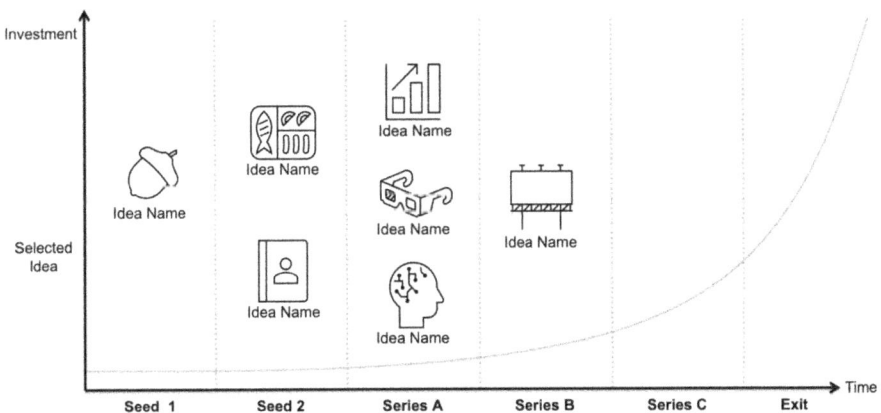

Figure 12-5. *Illustrative depiction of incubating teams and their current state*
Note: *The vertical position of the ideas does not indicate a level of investment. The "Investment" axis applies only to the investment curve*

Figure 12-5 is better. I can clearly understand which ideas are part of the initiative and their current state. There is value in that, and I have successfully used similar diagrams to communicate the current state of an initiative to executives, sponsors, and others. But it does *not* show whether the initiative's engine is working. It does not demonstrate flow. For example, how would I know whether an idea is evolving, or whether it entered the initiative at its current stage.

Figure 12-6 starts to provide a bit more information and begins to introduce flow. You can see that four of the ideas have advanced, as indicated by the arrows leading from a silhouette of the solution's icon (indicating its former position) to an icon indicating its current position. We know from the illustration's title that this indicates the movement which occurred in a specific quarter.

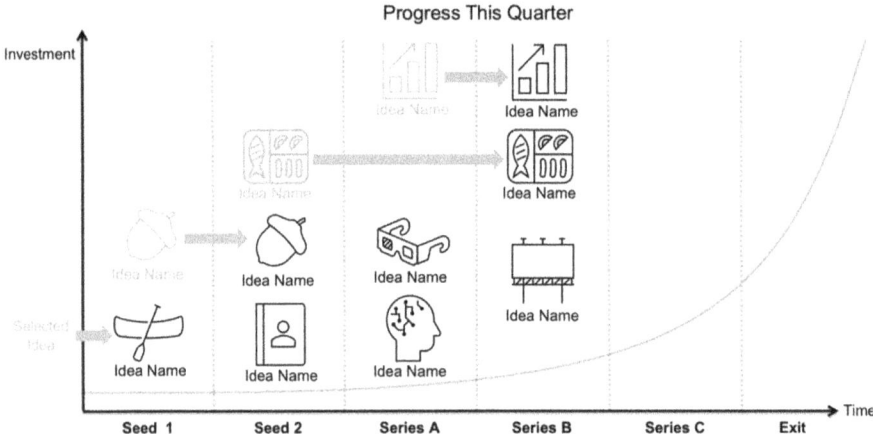

Figure 12-6. Illustrative depiction of the current state of ideas participating in a Seed-Series model and their progress over a period of time (quarterly progress shown)

We are getting closer. However, Figure 12-6 shows only forward progress. Teams sometimes discover the need to pivot, and that can result in the need to return to a previous stage.

Fortunately, this format can also be used to illustrate the impact of a pivot, which might necessitate repeating activities from a previous stage (Figure 12-7).

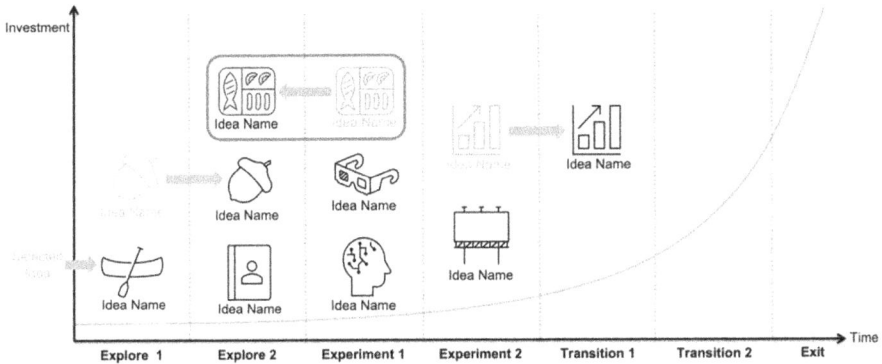

Figure 12-7. Illustrative depiction of the current state of ideas participating in an Explore–Experiment–Transition model and their progress over a period of time highlighting an idea that has pivoted back from Experiment 1 to Explore 2

We are making progress. Illustrations like those shown *could* be used to convey movement, and serve as the foundation for conversations about what moved, why, and which actions might be required as a result. But we are missing a key piece of information. How long has each idea been at each stage? There are several ways we could indicate that, from color changes, to highlights, to border shapes or shadows. The simplest solution might be to add the elapsed time an idea has been in its current stage above its icon, as shown in Figure 12-8 and Figure 12-9.

CHAPTER 12   MEASURING PERFORMANCE AND IMPACT

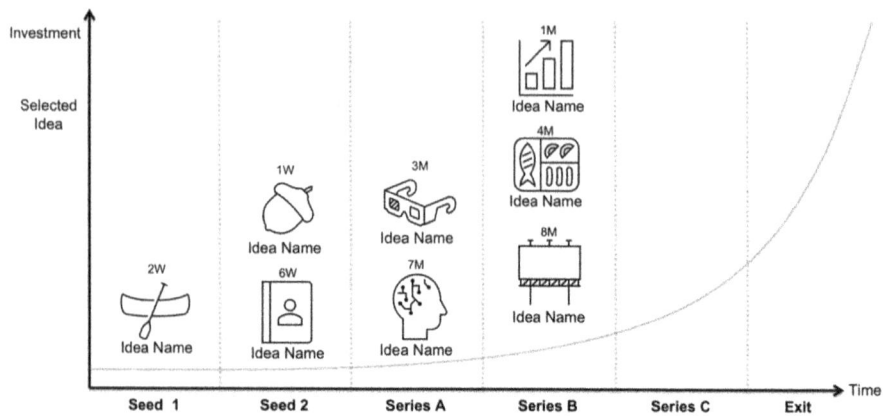

Figure 12-8. *Seed-series model status indicating the time a solution has been in its current stage in weeks (W) or months (M)*

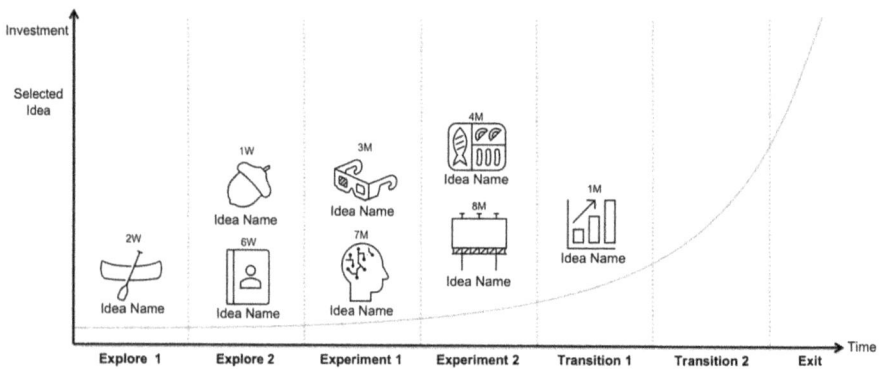

Figure 12-9. *Explore–Experiment–Transition model status indicating the time a solution has been in its current stage in weeks (W) or months (M)*

The example in Figure 12-10 combines these styles to help people understand how the initiative's engine is working at a high level. It shows where all incubating teams are in their evolution (each icon), how long they have been there (above the icon), what has recently transitioned to a new stage (silhouettes and arrows), when that transition occurred (date inside the arrow), and how much time the team spent in the previous stage (above the silhouette).

432

CHAPTER 12 MEASURING PERFORMANCE AND IMPACT

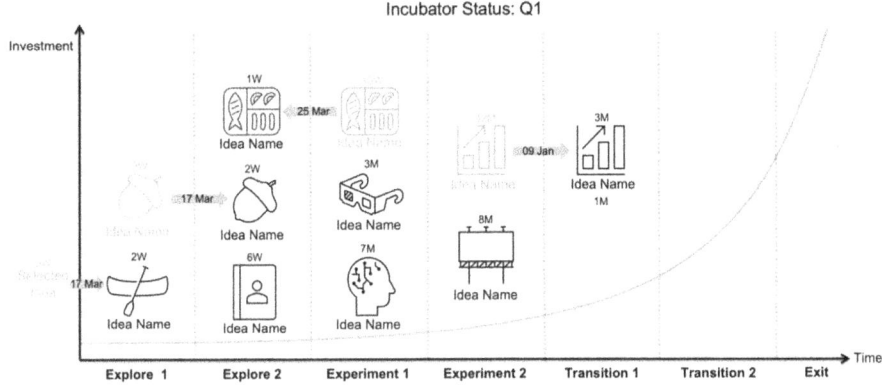

Figure 12-10. *Explore–Experiment–Transition model showing the current stage of all incubating teams and the flow that occurred within a specific time period (one quarter shown)*

I stepped through this primarily to ensure we have a common understanding of what I mean by flow. Hopefully you can see that idea/solution flow is a *key* indicator of the performance of these initiatives.

Incidentally, the style of communication used in Figures 12-5 through 12-10 can itself be useful. I have used various forms of these diagrams to convey the current state of ideas and/or flow to executives, stakeholders, and other interested people, and have found them to be quite effective. I have received very positive feedback when using the flow-style diagrams shown from 12-5 onward to communicate the performance of an initiative's engine to executives. When presenting to senior executives, I most often shared updates spanning from the last time I met the group to the day before the meeting, but quarterly and yearly versions were also effective.

But is that enough? (Spoiler: It isn't.) This format and style can be extremely effective in specific situations. However, we will need additional detail to analyze the initiative's performance more deeply. Furthermore, flow is not the only indicator of performance.

433

CHAPTER 12 MEASURING PERFORMANCE AND IMPACT

Initiative Performance Data

Here are some metrics to consider when measuring the performance and flow of your initiative:

1. **Promotion and communications metrics**
    - Number of events per period
        - For example, Fireside Chat, Town Hall, Lunch and Learn, newsletter...
        - Attendance or click-through
        - Referrals
    - Date of last promotional event
        - Length of time since last promotional event
            - Useful when troubleshooting why interest may be waning

2. **Pitch and entry metrics**
    - Number of pitch requests (applications to pitch)
        - Is this number increasing or decreasing?
            - May indicate loss of interest or the effectiveness of a focus or campaign
        - Date of each request
        - Origin demographics and diversity indicators (location, job function, gender...)
        - Date each pitch was deemed to be ready for a Pitch event

- Duration from submitted to readiness (Date Ready - Date Requested)
  - Longer duration could signify Initiative Team is overloaded or has issues and requires assistance or attention; may signify the pitch team is taking too long to respond to update requests
- Number of pitches
  - Is this number increasing or decreasing?
    - May indicate a change in the quality of pitches
    - May signal issues with Governance Team availability
  - Date of pitch
  - Length of time waiting to pitch (Pitch Date – Request Date)
    - Long delays could signify increased interest, insufficient attention to pitches by the Initiative Team, or lack of Governance Team availability (e.g., need to reschedule the pitch event day and time, need to re-engage the Governance Team)
  - Origin demographics and diversity indicators (location, job function, gender…)
- Number of ideas selected to enter
  - Date of each idea's selection
  - Date of Entry

- Time waiting to enter (Entry Date – Selection Date)
  - May indicate Initiative Team resource issues
  - May indicate long transition time requested by the team to which the incubating team members originally belonged
  - May indicate blockers and issues
    - Raises a question: Once resolved, can the Initiative Team prevent those from happening to subsequent incubating teams?
- Average time between selection and entry
  - Incubating teams waiting to enter with above-average wait times may require assistance or attention
  - Long delay may indicate Initiative Team is overloaded
  - May indicate a resource shortage
- Incubating team demographics and diversity indicators (location, job function, gender…)
- Is the number of entries increasing or decreasing?
  - May indicate quality of pitches
  - May signal issues with Governance Team availability
  - May signal intentional throttling

- Number of pitches redirected
  - Percentage of total pitches that were redirected
  - Number of redirect pitches that were resubmitted
- Number of pitches not accepted
  - Percentage of total pitches that were not accepted
- Pitch backlog
  - Number of pitch requests submitted, ready, and waiting to pitch
  - Average length of time between readiness and a pitch event (Date Pitched – Date Ready)
    - Longer durations could signify issues with the Initiative Team or with Governance Team availability

3. **Stage metrics**
   - Number of teams at each stage (e.g., Seed 1, Explorc 1)
   - Date each team entered each stage
   - Date each team exited each stage
   - Team duration in stage (Date Stage Exited – Date Stage Entered)
   - Total investment in each team at each stage

- Average duration in a stage
  - Over time, will indicate whether a team may be in a specific stage too long and might require assistance or attention
  - Too little time in a stage might prompt the Governance Team to be diligent in their Transition Request questions
  - May be used as a predictor of duration for future teams once sufficient data has been gathered
  - May be an indicator of whether the initiative's teams are learning fast enough, and direct the Initiative Team to act if they are languishing
- Investment
  - Average investment in each stage
    - May be used as a predictor of future stage investment requirements once sufficient data has been gathered
    - Can be used to estimate how many teams can incubate concurrently when planning
    - Can be an indicator of whether an incubating team is overspending (underspending can also be a signal)
  - Average number of people in each stage at stage entry
    - May be used as a predictor of future stage investment requirements once sufficient data has been gathered

CHAPTER 12   MEASURING PERFORMANCE AND IMPACT

- Average number of people in each stage at stage exit
  - May be used as a predictor of future stage investment requirements once sufficient data has been gathered
- Pivots
  - The number of times each incubating team pivots and must move back to an earlier stage
  - Average number of pivots (all teams)
  - The number of stages a pivoting team had to regress (e.g., Experiment 1 to Explore 1 = -2 stages)
  - Average stage regression (all teams)
- Pauses
  - Number of paused teams (shut downs)
  - Date of a team's pause
  - Stage an idea was at (e.g., Experiment 1) when paused
  - Total incubation duration for each paused team (Shut Down Date – Entry Date)
    - Can be an indicator of how efficiently non-viable ideas are identified
    - Can be a predictor of when ideas might reach a key inflection point
  - Average duration for paused teams
  - Total lifetime cost of each paused team

- Average lifetime cost of a pause
- Team size at pause
- Number of team members successfully given new assignments
  - Duration of time between exit and reassignment for each reassigned person
  - Total cost of bench time per pause
  - Average duration of time between exit and reassignment
  - Average total cost of bench time per pause
  - Percentage of people from paused initiative teams successfully reassigned
- Number of people who could not be reassigned (should be 0!)
  - Percentage of people from paused teams who were not reassigned
- Number of people waiting reassignment
- Number of pauses at each stage
- Percentage of ideas paused at each stage
- Total number of pauses
- Percentage of ideas that participated in the initiative that paused

• Exits
  - Number of successful exits
  - Date of each team's exit

- Duration of incubation through exit (Exit Date – Entry Date)
- Average duration for a successful exit
- Total lifetime cost of each exit
- Average lifetime cost of an exit
- Team size at exit
- Exit to Pause ratio (Number of Exits/Number of Pauses)
- Percentage success rate (Number of Exits/Number of Entries)
- Loaded cost of a successful exit
    - (Avg. Lifetime Cost of Pause * Number of Pauses per Exit) + (Avg. Cost of a Successful Exit)

This data enables analysis of an individual incubating team's performance compared to others, while also enabling analysis of the initiative's performance and flow overall against predicted and desired levels of performance.

When analyzing an individual team, these measures can be used to identify when that team *might* be spending too much time at a specific stage, or spending more money than expected. Be careful when analyzing individual teams in this way. This type of analysis provides useful indicators of performance, but it may not tell you everything.

For example, a team may be incubating an idea that requires a specialized, expensive piece of equipment. That added expense might cause their total expenses for a stage to be legitimately larger than most other teams. If everyone agreed to that expense during the Transition Request ceremony, then that higher expense should not be an issue.

The type of variance discussed above does not usually cause problems. However, people can forget about agreements like those, especially over time, so caution everyone to use these as indicators of interest as opposed to absolutes. In addition, some minor variance should be expected in virtually every incubation, so expect all teams to be somewhat above or below averages at specific points in time.

Analyzing this data in aggregate can deliver some very interesting insights. First, it can tell you how your initiative is performing compared to stated objectives and/or forecasts. For example, if you set a goal that every team should get through both Explore 1 and Explore 2 in three-to-four months and the average for your initiative is six-to-seven months, you might want to investigate that discrepancy and determine whether you need to address a need or issue, or update your forecast.

Finally, one of the benefits of keeping data at this level of detail is that it will be outstanding input for goal setting and financial forecasting. You will have detailed historical data on how long each stage takes, how many people it requires, and how much it costs. You can combine that with information about the current stages of incubating teams, and with the teams' own forecasts, to predict which teams will be at which stages in which portions of the following fiscal year.

Equipped with the knowledge of how much each stage costs, and how long each team will be in each stage, you will be able to create a realistic financial forecast. Once you have done that you can determine how many new ideas you will be able to accept in the next year (i.e., understand remaining funding), how far they will advance, and what they will cost. Then, you can use all that data as input when setting goals or OKRs.

Automating Data Capture

One way of collecting the data required for this type of analysis is to simply have someone keep track of it in a spreadsheet. It may seem like a lot of information, but I have done it and it's not as onerous as you might think.

However, automating the capture of most of this type of information, and augmenting that with comments or context can be a game changer. Automatically collecting data:

- Saves the time and effort that would normally be required to collect and record the data, which can be of *significant* benefit as your initiative grows and things really begin to move

- Is less error-prone

- Will result in more accurate data

- Can provide instantaneous update and availability of information, as new data can be shared the instant it is recorded

- May open new doors with regard to how you can make it available to those who need it

Let me share an example where all these benefits were achieved by utilizing a system that was already available. One team I worked with had implemented an off-the-shelf agile management software solution. The Initiative Team imported all of their stage checklists into that solution's Kanban function. This drove several immediate benefits:

- The Initiative Team could maintain and update the template checklists electronically.

- A central repository delivered a single version, and change logs and history protected the integrity of the information.

- Changes and updates to stage checklists were immediately available to everyone.

443

- Incubating teams entering a new stage could instantly activate an instance of the latest checklist, and customize it if necessary to meet their unique requirements.

- Every incubating team's updated checklist was immediately available to everyone for review the instant they created it (the incubating team, the Initiative Team, the Governance Team…).

- Incubating teams could leverage the system to keep notes regarding experiments (if they desired), and coordinate their activities by using the system to keep track of when they were working on an item, who owned it, and when it was completed.

This was obviously beneficial and convenient for incubating teams and others in an operational sense, but what does it have to do with measuring flow? There's more:

- As teams completed checklist items, the system automatically logged the date and time of completion and shared the updated status to all teams.

- Advisory Team, Governance Team, and Initiative Team members could conveniently see what an incubating team was working on, when they started working on it, what was completed, and what was left to be done in the stage – without disrupting the teams (this saved a lot of time and reduced unnecessary interruptions that may have interfered with creative flow).

- When all relevant items were complete and a team received approval to transition to the next stage, their new status was reflected in the system's dashboard, and the date and time was logged.

CHAPTER 12   MEASURING PERFORMANCE AND IMPACT

The data was collected largely as a by-product of the incubating team's activity, and it was immediately available to everyone. We made the easy-to-understand dashboard available to even the most senior sponsors and executives, and posted it with an easy-to-remember link to an internal site (e.g., https://<initiative-name>status.<their-domain-siffix>). It was a hit. The incubating teams did not have to waste time answering basic status questions, the Initiative Team did not have to scramble to create reports, and the executives and sponsors appreciated how simple it was to access the system.

The transparency this system delivered may have been the greatest benefit. No misconceptions. No lack of understanding the current state, nor concerns it was being hidden. Complete transparency. Complete trust.

Figure 12-11 provides an illustrative example of what the dashboard looked like, matching the status of the incubating ideas shown in Figure 12-8. Each of the boxes in the dashboard provided key information about one incubating idea such as the name of the incubation, its leader, the idea's high-level concept, its technology domain, its current stage, when it entered the initiative, when it entered its current stage, how far along it was in the achievement of its stage objectives, and other relevant information and comments. Incubation team leaders could also add highlights, such as key milestones, whether they had active users or paying customers, or whether they had received patents for their work. It seems like a lot, but it was presented in an efficient and powerful way, using very few words.

445

CHAPTER 12   MEASURING PERFORMANCE AND IMPACT

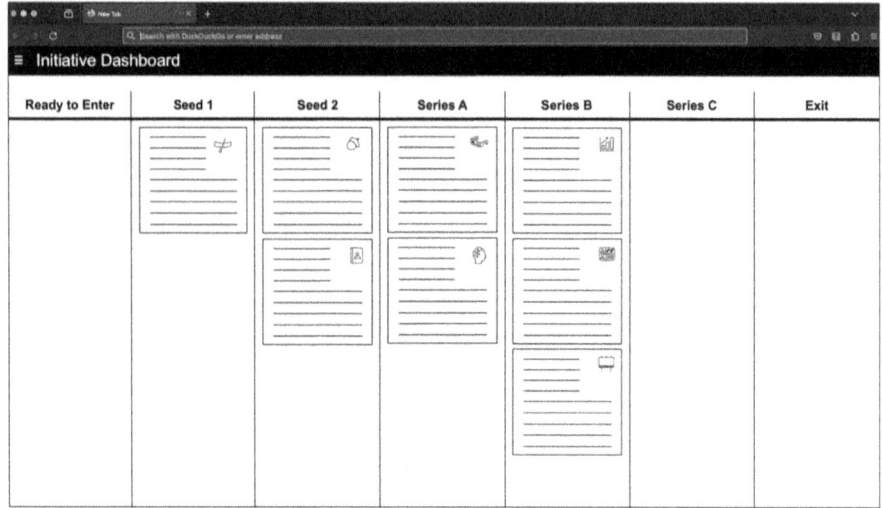

Figure 12-11. Initiative dashboard (illustrative)

In addition to what you see in Figure 12-11, users could click on any of the idea's cards and would be presented with more information, including access to the stage checklist the team was using and the status of each item in their list. It was better than we had hoped. It was operationally useful, captured much of the data as the work was being done, drove transparency, and collected flow and performance data that could be used in other forms of reporting.

Don't worry if you don't have access to a system like this. You can keep the data in Excel, Numbers, Sheets, or any other modeling tool you are comfortable with. I've used several, and each has its advantages.

Graphics are nice, but sometimes even a simple table might be all you need. At one point in one initiative, an executive team wanted a brief summary of what was incubating in the initiative, and the ability to view a bit more detail about each incubating solution if they felt the need to learn more. They wanted this added to a regular briefing document they received, so a simple table such as is shown in Figure 12-12 was all that was required.

CHAPTER 12 MEASURING PERFORMANCE AND IMPACT

Pitches (FY)	Entry	Seed 1	Seed 2	Series A	Series B	Series C	Exits and Pauses (FY)
12	1	2	3	3	0	0	0

Name	Description	Technology	Current Stage	Entered Stage	Entered Initiative	Patents Filed	Next Steps / Comments
Amazing Idea	AI engine for medical diagnoses	AmazingAI GPT, Neural Net, LLM7	Series A	January 2099	September 2098	5	450 active users, 91% retention rate after 6 months, transition to Series B targeted for February 2100
----	----	----	----	----	----	----	----
----	----	----	----	----	----	----	----
----	----	----	----	----	----	----	----

Figure 12-12. Illustrative status update

Whether you choose state of the art graphics and graphs, traditional dashboards, or more standard tables and sheets, make sure they communicate to your stakeholders in their language and effectively bring out the message(s) you need to deliver. As with other areas of specialty, don't be afraid to ask for help. Your Strategy, Marketing, or Communications colleagues will likely have experience in this area and can give you feedback, or perhaps even some assistance and direction.

Putting It All Together

Let's look at one more example of measuring performance before we move on to a discussion of value and effectiveness. When discussing what to collect, I referred to some average calculations for key areas such as:

- Average stage duration per team
- Average number of people per team per stage
- Average total cost per stage

If we were evaluating a fictitious team with the following characteristics:

- Current stage: Explore 2
- Time in stage (to date): 18 weeks

- Expenses to date: $100,000
- Number of people: 2

If the initiative's metrics included:

- Average Explore 2 duration per team: 14 weeks
- Average number of people per team per stage: 4
- Average total cost per stage: $174,000

Our system, our spreadsheet, or our people should be raising at least one red flag. This team has exceeded the average Explore 2 duration across all teams by 30% (18 weeks vs. 14 weeks), *and* they have not yet completed the stage. This alone would be ample cause for inquiry, and reason to ask whether the team needed assistance. Furthermore, they are currently running under the average budget, but they have only two team members (as opposed to the average of four). This suggests they are likely over budget for non-personnel expenses. Those should be tracked separately, so that should be simple to verify.

I want to emphasize that this type of analysis is not about metaphorically clobbering the members of an initiative team over their heads with a red pen. It is about identifying when they might be off track and helping them to succeed. Furthermore, we might investigate this specific case and determine there is a reason for their team size and expense level, and that they are actually on track. They may be working with expensive technology. They may have to perform regulatory testing which adds time at that stage. There are a host of potential justifiable reasons.

Be careful to interpret such anomalies only as signals of interest, and diligently investigate their cause. Better still, notice how the teams are trending *before* any red flags are raised, help them to get on track if necessary, and transparently communicate that these indicators might be exceeded to stakeholders so no escalation is required when it happens.

In addition, be sure to capture – and highlight – foreseeable anomalies in the incubating teams' stage budgets and plans before they transition to the next stage to avoid the need to address this type of anomaly as an escalation or emergency.

Performance Metrics and OKRs

I find initiative performance metrics frequently useful when setting OKRs. You may recall their use when discussing a fictitious OKR in Chapter 8. In the example shown in Figure 8-2, we set out to achieve the objective of launching an initiative. Amongst that objective's key results are adding two incubations, moving from three to five active incubating ideas, and accepting 15 pitches, the number we believed was required to find the two ideas. Both of those metrics are initiative performance and flow metrics.

Using performance and flow metrics in OKRs early in the initiative is an excellent way to help focus on the things that matter most. Not only does that type of focus help prime the initiative, it also helps identify your initiative's minimum requirements in other areas. In the preceding example, since I know I need to accept pitches, I know I will need to have all the material necessary for pitches ready, have a trained facilitator, have a venue booked (physical or virtual), and have a Governance Team or selection team ready by the date of the first pitch event. I also know selected teams will be entering the Explore stages by February, so I need to be ready with the material and infrastructure required for that stage (e.g., entry and stage checklists, training, resources…) before then.

I have also seen aggregated flow metrics used effectively in OKRs. For example, transitions into Seed 1 and Seed 2 could be added to a single "Incubation Entries" key result, Transitions from any stage of the Incubation Phase to any stage of the Startup Phase could be counted as "Transitions to Startup." The same could be done for the Explore, Experiment, or Transition phases. Aggregation of metrics at this level

CHAPTER 12   MEASURING PERFORMANCE AND IMPACT

might make the most sense for a yearly key result. For example, you may have one or more flow-related Key results like these in a fiscal year OKR:

- Host 25 Pitch Events
- Transition seven ideas to the Incubation Phase
- Transition four incubating teams to the Startup Phase
- Exit one solution

Actively watching performance and flow metrics is always useful and can help identify areas that need attention early in the life of your initiative. It can also surface things that are going well so you can leverage your success.

That's enough about the performance and flow of the initiative's engine. While a healthy engine is essential to the success of an initiative, it must also drive the impact it was created to deliver, and it must drive value. So let's review at impact-related metrics.

3. Measure Impact and Value

Why are you doing this? There was some impetus for you to expend all the effort required to create an initiative like this. There are countless reasons people launch these initiatives. Some of the reasons I most commonly encounter are:

- To build a pipeline for future revenue
- To deliver more modern, efficient government services and programs
- To open a new market or lead in a new market
- To extend existing product lines
- To address a competitive threat

- To counter unfavorable competitive messages or publicity
- To compensate for shrinking mature markets
- To create an innovative culture
- To increase the performance of specific teams (e.g., manufacturing, engineering...)
- To create a favorable market impression
- To develop a brand glow or brand halo
- To disrupt legacy product lines (competitors' and their own)
- To change team attitudes regarding innovation
- To demonstrate a commitment to creativity and innovation
- To send a message it's OK to try new things
- To teach teams effective habits

Some of these, like the first two in the list, are obvious. Others may be less so. Every organization has its own needs and priorities, and they are not always the most obvious in the list. Fortunately, you should have a very good idea of the value and impact expected from your initiative because you confirmed those things during your assessment. Your organization's leaders may even have decided upon the most important of them before you started.

You may have noticed a stark difference between some of the examples in the preceding list and the performance metrics discussed in the previous section. While the performance and flow metrics were all quantitative metrics, the impact and value metrics above are a mix of quantitative *and* qualitative measures.

CHAPTER 12 MEASURING PERFORMANCE AND IMPACT

Quantitative metrics are typically easily understood. A product created in the incubator is made available for sale. People buy it. The money they pay is revenue, and it can be counted. A federal government program targets delivering ten million dollars in aid. The aid is delivered through the solution created in the initiative, and it can be counted. A provincial government wants to deliver one million new licenses electronically through the solution created by an incubating team. The licenses are delivered can be counted. It's very straightforward.

But what about the qualitative measures. The "squishy stuff." That can be a bit more challenging, but it's never impossible. It just involves a bit of creativity and – most importantly – an agreement from everyone (stakeholders, executives, the Governance Team, the Initiative Team) regarding what will be measured and how.

Given the nature of these metrics it is a bit more difficult for me to enumerate *all* the things you might potentially measure. I will share some of those I most commonly encounter, and then give some illustrative examples of how some of the "squishier" things might be measured.

When thinking about measuring the value and impact of your initiative, consider:

- **Value delivered via the government program associated with your solution**
    - For example, aid delivered, number of service events, number of passports created or delivered, number of licenses delivered, reduction in the cost of a program as the result of your solution...
    - Value delivered/cost of the incubation

- ROI: Total value delivered by an exit/loaded cost of a successful exit
  - Loaded cost of a successful exit = (Avg. Lifetime Cost of Pause * Number of Pauses per Exit) + Avg. Cost of an Exit
- Average value delivered from all solutions/average cost of incubation
- Average value delivered from all solutions/loaded cost of a successful exit

- **Revenue from solutions or services created via the initiative**
  - Revenue/cost of the incubation
  - ROI: Revenue/loaded cost of a successful exit
  - Average revenue delivered from all solutions/average cost of incubation
  - Average revenue delivered from all solutions/loaded cost of a successful exit

- **Number of solutions exited to mature lines of business**
  - Revenue realized by the mature line of business
  - Changes in expenses realized by the mature line of business
  - Average revenue realized by mature lines of business
  - Average changes in expenses realized by mature lines of business

- **Number of product line extensions exited**
  - Changes in revenue due to the addition of the solution
  - Changes in expenses due to the addition of the solution
  - Average revenue change for all exited product line extensions
  - Average changes in expenses for all exited product line extensions
- **Technology exits**
  - For example, number of components that did not exit as stand-alone products, programs, or services but will be embedded in other solutions
  - Revenue or expense reduction as the result of a single exit
  - Average revenue or expense reduction across all exits
- **Exit metrics**
  - Number of successful exits
  - Date of each team's exit
  - Efficiency: Duration of incubation through exit (Exit Date – Entry Date)
  - Average duration for a successful exit
  - Total lifetime cost of each exit
  - Average lifetime cost of an exit
  - Team size at exit

- Exit to Pause ratio (number of Exits/number of Pauses)
- Percentage success rate (number of Exits/number of Entries)
- Loaded cost of a successful exit
- (Avg. Lifetime Cost of Pause * Number of Pauses per Exit) + Avg. Cost of an Exit)

- **Reduction in committed bets**
  - Waste reduction realized from not funding committed bets

- **Diversity of incubating teams**
  - Various dimensions (e.g., race, gender, location, occupation, seniority, age, education, line of business...)

- **Employee opinion survey metrics**
  - For example, perception the organization is innovative, operates with excellence, is modern, can create with speed, morale...; number of people who would recommend a friend or relative work for the company

- **Employee performance**
  - Improved performance and execution from people who exited the initiative and returned to their department or business unit
  - Promotions and awards to past initiative participants
  - Overall performance improvements in selected areas deemed to be influenced by the initiative

- **Patents**
  - Number of applications
  - Number filed with the patent office
  - Number of patents granted
- **Improvement of other programs and initiatives**
  - For example, how well does the initiative provide input to, or consume output from, other initiatives like scientific research, applied research, InnerSource, publications...
- **Improvements to the broader organization**
  - Adoption of new processes, procedures, technology, or tools developed or adapted by the initiative's teams (e.g., lightweight procurement, ability to accept online transactions...)
  - Updates to, or modernization of policy, procedure, or regulation resulting from incubating team activities (e.g., security assessment, privacy policies...)
- **Adoption of the initiative's best practices by other groups and initiatives**
  - For example, lean approaches, investment model, specific procedures, lean meetings...
- **Press attention and publicity**
  - Number of interviews
  - Number of positive or negative mentions
  - Attendance at press events

- Speaking invitations
- Attendee feedback

- **Brand contribution (also referred to as "brand halo" or "brand glow")**
  - Press mentions (counts and quotes)
  - Analyst mentions (counts and quotes)
  - Interview requests
  - Web site impressions
  - Customer interest
  - Customer survey responses

Value Migration

As with the performance metrics, some of these impact metrics will be easy to measure and will be useful early in the life of the initiative. Others may take time to achieve meaningful values, and some may be zero or unmeasurable early on. The most obvious of the latter are revenue or value delivery (the first two items in the impact metrics list). It is a brutal irony that these are also the most sought-after metrics, and the most frequent subject of sponsor and executive inquiry.

These will be top of mind even if you have obtained agreement and understanding that they will take some time to develop. Perhaps more time than most, if not all, other measures. As discussed in Chapter 9, you will need to ensure executives, leaders, stakeholders, and champions understand how – and when – these metrics are expected to evolve.

In Chapter 9, I provided an example of a value migration map as a means to accomplish this. I will not repeat that entire discussion here, but I would like to augment it slightly in the

CHAPTER 12   MEASURING PERFORMANCE AND IMPACT

context of measures and commitments. Figure 12-13 shows a value migration map with additional guidance. It provides a clear statement of the planned migration each fiscal year. Such guidance can be included with metrics and in executive and sponsor briefing material, and both the graphic and the explanation can be updated yearly to maintain a sliding window as the initiative evolves.

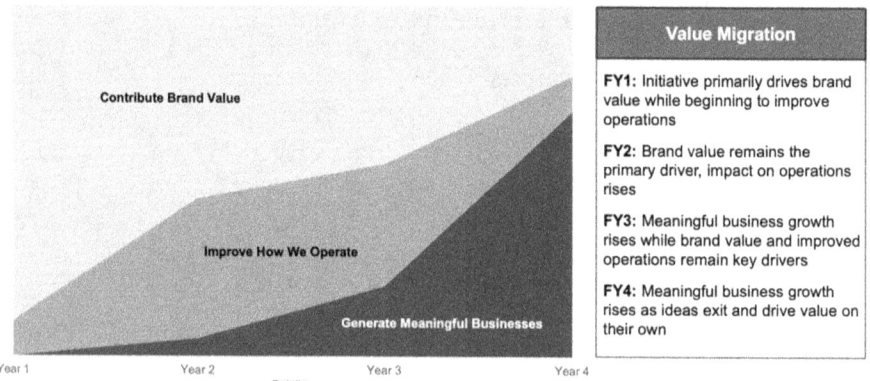

Figure 12-13. Value migration model with commitments (illustrative)

Putting It All Together

An initiative like this presents a host of opportunities for measurements. What's ironic about this is that there is sometimes a risk metrics will make the simple complex. Take the time to test your metrics, measures, and dashboards and make sure they are truly understood at every necessary level. Leverage the executives and leaders on the initiative's Advisory Team and Governance Team to provide you with candid feedback, and ask them for their own ideas. Once you do that, you should be able to make the complex simple.

CHAPTER 12   MEASURING PERFORMANCE AND IMPACT

For example, Figure 12-14 combines some of the complex performance and impact metrics into a powerful "model-at-a-glance" that can be used to communicate the value of the program, set expectations, and assess the performance of an incubating team at a high level.

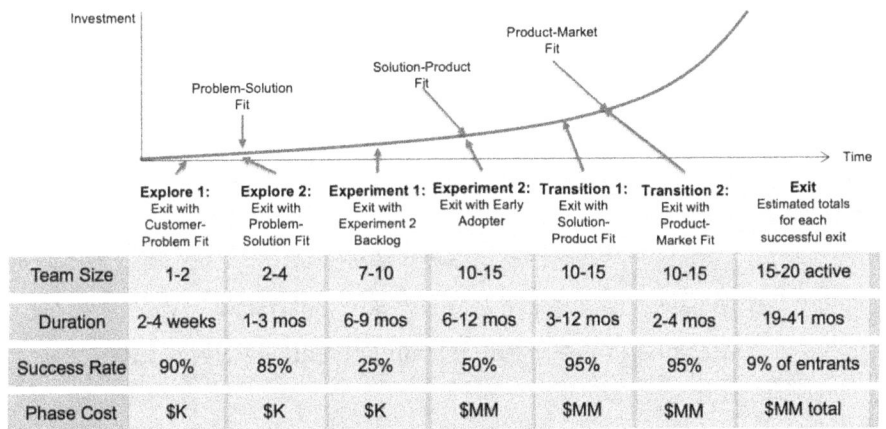

Figure 12-14. Initiative model-at-a-glance (illustrative)

Additional Considerations

Consider the following as you prepare your initiative's metrics and measures:

- The most effective metrics drive action:
    - For each metric ask what action you would take if it were higher than, lower than, or as, expected, or if it did not change.
        - If none of those states would prompt action, reconsider the metric's usefulness.

- Bias to transparency: Share everything (internally) unless there is a reason it cannot or should not be shared.

- Leverage the executives and leaders on the initiative's Advisory Team and Governance Team to:
  - Identify measures they require
  - Provide you with candid feedback and guidance regarding the presentation of metrics

- Collect everything you can.
  - You can stop collecting any time.
  - It is much easier to archive or delete data you do not need than to forensically recreate data you did not collect.

- Start collecting data as early as possible, even prior to the initiative's launch, if possible.

- Think through the stories you will need to tell about your initiative, its performance, and its value, and collect metrics that support those stories.

- Gain agreement on how qualitative metrics will be measured, and confirm the measurements are effective early on.

- Capture as much information as possible automatically and as a by-product of work.

- Don't wait until launch to think about measures, get ahead of it, create some mock-ups, and get agreement on your first generation (minimum viable measures) as early as you can.

- Don't be afraid to ask for help: People with experience in areas like strategy, communication, marketing, product management, press or analyst relations, business development, or finance may be able to help you determine the best way to measure, present, or visualize your information.

Summary

Initiatives of this nature provide a broad range of potential measures. Each measure tells a different story, and each may be more, or less, useful at different times in your initiative's life. Don't be overwhelmed by the breadth of possibilities.

To simplify things, think about the two major targets of measurements in your initiative: (1) The solutions incubating inside the initiative; (2) The initiative itself. Measure each solution across a continuum ranging from validated learning, through innovation metrics, through metrics used by their more mature cousins. Think about the initiative in terms of its performance and flow (its engine) and its impact and effectiveness (its value).

Realize that while an initiative's performance related metrics will be quantitative and easier to measure, its impact metrics will include both quantitative *and* qualitative elements. Qualitative measurements can be tricky and subjective, so get agreement on which will be measured and how. Don't be afraid to add a few new ones if you find them, but ask for confirmation of their value once you have them.

Well-selected metrics will not only help you deliver a better, more impactful initiative, they will ensure that people *know* the initiative is impactful and worthwhile. Transparency in their delivery will build confidence and trust in both the initiative and its team.

CHAPTER 12 MEASURING PERFORMANCE AND IMPACT

Measurement leads to learning, and learning leads to improvement. Continuous learning and improvement – a key lean entrepreneurship principle – is the topic of our final chapter.

CHAPTER 13

Continuous Learning and Improvement

Congratulations! You've launched your initiative. You're helping lead your organization into the future and enabling people to chase their creative dreams. Regardless of the size and scope of your initiative, it's no small feat. You've had to rally a diverse team around a vision; and I am confident you've had to slay a few dragons during the journey. But you made it, and it's perfect. Right?

As the well-known saying goes, "nobody's perfect." (Except my Mom.) I'm sure you may have begun to realize that there are a few things you would like to fine-tune at the very least. Furthermore, even *if* your initiative was perfect when you launched it, things change. Organizations change, needs change, political climates change, markets change, objectives change, and people find new opportunities where the application of their initiatives would be valuable.

Even if none of that happens, execution can drift over time. We need to be diligent. We need to regularly take the pulse of the initiative and understand how it is performing and whether it is contributing the value we expect. Then we need to adapt based upon what we learn (Figure 13-1).

CHAPTER 13   CONTINUOUS LEARNING AND IMPROVEMENT

In this Chapter

Continuous Learning and Improvement:

1. Retrospectives
2. Proactive learning
3. Leadership development
4. Summits and Off-sites
5. Introspection
6. Role clarification and alignment
7. Incremental learning

Figure 13-1. *What's in this chapter*

The measures you've captured will help direct you to some of the areas that would benefit from attention and adaptation. That's a start. Sometimes those measures will point you toward a simple remedy. For example, if your backlog of ready pitches is long and the average time between a pitch's readiness and the relevant pitch event is too long, maybe you need to add some pitch events to relieve the backlog or add more pitches to each event. Other times the metrics will direct you to a more systemic issue that may require fundamental changes to your initiative.

As discussed in the previous chapter, continuous learning and adaptation based upon measures is critical. But the metrics alone won't be enough; and they won't make a difference if you don't act on them.

Beyond the Metrics

Having thoughtful metrics is great. The incubating teams' metrics and the initiative's performance and impact metrics should drive great value for you and your initiative. But most metrics have shortcomings, and many won't tell you *everything* you need to know.

CHAPTER 13 CONTINUOUS LEARNING AND IMPROVEMENT

There are some things that will require you to explore more of the "squishy stuff" I discussed in the previous chapter. Furthermore, metrics will often tell you where to look, but not the root cause of their state or the action required to address any issues or opportunities they bring to light. They also won't directly tell you that you should be paying attention to something that you haven't been measuring.

I don't want to leave you with the false impression that metrics are useless. I've leveraged them to make enormous improvements in transformational initiatives. My point is only that we must think beyond the metrics to get the complete picture.

We also need to consider the human element, and the value of dialog over numbers, or even written comments. Consider, for example, a satisfaction survey of an initiative's participants. In it we could ask all participants to rate the initiative's services, resources, team… anything we wish. We could also ask for written comments and explanations.

A brief pulse survey of this nature can be extremely useful and informative. I've run these types of surveys many times and received great value from them. However, there are some things a survey of this nature won't tell you, and there are some risks. Some of the potential pitfalls with surveys are:

- They don't always tell the team running them everything they need to know.

- They do not (usually) provide answers to questions you did not ask.

- This is often where great insight is missed.

- Some people do not like to complete surveys.

- Some people are concerned survey responses will be used against them or their team.

- Some people game surveys (this might be their most risky drawback).

465

- The results *can* be misleading.
- Communication is asynchronous and there is no opportunity for rich dialog.
- Removing anonymity to allow for follow-up can impact their results.
- They can feel impersonal (especially in our context).
- They may not provide an opportunity to strengthen relationships and trust.

Again I feel the need to clarify that I have nothing against surveys. They can be very useful. Though we need to understand what they are good for, and where their shortcomings are. Let me share a few real-world examples where I have encountered issues with survey style metrics and a different technique told a more complete story.

Early in my career, I was collecting satisfaction surveys following a customer training session. The session had gone extremely well, and the customers were unanimously giving five out of five (5/5) marks on every measure. I was standing near one person who was completing the survey. They made the unsolicited comment that they thought the session was outstanding, but they were only going to give four out of five marks (4/5) because "nobody is perfect." (That's a pretty high bar.) That didn't really move the overall result, but it made me pay more careful attention to this type of tool. I'll bet there are some people who always give five out of five (5/5) even if they were disappointed, and I have since then run across people who always or usually give three out of five (3/5) to avoid conflict.

The impact of this type of behavior is probably inconsequential in the preceding examples, though that's not a given. Regardless, they serve as a cautionary tale at the very least. Later I encountered a more impactful example.

CHAPTER 13   CONTINUOUS LEARNING AND IMPROVEMENT

We were reviewing employee satisfaction surveys to look for areas we could improve and we noticed that the sentiment of one group – which had previously been extremely good – dropped noticeably. It didn't make sense. The group's morale seemed great, and they were performing exceptionally well. Their leader was very skilled and well liked. I had to look deeper. I had to visit the team.

In conversations with team members, they told me things were great. They were happy. The work was challenging and satisfying. They were growing. They liked their pay and benefits. I was even more confused than before I visited. I finally asked the right question, and the answer was surprising.

The team members *were* happy with everything. They had given lower ratings as a *preventative* measure. They thought if they rated things high conditions might get worse. That a good rating would lead to devolution. They were also sandbagging ratings for things like compensation or benefits, for example, because they felt marking those high would result in no increases in the following years, and in some cases because they thought the low ratings would result in compensation increases. This trended across an entire group.

The irony in this case is that some of their responses might have led to adjustments that they may not have liked. Fortunately, we asked the second order questions and were able to take appropriate actions, both to help the team understand we were looking for truthful and accurate responses to the surveys, and so we could address the things that were actually unsatisfactory.

In this example **retrospective analysis beyond the quantitative research** (the survey ratings) and the few opportunities the survey provided for comments **led us to the right answer, which led us to the right action**. The remainder of this chapter will focus on other ways in which you can augment your metrics and drive continuous learning and improvement.

CHAPTER 13   CONTINUOUS LEARNING AND IMPROVEMENT

1. Retrospectives

In my opinion retrospectives are one of the most powerful and valuable tools available to people leading transformative initiatives of any type. During a retrospective a group of people reflect on past and current events and/or performance within a well-defined context, analyze what has been going well, and identify areas where additional learning or improvement are advised or warranted. Good retrospectives deliver specific, actionable learning, and can be the cornerstone of continuous learning and improvement for any team.

Retrospectives:

- Foster continuous learning and improvement.
- Enable teams to rapidly learn from experience and course correct.
- Prevent exacerbation of issues and missteps.
- Minimize wasted time and resources.
- Enable participants to learn from one-another.
- Provide an opportunity to recognize great performance and team contribution.
- Identify areas of excellence which can be further leveraged.
- Surface areas for improvement that may not be widely known or understood.
- Proactively surface potential areas of conflict.
- Maintain and improve team cohesion and morale.

There are many different forms of retrospectives, but even the most basic can deliver all these benefits. The most basic of these, captured in the Toolkit as a "Classic Retrospective," follows a simple formula:

1. Gather.
2. Align on scope.
3. Discuss what went well.
4. Identify areas for improvement.
5. Identify actions to improve the identified areas.

The Toolkit includes an agenda for an hour-long classic retrospective, but they can be conducted in as little as ten or 30 minutes, depending upon the topic and the facilitation style used. In some cases teams omit step five from the ceremony and return to it later. For example, when short on time with a group you may not be able to convene often, you might use this approach to learn as much as you can while everyone is present. But don't omit the step altogether, and get to the action generation as soon as possible.

Note The Toolkit contains additional information regarding retrospectives and step-by-step instructions on how to conduct one.

Easy to Prepare, Easy to Conduct

Retrospective ceremonies are easy to conduct, and they take almost no time to prepare once you become comfortable with them. They do not require an experienced facilitator, but will benefit from one if available. In addition, they do not require a lot of preparation. Just bring some sticky notes and markers or pens (or flip charts or a whiteboard and markers) for an in-person retrospective, or create an instance of a virtual wall like the one in Figure 13-2 to conduct an online retrospective.

CHAPTER 13 CONTINUOUS LEARNING AND IMPROVEMENT

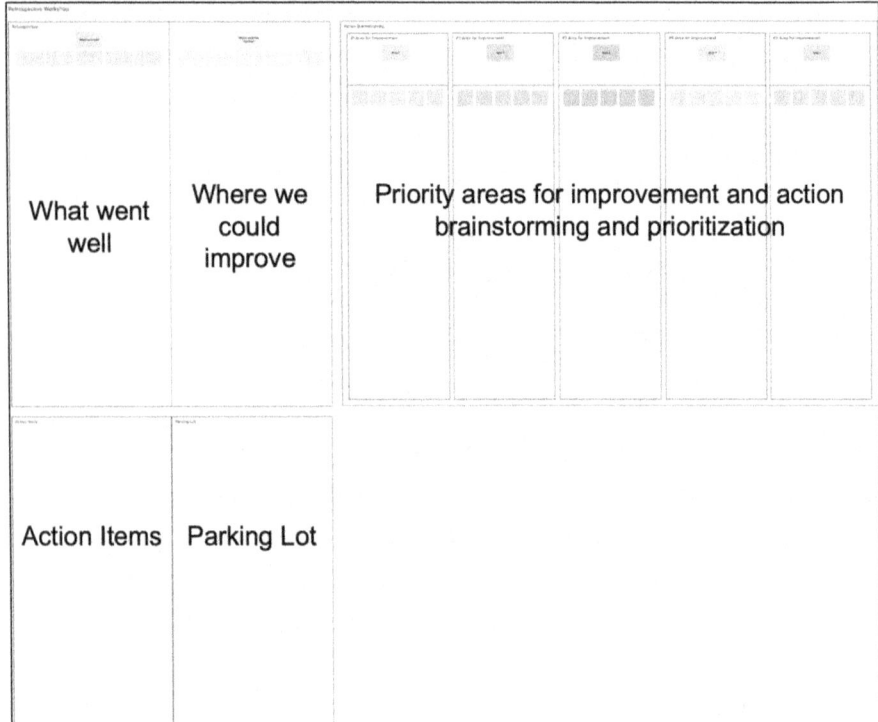

Figure 13-2. Sample classic retrospective virtual wall (illustrative)

Because they require little-to-no preparation, retrospectives are great for impromptu or in situ analyses. Just go to a whiteboard or flipchart, or grab some sticky notes, and you're ready.

Capture and Manage Actions

Henry Ford cautioned that vision without execution is hallucination. Heed that message as you run your retrospectives. I have seen many teams run excellent retrospectives, identify their pockets of excellence, discover areas for improvement that needed critical attention, and never follow up. Running retrospectives in that manner is an excellent way to lower morale and erode trust. What a wasted opportunity!

Even though they don't take a lot of time, retrospectives still take time people could spend doing something else important to them. Respecting others' time is a key tenet of lean entrepreneurship, and it's just the right thing to do. Make sure to develop and capture actions to address areas for improvement and opportunities and assign an owner and deadline to each.

You may not be able to address everything you discover, especially early on. If there are a lot of things to address, have the team prioritize them and select from the highest priority items. Then assign an owner to follow up and ensure the actions items are being addressed. Better still, put the actions in a Kanban or similar tool so everyone can watch the improvement in action.

Opening the group's subsequent retrospective by reviewing the actions that have been taken and their impact if it is known, is a good way to demonstrate the value derived from the team's time and input. In addition to solidifying trust and strengthening relationships, this may have the added benefits of increasing future retrospective participation (both in numbers and contribution) and increasing adoption of retrospective learning and continuous improvement elsewhere in the organization. It reinforces the value of the exercise.

Learn Everywhere

Run retrospectives for services, ceremonies, resources, teams, and the initiative overall. That is not to suggest you become a full-time retrospective facilitator. Find the constructs and cadence that make sense for you and the teams you work with. For example, you might run retrospectives:

- For individual ceremonies (e.g., 3P Reviews, Pitch Ceremonies) which include members of one or more affected teams (e.g., Initiative Team, Governance Team, each incubating team, and perhaps the Advisory Team)

- On the entire initiative with all teams present

- To obtain broad feedback from members of one specific group, either on a broad range of topics or one specific area (e.g., incubating team leaders, Governance Team members, Advisory Team members, Initiative Team members)

- Briefly at the end of a training session, summit, or off-site event in order to improve future, similar events

Just make sure you cover everything, and every team in some way. In addition, incubating teams should be running their own retrospectives to learn and improve how they are bringing their idea to life.

Though you should run retrospectives regularly, recurring retrospectives do not all have to be run with the same frequency. Find a cadence that works best for the team(s) involved and the entity or entities under review. I recommend a retrospective early in the life of any entity, team, or ceremony (e.g., one month into execution). I also suggest holding more frequent retrospectives early in the initiative or entity's life (e.g., monthly) and relaxing the cadence (e.g., to quarterly) once team rhythms develop and you are better able to assess the need for them.

Pay attention to mood, body language, morale, and other indicators as teams execute, and run ad hoc retrospectives if you sense they are changing or something is veering off course.

A Few Things I Learned from Initiative-Focused Retrospectives

I have received tremendous benefit from retrospectives involving a wide variety of assignments and teams, and find them especially beneficial for transformational initiatives of any kind. They have driven tremendous benefits to teams participating in initiatives like those discussed in this book such as:

- Identification of new partners in their organization
- Improved alignment with the organization's strategy
- Improved processes (e.g., creation of new lightweight processes)
- Streamlined collaboration with specific groups in the organization
- Discovery of the benefit of optionally adding a Governance Team member as an advisor to each incubating team
- Clearer, richer stage transition objectives
- Creation of a smoother approach to pauses
- Creation of the first incubation team leader Boot Camp

2. Proactive Learning

Though I consider retrospectives to be the mainspring of continuous learning and improvement, they are not the only useful tool. Retrospectives also have an Achilles heel. They only let you learn from things that have already happened.

That may be a bit confusing. Isn't all learning based upon what happened in the past? Wouldn't you need a time machine to learn from the future? Maybe. What if I suggested we *can* learn from something that *hasn't* happened?

There are several good techniques that will help us anticipate what *might* happen and what to do if it does occur. For example, fire drill, premortem, and Failure Mode and Effects Analyses (FMEA) techniques provide different methods of guiding teams through an exercise where they brainstorm on what future conditions might occur, how something might fail, what the cause of the failure might be, and what could be done to prevent it from happening. (A sample fire drill ceremony is included in the Toolkit.)

Sometimes the outcome of these ceremonies is an accurate, or directionally accurate, prediction of the future resulting in better preparedness when it happens. Other times, teams can identify and proactively prevent the potential cause of a future failure. In either case, these proactive learning techniques can drive a lot of value, save a lot of time and energy, and reduce embarrassment, cost, and/or stress. When an emergency occurs, stress is high, and there is enormous pressure to remedy the situation. A checklist made in a proactive learning session can substantially relieve that pressure and help ensure mistakes that might exacerbate the situation are not made.

3. Leadership Development

One of the best collateral benefits of running an initiative like this is the leadership development opportunities it presents. With a bit of deliberate attention, and not too much effort, your initiative can be as much about developing people as it is about developing new ideas.

Think about why that is important. If we assume you are looking for breakthrough ideas, we can begin with the estimate that approximately one or two in ten of the incubating solutions in your initiative will eventually succeed, at least at the outset. (The rate of successful exits should improve over time, as your Governance Team gets better at selecting ideas and teams. It might also be higher if you are incubating less risky ideas.)

Regardless of what you estimate your success rate will be, some incubating solutions will pause, which means a number of people on incubating teams will eventually return to the mature areas of the organization. Through your initiative, you can help them return as experienced leaders. Doing that is great for those people, and it is great for the organization. Furthermore, they will be able to take what they learned and help others to grow. It's exciting to watch that when it happens.

 A person's skills alone are usually not enough to provide them with a leadership opportunity. People also need the opportunity to *demonstrate* their abilities to others. Your initiative can provide both! In one accelerator, an exceptional incubating team leader brought their solution to an amazingly efficient and successful pause. We hoped they would become a serial intrapreneur. However, a senior executive had witnessed their exceptional performance and quickly offered that incubation team leader a new position in a mature line of business. That team leader was also given a double promotion to Vice President.

Consider providing team leaders with the opportunity to self-assess their leadership competencies, and make their own plan to fill gaps or bring in people with skills they lack to complete their minimum viable team. Self-assessments and competency modes of this nature:

- Ensure minimum viable team composition is considered during all stages of incubation
- Give each incubating team the best possible chance to succeed
- Leverage the initiative to develop people
- Provide consistent evaluation of skills and knowledge to enable unbiased evaluation, assessment, and development of people and teams
- Facilitate:
  - Selection of incubation team leaders
  - Recruiting and selecting team members to fill skill gaps

- Individual development and career growth through customized learning plans
- Promotion decisions and advancement
- Performance management

- Evaluation of leader performance and potential, and identification of areas for improvement and development

Figure 13-3 shows a high-level outline of some of the qualities of high-performing incubating team leaders.

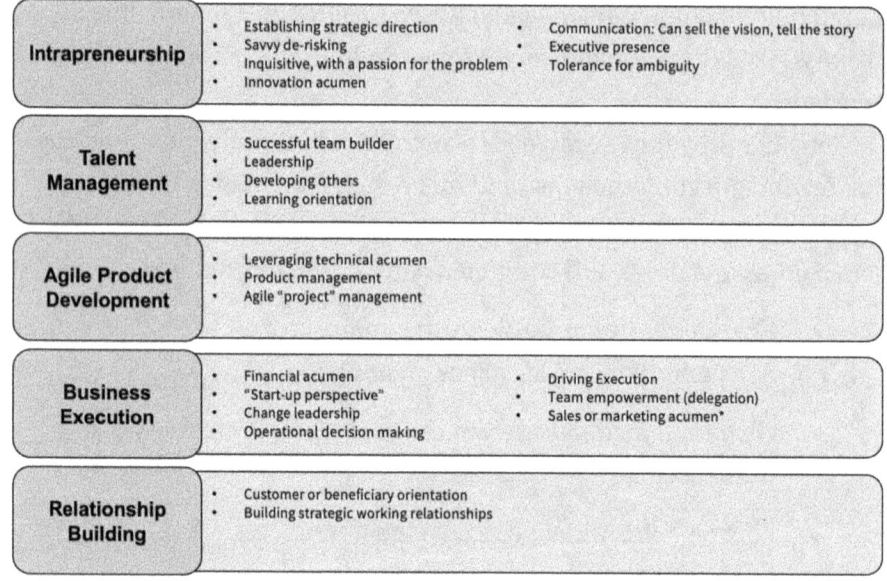

Figure 13-3. Innovation leadership competencies (illustrative)

Once gaps are identified, incubation team leaders can begin to fill them through traditional training, online training, mentoring, coaching, or other forms of education.

4. Summits and Off-Sites

Full calendars and frenetic day-to-day activities can make learning challenging for anyone. Initiative Team members must be deliberate about continuous learning and improvement, but getting caught up in daily activities or disruptions can be distracting; especially early on when the team is usually small (probably one person, perhaps one part-time person). For incubation team leaders the challenge can be even more difficult. They tend to be what is colloquially referred to as "player-coaches," making major contributions to day-to-day objectives as well as filling a leadership role. Ironically, they might benefit most from learning, but are often pulled away from it due to the demands of their team.

One way to remove these distractions is to pull people out of their day-to-day routine for a day or two to focus on learning. Summits and off-site events are simple ways to accomplish this.

Team Lead Summits (Founder Summits)

An incubating team leader's summit (sometimes referred to as a "Founder Summit") removes distraction and enables incubating team leaders to focus on learning and improvement by bringing them together in a location away from their teams and day-to-day responsibilities. A summit's agenda might include things like:

- Brief learning sessions led by subject matter experts in areas of broad interest (e.g., marketing, product management, leadership)
- Workshops to improve team leaders' skills
- Participant-led sessions that enable all participants help one incubating team address a difficult challenge or puzzle

- Participant-led sessions or workshops aimed at solving a shared problem or improving the initiative and its value to the incubating teams

- Open conversations and lean meetings or Lean Coffee style discussions

- Retrospectives on any plane (e.g., the initiative overall, specific puzzles or procedures...), and a brief (5-to-15-minute) retrospective on the summit itself at the end of the event

- Casual conversation and interaction between the leaders (sometimes referred to as "hallway sessions")

- Group design workshops

- Team building exercises

- Coaching from internal subject matter experts (group and/or one-to-one)

- Coaching from external experts (group and/or one-to-one)

The range of potential topics is practically limitless.

Setting the Agenda

Summits are typically planned by the Initiative Team, but planning should involve the incubating team leaders and other participants. One simple way to accomplish this is to solicit ideas as far in advance of the event as practical (e.g., two-to-four weeks). Collecting candidate agenda items can be as easy as posting a shared spreadsheet or Kanban. Once participants have submitted their ideas, I like to remove duplicates, organize the ideas into themes, post them to a shared location, and prioritize them by having the participants vote on the topics they believe are most important.

From time to time, the Initiative Team or Governance Team (via the Initiative Team) may have an agenda item or two they believe is important. These can be added to the agenda, but I have seen the greatest interest and success from these events when the agenda is primarily developed by the participants.

When building the agenda, don't forget to suggest topics that were discovered during retrospectives. Retrospectives can be a gold mine of inspiration for a summit, and why conduct retrospectives if you're not going to act on what you learn.

Schedule Far in Advance

As with other ceremonies, it is best to schedule summits as far in advance as possible. Should you choose to hold summits, you will likely only host one or two per year. Find a location and block everyone's time as early as you can. This will mitigate the risk of schedule conflicts, and booking a venue or room block early (if you need them) will often reduce the cost of the event dramatically; as will holding them in the target location's off-season.

Ownership Is Key

As you might expect, it is critical to have a single owner responsible for arranging and executing a summit. You can give them all the help they need or want. There can be a lot of moving parts, so attention to detail is key. Without a single owner, something is likely to be forgotten or fall behind.

Get Help

Don't be ashamed to ask for help or guidance from others whose primary job responsibilities involve arranging these types of events, or that you learn have experience for other reasons. People in your organization's travel or events department (if you have one) can provide guidance or assistance on the travel and venue logistics. People in the training, employee development, or people (HR) teams may be able to help with training, or even make themselves available as trainers or facilitators for one or more sessions.

Summit Benefits

I have found these summits to be extremely beneficial, not only to the incubating teams but also to the Initiative Team and others. They have led to substantial discoveries and initiative improvements, improved collaboration between the Initiative Team and incubation leaders, and led to insights I am sure would have otherwise been missed. They can also help the incubating team leaders better understand the initiative's broader objectives, and drive alignment on messaging.

For example, at one summit an incubating team leader asked a question during an open session that resulted in my helping them to understand the initiative's short-, mid-, and long-term objectives, how we expected value would migrate from year to year, and the ways in which we were explaining the initiative to the most senior executives. That provided all participants with better context and understanding. As a result, they were able to apply this knowledge to their own messaging and discussions and engage with those senior executives in a deeper and more meaningful way.

Summits can:

- Bring incubating teams together and help them learn from one-another

  - New teams can learn from the experience of teams that have been incubating longer.

  - Mature teams can learn from new teams who are unencumbered and unconstrained by experience.

- Provide training necessary to fill skill gaps or improve overall performance or efficiency

- Drive personal development and leadership development
- Fill training needs in a compressed and potentially more economically efficient way
- Build community amongst the incubating team leaders that results in better day-to-day collaboration and working relationships
- Provide an opportunity for incubating team leaders to learn tools, tricks, and resources that make their peers more effective and productive
- Reward incubating team leaders for their hard work, dedication, and ingenuity
- Advance the initiative's overall progress toward its objectives
- Identify and mitigate the initiative's risks and issues, and facilitate fine-tuning
- Relieve the pressure under which incubating team leaders, the Initiative Team, and others sometimes find themselves
- Drive alignment and ensure expectations are properly set
- Boost morale and drive more positive attitudes and emotions
- Reinforce lean thinking and good habits, and help identify and break bad ones
- Provide an opportunity for outreach to others who are not participating in the initiative

The last benefit in the list may not be obvious. When summits are planned in locations where the organization has a presence (e.g., an organization's office), the Initiative Team can create opportunities for the initiative's participants (e.g., incubating team leaders, the Initiative Team) to socialize with people who are not initiative participants. Something as simple as a buffet lunch can create opportunities for people to learn about the initiative from those participating in it. Those interactions are often a much more effective promotional event than having an Initiative Team member or sponsor speak about it. This type of social interaction also provides both incubating team members and those not participating in the initiative to learn from one-another and build working relationships which can carry on long past a leader's time in an incubating team.

Summits Don't Have to Break the Bank

Summits do not have to be expensive, and their location does not have to be lavish. They may not even have to involve travel depending upon the geographic dispersion of your initiative's leaders. If the leadership is geographically dispersed, holding summits in the areas of larger concentrations of incubating team leaders can keep costs low.

Summits do not have to be in "hotspot destinations." I have participated in successful leadership summits both in an organization's own meeting facilities and in nearby hotel meeting rooms. The former does not usually cost anything, and hotels will often offer a meeting room at no charge if your team is staying in their facility. Taking advantage of already scheduled organizational events that involve summit participants, or holding a summit in conjunction with an external conference or training event, might also be a way to keep expenses low.

Governance Team Off-Sites

Everyone *loves* off-site meetings. You get to spend two-to-four days watching people read slides to you that you could have read yourself in a couple of hours. You get to attend one- or two-hour long sessions where people read statistics and measures in long form that you can see on a dashboard in a few minutes. If you're lucky, they might even add context or highlight something interesting. It's exhilarating.

Most of us have been to off-site events where it feels as if the greatest achievement of the event is that you fall a week behind on the work required to achieve your objectives. Fortunately, that is not the kind of event I am referring to. Don't do those. It's irresponsibly cruel.

However, there will be times when you may need or want to get the Governance Team, and perhaps a few others, together to ensure the initiative is on track, solve tough puzzles, and set the initiative on a path toward success. An off-site might be the most efficient way to do that. Governance Team Off-sites are very similar in nature to Summits in that they might include elements of learning, planning, puzzle solving, troubleshooting, and fine-tuning.

Off-Site Logistics

Off-site logistics are similar, if not identical, to the summit logistics discussed earlier in this chapter. Like summits, off-sites should be scheduled as far in advance as possible. The Governance Team members should agree on the date, location, and agenda in advance of the event. As with summits, work with the Governance Team to brainstorm, prioritize, and select agenda items. The Initiative Team might also add items which they believe require the Governance Team's attention.

Focus the agenda almost exclusively on items that can only be accomplished with team members face-to-face and discussions which are better held in person. Use a prioritization and selection mechanism similar to what was discussed in the earlier "Setting the Agenda" section for choosing agenda items. Briefly:

1. Solicit ideas from participants.
2. Gauge interest in each (e.g., via voting).
3. Organize the agenda by themes.
4. Place themes in a logical order (each session feeds the next), and consider dependencies.
5. Confirm the agenda with participants, and adjust it, if necessary.

Don't make people sit too long. Be sure to include breaks. Back-to-back sessions are fine, but try not to go more than 90 minutes without a break. *Never* go beyond two hours without one. If the agenda items do not fill the time originally blocked for the event (e.g., two days of agenda for a three-day block), set the agenda to end early and inform the participants in advance. Make sure you consider travel schedules as well, and agree upon whether participants will arrive the evening before the event, and whether you will end early in consideration of departure schedules.

When preparing the agenda, make sure to include time for the participants to catch up with their day jobs and urgent matters. Schedule breaks in the morning and afternoon, set an hour or 90 minutes for lunch, and allow time at the end of the day for participants to catch up. This will help ensure people focus completely on each session and lower the probability people will have to temporarily step out of a session.

CHAPTER 13   CONTINUOUS LEARNING AND IMPROVEMENT

Avoid Presentation Poisoning

There is probably no quicker way to cause a senior team to reach for their laptops and mobile phones, and bury their faces in email and messages, than having people read reports aloud. Include items in your working agreement that state people will upload any necessary background material a week before the event (with updates permitted until the event begins), and that all participants will read the background material prior to the event. In my experience, this will remove the need for review of most of that type of material and enable the group to focus their time on necessary conversations and decisions. When it is necessary to show an exhibit, this will enable session leaders to immediately get to the heart of a discussion.

Put Budget and People Last on the Agenda

I have attended many off-sites and like events where the opening topic was finance and budgeting. It makes sense. It is a very important topic, and without investment there is no initiative. I believe the logic for this placement was that a group would begin by looking at what their budget was, and then build a plan based upon what they could afford. I suppose there is nothing wrong with that logic. But I have seen a different approach deliver better results.

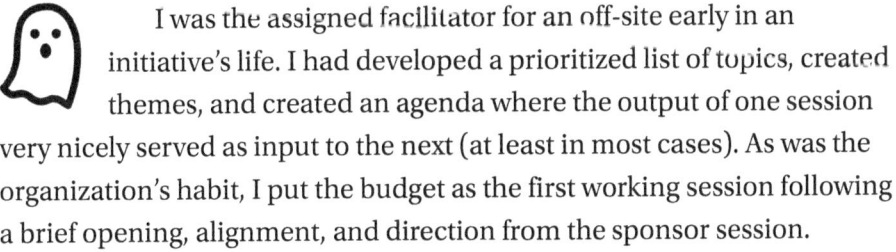

I was the assigned facilitator for an off-site early in an initiative's life. I had developed a prioritized list of topics, created themes, and created an agenda where the output of one session very nicely served as input to the next (at least in most cases). As was the organization's habit, I put the budget as the first working session following a brief opening, alignment, and direction from the sponsor session.

Fortunately, a very experienced colleague, for whom I had an enormous amount of respect, said something like, "Aw, you're not going to do that, are you? You're not going to put budget first?!" They commented on how it sucked the life out of off-sites and quarterly reviews and put everyone in the wrong context and the wrong frame of mind. What a gift!

485

I reworked the agenda and put the finance session second last, with a discussion of people as the very last item. It made an enormous difference. By the time we got to the finance sessions we knew exactly what we wanted to do. We had worked through the other items unconstrained in thought, and then were able to fine-tune the budget to accommodate our new priorities. It was a bit of a forehead-slapping moment. It made so much more sense once we had done it.

We also put people last. (It hurt me to write that.) Last only on the agenda! For the same reason, it made the discussion so much richer. We understood what we needed to achieve and were able to consider that when discussing people. We also had a very healthy culture of reward and recognition, so it was always great to end the off-sites discussing awards, promotions, increases, and other positive items. Ironically, putting people last (on the agenda) reinforced our goal of putting people first.

Be Opportunistic

People in Governance Teams often find themselves together for other events such as senior leadership meetings. Take advantage of those when you can.

Holding these events in an organization's offices ("on-site off-sites") can be a way to keep costs down while providing an opportunity for participants to socialize with the local teams. I worked with one team that deliberately held each off-site at a different company location so they could create these socialization opportunities regularly and broadly. Those events were very popular with the local teams.

Remember to keep the group as isolated and focused as possible during on-site off-sites, ensure your working agreement includes guidance to the team to be present during sessions, and remind them of this as the event commences.

The Facilitator Owns the Event

The person who will be the primary facilitator for an off-site event must be its owner. They can, of course solicit assistance when needed, but they should be accountable for the event. They should be the arbiter of record, and work with the Governance Team to resolve conflicts or agenda item disputes. They will be responsible for the flow, personality, and success of the event from start to finish.

Off-Site Benefits

Done well, off-sites can:

- Advance the Governance Team's work more rapidly
- Build better working relationships between Governance Team members and other participants
- Create a forum to enable high-potential people to become exposed to senior leaders
- Provide learning opportunities
- Generate ideas for the initiative's betterment
- Resolve disputes, conflicts, and differences of opinion in a safe and pleasant environment
- Preempt potential conflicts and issues
- Drive initiative awareness through socialization
- Create better relationships between the off-site's participants and local teams and employees
- Address sensitive issues that are better resolved in person (e.g., Governance Team performance, interpersonal issues, conflicts with or within incubating teams)

CHAPTER 13   CONTINUOUS LEARNING AND IMPROVEMENT

- Provide an opportunity for the Initiative Team and sponsors to thank the Governance Team and other volunteers

- Advance the initiative's overall progress toward its objectives

- Identify and mitigate the initiative's risks and issues, and drive fine-tuning

- Drive alignment and ensure expectations are properly set

  - For example, expectations for each stage of incubation often require reinforcement and realignment so Governance Team members evaluate and coach incubating teams appropriately.

- Reinforce lean thinking and good habits, and catch and break bad ones

5. Introspection

Introspection can be a powerful continuous learning and improvement tool. When combined with other tools and approaches the impact can be surprising. Since the term might be broadly interpreted, let me share an example of where the application of an introspective posture to an off-site delivered spectacular and unexpected results.

I had facilitated a few off-sites for a team. They were an extremely high-performing team with high emotional intelligence, and the outcomes of their off-site meetings were always impressive. Things were working well with this group, but I didn't want the off-sites to become routine. I thought that changing something in the team's approach might lead to new insights and outcomes.

CHAPTER 13 CONTINUOUS LEARNING AND IMPROVEMENT

After thinking through past events – and off-sites and retrospectives in general – I realized that teams often identify externalities that need to be addressed. That is, they identify areas for improvement where *they* do not play a role in the root cause. I also hypothesized that, for governance or oversight teams, externalities were far higher in number than were identified areas for improvement where the team itself played a role in the root cause. After all, they are not the ones doing the day-to-day work. I asked myself, "How can I leverage this potential insight?"

"Let's run an experiment!" That was one of my favorite mantras with that team, and it was well understood by all to be a request for agreement from the team that: (1) We would try something new. (2) It may not work. (3) We were all in agreement that it was worth trying. (4) There would be no personal consequences if it did not deliver the expected outcome. (5) We would inspect and adapt if it was not delivering what we had hoped. We would checkpoint early in the off-site, and we could always return to our tried-and-true approach if we felt the new one was not working. As the facilitator I was also implicitly committing to be prepared to take the team in a different direction if it did not work.

The experiment? "Let's assume that whatever we discover, whatever the issue, *WE* created the conditions that led to it." Even if we could not think of a way in which that could have happened, let's just begin with the assumption we were the root cause. The result was nothing short of astounding.

The introspective off-site was intense. The discussions were unbelievably rich, as we looked for ways we might have influenced outcomes. In a typical off-site this team would make approximately 18 major decisions, and capture approximately three dozen action items. In that off-site, we made twice as many major decisions (36) and captured 86 meaningful action items. We had wallpapered every wall and window with flip charts as we worked through the off-site's objectives and agenda. We were exhausted, but we were energized.

489

But why did that happen? Why was the event so productive? I thought about that a lot as I captured and analyzed the outcomes. I believe that **in assuming we were the root cause, we gave ourselves the power to act. We moved from passive to active posture and gave ourselves permission to address all of the issues or opportunities we identified.** If we were the cause, then surely we could be the solution. It was mind-blowing.

Though I strongly recommend applying the power of introspection to your continuous learning and improvement, I also caution against doing so too early. Get the team to the performing stage of Tuckman's model (see Chapter 10) before you take this approach. It can be intense, and you'll need the team's trust to execute it successfully. You might also need to inspect and adapt an introspective off-site in progress, so you might want to try an approach with a higher probability of success early on. But don't miss out on this tremendous opportunity for growth, and think of ways to apply it to self-reflection and other learning opportunities.

When We Are at Our Best/When We Are Not at Our Best

Another simple introspective exercise that can be useful involves individual team reflection on the characteristics that define them when they are at their best, or not at their best (or even at their worst). For example, someone might notice that when they are at their best, they are even-tempered, ask open-ended questions, take a positive tone, and are not judgmental. They might also notice that when they are having a bad day they can be short-tempered, overly critical, and directive.

A simple observation and brainstorming exercise, as illustrated in Figure 13-4, can discover these areas for improvement (when we are/I am not at our/my best) and strengths to be reinforced and leveraged (when we are/I am at our/my best) at an individual or team level.

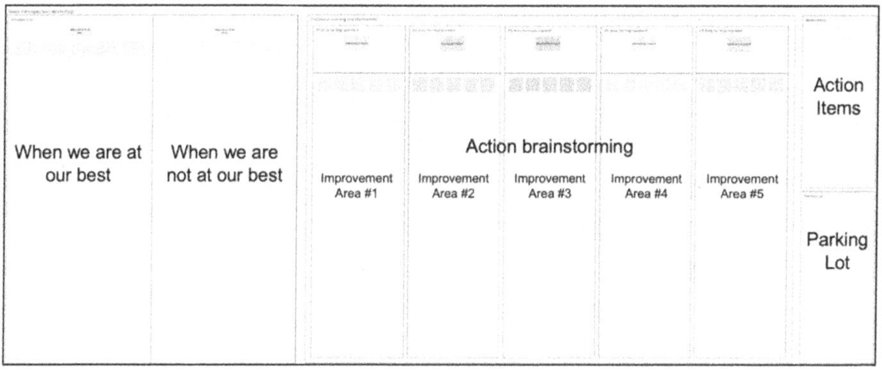

Figure 13-4. Example of an introspection exercise

To conduct this exercise at a team level, have each member of the team take a couple of minutes of reflection to capture the characteristics and behaviors they believe the team or its members manifest when they are at their best, without speaking to other team members. After the period of individual reflection, have team members post their ideas to a wall or whiteboard, group like ideas, and discuss items as necessary to ensure everyone understands what has been shared. Then repeat the process for what characterizes the team and its members when they are not at their best.

Once both groups of characteristics and behaviors have been discussed, develop strategies for reinforcing and leveraging the positive behaviors and characteristics, and addressing or preventing the blind spots and anti-patterns.

Note Additional information regarding this exercise is available in the Toolkit.

6. Role Clarification and Alignment

Clarity of roles in an initiative is paramount. Everyone has enough to do. They don't need to spend time on things someone else should be doing. In addition, people can become extremely annoyed when others execute outside their roles. It can lead to inefficiencies, duplication of work, or even serious interpersonal conflict.

Ironically, people operating outside their roles often neglect things that *are* within their purview. This can result in missed deadlines, failure to deliver or achieve objectives, and stress or serious interpersonal conflict. Even when the consequences are not that serious it can be annoying and counterproductive.

When it comes to role clarity within an initiative there can be other complicating factors. People new to a role can make incorrect assumptions. That may not be surprising, but remember that early in the initiative's life *everybody* will be in a new role. There will be a lot going on. Furthermore, role perception can drift, and expectations and assumptions can change over time. It can be a complex dynamic.

Role clarity cannot be left to chance. I have found a simple exercise can help align a team, or multiple teams on the responsibilities of a role, and help identify any gaps between roles or misalignment between teams (Figure 13-5).

CHAPTER 13 CONTINUOUS LEARNING AND IMPROVEMENT

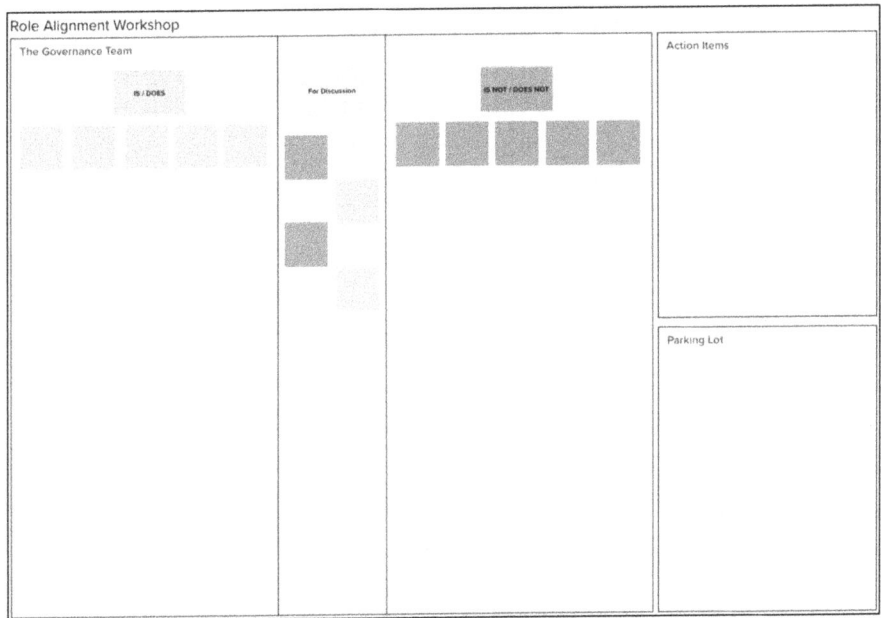

Figure 13-5. Sample role clarification and alignment exercise

The exercise begins with a brainstorm on what the role of the team or individual is. Create a section on a wall or whiteboard and label it "The *<team name/individual role>* IS/DOES:" (e.g., "The Governance Team IS/DOES:"). Give participants a few minutes to think about, and write down, all the things they believe the team is responsible for, and the actions it should be taking. Have them perform this first step without speaking with others. Once that step is complete, have everyone post their ideas to the wall (or write them on the whiteboard…) and give them time to look at what everyone has written. Next, have the team perform the same steps for an area marked "The role of the *<team name/individual role>* IS NOT/DOES NOT:"

Once both areas are complete, ask the team to identify anything in the IS/DOES or IS NOT/DOES NOT area they believe does not belong there and place them in the "For Discussion" area. Discuss each item in the "For Discussion" area as a team and resolve them on the spot. If you are

CHAPTER 13 CONTINUOUS LEARNING AND IMPROVEMENT

unable to do so for any item, need assistance, or run out of time, assign an action item, owner, and follow-up date for its resolution. If you are time constrained you can also quickly prioritize the identified items and get through as many as you can while the group is together.

> **Note** Additional information regarding this exercise is available in the Toolkit.

This simple exercise can be used to clarify individual or team roles. It can also be used when multiple teams are present to build alignment across teams and clarify misconceptions. For example, the Governance Team and Initiative Team members, and perhaps even incubating team leaders, could perform this exercise for the Governance Team (or all three teams). One team might also ask another to assess them in this way. For example, the Governance Team might be curious regarding what the incubating team leaders believe the Governance Team's role is.

This worthwhile exercise can be performed in as little as 15 to 30 minutes. While it can be used initially to help define a role, I have found it very useful for fine-tuning roles and driving clarity and alignment after teams have been executing for 6 to 12 months or more. I also use this exercise when I sense tension developing between teams or individuals that might be related to role clarity. For example, I have worked with leadership team members (outside the context of an initiative) to perform this exercise to clarify all their individual roles so they could reduce conflict and enable better, more efficient collaboration and execution.

7. Incremental Learning

Several times throughout this book I discussed how these initiatives can be built incrementally. You do not have to build everything for every stage at once. You do not have to have your communication and channels perfectly

CHAPTER 13 CONTINUOUS LEARNING AND IMPROVEMENT

defined at the outset. You do not have to have a full-sized Governance Team on the first day. I'm sure you get the point. This incremental approach creates an opportunity.

As you build the minimum viable version of each stage you can leverage what you learned from the stages and components you have previously built. Figure 13-6 shows a very simple illustration of this concept. Each of the three horizontal flows beginning with "Increment 1" represents a different point in time, with the topmost row being the earliest item in the evolution, and the bottom being the latest.

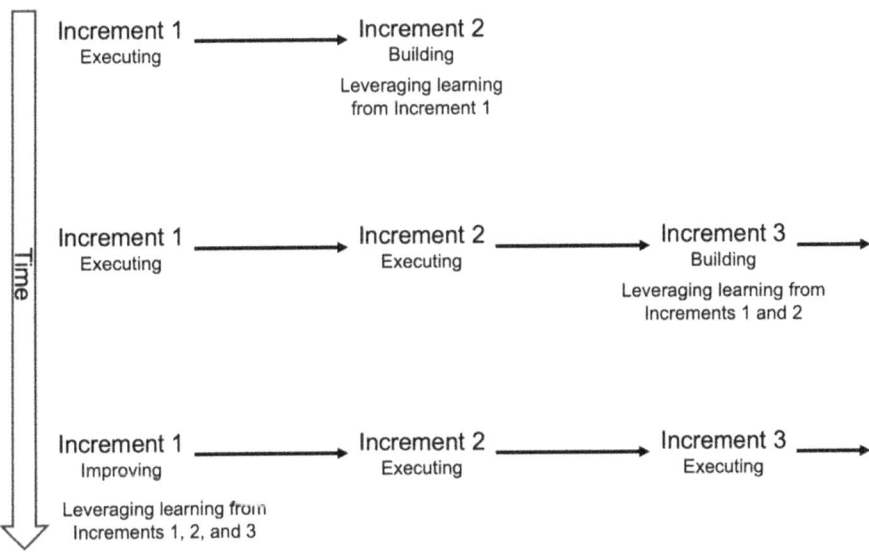

Figure 13-6. Leveraging incremental learning

You can see in the first row that the first increment (e.g., creation of pitch ceremonies and resources) is completed and executing, and the second (e.g., creation of entry stage checklists) is being built leveraging what was learned while building the first. In the second row, increments one and two are executing (e.g., the pitch and entry activities) and increment three (e.g., Explore 1 checklists, ceremonies, and artifacts) is being created based on learning acquired while building the first two.

495

This evolution will continue. At some point it will be time to revisit increment 1 (e.g., pitch readiness and events) and improve it. As you can see in the third row, that improvement can leverage all learning to date.

Additional Considerations

Consider the following as you build a continuous learning and improvement culture:

- Turn learning into action: Always capture specific action items, owners, and deadlines to ensure learning is leveraged.

- A Kanban (physical or online) is a great, simple way to keep everyone in sync and ensure all actions are captured.

- Assign an owner to the action list or Kanban to keep track of overall progress and ensure action item owners are completing their actions.

- Don't overlook traditional methods of learning such as online or in-person classes.

- Keep surveys simple, clear, and brief whenever possible, and ensure they are not your only way of learning.

- Start, stay, and stop on time when conducting retrospectives and other ceremonies and workshops.

- Every time you touch something look for ways it might be improved.

CHAPTER 13 CONTINUOUS LEARNING AND IMPROVEMENT

- Look for signs performance or utility is drifting (e.g., it is taking teams too long to prepare for 3P reviews) and follow up to identify potential issues and root causes via retrospectives or other means.

- Leverage metrics and measures to identify areas for improvement, and always turn that learning into action.

- Perform retrospectives more frequently early in an activity or initiative's life.

Summary

Nobody gets everything right the first time, and even if they did, performance, value, and satisfaction will drift over time. Don't be embarrassed if this happens, expect it, and employ a regimen of continuous learning and improvement to address it or prevent it from happening.

Retrospectives are the cornerstone of continuous learning and improvement. They are simple, require little preparation time, and can drive invaluable insight that leads to concrete action and improvement. Consider all aspects of the initiative when planning retrospectives. Find the right cadence for each team or target, but a higher frequency at the outset is almost always the better choice.

Turn learning into action! Don't waste valuable time and insight by not following up. Capture actions, owners, and deadlines for improvement activities as you learn, to ensure important improvements are made. An online or physical Kanban can help manage follow up activities, drive transparency, and ensure people see that their time is well spent.

CHAPTER 13 CONTINUOUS LEARNING AND IMPROVEMENT

Leverage proactive learning techniques to prevent bad things from happening, and so you can be better prepared to respond to events you cannot prevent. In addition, anticipate gaps in participants' skills and proactively provide training to close them. Make sure everyone understands their own roles and the roles of the teams they depend upon, and don't be afraid to run an alignment workshop if tensions are building.

Lightweight summits and off-sites can drive learning and performance and lead to marked improvements in the initiative, and they don't have to break the bank. Keep them simple and light, and don't feel the need to fill all the time set aside for them with busywork. Periodically adopt an introspective posture. The alternative perspective it provides can lead to substantial insights.

PART IV

Conclusion

CHAPTER 14

Conclusion

Thank you for reading this book.

One of the concerns I had when discussing what might be included in a book like this was how to strike a balance between putting enough information in the book to make it helpful while not including so much information it would be impossible for someone to find what they need. The wide variety of reasons people want to embark on an initiative like this, their varied organizational and team objectives, the numerous design options, and the many different types of ideas people want to nurture would necessitate covering many options and potential nuances. The fact that these transformative initiatives often involve the potential discomfort and uncertainty of change, which itself must be deliberately managed, meant potentially covering even more ground. Then I realized my thinking was a manifestation of a classic puzzle solving, project management, or program management misstep: I was thinking about how to do everything at once. I needed to break it down.

That brings us to the beginning of the end of our journey together.

You Don't Have to Do Everything at Once

You do not have to do everything. Your initiative does not have to include every option or every ceremony. Neither your Initiative Team nor your Governance Team needs to be large. The initiative described in *Lean Entrepreneurship* began with one part-time Initiative Team member and a five-to-six-person Governance Team.

CHAPTER 14   CONCLUSION

You don't have to bring in a large number of incubating teams at one time. You can start with one. You don't even have to cover all of the stages of incubation outlined in this book. You could have an initiative that ends after the first stage (customer–problem fit or beneficiary–problem fit) and turns validated ideas over to another area of your organization (with all of the caveats in Chapter 2 of this book and in *Lean Entrepreneurship*).

Furthermore, you don't even have to begin by doing all you plan to do.

Start Small, Build Incrementally

You can – and in my opinion you should – start small and build incrementally. That is exactly what you will be proposing your incubating teams do. *That* is lean.

What's great about practicing lean principles while building your initiative is that their incremental approach can be applied to any and every one of its dimensions. You can begin with small teams, or you might even begin without one of the teams in place (e.g., the Advisory Team) and add it when you need to. Match the size of the team with the initiative and grow only when you need to; but be careful not to take too much on.

You can build only the stages that you need (e.g., Seed 1, Explore 1), slightly ahead of when you need them. You can then use what you learn from the successes and mistakes you made building those to improve what you've built, while you do an even better job building the next stage. What may be less obvious is that you can also incrementally build each stage and aspect of your initiative. You can build a minimum valuable version of your pitch stage, then move on to a minimum valuable version of your Seed 1 or Explore 1 stage before returning to the pitch stage to make it richer. You can build a minimum valuable version of the entire initiative at first, then apply learning and incremental improvement where it's needed most.

Likewise, you don't have to apply *everything* in the book at once. You can select the chapters that best align with your interests. You can focus on specific sections within those chapters, and return for others if, and when, they make sense for your initiative.

It will also be worthwhile to verify the needs the initiative will be expected to fulfill, and align the participants, stakeholders, and sponsors early on. A rapid assessment pays for the time it takes each time you proactively discover or clarify an objective, or identify an area of actual, potential, or perceived misalignment. Assessments do not have to be long, heavy projects. A simple, small series of conversations with the right people might be all you need for a smaller initiative or pilot.

Get Help

You do not have to do this all by yourself, even if you are a one-person team. Leverage your personal network. Be on the lookout for others passionate about helping creative people bring new things to life and positioning your organization for future growth and relevance. Find domain experts to help with things outside your own area of expertise. Whether that is communication, strategy, procurement, legal, or people management, every small gift from one of those people can be a massive force multiplier; especially if you are a force of one.

What is difficult for you might be simple for someone with domain experience. What takes you a day – or more – might take a domain expert 15 minutes. Don't be ashamed or shy. Approach with humility and the phrase that pays ("I need your help") and you might be surprised at how much you can accomplish with very little resource of your own.

Be open and invite others who share your passion to join your team, if only virtually. Build your own informal group of advisors. Engage them regularly, but be mindful you don't overstretch their generosity; and always remember to thank them. Turn them into passionate champions and earlyvangelists for your initiative.

CHAPTER 14   CONCLUSION

Leverage pockets of excellence whenever you can. There are likely people already doing a good job at some of things that you set out to accomplish – or at least who know how to do so. Deliberately look for them. Ask others who their role models are. Engage those role models whenever you find them.

Be Opportunistic

Shamelessly leverage every unfair advantage being part of your organization affords you. Take advantage of existing benefits, training, resources, physical locations, meeting rooms, and subscriptions. Engage resource personnel such as trainers and coaches. Use organizational functions such as kick-off meetings, quarterly reviews, senior leadership meetings, senior executive or board meetings, training, or other sponsored events to provide a platform or venue for your initiative, or to promote it. Use existing town halls, fireside chats, newsletters, information sites, training events, and other existing communication channels to promote and advance your initiative; and leverage the expertise of their organizers when you can.

Encourage incubating teams to do the same, and to piggyback on the organization's presence in external events like trade shows and conferences when it might benefit them.

It Is Always About People and Trust

These initiatives are energized by people and fueled by trust. Look for opportunities to help people learn and grow. Catch them doing good things and recognize and reward positive behaviors publicly. Give attribution to people who come up with good ideas, never allow someone to take credit for someone else's ideas or work, and don't let people steal attribution by silently accepting praise for something they did not do. Present people with opportunities to demonstrate their abilities and expose them to others who can help them grow and advance.

Trust is earned and very easily lost. Do what you said you would do and expect that of others on your team. Accept that mistakes will be made, and be forthcoming when they occur. Everyone makes mistakes. When you are forthcoming people will understand, and they may be able to help you rectify the situation. That's something they cannot do if they don't know about it.

Bias to transparency in all you do. Instead of asking if there is any reason you should share something, ask if there any reason you should *not* share it. A combination of transparency and proactively sharing information when something goes wrong will help build and maintain trust, and maybe even get you some unsolicited assistance at a time you could truly use it.

Communication Is Paramount

Good communication is an absolute requirement for success. Good communication will enable you to find and attract participants, demonstrate the value of the initiative, and solicit help that will accelerate the initiative's progress and success.

Language matters. Communicate in the language of the group you are dealing with, and don't expect them to use your language. The latter is especially important when you are dealing with senior executives. They have a lot to do, so don't make them have to interpret your messaging.

Specific words can matter. Learn the organization's vocabulary and be on the lookout for positive and negative trigger words (e.g., the earlier example where the word "innovation" was interpreted as "break things" or failure). Be mindful of an organization's vocabulary even if you think (or know) a person or group is using a word incorrectly. I have seen things go very badly for people because of their use of a single word.

CHAPTER 14   CONCLUSION

Find the right forum and format to communicate with each person or group. Early on this might be as simple as a 15- or 30-minute conversation once a week or every couple of weeks. Later you might need to leverage broader and/or more formal platforms. Find the right form and frequency for each constituent, and confirm it is the right form and frequency.

Ensure your stakeholders and sponsors are aligned with what you are building early on. Don't worry about locking yourself in. You can build these things incrementally, and you can evolve even a one-stage, one incubating team initiative into a full-stage, multi-team initiative. Just prepare stakeholders for the change and align with them when it's time.

Do not overhype your initiative. It's great to be passionate, but set realistic expectations and confirm them with stakeholders and sponsors. Be transparent and forthcoming if anything changes or whenever there are setbacks. (I mentioned that earlier, but it's worth a second mention.) Of course, be transparent and forthcoming about the good news too.

Never go dark! Failure to communicate often leads to assumptions. Assumptions can lead to fear or discomfort. Fear and discomfort lead to unnecessary escalations and damage control exercises… or worse. It should not take much time and effort to stay in sync with people once you have established a forum, format, and cadence.

Good Governance Is Also Good Guidance

Yes, governance is ensuring that the leaders of an incubating team are being good custodians of the investment they have been entrusted with. But it's also about helping them achieve their objectives, which also advances the broader organization's objectives.

Encourage the Governance Team to be nurturing when appropriate. Governance Teams like to judge, so they may need some encouragement from the initiative's leaders and facilitators. Ensure they know which

CHAPTER 14 CONCLUSION

interactions should be mostly "coachy" (e.g., early 3P reviews) and which ones should be more "judgy" (e.g., transition requests). Select Governance Team members that can do both whenever possible.

Structure the initiative's governance to enable the Governance Team to learn what they need to while creating as little additional governance-related work as possible for incubating teams, and for the Governance Team itself. Capture as much of that information as possible as a by-product of incubating teams' incubation-related work. No work for the sake of work. No governance just for the sake of governance.

Be Willing to Let Go

I am very passionate about the things these initiatives entail. Bringing new ideas to life, innovation, helping people grow, giving people a chance to chase their creative dreams. These things energize me. But sometimes you must let some things go – even if you love them.

For example, as an Initiative Team leader or designer, you may create an artifact, resource, or system you are truly proud of. It may even be objectively excellent. But if it is not absolutely necessary for the advancement of teams and their ideas – or the initiative's objectives – it doesn't belong. Even if it is extremely good. Even if it was, at one time, very useful.

This can be tough. But just as we ask incubating teams to have strong opinions (or firm beliefs) weakly held, you may have to let go of things you are proud of. Reminiscent of the advice attributed to Coco Chanel cautioning people to look in the mirror before they leave the house and take one thing off, look at the initiative and ask whether things can be removed. You'll likely find a bunch of those as the initiative grows. Think of it like removing training wheels from a bicycle. It's time to celebrate, you just improved. Look for these opportunities to let go in all aspects of the initiative.

CHAPTER 14   CONCLUSION

Sadly, from time to time you may have to let go of an incubating team. I've liked all the teams I have worked with. Really liked them. A lot. It may not be easy, but the members of those incubating teams are not unlike the person who has just had the training wheels removed from their bicycle. They have acquired new skills and they now have the freedom to apply those anywhere they please.

Watch for Drift

Like the insidious committed bet I introduced in *Lean Entrepreneurship*, the state of your initiative, or the utility delivered by any aspect of it, can drift over time. Watch for warning signs that this may have happened. The initiative's tools and artifacts are meant to help and accelerate the incubating teams. However, what was meant to be an advantage to incubating teams can quickly become an encumbrance.

For example, if any of the initiative's participants start focusing on the artifacts or checklists more than their idea, something is wrong. If you even find they are *talking* about such things for an unusually long time or with unusual frequency, it might be worthwhile to check in with them. This caution applies to the Initiative Team and Governance Team as well as the incubating teams. Hyper focus on the initiative's procedures, tools, or artifacts by any of these groups can set the initiative off in the wrong direction.

If you are beginning to feel comfortable, as if everything is perfect, treat that as a signal that it might be time to check on things. It's a bit like those reality shows where people are voted out of a game by its other contestants. The moment one contestant feels comfortable marks the episode where they are voted out. Check in on the teams and their sentiment, look for signs, and run retrospectives to ensure you have not regressed or devolved.

Never Stop Learning

Continuous learning and improvement is a fundamental lean principle. Learning and improvement should begin when you begin, before the initiative is launched, and it should never stop. This includes both learning for personal growth and learning to improve the initiative.

Use retrospective learning to learn from the past and improve the future. Use proactive learning to learn from what might happen in the future and take preventative or mitigating measures. Look in the mirror periodically through introspective learning to provide a new perspective and give yourself the power to act. Then inspect and adapt!

Don't fail fast and break things. Learn fast and iterate! You're not failing if you're learning.

Take the First Step!

Regardless of the size and type you choose, these initiatives can be extremely rewarding. Though they are not always without challenge, I have always enjoyed them. They have rewarded me with amazing opportunities and provided me with some of my greatest professional experiences.

Through these initiatives, I have been exposed to people, places, and events I would not have otherwise encountered. Most importantly, they have introduced me to smart, passionate, creative, and interesting people. I count many of those people amongst my closest colleagues and friends.

Thank you, again, for taking time to read this book. I wish you the very best on your own journey, and please share your stories of success if you can. I look forward to learning about your victories.

Now, go build something great!

PART V

The Lean Entrepreneurship Toolkit

APPENDIX 1

Initiatives-at-a-Glance, One-Page Stage Overviews, and Stage Checklists

How to Use This Section

This section of the Lean Entrepreneurship Toolkit contains illustrative overviews and checklists for each stage of incubation for three illustrative incubation models. It is likely that not all items in any one checklist will be applicable to your incubation or initiative. Individuals and teams should make deliberate decisions about which items apply to their initiative and which do not, and use only those items that are applicable. You may find that items from different checklists in more than one scenario apply to your situation, and you might also wish to add new items to the checklists to suit your unique needs. Stage time estimates may require adjustment to suit your environment and meet your unique requirements.

APPENDIX 1   INITIATIVES-AT-A-GLANCE, ONE-PAGE STAGE OVERVIEWS, AND STAGE CHECKLISTS

Checklists should be used situationally, at the discretion of individuals and teams, to facilitate and accelerate the advancement of an idea or initiative, and to help achieve the most learning possible in the shortest time. These are meant to be illustrative starting points, not immutable directives.

APPENDIX 1 INITIATIVES-AT-A-GLANCE, ONE-PAGE STAGE OVERVIEWS, AND STAGE CHECKLISTS

Seed-Series Model–Private Sector Product or Service Scenario

Customer-Problem Fit (Seed 1)	Problem-Solution Fit (Seed 2)	Solution-Product Fit (Series A)	Product-Market Fit (Series B)	Exit to Scale (Series C)
Objective: Validate that problem is worth solving for the identified target market, via early adopters; prepare problem-solution fit activities	**Objective:** Validate solution's likelihood to delight early adopters	**Objective:** Prove ability to achieve traction with early adopters	**Objective:** Prove business model is viable and scalable, find an acquirer	**Objectives:** Execute on business case; align to acquirer requirements; exit the business to the acquirer
Key Questions to Answer: Is this problem worth solving?	**Key Question to Answer:** If we build this, will early adopters use it? Will they pay for it?	**Key Question to Answer:** Now that we've built it, did the early adopters come, and does it continue to attract new customers?	**Key Question to Answer:** Has our business scaled with the additional investment? Can it continue to scale? Is the business model viable?	**Key Question to Answer:** Were the acquisition commitments met?
Outcome: Sufficient evidence of problem-early adopter pair	**Outcomes:** Sufficient evidence that the problem-solution approach satisfies early adopters; clearly defined and scoped MVP; business model* baseline	**Outcome:** MVP; sufficient evidence of business model* traction	**Outcomes:** Market demand for the solution is accelerating; clear marketing and sales strategy; confirmed intent to acquire	**Outcomes:** Solution acquisition; exit from the initiative
Output:	**Output:**	**Output:**	**Output:**	**Output:**
• Marketing: Segmentation / Early Adopter Analysis; Lean Persona(s); Rough Market Sizing	• Marketing: positioning statement; business narrative/pitch; validated thinking on how you will reach early adopters; competitive landscape; pricing model	• Marketing: Website reveal; go-to-market plan; key engine of growth identified; early/evangelist purchase of solution	• Marketing: Evidence that GTM strategy is effective & will scale	• Traction: Traction model shows growth and scale targets defined in Series B were achieved
• Rough sizing of the likely scope of the problem at scale (e.g.: tens, hundreds, or millions of users)	• Traction: One-page traction model with assumptions outlined	• MVP released	• Traction: Target weekly growth rate & retention achieved; traction model goals met, evidence solution can scale	• Acquisition: Technical due diligence completed; input provided for business due diligence
• Traction: Estimated understanding of the user base and size	• Analysis of alternatives and competing solutions	• Early adopters	• Firm understanding of CAC, LTV, and COGs	• Documented final decision from acquirer for business to exit the initiative
• Updated lean canvas	• Validated MVP definition and initial backlog	• Sean Ellis Test baseline	• Acquisition: Pitch and executive summary	• Exit pitch
• Evidence the problem is painful enough people would adopt a new solution	• Initial proof of the market is large enough	• Traction Model shows that you've met your first goal	• Marketing: Input provided to business case and acquisition pitch	• Transfer of control of the business to the acquirer
• Analysis of existing alternatives	• Initial proof the solution solves the early adopter's problem	• Initial understanding of CAC, LTV, and COGs	• Contingent acquisition commitment	• Knowledge capture and preservation
• Rough market sizing	• Series A Plan	• Technical de-risking	• Clear sales and partner strategy	• Turnover of technology and artifacts to the acquiring business
• Traction: Animal You're Hunting		• Design for scale	• Technical debt assessment	• Completion of architecture for scale
• Seed 2 Plan		• Referenceable customers	• Series C Plan	
		• Series B backlog		
		• Series B Plan		

*May include free/non-monetary models.

Desirability → Feasibility → Viability
Incubation → Startup

APPENDIX 1 INITIATIVES-AT-A-GLANCE, ONE-PAGE STAGE OVERVIEWS, AND STAGE CHECKLISTS

Initiative Team Entry Preparation Checklist
(Initiative Team)

- ☐ Ensure team members are ready to travel (e.g.: executive approval, credit card acquisition)…
- ☐ Set up budget forecast and cost center
- ☐ Engage HR for Incubation Rotation
- ☐ Obtain approvals for team member participation
- ☐ Schedule first 3P review
- ☐ Ensure goal, objective, PMA, MBO, or OKR relief for incubating team members' original teams as appropriate
- ☐ Notify incubation team members' managers of entry acceptance
- ☐ Ensure team members are allocated to team as planned
- ☐ Create "project" in project management or agile management tool (e.g.: Jira™, Agile Central™, Rally™ …)
- ☐ Add Incubating Team leader to leadership Lean Coffee™ or lean meetings
- ☐ Update the initiative's email distribution lists
- ☐ Notify incubating team, Finance, and HR of pending entry and relevant changes
- ☐ Add new incubation to the initiative's dashboard
- ☐ Acquire office space or workspace if necessary
- ☐ Create messaging channel for new team, add this team to the initiative's collaboration channel(s)
- ☐ Verify team access to incubating team resources areas on internal systems (Wiki, SharePoint™ …)
- ☐ Schedule regular incubating team check-in sessions with Initiative Team
- ☐ Deliver Welcome Kit to incubating team leaders
- ☐ Ensure access to external subscriptions (e.g.: tools…), sub-accounts/users (complete permission forms if required)
- ☐ Spin up instance for new incubation landing page and link from central dashboards
- ☐ Deliver initiative compensation plan if applicable (e.g.: equity plan)

516

APPENDIX 1   INITIATIVES-AT-A-GLANCE, ONE-PAGE STAGE OVERVIEWS, AND STAGE CHECKLISTS

Incubating Team Entry Checklist
(New Incubator Participants)

- ☐ Welcome and Entry review (with Initiative Team)
- ☐ Read Eric Ries 'The Lean Startup'
- ☐ Read Ash Maurya's 'Running Lean', 3rd Edition
- ☐ Read, or listen to, Sam Altman's 'Startup Playbook' article (https://playbook.samaltman.com)
- ☐ Notify new incubating team's managers of their acceptance
- ☐ Begin competency model self-assessment
- ☐ Read Point Nine's "5 Ways to Build a $100 Million Business" Infographic (https://medium.com/point-nine-news/5-ways-to-build-a-100-million-business-c5066181bf50)
- ☐ Minimum Viable Team assessment (with Governance and/or Initiative Team)
- ☐ Establish business roles and reporting structure (incubating team founders/leaders)
- ☐ Establish business location and collocation requirements (incubating team founders/leaders)
- ☐ Seed 1 plan
- ☐ Solicit incubating team mentors and advisors
- ☐ Business name review
- ☐ Patent training if applicable
- ☐ Conduct an invention harvesting session
- ☐ Incubation Logistics (Initiative Team) (Help new team members understand how things are done)

APPENDIX 1   INITIATIVES-AT-A-GLANCE, ONE-PAGE STAGE OVERVIEWS, AND STAGE CHECKLISTS

Pause Checklist

- ☐ Communicate Pause decision or recommendation
- ☐ Distribute IP as appropriate (e.g.: deliver it to a common services or architecture group)
- ☐ Turn over ownership of any active research projects
- ☐ Assess code reuse (preserve knowledge, learning, and technology that may be reused)
- ☐ Assess new initiatives or business opportunities that might leverage the incubation's IP
- ☐ Return team members to their original or subsequent tasking if appropriate
- ☐ Update knowledge bases and/or other systems as appropriate to preserve knowledge and learning
- ☐ Consider and select recognition awards
- ☐ Cancel services and subscriptions or reassign ownership
- ☐ Preserve businesses, and other, contact databases as appropriate and while respecting privacy regulations, legislation, and guidelines
- ☐ Remove the incubation's mentions from internal systems or update its status
- ☐ Return or reassign equipment
- ☐ Remove internet presence
- ☐ Prepare and schedule business pivot if applicable
- ☐ Complete the turnover and funding allocation for active research projects (if applicable)

APPENDIX 1   INITIATIVES-AT-A-GLANCE, ONE-PAGE STAGE OVERVIEWS, AND STAGE CHECKLISTS

Seed 1: Customer-Problem Fit

Objectives:
- Validate the problem and needs are well understood and worth solving for the customers, users, and/or buyers via likely early adopters and those impacted
- Prepare for problem-solution fit activities

Key questions to answer:
- Is this a problem worth solving?
- Is the problem painful enough target users would switch from existing alternatives?
- Do we understand the problem or needs well enough to begin incubating?

Illustrative Activities and Outputs:
- Updated canvas
- Early adopter analysis
- Personas
- Scenarios
- Initial Seed 2 experiment definitions
- Experiment reports (plan for next step) if appropriate
- Partial validation plan (plan for next step) if appropriate
- Evidence of how early adopters are addressing the problem today
- Transition pitch

- Sufficient evidence to prove the problem exists, is well understood, is painful enough customers would switch to an alternative
- Estimated cost and resources for Seed 2
- Incubation Boot Camp training
- Rough market sizing
- Create incubating team's advisory team
- High-level competitive landscape
- Traction goal assessment

Estimated Duration: 2-4 weeks

Outcome:
Sufficient evidence of problem-early adopter pair
Updated business model canvas
Seed 2 plan

Operational Ownership:
Initiative Team

Governance:
Governance Team approval to transition to next phase

APPENDIX 1 INITIATIVES-AT-A-GLANCE, ONE-PAGE STAGE OVERVIEWS, AND STAGE CHECKLISTS

Seed 1 Checklist

- [ ] Complete incubation boot camp (incubating team SMEs, leaders, ops) training
- [ ] Identify your target market and early adopter segment (canvas "customer" and "early adopter" areas)
- [ ] Assess rough market sizing (e.g.: are you building your solution for 10s, 100s, 1,000s, or 1,000,000s of users)
- [ ] Form incubating team's advisory team and begin regular collaboration with them
- [ ] Desirability: Obtain initial proof the problem is painful, significant and needs to be solved by your target users or businesses, especially early adopters (validate lean canvas top boxes)
- [ ] Provide evidence that you understand how your early adopters are working around the problem today and their level of satisfaction with the workaround
- [ ] Establish a Seed 2 plan
- [ ] Identify Seed 1 assumptions & hypotheses and run Seed 1 experiments
- [ ] Perform a high-level survey of alternatives (competitive landscape)
- [ ] Understand the solution's market type
- [ ] Research knowledge bases and other relevant systems for existing knowledge and learning from prior initiatives
- [ ] Initial assessment of traction goals
- [ ] Create lean personas
- [ ] Conduct an invention harvesting session
- [ ] Understand the likely security and privacy needs
- [ ] Identify minimum viable team requirements and perform an MVT gap analysis

APPENDIX 1 INITIATIVES-AT-A-GLANCE, ONE-PAGE STAGE OVERVIEWS, AND STAGE CHECKLISTS

Seed 2: Problem-Solution Fit

Objective:
Validate the solution's likelihood to delight early adopters and that it would make things better, not worse

Key question to answer:
Will the solution meet the customer's needs, and would the intended users likely use it? Will the intended users pay for the solution?

Estimated Duration: 1-3 months

Outcome:
Sufficient evidence that the problem-solution approach satisfies early adopters, initial Startup phase scope, business model baseline

Illustrative Activities and Outputs:

- Solution narrative
- Pitch
- Validated learning with evidence of early adopter support for the concept
- Analysis of alternatives and competing ideas
- Traction model assumptions
- Prototyping
- Measurement hypotheses created
- Series A backlog
- Series A plan
- Pricing model hypothesis

- Seed 2 experiments completed
- Continued engagement with potential adopters
- Technical de-risking
- Technical architecture backlog
- Blockitecture
- Validated MVP definition
- Visual communication of the idea
- Initial proof the solution solves the early adopter's problem
- Initial proof of the market opportunity is large enough
- Viable business model hypothesis

Operational Ownership:
Initiative Team

Governance:
Governance Team 3P reviews

521

APPENDIX 1   INITIATIVES-AT-A-GLANCE, ONE-PAGE STAGE OVERVIEWS, AND STAGE CHECKLISTS

Seed 2 Checklist

- ☐ Read Ash Maurya's 'Scaling Lean'
- ☐ Business narrative / pitch
- ☐ Visually communicate the idea (e.g. models, storyboards)
- ☐ Initial proof that the solution solves the early adopters' problem(s)
- ☐ At least one viable business model identified
- ☐ Positioning statement
- ☐ Elevator pitch (positioning statement, why people should care about the solution)
- ☐ Initial proof that the impact or opportunity is big enough, based on your early adopters' perceived value of a solution
- ☐ Product (solution) backlog
- ☐ Understanding of how the team will reach its early adopters and partners
- ☐ Validated definition of the MVP
- ☐ Pricing model
- ☐ Search knowledge bases and other appropriate "lessons learned" libraries
- ☐ Architecture-level backlog
- ☐ Blockitecture creation
- ☐ Series A plan
- ☐ Identified risks to the current plan
- ☐ Invention harvesting
- ☐ Understand the potential security and privacy requirements for Series A

APPENDIX 1   INITIATIVES-AT-A-GLANCE, ONE-PAGE STAGE OVERVIEWS, AND STAGE CHECKLISTS

Series A: MVP, Early Adopter

Objective:
Build an MVP, prove likely feasibility, validate the business model, and demonstrate likelihood to attract early adopters

Illustrative Activities and Outputs:
- MVP released
- Sean Ellis Test with users (demand/value measurement)
- Customer (buyer and/or user) testimonials
- Create Series B backlog
- Transition pitch (sufficient evidence and artifacts to support early adopter traction and readiness for Series B)
- Series B plan
- Technical de-risking
- Continued engagement with Business Owners, Product Owners
- Go-to-market plan

Key questions to answer:
Is the solution feasible? Would people use it? Can it scale? Does the solution solve the problem? Does it drive value? Can we attract early adopters?

- Customer acquisition cost (CAC), customer lifetime value (LTV), cost of goods sold (COGS) understood
- Solution on track with traction and impact goals
- Acquisition of early adopters and earlyvangelists
- Privacy and security implications identified and tested
- Health and safety activities as appropriate and necessary
- Scaled architecture design, review, and guidance
- Understanding of costs at scale

Estimated Duration: 3-9 months

Outcome:
MVP delivered, early adopters and earlyvangelists acquired, validated learning supporting Series B preparedness, customer feedback to improve experience and adoption

Operational Ownership:
Initiative Team

Governance:
Governance Team 3P reviews
Some initiatives may require Extended Governance Team review or approval to transition to next phase

APPENDIX 1   INITIATIVES-AT-A-GLANCE, ONE-PAGE STAGE OVERVIEWS, AND STAGE CHECKLISTS

Series A Checklist

- [ ] Read Croll and Yoskovitz' "Lean Analytics" (incubating team leader or measurement assignee(s))
- [ ] Onboard development team or solution builders
- [ ] Incubating team trained
- [ ] Prior to MVP launch, positioning and messaging, activation flow, and business model are validated
- [ ] Marketing website is built and reviewed with incubating team advisors and Governance Team
- [ ] Go-to-market plan
- [ ] MVP is released
- [ ] Conduct Sean Ellis Test to gauge support and movement in sentiment
- [ ] Customer acquisition cost (CAC) understood
- [ ] Cost of goods sold (COGS) understood
- [ ] Customer lifetime value (LTV) understood
- [ ] Series B budget and plan
- [ ] Architecture review at scale
- [ ] Understanding of operational costs at scale, or cost to create and scale the solution
- [ ] Series B backlog
- [ ] Series B plan established
- [ ] Key engine of growth is identified with assumptions outlined
- [ ] An earlyvangelist has purchased the solution
- [ ] Solution is on target with traction & impact goals
- [ ] Referenceable early adopters
- [ ] Invention harvesting session
- [ ] Series B plan
- [ ] Understand the potential security and privacy requirements of Series B and at scale
- [ ] Health and safety activities as appropriate
- [ ] Executive summary (e.g.: presentation, document)

APPENDIX 1 INITIATIVES-AT-A-GLANCE, ONE-PAGE STAGE OVERVIEWS, AND STAGE CHECKLISTS

Series B: Solution-Product Fit

Estimated Duration: 3-12 months

Outcome:
Increasing demand, evidence go-to-market strategy is effective, confirmed intent to acquire the solution, clear marketing and sales strategy, evidence the solution can scale as needed

Operational Ownership:
Initiative Team

Governance:
Governance Team 3P reviews
Some initiatives may require Extended Governance Team approval to transition to next phase

Objective:
Prove the solution is viable, demonstrate it can scale, and confirm the business mode fundamentals are strong

Key questions to answer:
Can this scale? Does it continue to add value at scale? Will it be supportable? Does it support a viable business case?

Illustrative Activities and Outputs:
- Pass Sean Ellis Test
- Achieve monthly target retention rate
- Referrals from early adopters
- Evidence traction model has been validated with weekly target growth rates achieved
- Evidence of growth and ability to scale: Customer acquisition cost (CAC), customer lifetime value (LTV), cost of goods sold (COGS) understood
- Evidence go-to-market strategy is effective and will scale
- Clear sales and partner strategy
- Documented contingent acquisition commitment
- Acquisition requirements: Investor pitch, executive summary, input to business case, and Extended Governance Team deck
- Support readiness or support model
- Technical debt assessment
- Transition plan describing how the contingent agreement will be satisfied
- Series C plan
- Invention harvesting session

APPENDIX 1 INITIATIVES-AT-A-GLANCE, ONE-PAGE STAGE OVERVIEWS, AND STAGE CHECKLISTS

Series B Checklist (1/2)

- ☐ Product-market fit: Pass the Sean Ellis Test
- ☐ Product-market fit: Achieve targeted monthly retention rate
- ☐ Evidence of growth and ability to scale: CAC, LTV, COGS
- ☐ Evidence of growth and ability to scale: Traction model validated with target weekly growth rate achieved
- ☐ Evidence go-to-market strategy is effective and will scale
- ☐ Clear sales & partner strategy
- ☐ Early adopters have acquired the solution
- ☐ Acquisition requirement: Investor pitch
- ☐ Acquisition requirement: Executive summary
- ☐ Acquisition requirements: Input to business case and Extended Governance Team deck
- ☐ Acquisition requirement: Documented, contingent acquisition commitment
- ☐ Architecture review with focus on scaled deployment
- ☐ Technical de-risking of architecture and scaling
- ☐ Understanding of operational costs, cost of operation, cost to scale, nature of cost increases (if any) at scale (e.g.: linear, step, exponential)
- ☐ Evidence from testing required to confirm scale hypothesis
- ☐ Preliminary support model
- ☐ Referenceable early adopters

APPENDIX 1 INITIATIVES-AT-A-GLANCE, ONE-PAGE STAGE OVERVIEWS, AND STAGE CHECKLISTS

Series B Checklist (2/2)

- ☐ Identification of technical debt including code not suited for full-scale deployment, tools required for scale, and contracts and licenses requiring update for full scale deployment
- ☐ Transition plan for incubating team's exit
- ☐ Security and privacy requirements for acquisition understood
- ☐ Communications strategy
- ☐ Initial business due diligence
- ☐ Begin transition of source and IP to standard organizational repositories (as needed)
- ☐ Invention harvesting

APPENDIX 1   INITIATIVES-AT-A-GLANCE, ONE-PAGE STAGE OVERVIEWS, AND STAGE CHECKLISTS

Series C: Exit

Objective:
Complete acquisition and due diligence requirements, complete acquisition of the business, transfer business to the acquiring organization, move team to acquiring organization and/or next assignment

Illustrative Activities and Outputs:
- Evidence of continued growth and scale
- Technical due diligence completed
- Business due diligence completed
- Final decision to acquire the business is completed (affirmative)
- Invention harvesting
- Transfer of source control and IP to appropriate locations
- Transition plan execution completed

Key questions to answer:
Were the commitments agreed to in the Series B transition plan met? Is the solution ready to deploy and scale? Have all acquisition requirements been met? Is the receiving business ready to take over?

- Exit pitch (evidence and artifacts show exit criteria were met)
- Transfer full control to the acquiring business
- Turnover of technical artifacts
- Technical debt addressed if and as required by the acquisition plan
- Initial scale architecture completion
- Receiving team artifact requirements met
- Knowledge capture and preservation

Estimated Duration: 2-4 months

Outcome:
Evidence of continued growth and scale, technical due diligence complete, business due diligence complete, final acquisition complete

Operational Ownership:
Incubating Team
Incubating team transfers control to the acquiring business team

Governance:
Governance Team 3P reviews
Acquiring business team approval
Some initiatives may require Extended Governance Team approval to transition to Exit

APPENDIX 1 INITIATIVES-AT-A-GLANCE, ONE-PAGE STAGE OVERVIEWS, AND STAGE CHECKLISTS

Series C Checklist

- ☐ Evidence of continued growth and scale
- ☐ Documented business team agreement to acquire the solution
- ☐ Final decision to acquire the business completed (affirmative)
- ☐ Referenceable customers (users and/or buyers)
- ☐ Completed technical due diligence
- ☐ Completed business due diligence
- ☐ Business transition to the acquiring group
- ☐ Incubating team members were moved with the solution or redeployed to new assignments
- ☐ Series C transition request presentation (pitch)
- ☐ Pause checklist completed
- ☐ Invention harvesting
- ☐ Transfer of source code and IP to appropriate locations
- ☐ Acquisition contingency plan requirements met
- ☐ Acquiring business artifacts requirements met
- ☐ Control transferred to acquiring business
- ☐ Initial scale architecture completed
- ☐ Knowledge capture and preservation

APPENDIX 1 INITIATIVES-AT-A-GLANCE, ONE-PAGE STAGE OVERVIEWS, AND STAGE CHECKLISTS

Incubate–Startup–Accelerate Model–Private Sector Product or Service Scenario

Customer-Problem Fit (Incubate 1)	Problem-Solution Fit (Incubate 2)	Solution-Experiment Fit (Startup 1)	MVP, Early Adopter (Startup 2)	Solution-Product Fit (Accelerate 1)	Exit to Scale (Accelerate 2)
Objective: Validate that problem is worth solving via early adopters; prepare for problem-solution fit	**Objective:** Validate solution's likelihood to delight early adopters	**Objective:** Prove likely feasibility in a real-world environment and demonstrate likelihood to attract early adopters	**Objective:** Prove ability to achieve traction with early adopters	**Objectives:** Prove business model is viable and scalable, find an acquirer	**Objectives:** Execute on business case; align to acquirer requirements; exit the business to the acquirer
Key Questions to Answer: Who has this problem, and is it worth solving?	**Key Questions to Answer:** If we build this, will early adopters come? Will they pay?	**Key Questions to Answer:** Is the solution feasible? Now that we've built it, did the early adopters come? Can it scale?	**Key Questions to Answer:** Now that we've built it, did the early adopters come, and does it continue to attract new customers?	**Key Questions to Answer:** Has our business scaled with the additional investment? Can it continue to scale? Is the business model viable?	**Key Questions to Answer:** Were the acquisition commitments met?
Outcome: Sufficient evidence of problem-early adopter pair	**Outcomes:** Sufficient evidence that the proposed solution satisfies early adopters; initial Startup phase scope; business model baseline*	**Outcome:** Validated learning from experiments; sufficient traction, customer feedback, technical de-risking	**Outcomes:** MVP; sufficient evidence of business model* traction	**Outcomes:** Market demand for the solution is accelerating; clear marketing and sales strategy; confirmed intent to acquire	**Outcomes:** Solution acquisition; exit from the initiative
Output:	**Output:**	**Output:**	**Output:**	**Output:**	**Output:**
- Segmentation / early adopter analysis (understanding of who has the problem)
- Lean Persona(s)
- Rough sizing of the likely scope of the problem at scale (e.g.: tens, hundreds, or millions of users)
- Traction: Estimated understanding of the user base and size
- Evidence the problem is painful enough people would adopt a new solution
- Analysis of existing alternatives
- Rough market sizing
- Incubate 2 plan	- Marketing: positioning statement; business narrative/pitch; competitive landscape; pricing model
- Traction: One-page traction model with assumptions
- Analysis of alternatives and competing solutions
- Validated Startup 1 MVP definition and initial backlog
- Initial proof the market is large enough
- Initial proof of the solution solves the early adopter's problem
- One-page traction model with assumptions outlined
- Risk identification
- Startup 1 plan	- Experiment released in limited, controlled real-world context
- Earlyvangelist adoption
- Sean Ellis Test baseline
- Traction Model shows first goal was met
- Marketing: Website reveal; go-to-market plan; key engine of growth identified; initial understanding of cost and benefit of scaling
- Referenceable early adopters or earlyvangelists
- Startup 2 backlog, MVP definition, design for scale
- Startup 2 plan	- Marketing: Website reveal; go-to-market plan; key engine of growth identified; earlyvangelist purchase of solution
- MVP released
- Early adopters
- Sean Ellis Test (progress)
- Initial understanding of CAC, LTV, and COGs
- Technical de-risking
- Design for scale
- Referenceable customers
- Accelerate 1 backlog
- Accelerate 1 plan
- Evidence of growth and ability scale
- Traction model goals met, and proof usage can scale
- Firm understanding of cost and benefit at scale
- Engine of Growth identified	- Marketing: Evidence that GTM strategy is effective & will scale
- Sean Ellis Test passed
- Traction: Target weekly growth rate & retention achieved; traction model goals met, evidence solution can scale
- Firm understanding of CAC, LTV, and COGs
- Acquisition: Pitch and executive summary completed; input provided to business case and acquisition pitch
- Contingent acquisition commitment
- Clear sales and partner strategy
- Technical debt assessed
- Accelerate 2 plan
- Accelerate 2 backlog	- Traction: Traction model shows growth and scale targets defined in Accelerate 1 were achieved
- Acquisition: Technical due diligence completed; input provided for business due diligence
- Documented final decision from acquirer for business to exit the initiative
- Exit pitch
- Transfer of control of the business to the acquirer
- Knowledge capture and preservation
- Turnover of technology and artifacts to the acquiring business
- Completion of architecture for scale
- Technical debt addressed as required

*May include free/non-monetary models.

Desirability → Feasibility → Viability

APPENDIX 1   INITIATIVES-AT-A-GLANCE, ONE-PAGE STAGE OVERVIEWS, AND STAGE CHECKLISTS

Initiative Team Entry Preparation Checklist
(Initiative Team)

- ☐ Ensure team members are ready to travel (e.g.: executive approval, credit card acquisition)…
- ☐ Set up budget forecast and cost center
- ☐ Engage HR for Incubation Rotation
- ☐ Obtain approvals for team member participation
- ☐ Schedule first 3P review
- ☐ Ensure goal, objective, PMA, MBO, or OKR relief for incubating team members' original teams as appropriate
- ☐ Notify incubation team members' managers of entry acceptance
- ☐ Ensure team members are allocated to team as planned
- ☐ Create "project" in project management or agile management tool (e.g.: Jira™, Agile Central™, Rally™ …)
- ☐ Add Incubating Team leader to leadership Lean Coffee™ or lean meetings
- ☐ Update the initiative's email distribution lists
- ☐ Notify incubating team, Finance, and HR of pending entry and relevant changes
- ☐ Add new incubation to the initiative's dashboard
- ☐ Acquire office space or workspace if necessary
- ☐ Create messaging channel for new team, add this team to the initiative's collaboration channel(s)
- ☐ Verify team access to incubating team resources areas on internal systems (Wiki, SharePoint™ …)
- ☐ Schedule regular incubating team check-in sessions with Initiative Team
- ☐ Deliver Welcome Kit to incubating team leaders
- ☐ Ensure access to external subscriptions (e.g.: tools…), sub-accounts/users (complete permission forms if required)
- ☐ Spin up instance for new incubation landing page and link from central dashboards
- ☐ Deliver initiative compensation plan if applicable (e.g.: equity plan)

531

APPENDIX 1   INITIATIVES-AT-A-GLANCE, ONE-PAGE STAGE OVERVIEWS, AND STAGE CHECKLISTS

Incubating Team Entry Checklist
(New Incubator Participants)

- ☐ Welcome and Entry review (with Initiative Team)
- ☐ Read Eric Ries 'The Lean Startup'
- ☐ Read Ash Maurya's 'Running Lean', 3rd Edition
- ☐ Read, or listen to, Sam Altman's 'Startup Playbook' article (https://playbook.samaltman.com)
- ☐ Notify new incubating team's managers of their acceptance
- ☐ Begin competency model self-assessment
- ☐ Read Point Nine's "5 Ways to Build a $100 Million Business" Infographic (https://medium.com/point-nine-news/5-ways-to-build-a-100-million-business-c5066181bf50)
- ☐ Minimum Viable Team assessment (with Governance and/or Initiative Team)
- ☐ Establish business roles and reporting structure (incubating team founders/leaders)
- ☐ Establish business location and collocation requirements (incubating team founders/leaders)
- ☐ Incubate 1 plan
- ☐ Solicit incubating team mentors and advisors
- ☐ Business name review
- ☐ Patent training if applicable
- ☐ Conduct an invention harvesting session
- ☐ Incubation Logistics (Initiative Team) (Help new team members understand how things are done)

APPENDIX 1   INITIATIVES-AT-A-GLANCE, ONE-PAGE STAGE OVERVIEWS, AND STAGE CHECKLISTS

Pause Checklist

- ☐ Communicate Pause decision or recommendation
- ☐ Distribute IP as appropriate (e.g.: deliver it to a common services or architecture group)
- ☐ Turn over ownership of any active research projects
- ☐ Assess code reuse (preserve knowledge, learning, and technology that may be reused)
- ☐ Assess new initiatives or business opportunities that might leverage the incubation's IP
- ☐ Return team members to their original or subsequent tasking if appropriate
- ☐ Update knowledge bases and/or other systems as appropriate to preserve knowledge and learning
- ☐ Consider and select recognition awards
- ☐ Cancel services and subscriptions or reassign ownership
- ☐ Preserve businesses, and other, contact databases as appropriate and while respecting privacy regulations, legislation, and guidelines
- ☐ Remove the incubation's mentions from internal systems or update its status
- ☐ Return or reassign equipment
- ☐ Remove internet presence
- ☐ Prepare and schedule business pivot if applicable
- ☐ Complete the turnover and funding allocation for active research projects (if applicable)

533

APPENDIX 1 INITIATIVES-AT-A-GLANCE, ONE-PAGE STAGE OVERVIEWS, AND STAGE CHECKLISTS

Incubate 1: Customer-Problem Fit

Estimated Duration: 2-4 weeks

Objectives:
- Validate the problem and needs are well understood and worth solving for the customers, users, and/or buyers via likely early adopters and those impacted
- Prepare for problem-solution fit activities

Key questions to answer:
- Is this a problem worth solving?
- Is the problem painful enough target users would switch from existing alternatives?
- Do we understand the problem or needs well enough to begin incubating?

Outcome:
- Sufficient evidence of problem-early adopter pair
- Updated business model canvas
- Incubate 2 plan

Illustrative Activities and Outputs:
- Updated canvas
- Early adopter analysis
- Personas
- Scenarios
- Initial Incubate 2 experiment definitions
- Partial validation plan (plan for next step) if appropriate
- Evidence of how early adopters are addressing the problem today
- Transition pitch

- Sufficient evidence to prove the problem exists, is well understood, is painful enough customers would switch to an alternative
- Estimated cost and resources for Incubate 2
- Incubation Boot Camp training
- Rough market sizing
- Create incubating team's advisory team
- High-level competitive landscape
- Traction goal assessment

Operational Ownership:
Initiative Team

Governance:
Governance Team approval to transition to next phase

APPENDIX 1 INITIATIVES-AT-A-GLANCE, ONE-PAGE STAGE OVERVIEWS, AND STAGE CHECKLISTS

Incubate 1 Checklist

- [ ] Complete incubation boot camp (incubating team SMEs, leaders, ops) training
- [ ] Identify your target market and early adopter segment (canvas customer and early adopter segments)
- [ ] Assess rough market sizing (e.g.: are you building your solution for 10s, 100s, 1,000s, or 1,000,000s of users)
- [ ] Form incubating team's advisory team and begin regular collaboration with them
- [ ] Desirability: Obtain initial proof the problem is painful, significant and needs to be solved by your target users or business, especially early adopters (validate lean canvas top boxes)
- [ ] Provide evidence that you understand how your early adopters are working around the problem today and their level of satisfaction with the workaround
- [ ] Establish an Incubate 2 plan
- [ ] Identify Incubate 1 assumptions & hypotheses and run Incubate 1 experiments
- [ ] Perform high-level survey of alternatives (competitive landscape)
- [ ] Understand the solution's market type
- [ ] Research knowledge bases and other relevant systems for existing knowledge and learning from prior initiatives
- [ ] Initial assessment of traction goals
- [ ] Create lean personas
- [ ] Conduct an invention harvesting session
- [ ] Understand the likely security and privacy needs
- [ ] Identify minimum viable team requirements and perform an MVT gap analysis

APPENDIX 1 INITIATIVES-AT-A-GLANCE, ONE-PAGE STAGE OVERVIEWS, AND STAGE CHECKLISTS

Incubate 2: Problem-Solution Fit

Objective:
Validate the solution's likelihood to delight early adopters and that it would make things better, not worse

Key question to answer:
Will the solution meet the customer's needs, and would the intended users likely use it? Will the intended users pay for the solution?

Estimated Duration: 1-3 months

Outcome:
Sufficient evidence that the problem-solution approach satisfies early adopters, initial Startup phase scope, business model baseline

Illustrative Activities and Outputs:

- Solution narrative
- Pitch
- Validated learning with evidence of early adopter support for the concept
- Analysis of alternatives and competing ideas or projects
- Traction model assumptions
- Prototyping
- Measurement hypotheses created
- Startup 1 backlog
- Startup 1 plan
- Pricing model hypothesis

- Continued engagement with potential adopters
- Incubate 2 experiments completed
- Technical de-risking
- Technical architecture backlog
- Blockitecture
- Validated MVP definition
- Visual communication of the idea
- Initial proof the solution solves the early adopter's problem
- Initial proof of the market opportunity is large enough
- Viable business model hypothesis

Operational Ownership:
Initiative Team

Governance:
Governance Team 3P reviews

APPENDIX 1 INITIATIVES-AT-A-GLANCE, ONE-PAGE STAGE OVERVIEWS, AND STAGE CHECKLISTS

Incubate 2 Checklist

- [ ] Read Ash Maurya's 'Scaling Lean'
- [ ] Business narrative / pitch
- [ ] Visually communicate the idea (e.g. models, storyboards)
- [ ] Initial proof that the solution solves the early adopters' problem(s)
- [ ] At least one viable business model identified
- [ ] Positioning statement
- [ ] Elevator pitch (positioning statement, why people should care about the solution)
- [ ] Initial proof that the impact or opportunity is big enough, based on your early adopters' perceived value of a solution
- [ ] Product backlog
- [ ] Understanding of how the team will reach its early adopters and partners
- [ ] Validated definition of the MVP
- [ ] Pricing model
- [ ] Search knowledge bases and other appropriate "lessons learned" libraries
- [ ] Architecture-level backlog
- [ ] Blockitecture creation
- [ ] Startup 1 plan
- [ ] Identified risks to the current plan
- [ ] Invention harvesting
- [ ] Understand the potential security and privacy requirements for Startup 1

APPENDIX 1 INITIATIVES-AT-A-GLANCE, ONE-PAGE STAGE OVERVIEWS, AND STAGE CHECKLISTS

Startup 1: Solution-Experiment

Objective:
Prove likely feasibility and demonstrate likelihood to attract early adopters

Key questions to answer:
Is the solution feasible? Would people use it? Did it attract early adopters? Can the low-fidelity version be translated to viability at the necessary scale? Did it solve the problem? Does it drive value?

Estimated Duration: 3-9 months

Outcome:
Validated learning via small batch experiments in preparation for Startup 2
Customer (user and/or buyer) feedback to improve experience and adoption
Technical de-risking

Illustrative Activities and Outputs:

- Early deployment hypothesis and plan
- Solution may be released in a limited-time, controlled test
- Initial understanding of likely cost of Startup 2
- Startup 1 customer (buyer and/or user) testimonials
- Create Startup 2 backlog
- Initial Accelerate 1 plan (scaled deployment hypothesis)
- Small batch, rapid experiments
- Technical de-risking with low-cost, low-fidelity components
- Continued engagement with Business Owners, Product Owners
- Potential early adopters engaged
- Startup 2 plan
- Privacy and security implications identified and tested
- Health and safety activities as appropriate and necessary
- Initial scaled architecture hypothesis, review, and guidance

Operational Ownership:
Initiative Team

Governance:
Governance Team 3P reviews
Some initiatives may require Extended Governance Team review or approval to transition to next phase

538

APPENDIX 1   INITIATIVES-AT-A-GLANCE, ONE-PAGE STAGE OVERVIEWS, AND STAGE CHECKLISTS

Startup 1 Checklist

- ☐ Read Croll and Yoskovitz' "Lean Analytics" (Incubating team leader or measurement assignee(s))
- ☐ Onboard development team or solution builders
- ☐ Incubating team trained
- ☐ Prior to MVP launch, positioning and messaging, activation flow, and business model are validated
- ☐ Marketing website is built and reviewed with incubating team advisors and Governance Team
- ☐ Go-to-market plan hypothesis
- ☐ Startup 1 low-fidelity MVP is released
- ☐ Conduct Sean Ellis test to establish a baseline
- ☐ Customer acquisition cost (CAC) hypothesis
- ☐ Cost of goods sold (COGS) hypothesis
- ☐ Customer lifetime value (LTV) hypothesis
- ☐ Initial architecture review
- ☐ Initial understanding of operational costs at scale, or cost to create and scale the solution
- ☐ Startup 2 backlog
- ☐ Startup 2 plan
- ☐ Key engine of growth is identified with assumptions outlined
- ☐ An earlyvangelist has conditionally purchased or agreed to use your solution
- ☐ Solution is on target with traction & impact goals
- ☐ Invention harvesting session
- ☐ Understand the potential security and privacy requirements for likely solution and for Startup 2

APPENDIX 1   INITIATIVES-AT-A-GLANCE, ONE-PAGE STAGE OVERVIEWS, AND STAGE CHECKLISTS

Startup 2: MVP, Early Adopter

Objective:
Build an MVP, prove likely feasibility, validate the business model, and demonstrate likelihood to attract early adopters

Key questions to answer:
Is the solution feasible? Would people use it? Can it scale? Does the solution solve the problem? Does it drive value? Can we attract early adopters?

Estimated Duration: 6-12 months

Outcome:
MVP delivered, early adopters and earlyvangelists acquired, validated learning supporting Accelerate 1 preparedness, customer feedback to improve experience and adoption

Illustrative Activities and Outputs:
- MVP released
- Sean Ellis test with users (demand/value measurement)
- Customer (buyer and/or user) testimonials
- Accelerate 1 backlog
- Accelerate 1 plan
- Transition pitch (sufficient evidence and artifacts to support early adopter traction and readiness for Accelerate 1)
- Technical de-risking
- Customer acquisition cost (CAC), customer lifetime value (LTV), cost of goods sold (COGS) understood

- Continued engagement with business owners, product owners
- Go-to-market plan
- Solution on track with traction and impact goals
- Health and safety activities as appropriate and necessary
- Architecture review, and guidance
- Privacy and security implications identified and tested
- Understanding of cost at scale
- Scaled architecture design, review, and guidance
- Acquisition of early adopters and earlyvangelists

Operational Ownership:
Initiative Team

Governance:
Governance Team 3P reviews
Some initiatives may require Extended Governance Team approval to transition to next phase

APPENDIX 1   INITIATIVES-AT-A-GLANCE, ONE-PAGE STAGE OVERVIEWS, AND STAGE CHECKLISTS

Startup 2 Checklist

- [ ] MVP released
- [ ] Architecture review
- [ ] Conduct Sean Ellis test to gauge support and movement in sentiment
- [ ] Achieve targeted retention rate
- [ ] Go-to-market plan completed
- [ ] Evidence of growth and ability to scale: Understand user acquisition cost (CAC), Customer lifetime value (LTV), and cost of goods sold (COGS)
- [ ] Initial understanding of operational costs, cost of operation, cost to scale, nature of cost increases (if any) at scale (e.g.: linear, step, exponential)
- [ ] Architecture (for scale) review and guidance
- [ ] Solution is on target with traction & impact goals
- [ ] An early adopter has been acquired
- [ ] An earlyvangelist has purchased the solution
- [ ] Referenceable early adopters
- [ ] Accelerate 1 backlog
- [ ] Accelerate 1 plan established
- [ ] Understand security and privacy requirements of the solution
- [ ] Health and safety activities as appropriate and necessary
- [ ] Accelerate 1 budget estimate
- [ ] Executive summary (e.g.: presentation, document)
- [ ] Invention harvesting

APPENDIX 1   INITIATIVES-AT-A-GLANCE, ONE-PAGE STAGE OVERVIEWS, AND STAGE CHECKLISTS

Accelerate 1: Solution-Product Fit

Estimated Duration: 3-12 months

Objective:
Prove the solution is viable, demonstrate it can scale, and confirm the business model fundamentals are strong

Key questions to answer:
Can this scale? Does it continue to add value at scale? Will it be supportable? Does it support a viable business case?

Outcome:
Increasing demand, evidence go-to-market strategy is effective, confirmed intent to acquire the solution, clear marketing and sales strategy, evidence the solution can scale as needed

Illustrative Activities and Outputs:
- Pass Sean Ellis Test
- Achieve monthly target retention rate
- Referrals from early adopters
- Evidence traction model has been validated with weekly target growth rates achieved
- Evidence of growth and ability to scale: Customer acquisition cost (CAC), customer lifetime value (LTV), cost of goods sold (COGS) understood
- Evidence go-to-market strategy is effective and will scale
- Clear sales and partner strategy
- Documented contingent acquisition commitment
- Acquisition requirements: Investor pitch, executive summary, input to business case and Extended Governance Team deck
- Support readiness or support model
- Technical debt assessment
- Transition plan describing how the contingent agreement will be satisfied
- Accelerate 2 plan
- Invention harvesting session

Operational Ownership:
Initiative Team

Governance:
Governance Team 3P reviews
Some initiatives may require Extended Governance Team approval to transition to next phase

APPENDIX 1　INITIATIVES-AT-A-GLANCE, ONE-PAGE STAGE OVERVIEWS, AND STAGE CHECKLISTS

Accelerate 1 Checklist (1/2)

- ☐ Product-market fit: Pass the Sean Ellis Test
- ☐ Product-market fit: Achieve targeted monthly retention rate
- ☐ Evidence of growth and ability to scale: CAC, LTV, COGS
- ☐ Evidence of growth and ability to scale: Traction model validated with target weekly growth rate achieved
- ☐ Evidence that go-to-market strategy is effective and will scale
- ☐ Clear sales & partner strategy
- ☐ Early adopters have acquired the solution
- ☐ Acquisition requirement: Investor pitch
- ☐ Acquisition requirement: Executive summary
- ☐ Acquisition requirements: Input to business case and Extended Governance Team deck
- ☐ Acquisition requirement: Documented, contingent acquisition commitment
- ☐ Architecture review with focus on scaled deployment
- ☐ Technical de-risking of architecture scaling
- ☐ Understanding of operational costs, cost of operation, cost to scale, nature of cost increases (if any) at scale (e.g.: linear, step, exponential)
- ☐ Evidence from testing required to confirm scale hypothesis
- ☐ Preliminary support model
- ☐ Referenceable early adopters

APPENDIX 1 INITIATIVES-AT-A-GLANCE, ONE-PAGE STAGE OVERVIEWS, AND STAGE CHECKLISTS

Accelerate 1 Checklist (2/2)

- [ ] Identification of technical debt including code not suited for full-scale deployment, tools required for scale, and contracts requiring update for production deployment
- [ ] Transition plan for incubating team's exit
- [ ] Security and privacy requirements for acquisition understood
- [ ] Initial business due diligence
- [ ] Communications strategy
- [ ] Begin transition of source and IP to standard organizational repositories (as needed)
- [ ] Invention harvesting

APPENDIX 1   INITIATIVES-AT-A-GLANCE, ONE-PAGE STAGE OVERVIEWS, AND STAGE CHECKLISTS

Accelerate 2: Exit

Estimated Duration: 2-4 months

Objective:
Complete acquisition and due diligence requirements, complete acquisition of the business, transfer business to the acquiring organization, move team to acquiring organization and/or next assignment

Outcome:
Evidence of continued growth and scale, technical due diligence complete, business due diligence complete, final acquisition complete

Illustrative Activities and Outputs:

- Evidence of continued growth and scale
- Technical due diligence completed
- Business due diligence completed
- Final decision to acquire the business is completed (affirmative)
- Invention harvesting
- Transfer of source control and IP to appropriate locations
- Transition plan execution completed

Key questions to answer:
Were the commitments agreed to in the Accelerate 1 transition plan met? Is the solution ready to deploy and scale? Have all acquisition requirements been met? Is the receiving business ready to take over?

- Exit pitch (evidence and artifacts show exit criteria were met)
- Transfer full control to the acquiring business
- Turnover of technical artifacts
- Technical debt addressed if and as required by the acquisition plan
- Initial scale architecture completion
- Receiving team artifact requirements met
- Knowledge capture and preservation

Operational Ownership:
Incubating Team
Incubating team transfers control to the acquiring business team

Governance:
Governance Team 3P reviews
Acquiring business team approval
Some initiatives may require Extended Governance Team approval to transition to next phase

APPENDIX 1   INITIATIVES-AT-A-GLANCE, ONE-PAGE STAGE OVERVIEWS, AND STAGE CHECKLISTS

Accelerate 2 Checklist

- ☐ Evidence of continued growth and scale
- ☐ Documented business team agreement to acquire the solution
- ☐ Final decision to acquire the business completed (affirmative)
- ☐ Referenceable customers (users and/or buyers)
- ☐ Completed technical due diligence
- ☐ Completed business due diligence
- ☐ Business transition to the acquiring group
- ☐ Incubating team members were moved with the solution or redeployed to new assignments
- ☐ Accelerate 2 transition request presentation (pitch)
- ☐ Pause checklist completed
- ☐ Invention harvesting
- ☐ Transfer of source code and IP to appropriate locations
- ☐ Acquisition contingency plan requirements met
- ☐ Acquiring business artifacts requirements met
- ☐ Control transferred to acquiring business
- ☐ Initial scale architecture completed
- ☐ Knowledge capture and preservation

APPENDIX 1   INITIATIVES-AT-A-GLANCE, ONE-PAGE STAGE OVERVIEWS, AND STAGE CHECKLISTS

Explore–Experiment–Transition Model–Public Sector Program or Project Scenario

	Beneficiary-Problem Fit (Explore 1)	Problem-Solution Fit (Explore 2)	Solution-Experiment Fit (Experiment 1)	Early Adopter Fit (Experiment 2)	Solution-Product Fit (Transition 1)	Product-Operations Fit (Transition 2)
Objective	Validate that problem is worth solving via early adopters; prepare for problem-solution fit	Validate solution's likelihood to delight early adopters	Prove likely feasibility in a real-world environment and demonstrate likelihood to attract early adopters	Prove operational feasibility, likely production viability	Prove the solution can be supportable, confirm likelihood of viability, de-risk scaling, transfer leadership to deployment project owners	Confirm readiness; transition to deployment project
Key Questions to Answer	Who has this problem, and is it worth solving?	If we build this, will early adopters come?	Can it be built for real-world operations? Now that we've built it, did the early adopters come? Did it drive value?	Can it be built for operation in a viable, scalable way?	Can the solution be built for operation at real-world scale, does it continue to add value at scale, is it viable, and are deployment prerequisite requirements met?	Were Transition 1 commitments met? Is the solution ready to deploy at scale? Were readiness requirements met? Has the project team taken over?
Outcome(s)	Sufficient evidence of problem-early adopter pair	Sufficient evidence that the proposed solution satisfies early adopters; initial Experiment phase scope; business model baseline	Sufficient evidence of business model traction and beneficiary feedback; technical de-risking	Demand for the solution is accelerating; Intent to acquire confirmed; Scale de-risked	Increasing adoption and demand; agreement to sponsor; deployment readiness	Readiness pass; Deployment project approval
Output	• Segmentation / early adopter analysis (understanding of who has the problem) • Updated lean canvas • Rough sizing of the likely scope of the problem at scale (e.g.: tens, hundreds, or millions of users) • Traction: Estimated understanding of the user base and size • Explore 2 plan	• Solution Narrative/Pitch • Validated learning & early adopter solution support • Analysis of alternatives • One-page traction model with assumptions outlined • Validated MVP definition • Early concept de-risking • Risk identification • Experimental apparatus • Experiment 1 plan	• Experiment released in limited, controlled real-world context • Measurement apparatus • Sean Ellis Test baseline • Traction Model shows first goal was met • Initial understanding of cost and benefit of scaling • Referenceable beneficiaries • Experiment 2 plan	• Experiment released in time-limited broader, controlled real-world context • Evidence of growth and ability scale • Sean Ellis Test passed • Target growth rate & retention achieved • Traction model goals met, and proof usage can scale • Firm understanding of cost and benefit at scale • Pitch and executive summary completed • Contingent commitment to proceed with full project • Engine of Growth identified • Transition 1 plan	• Evidence the solution can likely be widely deployed and operate at scale • Project MVP and architecture defined • Technical due diligence completed • Input provided for business due diligence • Documented final decision from business to sponsor • Leadership transitioned to project or program team	• Approval for deployment • Readiness evidence • Operational readiness and training • Technical debt addressed as required • Business due diligence completed • Documented final sponsorship agreement • Knowledge capture • Ownership transitioned to project or program team • Incubation team redeployed
	Understand the problem	Understand the potential solution space	Understand the solution	Understand the real-world solution space	Understand the deployment and scale considerations	Create the conditions for successful deployment
	← Exploration →		← Experimentation →		← Transition →	
	← Desirability →		← Feasibility →		← Viability →	

APPENDIX 1   INITIATIVES-AT-A-GLANCE, ONE-PAGE STAGE OVERVIEWS, AND STAGE CHECKLISTS

Incubating Team Entry Checklist
(New Incubator Participants)

- ☐ Welcome and Entry review (with Initiative Team)
- ☐ Read Eric Ries 'The Lean Startup'
- ☐ Read Ash Maurya's 'Running Lean', 3rd Edition
- ☐ Read, or listen to, Sam Altman's 'Startup Playbook' article (https://playbook.samaltman.com)
- ☐ Read Point Nine's "5 Ways to Build a $100 Million Business" Infographic (https://medium.com/point-nine-news/5-ways-to-build-a-100-million-business-c5066181bf50)
- ☐ Minimum Viable Team assessment (with Advisory Team)
- ☐ Establish business roles and reporting structure (Incubating Team founders/leaders)
- ☐ Establish business location and collocation requirements (Incubating Team leaders)
- ☐ Explore 1 plan established
- ☐ Solicit Incubating Team mentors and advisors
- ☐ Initiative, program, or project name review
- ☐ Incubation Logistics (Initiative Team)
  (Help new team members understand how things are done)

APPENDIX 1   INITIATIVES-AT-A-GLANCE, ONE-PAGE STAGE OVERVIEWS, AND STAGE CHECKLISTS

Initiative Team Entry Preparation Checklist
(Initiative Team)

- ☐ Ensure team members are ready to travel (e.g.: executive approval, credit card acquisition)…
- ☐ Determine budget forecast and cost center
- ☐ Obtain approvals for team member participation
- ☐ Ensure goal, objective, PMA, MBO, or OKR relief for incubating team members' original teams as appropriate
- ☐ Notify incubation team members' managers of entry acceptance
- ☐ Ensure team members are allocated to team as planned
- ☐ Schedule first 3P Review
- ☐ Create "project" in project management or agile management tool (e.g.: Jira™, Agile Central™, Rally™ …)
- ☐ Add incubating team leader to leadership Lean Coffee™ or lean meetings
- ☐ Update the initiative's email distribution lists
- ☐ Notify incubating team, Finance, and HR of pending entry and relevant changes
- ☐ Add new incubation to the initiative's dashboard
- ☐ Create messaging channel for new team, add this team to the initiative's collaboration channel(s)
- ☐ Verify team access to incubating team resources areas on internal systems (Wiki, SharePoint™ …)
- ☐ Schedule regular incubating team check-in sessions with Initiative Team
- ☐ Deliver Welcome Kit to incubating team leaders
- ☐ Ensure access to external subscriptions (e.g.: tools…), sub-accounts/users (complete permission forms if required)
- ☐ Spin up instance for new incubation landing page and link from central dashboards

549

APPENDIX 1   INITIATIVES-AT-A-GLANCE, ONE-PAGE STAGE OVERVIEWS, AND STAGE CHECKLISTS

Pause Checklist

- ☐ Communicate Pause decision or recommendation
- ☐ Distribute IP as appropriate (e.g.: deliver it to a common services or architecture group)
- ☐ Turn over ownership of any active research projects
- ☐ Assess code reuse (preserve knowledge, learning, and technology that may be reused)
- ☐ Preserve and document back-end APIs
- ☐ Assess new initiatives or business opportunities that might leverage the incubation's IP
- ☐ Return team members to their original or subsequent tasking if appropriate
- ☐ Update knowledge bases and/or other systems as appropriate to preserve knowledge and learning
- ☐ Consider and select recognition and awards
- ☐ Cancel services and subscriptions or reassign ownership
- ☐ Preserve businesses, and other, contact databases as appropriate and while respecting privacy regulations, legislation, and guidelines
- ☐ Remove the incubation's mentions from internal systems or update its status
- ☐ Return or reassign equipment
- ☐ Prepare and schedule incubation pivot if applicable
- ☐ Complete the turnover and funding allocation for active research projects (if applicable)

APPENDIX 1   INITIATIVES-AT-A-GLANCE, ONE-PAGE STAGE OVERVIEWS, AND STAGE CHECKLISTS

Explore 1: Beneficiary-Problem Fit

Objectives:
- Validate the problem and needs are well understood and worth solving for the beneficiaries, users, and/or sponsors via likely early adopters and those impacted
- Prepare for problem-solution fit activities

Illustrative Activities and Outputs:
- Updated Canvas
- Early adopter analysis
- Personas
- Scenarios
- Initial Explore 2 test definitions (purpose, methods, what will be observed)
- Partial test report (plan for next step) if appropriate
- Partial validation plan (plan for next step) if appropriate

Key questions to answer:
- Is this a problem worth solving?
- Do we understand the problem or needs well enough to begin incubating?
- Are the incubating team and sponsors aligned on the problem or needs?

- Transition pitch
- Sufficient evidence to prove the problem exists, is well understood, is painful enough to solve, and has technology components
- Estimated cost and resources for Explore 2
- Articulate benefits toward organization's mission achievement

Estimated Duration: 2-4 weeks

Outcome:
Sufficient evidence of problem-early adopter pair
Updated business model canvas
Explore 2 plan

Operational Ownership:
Initiative Team

Governance:
Governance Team approval to transition to next phase

551

APPENDIX 1 INITIATIVES-AT-A-GLANCE, ONE-PAGE STAGE OVERVIEWS, AND STAGE CHECKLISTS

Explore 1 Checklist

- ☐ Complete incubation boot camp (incubating team SMEs, leaders, ops) training
- ☐ Identify your target "market" and early adopter segment (canvas beneficiary and early adopter segments)
- ☐ Assess rough business model scoping (e.g.: are you building your solution for 10s, 100s, 1,000s, or 1,000,000s of users)
- ☐ Form incubating team's advisory team and begin regular collaboration with them (incubating team lead, "deal-maker")
- ☐ Obtain initial proof that the problem is painful, significant & needs to be solved by your target users or business, especially early adopters (ie: validate desirability via the PS lean canvas)
- ☐ Provide evidence that you understand how your early adopters are working around the problem today & their level of satisfaction with the workaround
- ☐ Establish an Explore 2 plan
- ☐ Identify Explore 1 assumptions & hypotheses and run Explore 1 experiments
- ☐ Perform high-level survey of alternatives (competitive landscape)
- ☐ Research knowledge bases and other relevant systems for existing knowledge and learning from prior initiatives
- ☐ Initial assessment of traction goals
- ☐ Create lean personas
- ☐ Understand the likely security posture of the likely solution
- ☐ Understand the likely privacy posture of the likely solution
- ☐ Understand the likely legal posture of the likely solution
- ☐ Identify minimum viable team requirements and perform an MVT gap analysis

APPENDIX 1 INITIATIVES-AT-A-GLANCE, ONE-PAGE STAGE OVERVIEWS, AND STAGE CHECKLISTS

Explore 2: Problem-Solution Fit

Objective:
Validate the solution's likelihood to delight early adopters and that it would make things better, not worse

Key question to answer:
Will this meet the beneficiaries' needs, and would the intended users likely use it?

Estimated Duration: 1-3 months

Outcome:
Sufficient evidence that the problem-solution approach satisfies early adopters, initial Experiment phase scope, business model baseline

Illustrative Activities and Outputs:

- Solution narrative
- Pitch
- Validated learning with evidence of early adopter support for the concept
- Analysis of alternatives and competing ideas or projects
- Adoption model (traction model) assumptions
- Early concept de-risking (low-fidelity)
- Prototyping
- Measurement hypotheses created
- Experiment 1 backlog

- Experiment 1 plan
- Continued engagement with Product/business owners and potential adopters
- Explore 2 experiments completed
- Technical de-risking with low-cost, low-fidelity components
- Initial experiments
- Experimental apparatus
- Technical architecture discussions begin
- Blockitecture
- Business architecture discussions begin

Operational Ownership:
Initiative Team

Governance:
Governance Team 3P reviews
Some initiatives may require Extended Governance Team approval to transition to next phase

APPENDIX 1 INITIATIVES-AT-A-GLANCE, ONE-PAGE STAGE OVERVIEWS, AND STAGE CHECKLISTS

Explore 2 Checklist

- ☐ Read Ash Maurya's 'Scaling Lean'
- ☐ Executive pitch (offering narrative)
- ☐ Visually communicate the idea (e.g. models, storyboards)
- ☐ Initial proof that the solution solves the early adopters' problem(s)
- ☐ At least one viable business model identified
- ☐ Elevator pitch (positioning statement, why people should care about the solution)
- ☐ Initial proof that the impact or opportunity is big enough, based on your early adopters' perceived value of a solution
- ☐ Architecture-level backlog
- ☐ Understanding of how the team will reach its early adopters and partners
- ☐ Validated definition of the MVP
- ☐ Search knowledge bases and other appropriate "lessons learned" libraries
- ☐ Consult with an/the architecture team regarding relevant, existing ecosystems
- ☐ Blockitecture creation
- ☐ Conduct exploration of whether an existing solution, ongoing project, or COTS solution could address all or part of the problem
- ☐ Experiment 1 plan established
- ☐ Identified risks to the current plan
- ☐ Understand the potential security posture of the likely solution and requirements for Experiment 1
- ☐ Understand the potential privacy posture of the likely solution and requirements for Experiment 1
- ☐ Understand the potential legal posture of the likely solution and requirements for Experiment 1

APPENDIX 1   INITIATIVES-AT-A-GLANCE, ONE-PAGE STAGE OVERVIEWS, AND STAGE CHECKLISTS

Experiment 1: Solution-Experiment

Objective:
Prove likely feasibility in a real-world operational environment and demonstrate likelihood to attract early adopters

Illustrative Activities and Outputs:
- Early deployment hypothesis and plan
- Solution may be released in a limited-time, controlled test
- Initial understanding of likely cost of Experiment 2
- Experiment 1 beneficiary (sponsor and/or user) testimonials
- Create Experiment 2 backlog
- Initial Transition 1 plan (scaled deployment hypothesis)
- Small batch, rapid experiments
- Technical de-risking with low-cost, low-fidelity components
- Continued engagement with business owners and product owners

Key questions to answer:
Can the solution run in a real-world environment? Would people use it if it did? Did it work in a real-world context? Did it solve the problem? Does it drive value?

- May include initial, limited, fenced connection to back-end production systems
- Potential adopters engaged
- Create Experiment 2 plan
- Authority to Operate, or similar approval, if required
- Initial Privacy Impact Assessment, or similar review, if required
- Health and safety activities as appropriate and necessary
- Initial architecture hypothesis, review, and guidance

Estimated Duration: 6-9 months

Outcome:
Validated learning via small batch experiments in preparation for Experiment 2
Beneficiary (user and/or sponsor) feedback to improve experience and adoption
Technical de-risking

Operational Ownership:
Initiative Team
Operations and architecture teams engage for learning and input

Governance:
Governance Team 3P reviews
Some initiatives may require Extended Governance Team approval to transition to next phase

APPENDIX 1   INITIATIVES-AT-A-GLANCE, ONE-PAGE STAGE OVERVIEWS, AND STAGE CHECKLISTS

Experiment 1 Checklist

- [ ] Read Croll and Yoskovitz' "Lean Analytics" (Incubating team leader or measurement assignee(s))
- [ ] Onboard development team or solution builders
- [ ] Incubating team trained
- [ ] Prior to MVP launch, positioning and messaging, activation flow, and business model are validated
- [ ] Communications (information) website is built and reviewed with incubating team advisors
- [ ] "Go-to-operations" plan is ready
- [ ] Experiment 1 MVP is released
- [ ] Initial architecture review
- [ ] Conduct Sean Ellis test to establish a baseline
- [ ] Cost of acquiring users (CAC) is understood
- [ ] Initial understanding of operational costs at scale, or cost to create and scale the solution
- [ ] Initial understanding of beneficiary lifetime value
- [ ] Experiment 2 backlog
- [ ] Experiment 2 plan established
- [ ] Project management approvals (if required)
- [ ] Authority to operate for Experiment 2 (if required)
- [ ] Key engine of growth is identified with assumptions outlined, when appropriate
- [ ] A sponsor has conditionally purchased, agreed to use, or agreed to fund your solution
- [ ] Solution is on target with traction & impact goals
- [ ] You have referenceable early adopters
- [ ] Understand the potential security posture of the likely solution and requirements for Experiment 2
- [ ] Understand the potential privacy posture of the likely solution and requirements for Experiment 2
- [ ] Understand the potential legal posture of the likely solution and requirements for Experiment 2

APPENDIX 1 INITIATIVES-AT-A-GLANCE, ONE-PAGE STAGE OVERVIEWS, AND STAGE CHECKLISTS

Experiment 2: Early Adopter

Objective:
Prove operational feasibility, confirm likelihood to attract early adopters, prove likely production viability

Key questions to answer:
Is there strong evidence the solution can be built for a real-world context, and that people will use it? Can it likely scale in a production context? What evidence shows it solves the problem and drives value?

Estimated Duration: 6-12 months

Outcome:
Validated learning supporting Transition 1 preparedness, beneficiary feedback to improve adoption and experience, backlog for Transition 1, an early adopter and potential earlyvangelist

Illustrative Activities and Outputs:

- Solution released in a limited time, controlled test (broader than Experiment 1)
- Sean Ellis test with users (demand/value measurement)
- Understanding of the likely cost of the Transition phase
- Initial understanding of the likely cost of a production deployment
- Transition pitch (sufficient evidence and artifacts to support early adopter traction and readiness for Transition 1)
- Technical de-risking with mid-cost, mid-fidelity components
- Initial deployment plan (hypothesis)
- Create Transition 1 plan
- Define Transition 1 experiments to validate plans and hypotheses, if necessary
- Authority to operate or other approvals as required
- Privacy Impact Assessment or other privacy approvals as required
- Transition 1 backlog
- Health and safety activities as appropriate and necessary
- Production architecture hypothesis, review, and guidance

Operational Ownership:
Initiative Team
Operations and architecture teams engage for learning and to provide guidance

Governance:
Governance Team 3P reviews
Some initiatives may require Extended Governance Team approval to transition to next phase

APPENDIX 1   INITIATIVES-AT-A-GLANCE, ONE-PAGE STAGE OVERVIEWS, AND STAGE CHECKLISTS

Experiment 2 Checklist

- ☐ Experiment 2 pilot is released
- ☐ Architecture review with focus on advising for Transition 1 and operational preparedness
- ☐ Product-Operations fit: Conduct Sean Ellis test to gauge support and movement in sentiment
- ☐ Product-Operations fit: Achieve targeted retention rate
- ☐ Evidence of growth and ability to scale: Understand user acquisition cost (CAC), and/or cost of production deployment (COGS)
- ☐ Initial understanding of operational costs, cost of operation, cost to scale, nature of cost increases (if any) at scale (e.g.: linear, step, exponential)
- ☐ Production architecture hypothesis, review, and guidance
- ☐ Engage project or program management resources in preparation for Transition phase

- ☐ Solution is on target with traction & impact goals
- ☐ An early adopter has agreed to use or sponsor the solution, champion the solution, or fund the initiative
- ☐ Referenceable beneficiaries, users, or sponsors
- ☐ Transition 1 backlog
- ☐ Transition 1 plan
- ☐ Authority to operate for Transition 1
- ☐ Privacy Impact Assessment for Transition 1
- ☐ Security assessment for Transition 1 (if required)
- ☐ Legal assessment for Transition 1
- ☐ Health and safety activities as appropriate and necessary
- ☐ Transition 1 budget estimate
- ☐ Executive summary (e.g.: presentation, document)

APPENDIX 1 INITIATIVES-AT-A-GLANCE, ONE-PAGE STAGE OVERVIEWS, AND STAGE CHECKLISTS

Transition 1: Solution-Product Fit

Estimated Duration: 3-12 months

Outcome:
Increasing demand, updated production solution definition, artifacts for turnover to project team, agreement of adoption from a sponsor/program team, business team, and operations, and project team ownership

Operational Ownership:
Initiative Team
Project Manager or Program Manager
Business Team
Operations and architecture teams engage for learning and to provide guidance

Governance:
Governance Team 3P reviews
Some initiatives may require Extended Governance Team approval to transition to next phase

Objective:
Transfer of control: Prove the ability to drive adoption and value, prove the solution can be supportable, confirm likelihood of viability, de-risk scaling, transfer leadership to project or program owners

Key questions to answer:
Can it scale? Does it continue to add value at scale? Does it work well with existing systems? Will it be supportable? Does it support a viable business case? Is it ready for the project/program team's ownership?

Illustrative Activities and Outputs:
- Evidence the solution can be widely deployed and can operate at scale
- Retention of users & sponsors
- Referrals from early adopters
- Solid understanding of the path to production
- Contingent agreement by a sponsor to adopt the solution in production
- Business team and project management team actively engages
- Evidence program or project team criteria was satisfied
- Pilot completion
- Transfer of leadership to program or project management lead
- Evidence to support any necessary project or program management artifacts
- Architecture review including support readiness or support model and technical debt assessment
- Verify compliance with relevant legislation, policy, or regulations
- Identify possible training needs
- Transition plan describing how the contingent agreement will be satisfied and how operational turnover will be completed
- Feedback on Experiment 2 results
- Incubating team begins to scale down

559

APPENDIX 1   INITIATIVES-AT-A-GLANCE, ONE-PAGE STAGE OVERVIEWS, AND STAGE CHECKLISTS

Transition 1 Checklist (1/2)

- [ ] An early adopter has agreed to use the solution
- [ ] Contingent agreement for project/program sponsorship or funding by a program or line of business team
- [ ] On-board project or program management resource(s)
- [ ] Transition leadership and ownership to the project or program management lead
- [ ] Architecture review with focus on operational preparedness and scaled deployment
- [ ] Technical de-risking of architecture scaling if appropriate
- [ ] Understanding of operational costs, cost of operation, cost to scale, nature of cost increases (if any) at scale (e.g.: linear, step, exponential)
- [ ] Evidence from testing required to confirm scale hypothesis as required
- [ ] Preliminary support model
- [ ] Go-to-operations (go-to-production) deployment hypothesis is updated with assumptions outlined, when appropriate
- [ ] Adoption hypothesis (traction model) and current state analysis
- [ ] Evidence that go-to-operations strategy (driving adoption) is effective and will likely scale
- [ ] Solution is on target with impact goals
- [ ] Referenceable early adopters
- [ ] Completed technical due diligence, including any testing or diligence outlined in the contingent sponsorship agreement
- [ ] Identification of technical debt including code not suited for full-scale deployment, tools required for scale, and contracts or licenses requiring update for production deployment

APPENDIX 1   INITIATIVES-AT-A-GLANCE, ONE-PAGE STAGE OVERVIEWS, AND STAGE CHECKLISTS

Transition 1 Checklist (2/2)

- [ ] Transition plan for incubating team's exit
- [ ] Authority to operate for project or program (if the solution has changed)
- [ ] Privacy Impact Assessment (or similar) for project (if the solution has changed)
- [ ] Security assessment (if necessary)
- [ ] Updated deployment architecture (if the solution has changed)
- [ ] Communications strategy
- [ ] Any evidence required by receiving project or program teams
- [ ] Technical transition plan
- [ ] Transition of technology, documentation, and code to the project or program team
- [ ] Initial input for business case and other program requirements (if applicable)
- [ ] Receiving project or program team artifact gap analysis and evidence collection
- [ ] Initial business due diligence
- [ ] Begin transition of source and IP to standard organizational repositories
- [ ] Begin transition of evidence and findings to the appropriate knowledge base or other libraries as appropriate
- [ ] Initial drafts and feedback on documents or evidence required by program or project management teams

APPENDIX 1 INITIATIVES-AT-A-GLANCE, ONE-PAGE STAGE OVERVIEWS, AND STAGE CHECKLISTS

Transition 2: Product-Operations

Estimated Duration: 2-4 months

Objective:
Transition to program or project team; Transition full control to program/project management and execution teams, pay down technical debt, prepare for scale, wind down incubation team

Key questions to answer:
Were the commitments agreed to in the transition plan met? Is the solution ready to deploy and scale? Have all receiving team requirements been met? Is the receiving team ready to take over?

Outcome:
Solution is designed to scale, business case is ready to turn over, receiving business organization, operations, and project teams agree on project readiness, incubation team is redeployed

Illustrative Activities and Outputs:
- Receiving program or project team, or governing body, approval
- Transition targets set in Transition 1 agreement with business, project, and operations teams met
- Documented business or program commitment for adoption
- Technical due diligence completed
- Transition plan execution completed
- Exit pitch (evidence and artifacts show exit criteria were met)
- Transfer full control to the new program/project management and execution teams
- Turnover of technical artifacts

- Prepare for compliance with relevant legislation, policy, or regulations or identify needs (as stipulated in the transition plan)
- User, partner, and operational training and preparedness
- Operational readiness (processes or procedures created if necessary)
- Technical debt addressed if and as required by the transition plan
- Initial scale architecture completion
- Receiving team artifact requirements met
- Knowledge capture and preservation
- Some Transition 2 activity may execute concurrently with Transition 1

Operational Ownership:
Project or Program Manager
Business Team
Incubating Team
Operations Team, and Architecture Teams engage for turnover, support, and input

Governance:
Governance Team 3P reviews
Some initiatives may require Extended Governance Team approval to transition to next phase
Some initiatives may require program or project team approval

APPENDIX 1 INITIATIVES-AT-A-GLANCE, ONE-PAGE STAGE OVERVIEWS, AND STAGE CHECKLISTS

Transition 2 Checklist

- ☐ Approved production architecture
- ☐ Documented business team agreement to sponsor next stage
- ☐ Referenceable beneficiaries (users and/or sponsors)
- ☐ Completed technical due diligence
- ☐ Completed business due diligence
- ☐ Received approvals required by receiving program/project team and/or governing bodies
- ☐ Full solution transition to the receiving team
- ☐ Incubating team members redeployed to new assignments
- ☐ Project or program budget estimates complete
- ☐ Executive summary presentation
- ☐ Pause checklist completed
- ☐ Business case completed (if required)
- ☐ Standard operating procedures delivered
- ☐ KPIs identified
- ☐ Risk assessments completed
- ☐ Cost estimates completed
- ☐ Initial project or program deployment plan
- ☐ Architecture assessment (for full-scale deployment)

APPENDIX 2

Ceremonies

APPENDIX 2   CEREMONIES

Ceremonies at-a-Glance

APPENDIX 2 CEREMONIES

Ceremonies at-a-Glance

	1. Pitch Ceremony	2. 3P Review	3. Retrospectives
	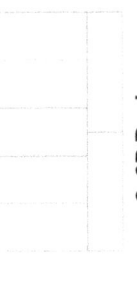		
Participants	• Incubating team leaders • Initiative Team	• Incubating team leaders • Governance Team • Others	• Participants in the subject of the retrospective • Other subject matter experts or people impacted
Objectives	• Prioritize and select incubation ideas • Ensure the incubation team is ready	• Determine whether the incubation should pivot, pause, or persist • Maintain incubating team focus and ensure progress toward objectives • Incubating team and Governance Team alignment	• Continuous learning and improvement • Drive team efficiency • Improve collaboration • Improve morale • Incubation framework or incubator improvement
Outcomes	• Approval to begin Seed 1, Incubate 1, or Explore 1	• Direction and assistance from Advisors • Approval to begin next stage	• Specific actions to help improve the team, work, framework, or initiative
Duration	• 30 minutes per pitch	• 30 minutes	• 60 minutes

APPENDIX 2   CEREMONIES

Ceremonies at-a-Glance

	4. Fire Drill (Optional)	5. Introspection (Optional)	6. Role Clarification (Optional)
Participants	• Incubating team • Architecture, operations, security, or other experts • Solution or system users	• Members of a single team	• Members of one or more teams who work together and must clearly understand one-another's roles
Objectives	• Identify specific ways a solution might fail • Identify the potential root causes of the hypothetical problem • Focus the team on the critical few issues • Identify mitigation strategies	• Understand the behaviors and characteristics that define the team's peak performance • Understand the behaviors and characteristics that undermine the team's performance	• Clearly identify the responsibilities of a specific role or team • Clearly identify what is excluded from a specific role or team's responsibilities • Resolve misalignment between participants
Outcomes	• Identification of potential risks and mitigation actions • Action plan	• Understanding of team needs • Action plan	• Clear definition of one or more roles
Duration	• 1 – 2 hours	• 1 – 1.5 hours	• 30 – 45 minutes per role

APPENDIX 2 CEREMONIES

1. Pitch Ceremony

APPENDIX 2   CEREMONIES

Pitch Ceremony

- The Pitch Ceremony is used to:
  - Aid with selection of projects for incubation
  - Determine whether an idea and team are ready for incubation
  - Assess the incubating team's composition
  - Identify actions required to ensure the incubating team will be ready to incubate upon entry

- The Incubation Advisory Team:
  - Reviews one or more brief presentations of ideas that are candidates for incubation
  - Evaluates the merit of the idea, its value, and its relevance to the organization's mission or strategy
  - Determines whether the team is ready to begin incubation
  - Decides whether the idea will begin incubation and when
  - Assesses whether the team composition is sufficient

Pitch Ceremony Definition of Done

- One or more teams has presented their idea
- For each pitch, the Governance Team has:
  - Evaluated the merit of the idea, its value, and its relevance to the organization's mission or strategy
  - Determined whether the team is ready to begin incubation
  - Decided whether the idea will begin incubation and when
  - Assessed whether the team composition is sufficient
  - Provided direction to the team (e.g.: suggested changes to the approach, team members)
  - Deliberated on whether the idea is ready to enter the initiative
  - Determined when the idea can enter the initiative
  - Informed the team of their decision
- All parking lot items are assigned owners and deadlines as they are identified (in process)

APPENDIX 2   CEREMONIES

Pitch Ceremony Agenda
(Approximately 30 minutes)

1. <u>Uninterrupted</u> Pitch Team Presentation (10 minutes)
2. Governance Team Questions and Discussion (10-20 minutes*)
3. Governance Team Deliberation (5-10 minutes*, in camera)
4. Communicate Governance Team Decision (5 minutes)

*The Governance Team may need additional time during their first few Pitch ceremonies. Times should approach 30 minutes as the team norms on roles and interests, and as they become accustomed to the ceremony.

APPENDIX 2   CEREMONIES

2. 3P Review Ceremony

APPENDIX 2   CEREMONIES

3P Review Ceremony

- The purpose of the Pivot, Pause, or Persevere Review ceremony is to:
  - Establish a working cadence for the incubating team and the Governance Team
  - Ensure alignment of the incubating team and the Governance Team
  - Enable the incubating teams to request assistance with obstacles, resources, or needs
  - Evaluate and discuss whether an incubation should pause, pivot, or stay on its current course
  - Determine whether an incubating team is ready to advance to the next stage
  - Drive responsible, lightweight governance

APPENDIX 2   CEREMONIES

3P Review
(Approximately 30 minutes for regular reviews)

- 3P Reviews typically take one of the following formats:
  - **15-15:** Up to fifteen minutes of uninterrupted presentation by the incubating team followed by up to fifteen minutes of open dialogue and Q&A from the Governance Team
    - This is typically the format of a routine 3P review
  - **10-20:** Up to ten minutes of uninterrupted presentation by the incubating team followed by up to twenty minutes of open dialogue and Q&A from the Governance Team
    - This is an alternate format for teams during heavy periods of building
    - This could also be modified to have ten minutes of open dialog (10-10)
  - **30-30:** Up to thirty minutes of uninterrupted presentation by the incubating team followed by up to thirty minutes of open dialogue and Q&A from the Governance Team
    - This is typically the format of a 3P review requesting a transition from one stage to another (e.g.: from Explore 2 to Experiment 1, Seed 2 to Series A, or Incubate 2 to Startup 1)
    - The addition of 10-15 minutes at the end of 3P reviews where teams are requesting transition to the next stage is recommended to provide time for the Governance Team to deliberate on the request
- 3P reviews are recommended monthly, especially in Seed, Explore, or Incubate stages

575

APPENDIX 2 CEREMONIES

Illustrative Working Agreement
(1/2)

- Each incubating team leader owns their 3P session, including the follow-up and/or redirect items that are identified within
- The 3P meeting is a "safe place" (i.e., what happens in the 3P meeting stays in the 3P meeting)
- We will stick to the agenda
- We will finish on time
- We will be in our seats and be ready to begin at least one minute before start times
- We will mute microphones when not speaking
- We will associate our actual name with our videoconference or audio connection (helps with context, makes follow-up easier)
- Each incubating team leader will upload a draft of their materials to the event library two business days prior to the event so participants can prepare for the meeting, three days in advance for transition requests

APPENDIX 2 CEREMONIES

Illustrative Working Agreement
(2/2)

- Incubating team leaders may update their material at any time prior to the commencement of their review, but should highlight any substantial changes during the review
- Governance Team members will review the uploaded material prior to the 3P meeting
- Reviews will be cancelled if materials are not posted 24 hours prior to the event
- For significant pivots and transition requests, the session will be cancelled if materials are not posted by three business days prior to the event
- We will not interrupt business teams during the "uninterrupted review" portion of the ceremony
- Only Governance Team and incubating team members will speak during the Q&A portion unless the Governance or the incubating team invite others to do so

APPENDIX 2   CEREMONIES

3P Definition of Done

- The incubating team has reviewed or made available in their material:
  - An update regarding actions taken from the previous 3P review
  - Their progress since the last 3P meeting
  - A review of experiments since the last review and what was learned as a result
  - Planned experiments and next steps, and what they believe they will learn as a result
  - Relevant metrics (e.g., validated learning, innovation metrics…)
  - The stage-appropriate checklist or Kanban, updated to show their progress
  - An updated Lean Canvas
- All decisions requested by the incubating team have been addressed
- All action items are assigned owners and deadlines as they are identified

APPENDIX 2   CEREMONIES

3P Agenda

1. **Uninterrupted Incubating Team Presentation (10, 15, or 30 minutes)**
   - Welcome and Meeting Objectives
     - Confirm context and objectives; state decisions that should be made
   - Progress and Results from Experiments (Incubating Team)
     - Actions that were presented as next steps during the last 3P meeting
     - What was done since the last 3P meeting
     - What was learned
     - What the business team plans to do next
     - What the business team believes they will lean from those actions (or what will be accomplished...)
     - Any issues or anticipated obstacles the team may require assistance with
     - Updated checklists

2. **General Discussion (10, 15, 20, or 30 minutes)**
   - Q&A, exploration of results and metrics, solicit advice
   - Next Steps
     - What will be done by the next meeting
     - What the incubating team believes they will learn
     - What results the incubating team expects from the experiments
     - Actions required prior to the next meeting

579

APPENDIX 2   CEREMONIES

Sample 3P Review Flow

Note: Incubating Teams need not review every slide or artifact they provide for a 3P review.

Since all artifacts will be supplied in advance, it is expected that all incubating team and Governance Team members will have reviewed them prior to the 3P review and will be prepared to ask about anything the incubating team does not cover during their uninterrupted presentation if necessary.

APPENDIX 2 CEREMONIES

Today's Objectives
Illustrative

- Current state
  - <Provide context required for participants to understand the material that follows>
- Discussion
  - <Items that will be discussed during the review and the objectives of the discussion>
- Decisions requested
  - <Decisions or support will the team be asking the Governance Team for, including approval to proceed to the next stage when appropriate>
  - <"Persist" is an implied request, so teams should be explicit when recommending a "pause" or "pivot" decision>
- Support required
  - <Explicit requests for support from the Advisory Team (e.g.: resources, assistance socializing with executives...)>

581

Actions from the previous 3P review

1. **<Description of Action 1>**
   - Status:
   - Learning or outcome: <If appropriate>
   - Next Steps: <If appropriate>
2. **<Description of Action 2>**
   - Status:
   - Learning or outcome: <If appropriate>
   - Next Steps: <If appropriate>
3. …

APPENDIX 2 CEREMONIES

What was learned

Summary

Action	Learning
What the team did	1. Things the team learned since their last update 2. What metric(s) are being used to assess the impact of the experiment or change (the "one metric that matters") 3. Evidence of the impact (e.g.: Explore 1: Evidence of the customer's pain and need for a solution) 4. Risks 5. Other relevant items (Can be supported by evidence in the appendix)

583

APPENDIX 2   CEREMONIES

Validated Hypotheses

EXAMPLE

Question	Hypothesis	Result
Do *potential customers* have this problem?	At least 60% of *target customers* are looking to solve this problem?	**Validated** 23 of 30 interviewed (77%)
How are *potential customers* working around the problem?	>30% of *target customers* are using manual workaround #1	**Validated** 12 of 30 interviewed (40%)
	>25% of *target customers* are doing nothing	**Not Validated** 2 of 30 interviewed (7%)
	>30% of *target customers* are using workaround #2	**Not Validated** 4 of 30 interviewed (13%)
	<10% of *target customers* are using Excel™	**Not Validated** 14 of 30 interviewed (47%)
Will decreasing the AI model evaluation time result in increased use of the service?	Decreasing evaluation time to below 1 second will increase click-through by 20%	**Validated** Click-through increased from 30 users/hr to 45 users/hr (+50%)
Will simplifying the user interface reduce errors and result in fewer abandons?	Reducing prompt text by 50% will decrease abandons by 50%	**Not Validated** Abandons declined from 5/hr to 3/hr (−40%)

Note: "Not Validated" results should not be interpreted as a failed experiment. They indicate only that the result was other than expected, and often lead to discoveries more exciting than initially hypothesized. They may also indicate that an hypothesis was directionally correct, though specifically inaccurate. This may be insignificant when numbers are small (e.g.: expected 3 of 5, observed 3 of 6). Furthermore, "Not Validated" results may be sufficient to justify action (e.g.: expected 75% to have a problem, 70% have the problem). In such cases the result *may* be considered "Validated", with explanation.

APPENDIX 2   CEREMONIES

Next Steps
Summary

Action	Learning
What the team will do (upcoming experiments, falsifiable hypotheses)	1. Things the team expects to learn from the experiment, expected outcomes 2. Hypothesis tree if appropriate 3. Other relevant items (Can be supported by items in the appendix such as in-progress experiment reports)

APPENDIX 2   CEREMONIES

Business Model

- Include an up-to-date version of the canvas here
- Highlight updates (e.g.: highlighting text, text color change, arrows, circling text...)

APPENDIX 2 CEREMONIES

Seed 1 Checklist

- ☐ Complete incubation boot camp (incubating team SMEs, leaders, ops) training
- ☐ Identify your target market and early adopter segment (canvas "customer" and "early adopter" areas)
- ☐ Assess rough market sizing (e.g.: are you building your solution for 10s, 100s, 1,000s, or 1,000,000s of users)
- ☐ Form incubating team's advisory team and begin regular collaboration with them
- ☐ Desirability: Obtain initial proof the problem is painful, significant and needs to be solved by your target users or businesses, especially early adopters (validate lean canvas top boxes)
- ☐ Provide evidence that you understand how your early adopters are working around the problem today and their level of satisfaction with the workaround
- ☐ Establish a Seed 2 plan
- ☐ Identify Seed 1 assumptions & hypotheses and run Seed 1 experiments
- ☐ Perform a high-level survey of alternatives (competitive landscape)
- ☐ Understand the solution's market type
- ☐ Research knowledge bases and other relevant systems for existing knowledge and learning from prior initiatives
- ☐ Initial assessment of traction goals
- ☐ Create lean personas
- ☐ Conduct an invention harvesting session
- ☐ Understand the likely security and privacy needs
- ☐ Identify minimum viable team requirements and perform an MVT gap analysis

APPENDIX 2 CEREMONIES

Explore 1 Checklist

- [ ] Complete incubation boot camp (incubating team SMEs, leaders, ops) training
- [ ] Identify your target "market" and early adopter segment (canvas beneficiary and early adopter segments)
- [ ] Assess rough business model scoping (e.g.: are you building your solution for 10s, 100s, 1,000s, or 1,000,000s of users)
- [ ] Form incubating team's advisory team and begin regular collaboration with them (incubating team's lead, "deal-maker")
- [ ] Obtain initial proof that the problem is painful, significant & needs to be solved by your target users or business, especially early adopters (ie: validate desirability via the PS lean canvas)
- [ ] Provide evidence that you understand how your early adopters are working around the problem today & their level of satisfaction with the workaround
- [ ] Establish an Explore 2 plan
- [ ] Identify Explore 1 assumptions & hypotheses and run Explore 1 experiments
- [ ] Perform high-level survey of alternatives (competitive landscape)
- [ ] Research knowledge bases and other relevant systems for existing knowledge and learning from prior initiatives
- [ ] Initial assessment of traction goals
- [ ] Create lean personas
- [ ] Understand the likely security posture of the likely solution
- [ ] Understand the likely privacy posture of the likely solution
- [ ] Understand the likely legal posture of the likely solution
- [ ] Identify minimum viable team requirements and perform an MVT gap analysis

APPENDIX 2 CEREMONIES

Evidence

This page is a reminder to include relevant evidence and not, itself, a tool or artifact

- Include artifacts created throughout the stage or relevant summaries
- Artifacts may be included inline, especially if they will be highlighted or discussed
- Artifacts may be included in an appendix (e.g.: as supporting evidence)

APPENDIX 2   CEREMONIES

Governance Team Requests

- It is not necessary to include a slide for this portion of the discussion
- This slide is here as a reminder for the incubating teams to leverage their Governance Team, Advisory Team, and executive resources
- Incubating teams often need to be reminded that their executives are a resource to them and can help the incubating team achieve its objectives (e.g.: by unblocking them, connecting them to other teams, obtaining resources, socializing with other organizations, business units, or departments and/or with senior executives)

Open Discussion and Questions

- Governance Team members and explicitly invited participants may now ask questions of the incubating team and explore material, metrics, experiments, and learning in more detail
- The incubating team may continue to solicit advice and assistance from the Governance Team or Advisory Team as required based upon the discussion

APPENDIX 2 CEREMONIES

Plan for <Next Stage>
Add when requesting approval to proceed to the next stage

- Include
  - Evidence required according to the current stage's checklist
    - Likely already provided or included in an appendix
    - Some checklist items may have been previously declared non-applicable
  - Timeline estimates
  - Identified risks
  - Metrics for the upcoming stage
  - Investment requirements or budget

Action Items and Next Steps

- The incubating team leader will recap key items resulting from the discussion including, though not limited to:
    - Issues which were identified
    - Actions and owners (including actions requested of the Governance Team)
    - Blockers
    - Decisions
- This will ensure that the Governance Team and incubating team are aligned on what was discussed and the path forward

APPENDIX 2   CEREMONIES

3. Classic Retrospective

APPENDIX 2 CEREMONIES

Classic Retrospective

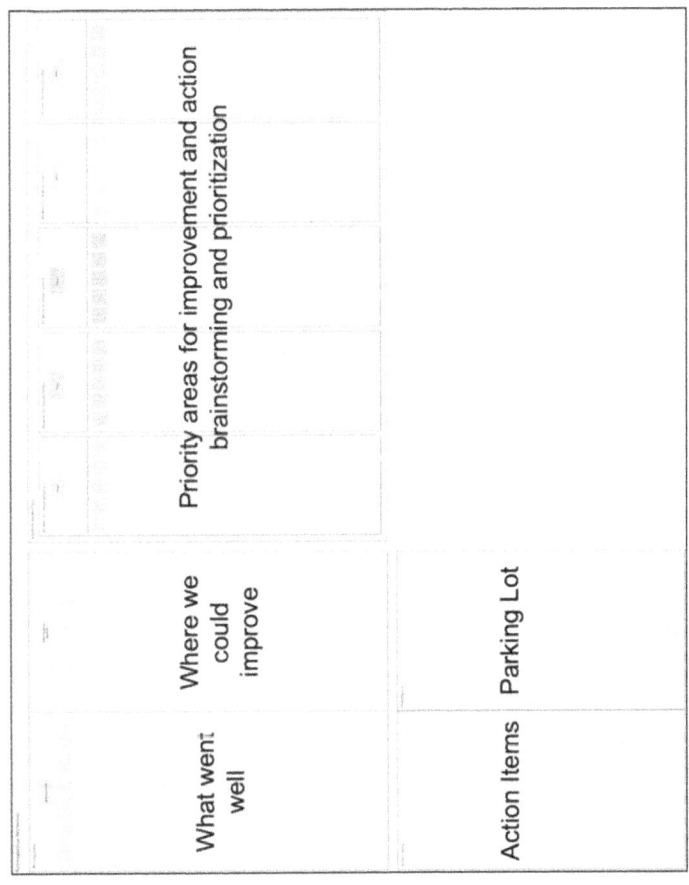

APPENDIX 2   CEREMONIES

Retrospective Agenda
Sample

1. Gathering (5 minutes)
2. Setting the scope and confirming a shared understanding (5 minutes)
3. What went well? (10-15 minutes)
4. Where could we improve? (10-15 minutes)
5. What actions can we take to improve? (10-15 minutes per item to be reviewed)*

Notes: Times for items 3 and 4 can be adjusted for team size, team composition, topic, and time allotment.
*In some cases action brainstorming *can* be performed in a follow-on meeting.

APPENDIX 2   CEREMONIES

Step 1: Gathering
5 minutes

The gathering portion of the agenda gives people time to:

- Change locations (in-person)
- Connect to the meeting or change meeting tools (remote)
- Resolve connection issues (remote)
- Switch context to the topic of the retrospective
- Prepare for the session
- The facilitator should ensure people are greeted and begin setting the session's tone

APPENDIX 2   CEREMONIES

Step 2: Confirming Scope
5 minutes

- It is critical that participants understand the retrospective's target
- The facilitator should:
  - Display and clearly state the session's purpose
  - Add any context necessary to ensure those present understand it
  - Ask the team whether they all understand the purpose and scope
  - Answer any questions on the scope and
  - Keep this section of the discussion focused on the scope
  - Set the agenda
  - Reinforce key elements of the working agreement (e.g.: all voices are equal, no finger-pointing)
- Prior to the meeting the facilitator should distribute, or make available:
  - The retrospective's purpose statement
  - Working Agreement
  - Definition of Done
  - Other artifacts that might help people prepare for the discussion

598

APPENDIX 2   CEREMONIES

Note: Examples of these artifacts are included in the Tools and Artifacts section of the Toolkit.

Step 3: Explore what went well
10-15 minutes

- **Purpose: Capture the things that went well or are going well**
  - Learn things that may help with future execution
  - Reinforce and continue positive behavior and actions
  - Celebrate accomplishments
- **Exploring the positives first is critical to ensuring the team has a positive mindset as they discuss areas for improvement and more sensitive items**
- **The facilitator should:**
  - Ensure the tone remains positive and reinforce the working agreement as necessary
  - Ensure there is broad participation and that nobody is monopolizing the time
  - Ensure the learning is captured (with anonymity) and recorded
  - Ensure action items are recorded as they arise
  - Keep the discussion focused on what went well

Step 3: Artifacts and execution

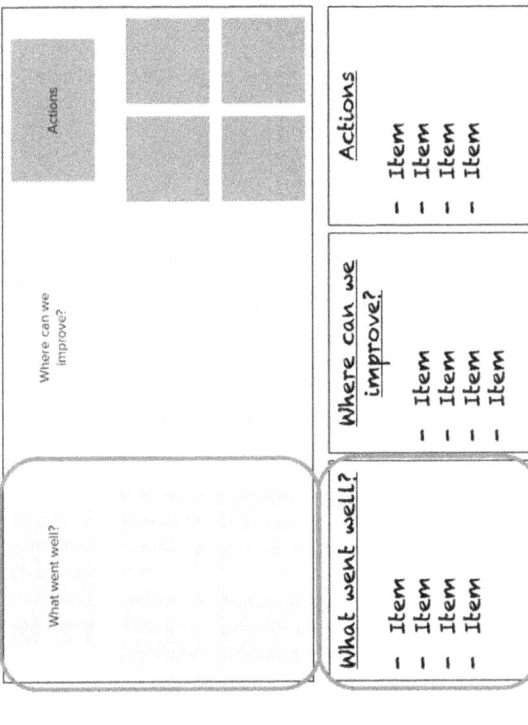

1. An area for recording what went well, areas to improve, and actions should be set up prior to the session (e.g.: flip charts, stickies, electronic whiteboard)
2. Participants suggest items to be added to "What went well?"
3. The facilitator records the items
4. Alternatives
   A. Participants place the sticky on the wall (or equivalent) and describe their contribution one at a time or round robin style
   B. Participants place all of their sticky notes on the wall at once
5. The section ends when the time allotted expires or there are no more ideas

APPENDIX 2   CEREMONIES

Step 3: Review, Discussion, Affinity Mapping
(Optional)

To add acuity to what is learned, add the optional steps on this page and the next to your retrospective.

1. If you have not discussed them as a group, read all of the items that others have added to the wall
2. Participants should be encouraged by the facilitator to ask questions about any items they read though do not understand
3. Discussion of any items which are called out for clarity should be limited to ensuring participants understand what the item refers to
4. The facilitator should stop any discussion of the merits of any of the items which were added during brainstorming
5. Group together items that are similar or the same (e.g.: stick related sticky notes together or cross out redundant items from lists)

Step 3: Prioritization
(Optional)

To add acuity to what is learned, prioritize the learning from this step. This does not imply items which receive fewer, or no, votes are not important nor that those items will not be addressed. This informs the team of the items which might be addressed first, or soonest.

1. Each person will be given three votes
2. Place a dot on each sticky (or next to the line captured by the facilitator) for the ideas you believe were the most impactful or important
3. Each person may place their votes on one item or up to three items

APPENDIX 2   CEREMONIES

Step 4: Explore areas for improvement
10–15 minutes

- **Purpose: Capture areas that could improve**
  - Learn things that may help with future execution
  - Identify and avoid areas of potential future conflict
- **Exploring the positives first is critical to ensuring the team has a positive mindset as they discuss areas for improvement and more sensitive items**
- **The facilitator should:**
  - Ensure the tone remains positive and reinforce the working agreement as necessary
  - Ensure there is broad participation and that nobody is monopolizing the time
  - Ensure the learning is captured (with anonymity) and recorded
  - Ensure action items are recorded as they arise
  - Keep the discussion focused on what could be improved
  - Ensure people understand that identifying something that could be improved does not mean that it, or anyone connected to it, has failed

APPENDIX 2 CEREMONIES

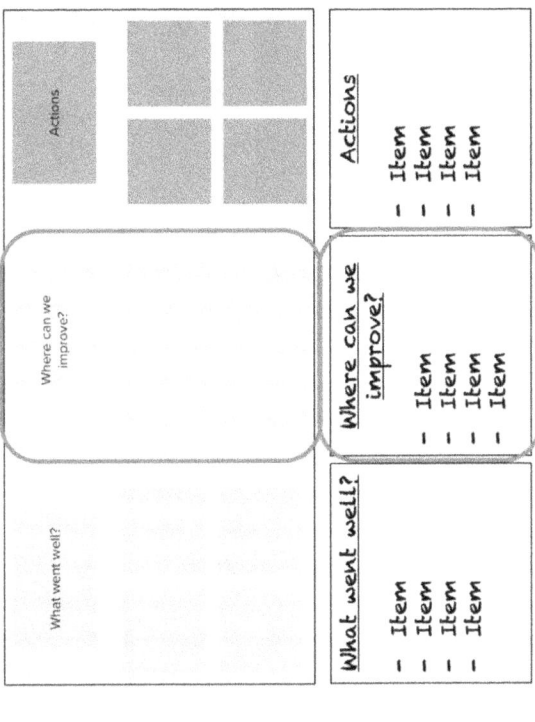

Step 4: Artifacts and execution

1. An area for recording what went well, areas to improve, and actions should be set up prior to the session (e.g.: flip charts, stickies, electronic whiteboard)
2. Participants suggest items to be added to "What can we improve?"
3. The facilitator records the items
4. Alternatives
   A. Participants place the sticky on the wall (or equivalent) and describe their contribution one at a time or round robin style
   B. Participants place all of their sticky notes on the wall at once
5. The section ends when the time allotted expires or there are no more ideas

605

Step 4: Review, Discussion, Affinity Mapping
(Optional)

To add acuity to what is learned, add the optional steps on this page and the next to your retrospective.

1. If you have not discussed them as a group, read all of the items that others have added to the wall
2. Participants should be encouraged by the facilitator to ask questions about any items they read though do not understand
3. Discussion of any items which are called out for clarity should be limited to ensuring participants understand what the item refers to
4. The facilitator should stop any discussion of the merits of any of the items which were added during brainstorming
5. Group together items that are similar or the same (e.g.: stick related sticky notes together or cross out redundant items from lists)

Step 4: Prioritization
(Optional)

To add acuity to what is learned, prioritize the learning from this step. This does not imply items which receive fewer, or no, votes are not important nor that those items will not be addressed. This informs the team of the items which might be addressed first, or soonest.

1. Each person will be given three votes
2. Place a dot on each sticky (or next to the line captured by the facilitator) for the ideas you believe were the most impactful or important
3. Each person may place their votes on one item or up to three items

Step 5: Brainstorm Actions
10–15 minutes

- **The purpose of this session is to identify actions that can:**
  - Leverage things that are going well
  - Take advantage of things learned during the retrospective
  - Adapt to improve things that can be improved
- **This is sometimes performed in a separate session**
  - e.g.: When a team that wishes to improve invites a cross-organization group which will not be involved in implementing the changes to the retrospective
- **Actions that arise earlier in the retrospective should be captured as identified**
  - Do not wait for this section of the retrospective
- **The facilitator should:**
  - Ensure the tone remains positive and reinforce the working agreement as necessary
  - Ensure there is broad participation and that nobody is monopolizing the time
  - Ensure each action has clear description, an owner, and a deadline

APPENDIX 2 CEREMONIES

Step 5: Artifacts and execution

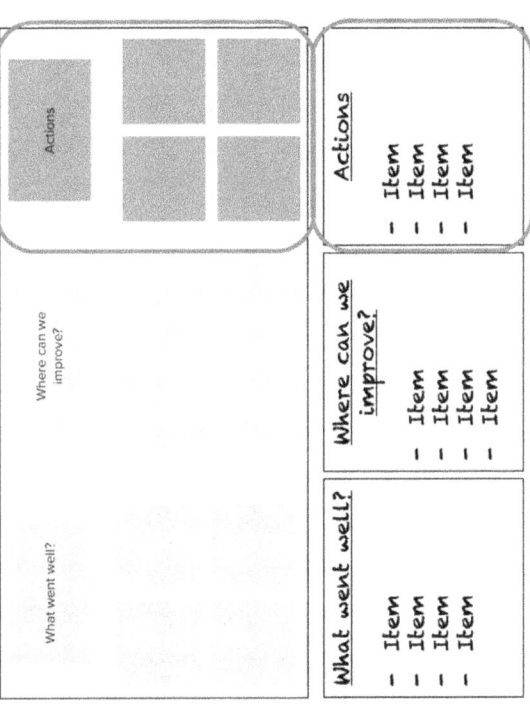

1. An area for recording what went well, areas to improve, and actions should be set up prior to the session (e.g.: flip charts, stickies, electronic whiteboard)
2. The facilitator can conduct a simple brainstorming exercise:
   1. Participants add suggested actions to the wall or board for 2-3 minutes
   2. Actions that are alike are grouped (5 mins) by the team
   3. Optional: Prioritize the actions by giving participants 1-3 votes to assign to the actions they believe most important
   4. If the meeting format cannot accommodate brainstorming the facilitator could record actions that are suggested by participants

APPENDIX 2   CEREMONIES

Step 5: Alternative Method

While the previously discussed method will result in actions in consideration of the overall retrospective, this method will help the team develop specific actions to address each of the most critical areas for improvement.

1. Select the area for improvement item from Step 4 that had the most votes and place it in the action brainstorm area
2. Conduct the Step 5 exercise as described on the previous page, but only for the selected item
3. Time permitting, repeat the exercise for the area for improvement from Step 4 with the second highest number of votes
4. Time permitting, repeat the exercise for the area for improvement from Step 4 with the third highest number of votes
5. Time permitting, you may decide to address additional items

When to hold retrospectives

- At the end of a workshop, offsite, or other event
- Shortly after introduction of something new
  - e.g.: New process, new tool, new ceremony
- Out of cycle
  - Every 2, 4, or 6 weeks, not at a milestone or event
  - Match your operational cadence
  - Randomly
- Following a key milestone
- At the end of an initiative, project, or process
- When you want to take a group's pulse
- When you sense a team is drifting from good habits
- Impromptu

APPENDIX 2   CEREMONIES

Things to consider (1/2)

- **Start with what went well – Always!**
  - Sets a positive tone for entry into the "how we could improve" section with a productive mindset
  - Focus on continuous learning and improvement
  - It's often more difficult than capturing areas for improvement

- **Facilitators may need to actively solicit contributions**
  - This may especially be necessary for teams new to retrospectives or new teams
  - This is often required when participants are working on "What went well?"
  - Use techniques like, "We have 8, let's see if we can get to 10", round robin contribution

- **Give participants a minute or two of think time before steps 3 and 4**
  - Ask them to write their thoughts down before anyone speaks
  - This helps avoid early groupthink and missed items
  - For physical or virtual sticky notes, have them write their ideas on the notes ahead of team posting
    - Participants can continue to add new ideas during active posting

Things to consider (2/2)

- **No finger-pointing**
  - This should be a positive experience, reinforce continuous learning and improvement
- **No personal attacks**
  - "We might benefit from more frequent communication" vs. "You never tell us what you're doing"
  - "A shared OKR might help us to…" vs. "Your team isn't pulling its weight"
- **All types of feedback are welcomed**
  - Do not limit feedback to the deliverables and the processes (no walls)
  - Unexpected feedback could lead to surprising discoveries

APPENDIX 2   CEREMONIES

Other Retrospective Styles

Why use alternative retrospective styles?

- **Teams conducting the same style of retrospective many times may:**
  - Become bored with the retrospective style
  - Lose interest
  - Fail to prepare
  - Stop thinking creatively or outside their roles

- **By asking the team to reflect using a different perspective, alternative retrospective styles can:**
  - Lead to previously undiscovered insights
  - Break bad or lazy retrospective habits by changing the routine
  - Create a safe and open space for people with different personalities and communication styles
  - Add variety and keep the team interested

- **Alternative styles may better surface value or opportunity for improvement in the incubation framework or approach**

APPENDIX 2 CEREMONIES

Alternative Formats (1/2)
Great for impromptu retrospectives

Wind in our Sails

- **Goals:** What the team was trying to accomplish (context)
- **Accelerators:** What accelerated progress
- **Barriers:** What blocked progress
- **Impediments:** What impeded progress or slowed things down
- **Lessons:** What the team learned

3Ls

- **Learned:** Lessons learned along the way (things to avoid *and* things to leverage)
- **Lacked:** What you wish you had but did not have
- **Loved:** What you loved about the work

4Ls

- **Loved:** What you loved about the work
- **Longed for:** What you wish you had but did not have
- **Loathed:** Things to avoid
- **Learned:** Lessons learned along the way (things to avoid *and* to leverage)

616

APPENDIX 2 CEREMONIES

Alternative Formats (2/2)
Great for impromptu retrospectives

What? So What? Now What?

- **What:** What happened? (Observations, what you saw, things that stood out)
- **So what:** What are the consequences? What conclusions or hypotheses result?
- **Now what:** What actions can you take in response to your observations?

Post-Love-Learn

- **Post:** How would you describe what you saw in a social media post or hashtag?
- **Love:** What did you love about what you saw?
- **Learn:** What would you change? (Constructive, positive feedback)
- Great for impromptu feedback

+ / ▲

- **+ :** Things that we liked, that went well
- **▲ :** Things we could improve?
- Great for evaluating a workshop, session, or at the end of the day for multi-day meetings or classes
  - Great for inspecting and adapting in situ

617

APPENDIX 2　CEREMONIES

4. Fire Drill

Assess potential failures and their impact and develop prevention and mitigation strategies

Fire Drill

A brainstorming exercise that:

- Identifies specific ways a product, process, initiative, or service might fail
- Develops actions to:
  - Mitigate or prevent potential failures
  - Reduce the probability of the occurrence of identified types of failure
  - Prepare a plan to respond to unpreventable failures when they occur

APPENDIX 2   CEREMONIES

Fire Drill Agenda
Sample

1. Gathering
2. Setting the scope and mindset, and confirming a shared understanding
3. Root cause analysis: Why did it fail?
4. Risk mitigation: How can we mitigate or eliminate the risk of failure?
5. Action: What next steps are required to implement our risk mitigation strategy?

APPENDIX 2 CEREMONIES

Step 1: Gathering
5 minutes

The gathering portion of the agenda gives people time to:

- Change locations (in-person)
- Connect to the meeting or change meeting tools (remote)
- Resolve connection issues (remote)
- Switch context to the fire drill exercise
- Prepare for the session
- The facilitator should ensure people are greeted and begin setting the session's tone

Step 2: Confirming Scope
5 minutes

- **It is critical that participants understand the session's objectives**
- **The facilitator should:**
  - Display and clearly state the session's purpose
  - Add any context necessary to ensure those present understand it
  - Ask the team whether they all understand the purpose and scope
  - Answer any questions on the scope
  - Keep this section of the discussion focused on the scope
  - Set the agenda
  - Reinforce key elements of the working agreement (e.g.: all voices are equal, no finger-pointing)
- **Prior to the meeting the facilitator should distribute, or make available:**
  - The meeting purpose statement
  - Working Agreement
  - Definition of Done
  - Other artifacts that might help people prepare for the discussion

APPENDIX 2 CEREMONIES

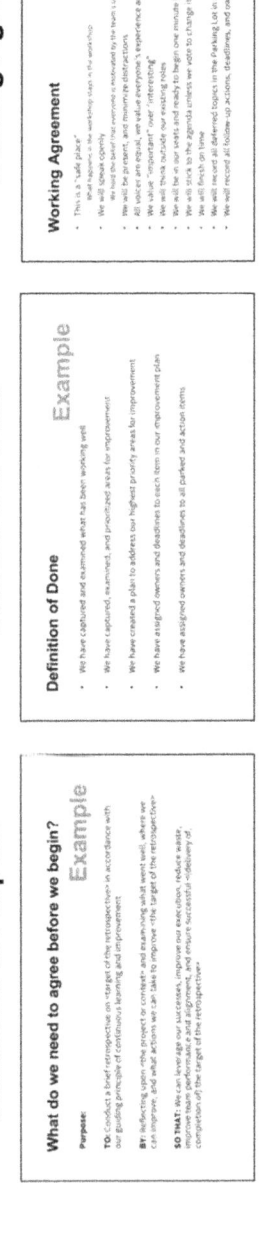

Note: Examples of these artifacts are included in the Tools and Artifacts section of the Toolkit.

623

Step 3: Establish the appropriate mindset

1. The facilitator aligns the team by explaining that the workshop's scenario is a failure or disaster that has already happened
   - The facilitator should *not* describe a specific scenario, just that *something* has happened to cause a failure, that the facilitator is not sure what caused it, and it's the team's job to figure out what that may have been
2. The facilitator should explain that looking for root causes is not being negative
   - In this scenario the entity under review has already failed, and the team is looking for ways to troubleshoot it and get things back on track (that's being positive)
   - Most people don't want to be perceived as being negative, so this may require reinforcement
3. Throughout the exercise facilitator should:
   - Ensure the tone remains positive and reinforce the working agreement as necessary
   - Ensure there is broad participation and that nobody is monopolizing the time
   - Ensure the learning is captured (with anonymity) and recorded
   - Ensure action items are recorded as they arise
   - Keep the discussion focused

Step 4: Brainstorm possible causes of failure

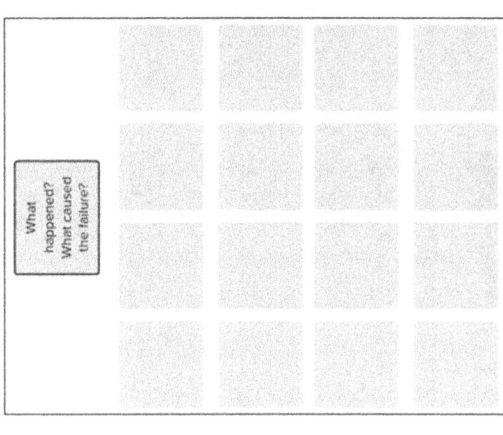

1. The facilitator asks the group what might have happened to cause the failure?
   - The facilitator reinforces there are *no* bad answers and encourages participants to collect a few "dumb ones"
   - The objective is to cast a wide net, and capture as many ideas as possible
2. To avoid groupthink initially, have people take an appropriate amount of time (e.g.: 5-7 minutes) to capture ideas on their own
   - e.g.: write them on a sticky note but not share it with the group

APPENDIX 2   CEREMONIES

Step 5: Review, Discussion, Affinity Mapping

1. Have the group share their ideas by using one of the following techniques:
   A. In round robin, each person to places one note on a wall and explains it briefly to the group
      - Continue until all ideas have been shared
      - Group like ideas and eliminate duplicates as ideas are added
   B. Have all participants add their ideas to the wall or board at once
      - Participants remain at the wall and read all the items others have added
      - Participants informally discuss what they have read as a group
      - Group like ideas and eliminate duplicates as the group reviews the ideas together

   Note: In both cases permit participants to add new ideas as they are inspired by the discussion

2. Participants should be encouraged by the facilitator to ask questions about any items they read and do not understand

3. Discussion of any items which are called out for clarity should be limited to ensuring participants understand what the item refers to

4. The facilitator should stop any discussion of the merits of any of the items which were added during brainstorming

APPENDIX 2   CEREMONIES

Step 6: Prioritization of causes of failure
(Optional)

To add acuity to what is learned, prioritize the causes of failure. This does not imply items which receive fewer, or no, votes are not important nor that those items will not be addressed. This informs the team of the items which they may wish to addressed first, or soonest.

1. Each person will be given three votes
2. Place a dot on each sticky note (or next to the line captured by the facilitator) for the ideas you believe were the most impactful or important
3. Each person may place their votes on one item or up to three items

Note: This step is mandatory if you plan to use the alternative method documented following Step 10 of this ceremony, which focuses on the highest priority causes of failure.

627

APPENDIX 2   CEREMONIES

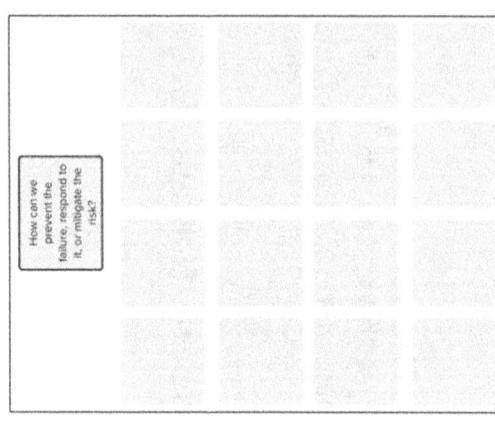

Step 7: Brainstorm possible remedies

1. The facilitator asks the group to consider how any or all failures captured in Step 5 could be prevented, their risks mitigated, or how the team could prepare to address the failure if it occurs

2. Participants suggest one or more of the following ways to mitigate each risk:

   A. Employ one or more specific **preventative actions** to reduce the probability the problem will occur

   B. Deploy one or more specific **contingency actions** to limit the impact of the problem should it occur

   C. Deploy one or more specific **detection mechanisms** that can identify an occurrence of the problem, detect the problem earlier than can it can currently be detected, or predict the likely future occurrence

3. To avoid groupthink initially, have people take an appropriate amount of time (e.g.: 5-10 minutes) to capture ideas on their own

   - e.g.: write them on a sticky note but not share it with the group

628

Step 8: Review, Discussion, Affinity Mapping

1. Have the group share their ideas by using one of the following techniques:
   A. In round robin, each person to places one note on a wall and explains it briefly to the group
      - Continue until all ideas have been shared
      - Group like ideas and eliminate duplicates as ideas are added
   B. Have all participants add their ideas to the wall or board at once
      - Participants remain at the wall and read all the items others have added
      - Group like ideas and eliminate duplicates as the group reviews the ideas together

   Note: In both cases permit participants to add new ideas as they are inspired by the discussion

2. Participants should be encouraged by the facilitator to ask questions about any items they read though do not understand

3. Discussion of any items which are called out for clarity should be limited to ensuring participants understand what the item refers to

4. The facilitator should stop any discussion of the merits of any of the items which were added during brainstorming

Step 9: Prioritization of potential remedies

To add acuity to what is learned, prioritize the potential remedies. This does not imply items which receive fewer, or no, votes are not important nor that those items will not be addressed. This informs the team of the items which they may wish to address first, or soonest.

1. Each person will be given three votes
2. Place a dot on each sticky note (or next to the line captured by the facilitator) for the ideas you believe were the most impactful or important
3. Each person may place their votes on one item or up to three items

APPENDIX 2   CEREMONIES

Action	Owner	Deadline
Action 1	Owner 1	Deadline 1
Action 2	Owner 2	Deadline 2
Action 3	Owner 3	Deadline 3
Action n	Owner n	Deadline n

Step 10: Create an action plan

1. Assign an owner and target date to each for each of the highest priority remedies from Step 9
2. Assign an owner for the entire plan to ensure action item owners follow-up on their assignments and the team is informed of progress

631

APPENDIX 2 CEREMONIES

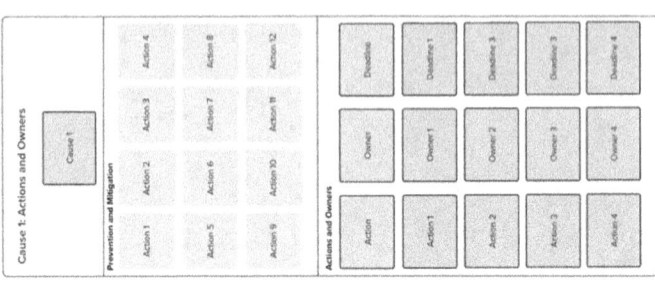

Steps 7-10: Alternative method

1. The facilitator selects the highest priority cause from Step 6
2. The facilitator leads the team through steps 7, 8, 9, and 10 for that one high priority item only
3. The facilitator then selects the next highest priority item from Step 6 and leads the team through steps 7, 8, 9, and 10 for that one item only
4. Steps 7, 8, 9, and 10 are performed on each item from Step 6 in priority order, or on a selected number of causes of failure (e.g. the top 5 items)

Note: This alternative method creates focus on a single cause at a time and *may* result in richer analysis of each item that is reviewed. However, this option *may* also constrain the team's thinking when brainstorming potential remedies.

APPENDIX 2   CEREMONIES

5. Team Introspection Workshop

Improve team performance, morale, and collaboration with others through self-reflection

APPENDIX 2   CEREMONIES

Action Items					Parking Lot
Improvement Area #1	Improvement Area #2	Improvement Area #3	Improvement Area #4	Improvement Area #5	

Action brainstorming

When we are at our best
When we are not at our best

634

Team Introspection Workshop

A brainstorming exercise that:

- Identifies areas of high performance which can be fostered and leveraged
- Delivers concrete actions to improve the team's behavior or performance
- Addresses performance or morale reducing negative behaviors if they are identified

<u>Note:</u> This workshop is best conducted by a skilled facilitator or someone who has developed a high degree of trust with the team

APPENDIX 2   CEREMONIES

Team Introspection Agenda
Sample

1. Gathering
2. Setting the scope and mindset, and confirming a shared understanding
3. Self-reflection: When we are at our best…
4. Self-reflection: When we are not at our best…
5. Action: What can we do to improve?

APPENDIX 2   CEREMONIES

Step 1: Gathering
5 minutes

The gathering portion of the agenda gives people time to:

- Change locations (in-person)
- Connect to the meeting or change meeting tools (remote)
- Resolve connection issues (remote)
- Switch context to the topic of the exercise
- Prepare for the session
- The facilitator should ensure people are greeted and begin setting the session's tone

Step 2: Confirming Scope
5 minutes

- **It is critical that participants understand the session's objectives**
- **The facilitator should:**
  - Display and clearly state the session's purpose
  - Add any context necessary to ensure those present understand it
  - Ask the team whether they all understand the purpose and scope
  - Answer any questions on the scope and
  - Keep this section of the discussion focused on the scope
  - Set the agenda
  - Reinforce key elements of the working agreement (e.g.: all voices are equal, no finger-pointing)
- **Prior to the meeting the facilitator should distribute, or make available:**
  - The meeting purpose statement
  - Working Agreement
  - Definition of Done
  - Other artifacts that might help people prepare for the discussion

APPENDIX 2   CEREMONIES

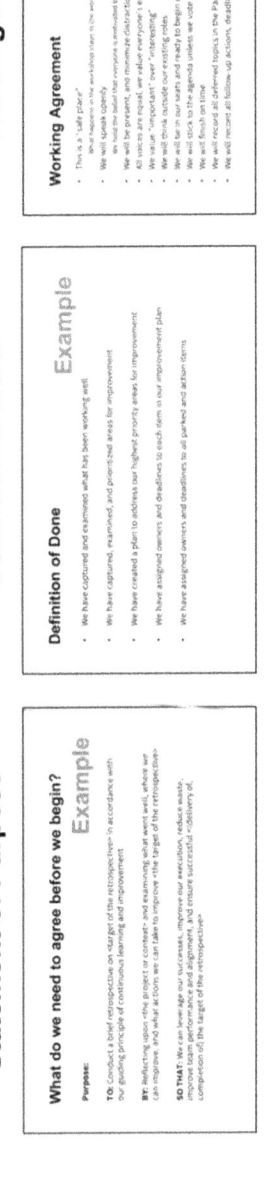

Note: Examples of these artifacts are included in the Tools and Artifacts section of the Toolkit.

APPENDIX 2   CEREMONIES

Step 3: Brainstorm: "When we're at our best..."

1. The facilitator asks the group to think about the behaviors that characterize the team at their best
   - Ask each person to picture the team's best day(s)
     - What happened? What was the impact?
     - What behaviors caused the good things to happen?
     - What actions did the team take?
     - What did the team feel?
     - How did others respond? How did they feel?
     - What did others say about them?

2. The facilitator reinforces there are *no* bad answers and encourages participants to collect a few "dumb ones"
   - The objective is to cast a wide net, and capture as many ideas as possible

3. To avoid groupthink initially, the facilitator asks people take an appropriate amount of quiet time (e.g.: 3-5 minutes) to capture ideas on their own
   - e.g.: write them on a sticky note but not share it with the group
   - Ask people to be silent as they finish

APPENDIX 2   CEREMONIES

Step 4: Review, Discussion, Affinity Mapping

1. Have all participants add their ideas to the wall or board at once
2. Ask participants to remain at the wall and read all the items that gave been added and group any identical or similar items together
   - Encourage discussion
   - Permit participants to add new ideas as they are inspired by the discussion
   - Using this method avoids putting pressure on an individual by asking them to read their ideas aloud
     - This will be more important during Step 7
3. Participants should be encouraged by the facilitator to ask questions about any items they read though do not understand
4. Discussion of any items which are called out for clarity should be limited to ensuring participants understand what the item refers to
5. The facilitator should stop any discussion of the merits of any of the items which were added during brainstorming

641

Step 5: Prioritization of best qualities
(Optional)

To add acuity to what is learned, prioritize the "best" behaviors. This does not imply items which receive fewer, or no, votes are not important nor that those items will not be addressed. This informs the team of the items which they may wish to address first, or soonest.

1. Each person will be given three votes
2. Place a dot on each sticky note (or next to the line captured by the facilitator) for the ideas you believe were the most impactful or important
3. Each person may place their votes on one item or up to three items

APPENDIX 2 CEREMONIES

Step 6: Brainstorm: "When we're not at our best..."

"When we're at our worst..."

1. The facilitator asks the group to consider the behaviors that characterize the team when they're not at their best
   - Ask each person to picture the team's worst day(s)
     - The facilitator reminds the team this is a positive exercise aimed at making the team better, all input is given with positive intent
     - What happened? What was the impact?
     - What behaviors caused the bad/less good things to happen?
     - What actions did the team take? What did the team feel?
     - How did others respond? How did they feel?
     - What did others say about them?

2. The facilitator reinforces there are *no* bad answers and encourages participants to collect a few "dumb ones"
   - The objective is to capture as many ideas as possible

3. To avoid groupthink initially, the facilitator asks people take an appropriate amount of quiet time (e.g.: 3-5 minutes) to capture ideas on their own
   - e.g.: write them on a sticky note but not share it with the group
   - Ask people to be silent as they finish

643

APPENDIX 2   CEREMONIES

Step 7: Review, Discussion, Affinity Mapping

1. Have all participants add their ideas to the wall or board at once
2. Ask participants to remain at the wall and read all the items that gave been added and group any identical or similar items together
   - Using this method avoids putting pressure on an individual by asking them to read their ideas aloud
   - Encourage discussion
   - Permit participants to add new ideas as they are inspired by the discussion
3. Participants should be encouraged by the facilitator to ask questions about any items they read though do not understand
4. Discussion of any items which are called out for clarity should be limited to ensuring participants understand what the item refers to
5. The facilitator should stop any discussion of the merits of any of the items which were added during brainstorming

Step 8: Prioritization of areas for improvement

To add acuity to what is learned, prioritize the areas for improvement. This does not imply items which receive fewer, or no, votes are not important nor that those items will not be addressed. This informs the team of the items which they may wish to address first, or soonest.

1. Each person will be given three votes
2. Place a dot on each sticky note (or next to the line captured by the facilitator) for the ideas you believe were the most impactful or important
3. Each person may place their votes on one item or up to three items

APPENDIX 2   CEREMONIES

Step 9: Brainstorm possible actions

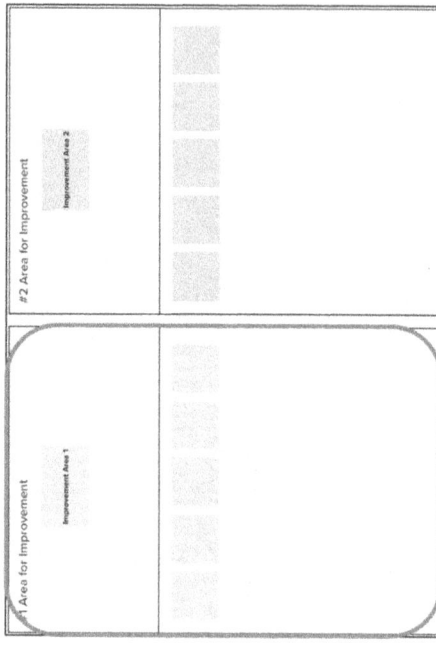

1. Select the area for improvement from Step 8 that had the most votes and place it in the #1 Area for improvement section of the wall

2. Ask the team to take 3-5 minutes to brainstorm on actions the team could take to address the areas for improvement, and place their ideas directly on the wall below the sticky note(s) containing the area for improvement

Step 10: Review, Discussion, Affinity Mapping

1. Ask participants to remain at the wall and read all the items that gave been added and group any identical or similar items together
   - Encourage discussion
   - Permit participants to add new ideas as they are inspired by the discussion
2. Participants should be encouraged by the facilitator to ask questions about any items they read though do not understand
3. Discussion of any items which are called out for clarity should be limited to ensuring participants understand what the item refers to
4. The facilitator should stop any discussion of the merits of any of the items which were added during brainstorming

APPENDIX 2   CEREMONIES

Step 11: Prioritization of potential actions

To add acuity to what is learned, prioritize the actions. This does not imply items which receive fewer, or no, votes are not important nor that those items will not be addressed. This informs the team of the items which they may wish to address first, or soonest.

1. Each person will be given three votes
2. Place a dot on each sticky note (or next to the line captured by the facilitator) for the ideas you believe were the most impactful or important
3. Each person may place their votes on one item or up to three items
4. Do one of the following:
   A. Assign one person to own the entire area of improvement and a deadline for follow-up
      • Step 10 is optional if you choose this method
   B. Assign an individual owner to each of the high priority actions
5. Repeat steps 9-11 for each of the next high-priority items

APPENDIX 2   CEREMONIES

6. Role Alignment Workshop

Improve execution, collaboration, and morale through detailed role alignment

APPENDIX 2 CEREMONIES

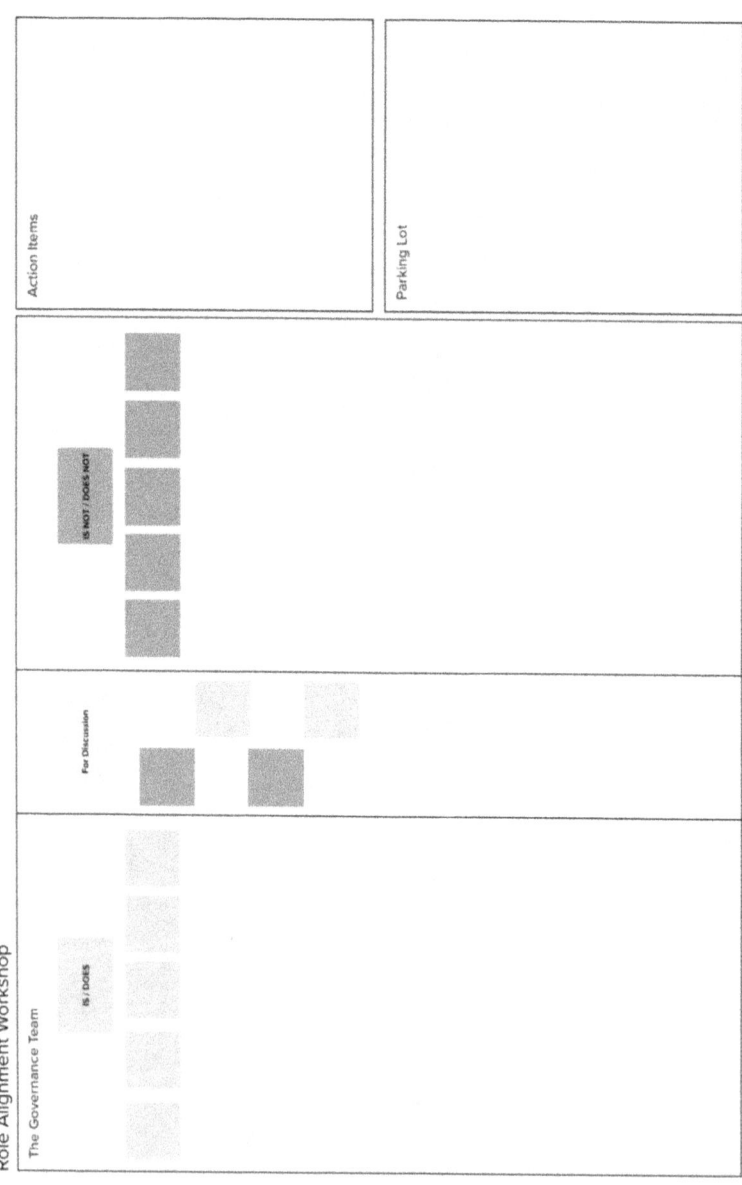

APPENDIX 2　CEREMONIES

Role Alignment Workshop

A brainstorming exercise that:

- Improves execution and morale through alignment
- Develops an explicit, shared understanding of what a team or individual's role is, and what it is not
- Develops an explicit, shared understanding of what a team or individual's tasks and responsibilities are, and what they are not
- Addresses role related misalignment, assumptions, and conflict through open discussion on areas of misalignment or disagreement

Role Alignment Workshop Agenda
Sample

1. Gathering
2. Setting the scope and mindset, and confirming a shared understanding
3. Brainstorming: What the team or individual role is and is not, and what the team or individual in that role does or does not do
4. Identification of areas for discussion
5. Discussion and resolution

APPENDIX 2 CEREMONIES

Step 1: Gathering
5 minutes

The gathering portion of the agenda gives people time to:

- Change locations (in-person)
- Connect to the meeting or change meeting tools (remote)
- Resolve connection issues (remote)
- Switch context to the topic of the exercise
- Prepare for the session
- The facilitator should ensure people are greeted and begin setting the session's tone

Step 2: Confirming Scope
5 minutes

- **It is critical that participants understand the session's objectives**
- **The facilitator should:**
  - Display and clearly state the session's purpose
  - Add any context necessary to ensure those present understand it
  - Ask the team whether they all understand the purpose and scope
  - Answer any questions on the scope and
  - Keep this section of the discussion focused on the scope
  - Set the agenda
  - Reinforce key elements of the working agreement (e.g.: all voices are equal, no finger-pointing)
- **Prior to the meeting the facilitator should distribute, or make available:**
  - The meeting purpose statement
  - Working Agreement
  - Definition of Done
  - Other artifacts that might help people prepare for the discussion

APPENDIX 2   CEREMONIES

Step 2: Artifacts

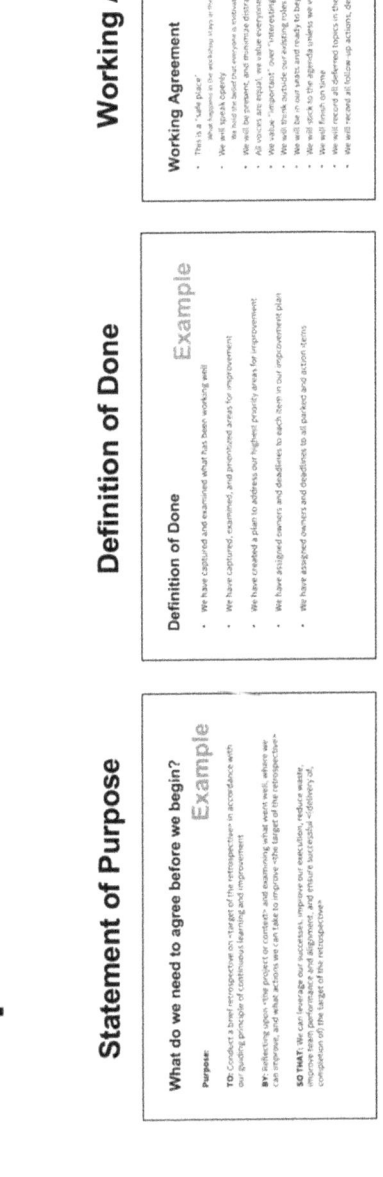

Note: Examples of these artifacts are included in the Tools and Artifacts section of the Toolkit.

APPENDIX 2   CEREMONIES

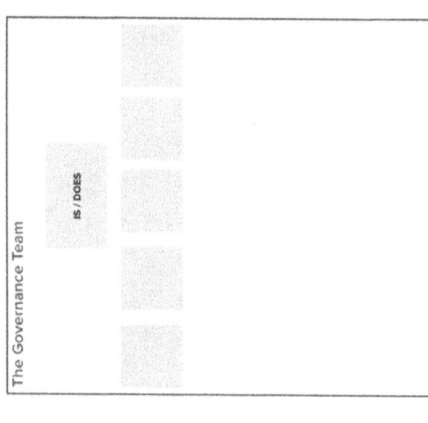

Step 3: Brainstorm: Role characteristics

1. The facilitator asks the group to think about the individual or team role under review and what each person believes does, and does not characterize the role
   - It may help participants to think in the form: The Governance Team role is…; The Governance Team role is not…; The CTO does…; The CTO does not…
   - Alternative method: Brainstorm first only for IS/DOES and separately for IS NOT/DOES NOT
   - **Note:** Using different color sticky notes for the IS/DOES and IS NOT/DOES NOT items may simplify or enhance Step 5
2. The facilitator reinforces there are *no* bad answers and encourages participants to collect a few "dumb ones"
   - The objective is to capture as many ideas as possible
3. To avoid groupthink initially, the facilitator asks people take an appropriate amount of quiet time (e.g.: 3-5 minutes) to capture ideas on their own
   - e.g.: write them on a sticky note but not share it with the group

Step 4: Review, Discussion, Affinity Mapping

1. Have all participants add their ideas to the wall or board at once
2. Ask participants to remain at the wall and read all the items that gave been added, and group any identical or similar items together
   - Encourage discussion
   - Permit participants to add new ideas as they are inspired by the discussion
3. Participants should be encouraged by the facilitator to ask questions about any items they read though do not understand
4. Discussion of any items which are called out for clarity should be limited to ensuring participants understand what the item refers to
5. The facilitator should stop any discussion of the merits of any of the items which were added during brainstorming

APPENDIX 2   CEREMONIES

Step 5: Identification of misalignment

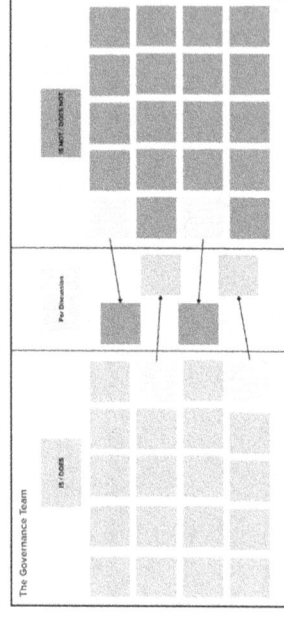

1. Participants return to the wall and:
   A. Identify any items in the IS/DOES area that they believe are not, or should not be, associated with the role and move them to the "For Discussion" zone in the center
   B. Identify items in the IS NOT/DOES NOT area that they believe are, or should be, associated with the role and move them to the "For Discussion" zone in the center

APPENDIX 2   CEREMONIES

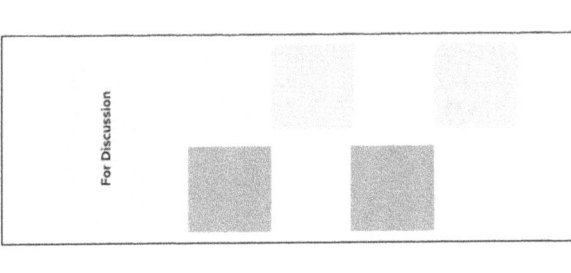

Step 6: Discussion and alignment

1. The facilitator selects an item from the "For Discussion" zone and leads a discussion to:
   A. Ensure all participants share a common understanding of what the item is
   B. Provide an opportunity for the person(s) who moved the item into the discussion zone, to explain why they moved it
   C. Lead an open dialog to determine whether the item should be included or excluded from the role
   D. Use a fist-of-five vote (or similar technique) to lead the group to a final decision
2. The facilitator selects another item from the discussion zone and repeats items A through D
3. Alternative Method: If there are too many items in the discussion zone to address in the time available teams may prioritize the items as outlined on the next page and select them in priority order

Alternative: Prioritization of discussion items
(Optional)

If there is insufficient time to discuss all discussion items, prioritize the "For Discussion" items. This does not imply items which receive fewer, or no, votes are not important nor that those items will not be addressed. This informs the team of the items which they may wish to address first, or soonest.

1. Each person will be given three votes
2. Place a dot on each sticky note (or next to the line captured by the facilitator) for the ideas you believe were the most impactful or important
3. Each person may place their votes on one item or up to three items

APPENDIX 3

Tools and Artifacts

Purpose Statement

- Every meeting or workshop should have a purpose consisting of:
  - **TO:** A clear, concise statement of what the meeting or workshop will accomplish (objective)
  - **BY:** A clear statement of how the objective will be achieved
  - **SO THAT:** A statement describing why achieving the objective is important, and that adds context that will help frame the work and drive a more valuable outcome
- The purpose should be distributed prior to the beginning of the meeting or workshop, preferably when the meeting or workshop is scheduled

---

What do we need to agree before we begin?

Purpose:

TO: Conduct a brief retrospective on <target of the retrospective> in accordance with our guiding principle of continuous learning and improvement

BY: Reflecting upon <the project or context> and examining what went well, where we can improve, and what actions we can take to improve <the target of the retrospective>

SO THAT: We can leverage our successes, improve our execution, reduce waste, improve team performance and alignment, and ensure successful <(delivery of, completion of) the target of the retrospective>

What do we need to agree before we begin?

Example

Purpose:

TO: Conduct a brief retrospective on <target of the retrospective> in accordance with our guiding principle of continuous learning and improvement

BY: Reflecting upon <the project or context> and examining what went well, where we can improve, and what actions we can take to improve <the target of the retrospective>

SO THAT: We can leverage our successes, improve our execution, reduce waste, improve team performance and alignment, and ensure successful <(delivery of, completion of) the target of the retrospective>

APPENDIX 3   TOOLS AND ARTIFACTS

Working Agreement

- Every meeting or workshop should have a working agreement
- Working agreements are a shared understanding of how a team or group will work together
- They define what each person can expect from the others and how the team's values will be manifested
- Teams should develop working agreements together
- Working agreements *can* be seeded and distributed for review ahead of time for discrete events such as workshops

---

Working Agreement

- This is a "safe place"
  - What happens in the workshop stays in the workshop
- We will speak openly
  - We hold the belief that everyone is motivated by the team's success
- We will be present, and minimize distractions
- All voices are equal, we value everyone's experience and input, there is no rank present
- We value "important" over "interesting"
- We will think outside our existing roles
- We will be in our seats and ready to begin one minute before start times
- We will stick to the agenda unless we vote to change it
- We will finish on time
- We will record all deferred topics in the Parking Lot in real time
- We will record all follow-up actions, deadlines, and owners in the "Action" chart

APPENDIX 3   TOOLS AND ARTIFACTS

Working Agreement

Example

- This is a "safe place"
  - What happens in the workshop stays in the workshop
- We will speak openly
  - We hold the belief that everyone is motivated by the team's success
- We will be present, and minimize distractions
- All voices are equal, we value everyone's experience and input, there is no rank present
- We value "important" over "interesting"
- We will think outside our existing roles
- We will be in our seats and ready to begin one minute before start times
- We will stick to the agenda unless we vote to change it
- We will finish on time
- We will record all deferred topics in the Parking Lot in real time
- We will record all follow-up actions, deadlines, and owners in the "Action" chart

665

APPENDIX 3 TOOLS AND ARTIFACTS

Definition of Done

- Every major meeting or workshop should have a definition of done
- A definition of done is a concise list of what must be accomplished for a team or group to consider a meeting or workshop to be completed
- The definition of done should be distributed prior to the beginning of the meeting or workshop, preferably when the meeting or workshop is scheduled

Definition of Done

- We have captured and examined what has been working well
- We have captured, examined, and prioritized areas for improvement
- We have created a plan to address our highest priority areas for improvement
- We have assigned owners and deadlines to each item in our improvement plan
- We have assigned owners and deadlines to all parked and action items

APPENDIX 3 TOOLS AND ARTIFACTS

Definition of Done   *Example*

- We have captured and examined what has been working well
- We have captured, examined, and prioritized areas for improvement
- We have created a plan to address our highest priority areas for improvement
- We have assigned owners and deadlines to each item in our improvement plan
- We have assigned owners and deadlines to all parked and action items

Assessment Goal Examples
(1/2)

- Identify the key challenges, issues, and impediments to bringing new ideas to life
- Identify and/or confirm the problem(s) to be solved
- Identify themes and commonalities and their significance and impact
- Identify and understand priorities at all levels
- Identify potential detractors and champions
- Learn about any current and past initiatives, and whether and why they were successful or unsuccessful
- Understand the outcomes participants and stakeholders hope to achieve
- Understand the value the participants expect
- Identify the "what's in it for me" (the "win") for each stakeholder or participant group
- Understand the timeframes within which each participant or stakeholder expects to achieve their desired outcomes

Assessment Goal Examples
(2/2)

- Confirm the type of initiative that will most likely address the problem at hand (e.g.: toolkit, framework, approach, incubator...)
- Confirm the type(s) of new ideas that will be brought to life via your initiative (e.g.: breakthrough, adjacent, projects, programs...)
- Identify any potential obstacles or friction to the delivery of the initiative
- Identify any potential accelerators
- Begin change management activities
- Gather data and evidence that will help with the transformation (change) activities
- Gather material that will support a stronger case for the initiative
- Test and refine early messaging
- Introduce yourself to influencers, stakeholders, and participants
- Establish new relationships and build trust

APPENDIX 3 TOOLS AND ARTIFACTS

A Simple Approach to Secondary Research
(1/2)

1. Find as much information as you can related to current and past initiatives (e.g.: studies, white papers, PowerPoint™ presentations, videos, executive summaries, after action reports)

2. Look for information from initiatives that appear similar to what your current hypotheses lead you to believe you might create, and anything that might be somewhat related to your purpose (e.g.: you may be building an incubator and find helpful information from past efforts related to an innovation contest or hackathon)

3. Examine information related to currently active initiatives, programs, and tools (e.g.: project management frameworks, current approval processes), and get color regarding their effectiveness, popularity, and whether there were mismatched expectations or unmet needs

   - Find out what people like and dislike about them
   - Investigate the value they deliver and the value people in the organization believe they deliver, and note any differences and gaps

APPENDIX 3　　TOOLS AND ARTIFACTS

A Simple Approach to Secondary Research
(2/2)

4. Analyze both past success and failure and determine why things failed or succeeded (e.g.: timing, personalities, team, leadership, participants, skill requirements, vocabulary mismatch, funding, wrong solution, training, sabotage)

5. Consider the differences between past and current conditions

6. Question how things might be different now, and what may have changed
   - Something that failed in the past may succeed in the future, so what would be different this time
   - Something that worked in the past, may not work in the future

7. Determine which currently available processes, programs, and/or frameworks, if any, your initiative will have to coexist with, adhere to, or work with as a supplier (provide input to) or consumer (accept output from)

Simple Four Week Assessment Schedule

Week 1: Preparation; secondary research; interview guide creation; interview scheduling

Week 2: Interviews; continue/complete secondary research; note enrichment; preliminary synthesis

Week 3: Interviews; complete secondary research; note enrichment; preliminary synthesis

Week 4: Final synthesis; preparation and delivery of findings

APPENDIX 3 TOOLS AND ARTIFACTS

Potential Assessment Interview Topics

(1/2) Illustrative

The current state

- Currently used methods, approaches, and methodologies
- What is going well, what is working
- What is not going well, what is not working
- Needs, challenges, and conflicts

What has worked well in the past

- What went well, and why
- What failed, and why
- Whether success or failure was experienced at an individual, team, department, and/or organizational level
- Trap doors and pitfalls that were discovered

Potential Assessment Interview Topics

(2/2) Illustrative

Opportunities for improvement

- Gaps in skills, funding, resources, people…
- Challenges
- Needs
- Clarify whether each opportunity for improvement is experienced at an individual, team, department, and/or organizational level

Future vision

- What does success look like
- What would participants do if there were no constraints

Value

- What value the participant hopes or expects the initiative will achieve

Frequently Valuable Interview Questions
(1/3)

If you could get everyone doing one thing consistently, what would that be?
- Elicits positive behavior that, applied consistently, will have a substantial positive impact
- Often helps identify pockets of excellence in execution and/or expertise

If you could change one thing – but only one thing – what would that one thing be?
- Helps highlight priorities
- Surfaces positive or negative conditions

As you think about your mission, what keeps you up at night?
- Surfaces the highest priority item
- Aids prioritization, planning, and messaging preparation

What is your greatest challenge?
- Often surfaces cross-team or cross-organization challenges and conflicts
- Can expose key design requirements
- Can offer insight into participant motivation

Frequently Valuable Interview Questions
(2/3)

Is there anything you need that you don't have now?
- Can surface immediately actionable needs and drive short-term wins
- Can identify obstacles that require immediate, or near-term, attention

Is there anything you would like to ask me about?
- Demonstrates openness
- May surface exploration targets that were not yet identified

Is there anything you expected me to ask you about that I have not?
- Identifies missed areas, gaps, and blind spots
- Many participants answer, "no"
- The few participants per assessment who have an answer usually provide amazing insight

Would it be OK if I follow up with you?
- Establishes permission for further discussion and exploration
- Potentially creates the opportunity for a deeper working relationship

Frequently Valuable Interview Questions
(3/3)

Is there anyone else you think I should speak with?

- Identifies stakeholders and influencers you may have missed
- Identifies potential new sources of knowledge, subject matter experts, champions and/or detractors
- Can identify people or teams which might be insulted or feel slighted if overlooked
- May help avoid political infighting

APPENDIX 3 TOOLS AND ARTIFACTS

Sample Assessment Interview Guide Structure
(1/3)

Organization Name - Initiative Name - Interview Guide

02 January 2028

Structure - (45 mins)

1. Gathering and personal introductions (3 mins)
2. Introduction and context (2 mins)
3. Current approach (10 mins)
4. What's going well (10 mins)
5. Opportunities for improvement (10 mins)
6. Future vision (10 mins)
7. Value expectations (10 mins)
8. Closing (5 mins)

Sample Assessment Interview Guide Structure

(2/3)

Introduction and Context (2 mins)

- Introduction line 1
- Introduction line 2
- …
- Last line of introduction
  <**Pause here for comments and confirmation**>

Current Approach (10 mins)

Explore current methods, methodologies, and approaches

(Opening statement to introduce the section and add context if necessary.)

- First question of the section
- Second question
- Third question
  <**MOVE TO NEXT SECTION IF PAST 10 MINS**>
- Fourth question
- …
- Last question of the section

APPENDIX 3 TOOLS AND ARTIFACTS

Sample Assessment Interview Guide Structure (3/3)

What's going well (10 mins)

Introductory statement and context
- First question of the section
- …

[Remainder of the interview guide…]

APPENDIX 3   TOOLS AND ARTIFACTS

Sample Interview Guide
(1/17)

Note: This example is intended to help you think through the questions you should ask during your assessment and how an interview guide can be assembled and structured. It will require editing and is not intended to be used as is. The questions and their sequence will need to be adjusted to meet the specific objectives of your assessment.

Some sections contain more questions than could be asked in the time allotted. This was done in this document to provide a broader variety of examples, but I often do that to provide options that enable adjustment to suit the person being interviewed and the nature of the conversation.

681

APPENDIX 3   TOOLS AND ARTIFACTS

Sample Interview Guide
(2/17)

Sample Assessment Interview Guide Draft

31 Dec 2056

Structure (Needs to be adjusted – Current timing is 80 minutes!)

1. Gathering and personal introductions (3 mins)
   - Informal
   - Interviewee's role...
2. Introduction and context (2 mins)
3. Current approach (10 mins)
4. What's going well (10 mins)
5. Opportunities for improvement (10 mins)
6. Future Vision (10 mins)
7. Value from the program (10 mins)
8. Team structure and working across teams (10 mins, optional)
9. Closing (10 mins)

APPENDIX 3   TOOLS AND ARTIFACTS

Sample Interview Guide
(3/17)

Introduction and Context (5 mins)

- <Assessment specific opening context and background…>

- To do that, we want to take a look at what's been happening
- Over the past [six-to-twelve months] or so – and perhaps beyond when it makes sense -
- And draw on your experience – and other relevant history
- To explore where you would like to take things
- So the purpose of our conversation this morning is to begin this discussion

- I would like to ask you a few questions to help me to understand
- What has been going well
- Areas where you feel you could improve
- Or that are causing frustration
- Things you expected to see or do that may not yet have started
- And opportunities you believe this team could take advantage of

683

APPENDIX 3   TOOLS AND ARTIFACTS

Sample Interview Guide
(4/17)

- I also want to let you know that our conversation this morning
- Will be completely confidential –

- I will capture your input anonymously
- And I will aggregate with all of the other feedback
- The source of the information will not be shared with anyone

- We want to capture the true state of things –
- The good – the not as good –
- The opportunities we may have missed – and those still ahead of us

- I will not divulge specific answers by specific people in any reports
- I will aggregate and summarize the information when that is appropriate

Sample Interview Guide
(5/17)

<Pause for comments and questions>

- Is there anything else you would like to be sure we cover?

- If you feel others would have different perspectives, please feel free to share those, but please distinguish between those – and always begin with your own opinion if you can

Current approach

- Explore current methods, approaches and methodologies

- I would like to begin by getting to know a bit more about what your do, and how things work in your organization

APPENDIX 3   TOOLS AND ARTIFACTS

Sample Interview Guide
(6/17)

- How do ideas arrive? How do they find you?
- What types of ideas tend to come to your team? (Are there different kinds of ideas that come to your team?)
- How do new ideas find you and your team?
- What happens once you receive them?
- Do you have a consistent approach for new ideas?
- What approach do you currently follow? Do you follow a specific methodology?

APPENDIX 3　　TOOLS AND ARTIFACTS

Sample Interview Guide
(7/17)

- Are there other innovation programs in progress?
- What are those?
- What's going well?
- What might you improve?
- Will they conflict with this initiative? Could they be complimentary?
- Have you run innovation or incubation programs like this in the past?
- What were the results? (Positive? Negative?)
- Why do you believe they did or did they not succeed?
- If it succeeded – why aren't you doing that now?

APPENDIX 3   TOOLS AND ARTIFACTS

Sample Interview Guide
(8/17)

- Is there pent-up demand for incubation?
- Are you aware of ideas that people are trying to promote or sell?
- How many do you believe will be there?

- Are their currently active incubations or teams or people trying to run skunkworks?
- Are they of interest, perhaps as seed initiatives?
- Do they have funding?

<GOOD TIME TO CHANGE SECTIONS TO OPTIMIZE TIME>

- Is the process documented? Anything you can share?
- Is that same approach followed by other teams?

Sample Interview Guide
(9/17)

- Are there things you do differently?
- What tools or methodologies do you use?
- Are you happy with them?
- Are they used consistently across teams?
- Are there things you think would be good for all teams to use?
- What types of ideas do you typically receive?
- Do you approach different types of ideas differently?

APPENDIX 3 TOOLS AND ARTIFACTS

Sample Interview Guide
(10/17)

What's going well

Let's explore what's really working.

Our context here is both you and your team, and the overall group.

It would be great if you could address and highlight differences when they exist.

- Can you tell me about things you believe are working well for your team – and perhaps others?

- If you could get everyone doing only one thing, and doing in consistently, what would it be?

- Are there others?

APPENDIX 3   TOOLS AND ARTIFACTS

Sample Interview Guide
(11/17)

Opportunities for improvement

Let's explore areas where we might improve.

Our context here is both you and your team, and the overall group.

It would be great if you could address and highlight differences when they exist.

- What do you believe might be better, could be improved, or perhaps isn't working as well as you think it can or would like it to?
- Is there anything you need that you don't have now?
- Could be process, (funding), resource, people, skills, access – anything.
- What is your greatest challenge?

APPENDIX 3 TOOLS AND ARTIFACTS

Sample Interview Guide
(12/17)

- Is there anything that's keeping you from doing your best or slowing you down? Maybe even something that's simple and slowing you down?

- If you could change one thing, what would it be?

- Do you think there's anything that we are letting slip past us? Something we're missing that we really could take advantage of? Something that might really be beneficial to the company or our customers?

- As you think about your mission, what keeps you up at night?

APPENDIX 3 TOOLS AND ARTIFACTS

Sample Interview Guide
(13/17)

Future Vision

- I would like to get a bit hypothetical for a moment.
- If we assume for a moment that you could have access to unlimited resources, skills, funding, talent… anything you might need
- What would you do?
- If you had complete control of everything for a day, what would you change?
- What does "breakthrough innovation" mean to you?
- Do you believe others would define it the same way?

693

APPENDIX 3 TOOLS AND ARTIFACTS

Sample Interview Guide
(14/17)

Value from the Program

- What value are you looking for this initiative to deliver?

- What value are others hoping to realize?

- What are you hoping to exit from your incubator? (Breakthrough products? New features? Internal systems?)

- Who will be looking for these results? How will they measure success?

- Is there any value to a brand contribution ("brand halo") through this initiative?

- Are there key areas you hope to get ideas or innovation in?

APPENDIX 3 TOOLS AND ARTIFACTS

Sample Interview Guide
(15/17)

- Do you have any other objectives?
  - Examples for interviewer context, don't offer these as suggestions unless the person cannot think of anything... try not to lead them
    - Improve customer perception as an innovative company
    - Improve employee perception of the innovative nature of our organization
    - Let employees know it's OK - and encouraged - to innovate

- Attention span: How long before you have to show results from an incubation?
  - Who needs to see those results
  - When do they need to see results?
  - What type of results would be acceptable?
    - Moving an idea forward (e.g.: Seed 1 to Seed 2)?
    - Bringing something to market?
    - Getting good press?
    - New product in test with customers? New prototype? Customer feedback? New idea is progressing well through the incubation process?

Sample Interview Guide
(16/17)

Team Structure (Optional)

- What about working across teams? Do you do much cross functional work?

- How often do you work with other teams – or do different teams work together? How does that work?

- Not asking about specific teams here, just a general question. Are there things that get in the way when you're working with other teams?

- Are they structural impediments? Process impediments?

- How is your team structured? Not the org structure, how you approach work?

- Are other teams structured the same way?

APPENDIX 3 TOOLS AND ARTIFACTS

Sample Interview Guide
(17/17)

Closing and final insights

- As you think about this, what is keeping you up at night? (If not asked earlier)

- Is there anything you expected me to ask you about that I have not?

- Would be OK to follow up with you if I need clarification later on or have additional questions?

- Is there anyone else I should speak with?

APPENDIX 3   TOOLS AND ARTIFACTS

Video Assessment Pre-Interview Checklist
(1/5)

Make sure the camera is connected, set, and tested
- I prefer an external camera, as it provides more flexibility for angles, framing, and positioning

Make sure you are well framed and centered
- Avoid strange angles, people will be distracted if you are a giant eyeball or nose
- Ensure your head is not cut off (high or low)
- Frame yourself with space on all four sides in case the video conference software crops part of your image

Ensure lighting is good
- Make sure you are not backlit
- Three well-placed light sources will usually be enough to address lighting issues

Look behind you! (Clear your frame)
- Know what is in frame behind you when you broadcast
- Ensure your work area looks tidy, clean, and professional
- Ensure there is no confidential or personal information in view
- Ensure there is nothing distracting behind you
- Do this every time you are about to begin a session!

Video Assessment Pre-Interview Checklist
(2/5)

Make sure the proper mic is connected, selected, and tested

- I find an external mic better than most built-in mics, and less apt to capture typing noises
- Beware that some mechanical keyboards can be distractingly loud, and position of the keyboard relative to the mic may matter

Ensure the network is properly configured

- Use a wired connection if possible
- If you have been switching between wired and wireless networks, it may be a good idea to reboot your machine with the connection type you plan to use (e.g.: wired) active, as I have found some video conferencing software can fail or perform poorly otherwise (I usually do this the evening before an interview, or early in the morning, in case there are problems)

Reboot the modem your internet provider supplied (when working from home)

- This can improve performance in some cases (your situation may differ)
- I usually do this the evening before an interview, or early in the morning, in case there are problems

Have a backup internet connection, if possible

- e.g.: I have tested that the hotspot capability on my mobile phone is good enough for some types of video conferences, and set it up prior to online sessions so I can switch quickly if necessary

Video Assessment Pre-Interview Checklist

(3/5)

Ensure others know an interview is being conducted (especially when working from home)

- This will prevent people from walking in on your interview or disrupting it with loud or distracting noises
- I use an "on air" light outside my office in case people who are unaware of the scheduled interview visit unexpectedly
- Don't panic if someone does come in, just use a calm, professional tone to let them know you are conducting an interview

Ensure keyboard, mouse, and other peripheral batteries are fully charged

Have a second laptop or desktop available, if possible

- I prepare a second machine and launch the video conferencing software, but do not join the session

Turn off or pause backups, automatic updates, anti-virus scans, and maintenance activities during the interview

- If your machine's maintenance is scheduled by a corporate administrator it might be a good idea to check for, and apply, pending maintenance the day prior to the interview

APPENDIX 3   TOOLS AND ARTIFACTS

Video Assessment Pre-Interview Checklist (4/5)

Shut down unnecessary applications

- They may be distracting
- They may cause performance issues, depending upon your system
- Hiding your browser's tabs or favorites may also be appropriate, depending upon what you may share

Open applications that will, or may, be used during the interview, and have material ready

- e.g.: If you are going to show an illustration, have it ready to share
- Ensure you have tested sharing them using the video conference application and configuration you will use during the interview

Configure your desktop or laptop workspace to maintain eye contact

Turn off or extend system time-out periods as needed

- This will prevent disruptions
- This will also remove the distraction caused by the need for you to keep tapping a display or hitting a key to keep the system from going to sleep

701

Video Assessment Pre-Interview Checklist

(5/5)

Silence messages, notifications, email alerts, and pop-ups for the duration of the interview

- They can be distracting
- They can be embarrassing (your friends and colleagues may not know you are sharing)
- I have seen some very embarrassing, and extremely not suitable for work, messages and spam email notifications pop up while people were sharing slides or illustrations
- Share specific applications, not your desktop or workspace

Dress professionally, even if you are working from home

APPENDIX 3   TOOLS AND ARTIFACTS

Tips for Conducting Interviews
(1/5)

1. **BRING HIGH, POSITIVE ENERGY!**
   - Be your authentic self, but dial your positivity up as high as you authentically can
   - Both the participant's and interviewer's energy levels will fall throughout the interview, so it is important to start high
   - Put bad days in your desk drawer before an interview begins, (unfortunately) they will be there when it's over

2. **Confirm the participant is still available for the scheduled period**
   - Sometimes participants develop schedule conflicts after they have confirmed their availability
   - It is best to know that your sixty-minute interview has become thirty-minutes before you ask your first question so you can adjust priorities or reschedule it

3. **Let participants know you will be taking notes, and how you will do that**
   - Never record audio or video without prior informed consent
   - When typing notes I ask participants to let me know if my typing is bothering them (I use an external mic positioned away from the keyboard to prevent that from happening, but I always ask)

4. **Have a crisp personal bio and elevator pitch ready**
   - Participants sometimes ask an interviewer to share a little personal information, or ask about the initiative, so be prepared to answer those questions in a simple sentence or two

703

APPENDIX 3   TOOLS AND ARTIFACTS

Tips for Conducting Interviews
(2/5)

5. Listen

- Use active listening techniques
- Ask probing questions based upon participant responses
- Don't rush through your interview guide and accept all answers at face value; listen to the participant's answers and, when appropriate, explore those more deeply (Don't just say, "OK" and move to the next question)
- Your guide should contain notes on how to stay on time if you follow an unforeseen path
- Participants frequently answer questions before they are asked, so don't ask questions they have already answered when you encounter them in your guide

6. Your interview guide is only a guide

- Don't be subservient to it, phrase your questions in a manner consistent with the conversation, then go where the conversation leads (as long as it's a relevant place)
- Tailor your priorities based upon the participant's role, experience, and knowledge (e.g.: practitioner vs. senior executive)
- Focus on information you can only obtain through an interview
- Don't feel the need to dive deeply into well-explored areas with every participant; use that time to cover new ground
- Leverage your preparation, and the guide, to ensure the most critical information is captured

APPENDIX 3 TOOLS AND ARTIFACTS

Tips for Conducting Interviews
(3/5)

7. **Pay attention to the participant's body language**
   - Listen with your eyes
   - A change in body language can let you know there is more to an answer than the words that were spoken, and catching that can help you to identify areas to probe
   - It may help you detect when a participant is giving you an answer they believe they are "supposed" to give versus telling you how they really feel
   - Watch for reactions to your questions and style, observe how you are being perceived
   - This is more challenging in video interviews, but not impossible

8. **An assessment interview is a conversation**
   - Be present, welcoming, warm, and engaged, and don't be cold and clinical
   - Rehearse, and try not to dryly read questions

9. **It's not about you (the interviewer)**
   - Keep your comments brief, though not rude, even in pedagogical style interviews
   - When asked a complex question, provide a brief response and offer to follow up

705

APPENDIX 3   TOOLS AND ARTIFACTS

Tips for Conducting Interviews
(4/5)

10. It is about you (the interviewer)

- This will likely be the first time many participants will meet you, and first impressions matter
- Be authentic
- Bring your best self

11. Save controversial or challenging questions until late in the interview, or near its end

- It gives the participant a chance to get "warmed up" and into a good mindset
- It gives the interviewer an opportunity to build trust and rapport before challenging a participant
- It reduces the risk of moving the conversation off course or poisoning the interview
- Carefully framing the question and acknowledging its controversial nature can help (e.g.: "I realize this is a bit of a sensitive area, but I would really like your insight...")
- You will not likely have overly controversial questions in this type of interview, but keep this in mind since some questions might be more sensitive or challenging than others

APPENDIX 3　TOOLS AND ARTIFACTS

Tips for Conducting Interviews
(5/5)

12. Take note of new learning and knowledge gaps, and follow-up

- Capture information regarding new topics, political conditions, technology, techniques, and anything you learn, whether or not you see a direct connection to your initiative
- Note when a participant mentions a process, group, or technology that you are unaware of, and make an action item to learn more about it following the interview
- Ask participants where you might learn more about a topic when appropriate
- To economize time, keep a follow-up list and ask questions at the end of the interview, or in a follow-up note
- Closing these gaps will often help with subsequent interviews, communication planning, and designing your initiative

APPENDIX 3   TOOLS AND ARTIFACTS

Sample Assessment Report Structure
(1/2)

1. **Introduction:** A one page summary that provides the context of the assessment including what was done (the assessment's basic parameters), the structure of the findings, and how to use the findings (e.g.: what to read if you want an overview, what to read if you need detail)

2. **Executive summary:** A one page summary of the top discoveries, conclusions, and recommendations; usually consisting of one bullet for each major theme

3. **Summary of findings (themes):** The highest level of detail of each finding, usually consisting of one page of additional detail for each bullet in the executive summary (each major theme)

4. **Detailed findings:** The detailed findings and evidence that led to the conclusions which were expressed as the major themes, normally consisting of one or more pages of detail related to each bullet in the summary of findings

5. **Appendix:** Additional detail, helpful artifacts, and/or answers to key questions (top ten lists)

APPENDIX 3 TOOLS AND ARTIFACTS

Sample Assessment Report Structure
(2/2)

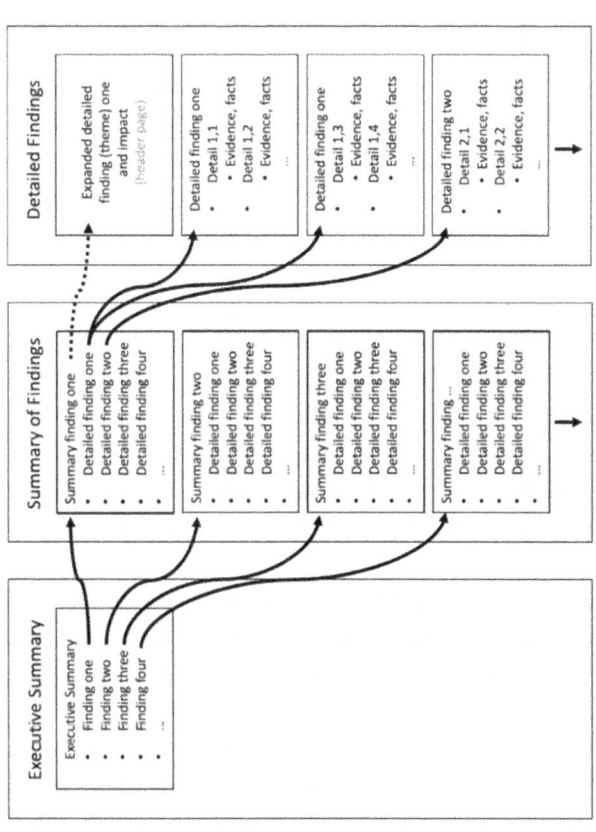

Candidate Assessment Finding Themes
(1/5)

Problems

- What problem(s) does the organization hope to address with your initiative? Does it (do they) actually exist? Is it (are they) painful enough people would act to solve them?
- What is the impact of the problems the organization (team...) faces? What threats do they pose?
- Are there adjacent or non-adjacent problems or organizational dysfunction that might impact the initiative?
- What are the primary concerns of people, teams, and/or the organization? What "keeps them up at night"?
- What external threats and risks is the organization dealing with?

Candidate Assessment Finding Themes
(2/5)

Expectations and aspirations

- What outcomes do people want the initiative to deliver?
- What value do people expect from the initiative? How will it be measured?
- What are the differences in expectations across people, different roles, different departments, different regions? Are they in conflict?

Organizational values

- What does the organization value?
- What do employees value?
- Are the organization and employee values different? How? Are there conflicts?
- Are the values interpreted differently across teams, departments, by managers…?
- What is the organization's attitude toward new idea incubation or innovation?
- What is really happening?
- What is rewarded?

Candidate Assessment Finding Themes
(3/5)

Performance and execution

- Are there synergistic individual or team strengths, or pockets of excellence? Where?
- Are there obstacles or impediments to execution? How prevalent are they?
- What do people believe they are doing? What are they actually doing?
- Is there consistently good execution in specific areas?
- Is there consistently poor execution in specific areas?
- Are there potential champions?
- Is there anyone who would want your new initiative to fail? Why?
- What, if anything, is holding the people, teams, groups, or organization back?

Candidate Assessment Finding Themes
(4/5)

People

- Does the current team have the skills required for the initiative?
- Can the current team acquire skills to fill any gaps? How quickly?
- Are there required skills which cannot be acquired in a reasonable timeframe?
- How is morale?
- What, if any, conflict exists between people, teams, departments, leaders, or leadership teams?
- Is there healthy or unhealthy competition between people or groups?

Opportunities

- What are the opportunities for early wins that could help build momentum and credibility?
- Are new ideas currently incubating somewhere which could seed your initiative?

Candidate Assessment Finding Themes
(5/5)

Opportunities (continued)

- Are other people or teams attempting to address similar issues? Could they become partners?
- Are there compatible initiatives and incentives which could be leveraged? (e.g.: HR programs or focus)
- Are there emerging organizational goals or core values which might be leveraged?
- Are there people with experience in similar initiatives or in bringing new ideas to life?

How frequently was each theme, fact, or example mentioned?

- Were there commonalities across those who mentioned it (position, role, location...)?
- Were there differences?
- Which themes are strong? Which are weak? Which weak ones should be further explored?

Sample Artifact Summary

Artifact	Description	Ceremony	Collab	Explore 1	Explore 2	Experiment 1	Experiment 2	Transition 1	Transition 2
Public Sector Lean Canvas	Capture, communicate, and de-risk a business model		Y	★	✓	✓	✓	✓	✓
Lean Canvas	Capture, communicate, and de-risk a business model		Y	★	✓	✓	✓	✓	✓
Classic Retrospective	Drives continuous earning and improvement	Retro	Y	★					

- **Artifact:** The common name(s) of the tool or artifact

- **Description:** A brief description of the purpose for which the tool is commonly used and, optionally, comments from teams who have found it useful (alternatively, comments might be added in a separate column)

- **Ceremony:** The label, index, or name of the ceremony or ceremonies that will help teams use the tool or complete the artifact

- **Collab:** Whether there is a pre-defined template in the organization's collaboration tool (e.g.: Mural™, Miro™, Figma™)

- **Explore 1 - Transition 2:** A check mark in a cell in a stage's column indicates the tool may be useful during the stage; a star indicates the earliest stage during which the tool or artifact is likely to be introduced

APPENDIX 3 TOOLS AND ARTIFACTS

APPENDIX 3   TOOLS AND ARTIFACTS

Design Workshop Layout
The workshop is described in detail in Chapter 7

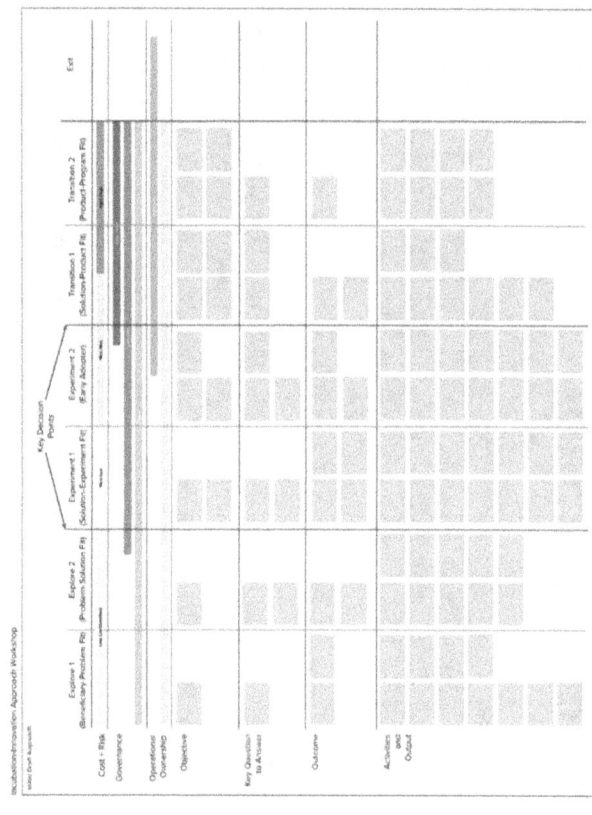

APPENDIX 3 TOOLS AND ARTIFACTS

Cross-Team Engagement Model (Illustrative)
(1/3) Private Sector Product Exit Example

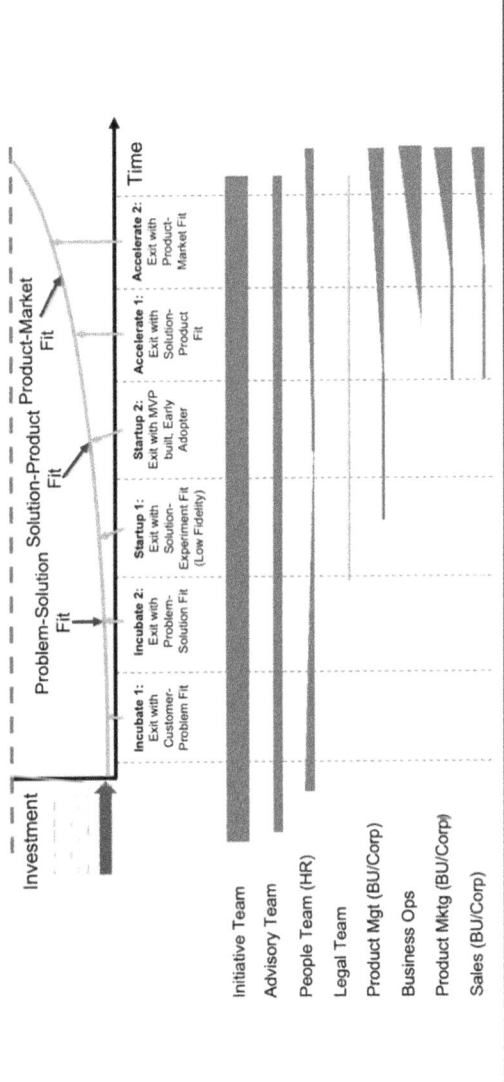

1. The blue bar begins where each team is most likely to engage
2. The height of each bar indicates a team's likely level of engagement (higher bar = higher level of engagement)

Note: Additional information and context is available in Chapter 7.

717

APPENDIX 3   TOOLS AND ARTIFACTS

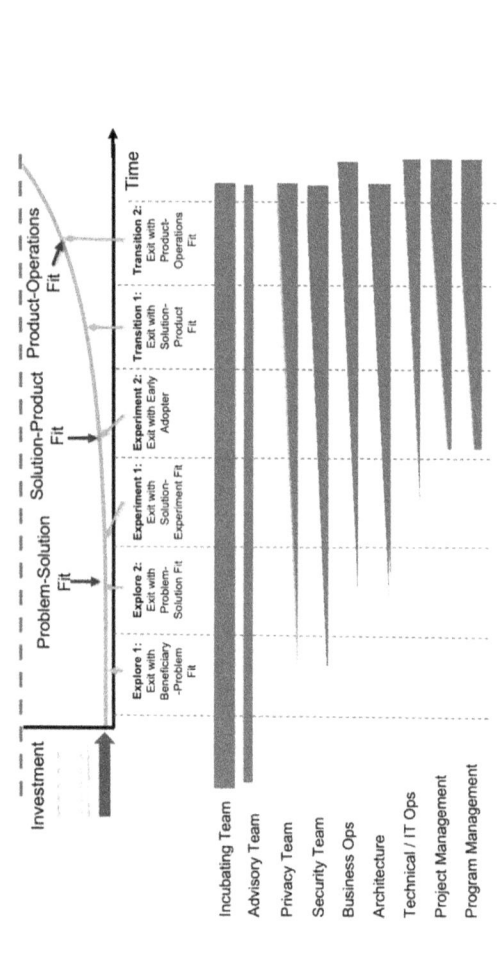

APPENDIX 3 TOOLS AND ARTIFACTS

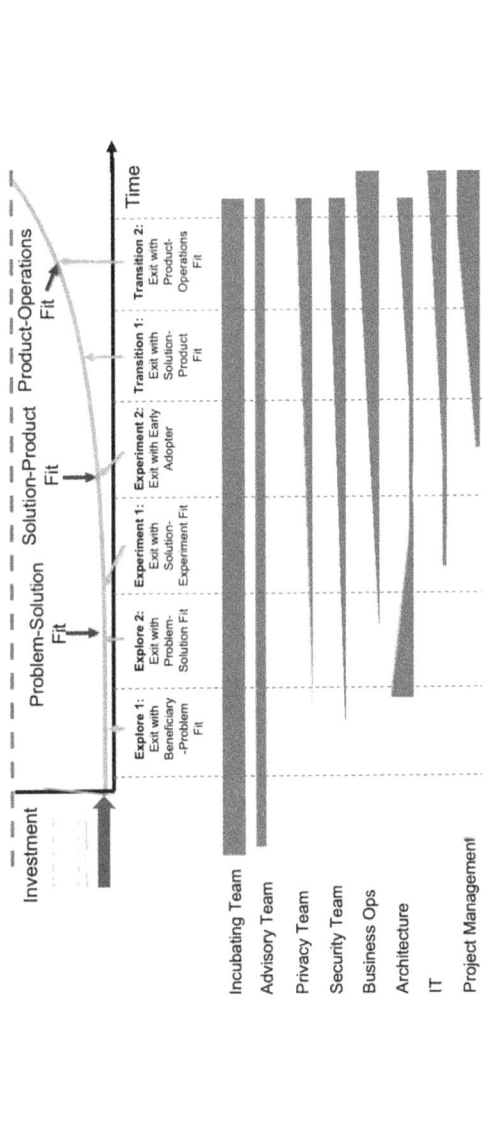

APPENDIX 3 TOOLS AND ARTIFACTS

Stakeholder Analysis

Name	Strongly Opposed	Somewhat Resistant	Neutral	Somewhat In Favor	Strongly Supportive	Rationale
Tina Sponsor					CR	The reason
Omar Executive		C	→ C	R		Another reason
Marta Detractor	C			R		More reasons
Goodwin Standing			CR			Other reasons
Greta Position			R	C		More Reasons

Preparing a simple stakeholder analysis:

1. Place an "C" to indicate a stakeholder's current sentiment
2. Discuss and record the rationale for placing the stakeholder in their current position
3. Place an "R" to indicate the level of sentiment you believe the stakeholder must have (required) for a successful initiative
4. Identify gaps between current and desired sentiments for each stakeholder
5. Indicate how individuals are linked to each other, draw lines to indicate an influence link using an arrow to indicate who influences whom (optional)
6. Create a plan for closing sentiment gaps or maintaining existing levels of sentiment as appropriate
7. Assign an owner to each action in the plan

Communication Plan

Audience	Objectives	Message	Format	Date	Frequency	Location	Owner

Simple communication plan:

- **Audience:** Who needs to receive your message?
- **Objectives:** What do you want or need the audience to do? What actions to you want or expect them to take?
- **Message:** What will your audience need to know in order to cause them to take the desired action?
- **Format:** How will you deliver the message (media, form)? (e.g.: Presentation, newsletter, social media, group message)
- **Date:** When will the message be delivered (or delivered for the first time)?
- **Frequency:** How often will the message be delivered? (e.g.: Once, monthly….)
- **Location:** Where will the message be delivered? (e.g.: Which specific media, which specific newsletters)
- **Owner:** Who will be responsible for the creation and delivery of the message?

APPENDIX 3 TOOLS AND ARTIFACTS

Communication Plan (Relationship Oriented)

Relationship	Owner	Objectives	Frequency

Simple communication relationship plan:

- **Relationship:** Who needs to be kept informed of information regarding the initiative?
- **Owner:** Who, from our team, will ensure the person will be kept informed and manage and foster the relationship?
- **Objectives:** Why must the person be kept informed? What actions do we need them to take? (e.g.: support, approve....)
- **Frequency:** How often should the person with whom we have a relationship be kept up to date?

APPENDIX 3   TOOLS AND ARTIFACTS

Communicating Idea Placement (Illustrative)
(1/3)

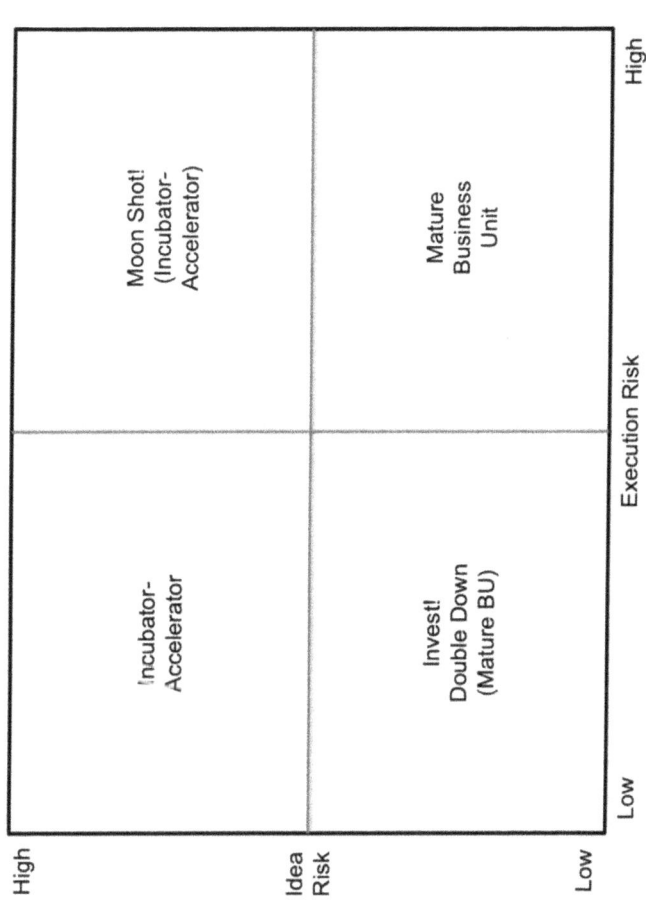

APPENDIX 3 TOOLS AND ARTIFACTS

Communicating Idea Placement (Illustrative)
(2/3)

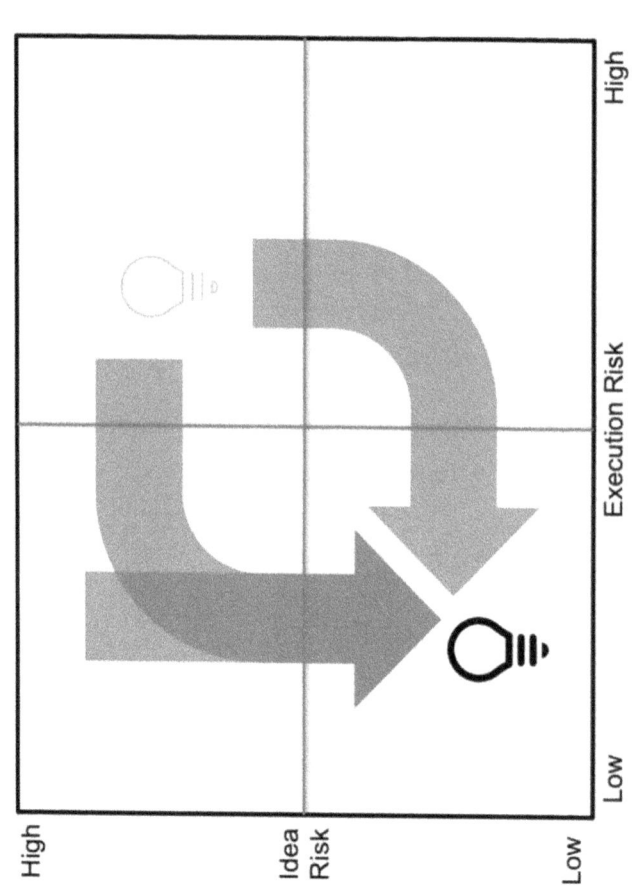

APPENDIX 3 TOOLS AND ARTIFACTS

Communicating Idea Placement (Illustrative)
(3/3)

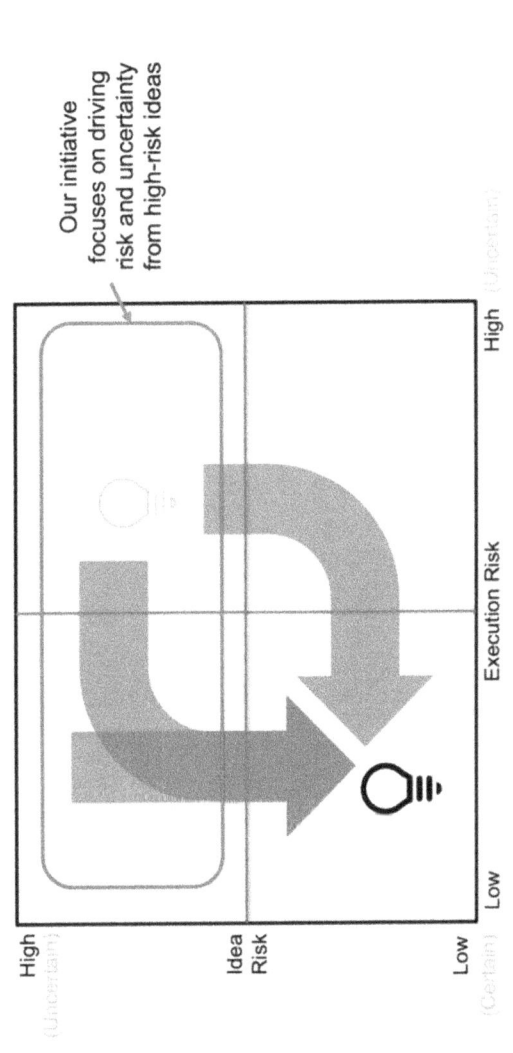

APPENDIX 3   TOOLS AND ARTIFACTS

Value Migration Model (Illustrative)
Additional information and context are available in Chapter 9 and Chapter 12

Value Migration

- **FY1:** Initiative primarily drives brand value while beginning to improve operations
- **FY2:** Brand value remains the primary driver, impact on operations rises
- **FY3:** Meaningful business growth rises while brand value and improved operations remain key drivers
- **FY4:** Meaningful business growth rises as ideas exit and drive value on their own

Contribute Brand Value

Improve How We Operate

Generate Meaningful Businesses

Year 1   Year 2   Year 3   Year 4

Illustrative

APPENDIX 3　TOOLS AND ARTIFACTS

Initiative Role Summary (Illustrative)

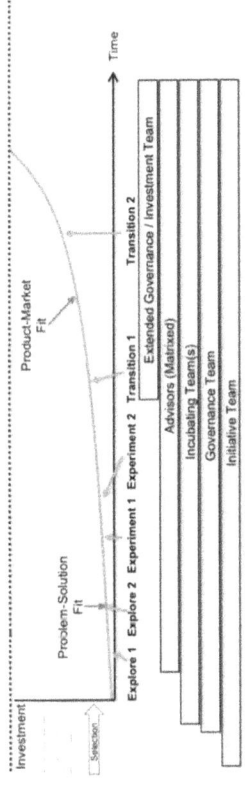

- **Initiative Team drives the initiative**
  - First point of contact for aspiring intrapreneurs, establishes and maintains cadence
  - Creates program artifacts, measures, and OKRs/KPIs
  - Drives retrospectives and inspects and adapts the program
  - Unblocks incubating teams
  - May have some bench expertise (e.g., business development, design, marketing)
- **Governance Team provides end-to-end oversight**
  - Evaluates pitches and selects ideas for entry
  - Conducts regular 3P (pivot, pause, or persist) reviews
  - Approves budget, objectives, and timelines at each investment round
  - Stage-specific checklists ensure focus on outcomes vs. output
  - Ensures teams remain customer-focused
  - Guides the overall direction of the initive
- **Extended Governance or Investment Team guides larger investments**
  - Transition 1, Transition 2, and Exit
- **Incubating Team brings ideas to life**
  - Incubates idea through all stages (Entry to Exit)
  - (Optional) Ad hoc assistance from Maker Team
- **Advisory Team provides matrixed direction and assistance from Entry to Exit**

727

APPENDIX 3 TOOLS AND ARTIFACTS

Calculating Governance Team Time Requirements (Illustrative Example)

Task	Hours Required
One Pitch Ceremony per month, up to four pitches + slack time (2-2.5 hours)	2.5
Five 3P reviews + slack time (2.5-3.5 hours)	3.5
Monthly meeting (1 hour)	1
Total time requirement per month (hours)	7

Validated Hypothesis Summary

Question	Hypothesis	Result
Do *potential customers* have this problem?	At least 60% of *target customers* are looking to solve this problem?	**Validated** 23 of 30 interviewed (77%)
How are *potential customers* working around the problem?	>30% of *target customers* are using manual workaround #1	**Validated** 12 of 30 interviewed (40%)
	>25% of *target customers* are doing nothing	**Not Validated** 2 of 30 interviewed (7%)
	>30% of *target customers* are using workaround #2	**Not Validated** 4 of 30 interviewed (13%)
	<10% of *target customers* are using Excel™	**Not Validated** 14 of 30 interviewed (47%)
Will decreasing the AI model evaluation time result in increased use of the service?	Decreasing evaluation time to below 1 second will increase click-through by 20%	**Validated** Click-through increased from 30 users/hr to 45 users/hr (+50%)
Will simplifying the user interface reduce errors and result in fewer abandons?	Reducing prompt text by 50% will decrease abandons by 50%	**Not Validated** Abandons declined from 5/hr to 3/hr (-40%)

Note: "Not Validated" results should not be interpreted as a failed experiment. They indicate only that the result was other than expected, and often lead to discoveries more exciting than initially hypothesized. They may also indicate that a hypothesis was directionally correct, though specifically inaccurate. This may be insignificant when numbers are small (e.g.: expected 3 of 5, observed 3 of 6). Furthermore, "Not Validated" results may be sufficient to justify action (e.g.: expected 75% to have a problem, 70% have the problem). In such cases the result may be considered "Validated", with explanation.

APPENDIX 3 TOOLS AND ARTIFACTS

Validated Hypothesis Summary (Extended)

Question	Hypothesis	Result	Learning / Conclusion	Next Steps
Do *potential customers* have this problem?	At least 60% of *target customers* are looking to solve this problem?	**Validated** 23 of 30 interviewed (77%)	People have the problem and they are willing to take action to switch from existing alternatives.	Persevere! Continue to problem-solution validation experiments
How are *potential customers* working around the problem?	<10% of *target customers* are using Excel™	**Not Validated** 14 of 30 interviewed (47%)	Excel™ users are a larger percentage of the potential customer base than expected	Further investigate Excel™ users and their implications Consider a function to migrate Excel™ users to our solution
Will decreasing the AI model evaluation time result in increased use of the service?	Decreasing evaluation time to below 1 second will increase click-through by 20%	**Validated** Click-through increased from 30 users/hr to 45 users/hr (+50%)	Users are response-time elastic.	Make the test module production ready and move it to the production codebase Retest response times
Will simplifying the user interface reduce errors and result in fewer abandons?	Reducing prompt text by 50% will decrease abandons by 50%	**Not Validated** Abandons declined from 5/hr to 3/hr (-40%)	Result justifies including this in production. Continue to look for improvements	Prepare the test module and migrate it to production Continue to look for ways to reduce abandons

Note: "Not Validated" results should not be interpreted as a failed experiment. They indicate only that the result was other than expected, and often lead to discoveries more exciting than initially hypothesized. They may also indicate that a hypothesis was directionally correct, though specifically inaccurate. This may be insignificant when numbers are small (e.g.: expected 3 of 5, observed 3 of 6). Furthermore, "Not Validated" results may be sufficient to justify action (e.g.: expected 75% to have a problem, 70% have the problem). In such cases the result may be considered "Validated", with explanation.

APPENDIX 3 TOOLS AND ARTIFACTS

Communicating an Initiative's Progress
(1/10)

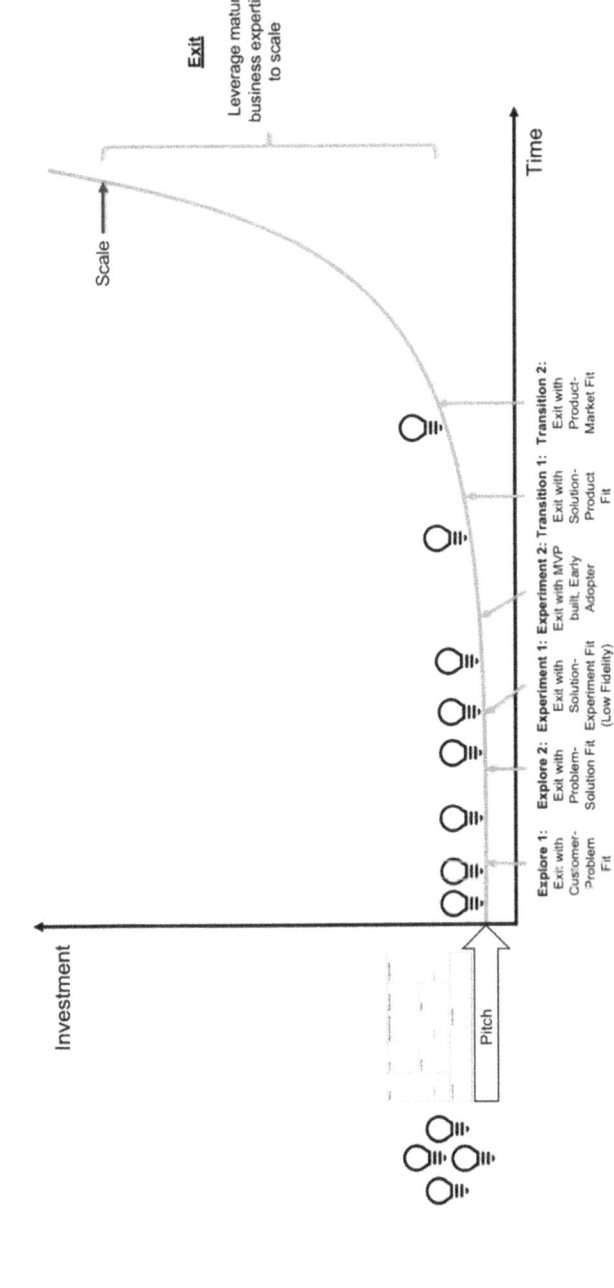

Note: Additional context is available in Chapter 12

APPENDIX 3   TOOLS AND ARTIFACTS

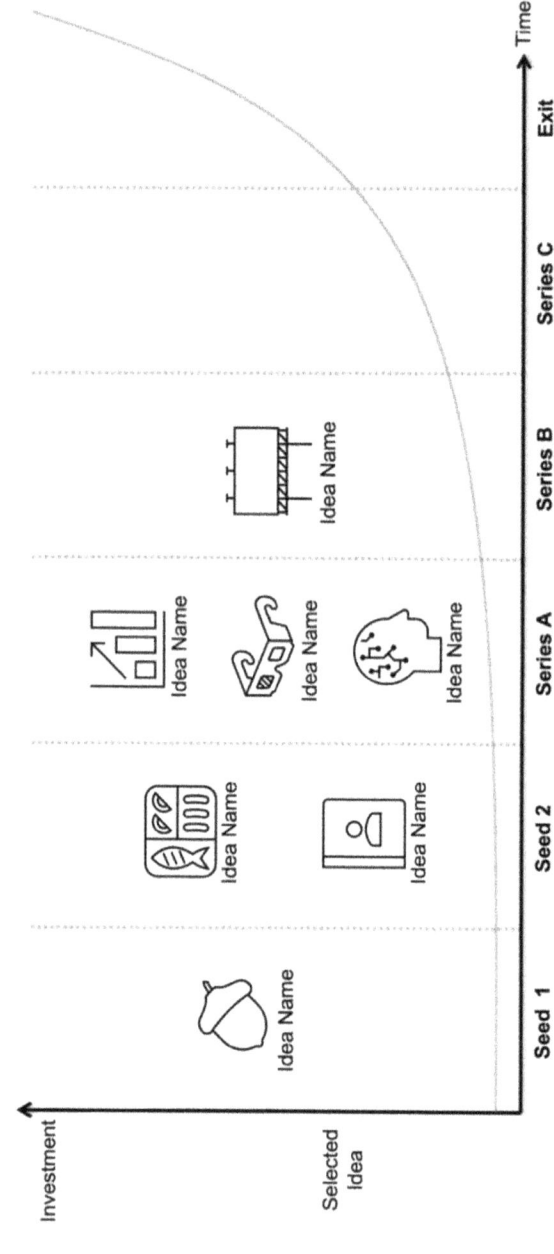

APPENDIX 3 TOOLS AND ARTIFACTS

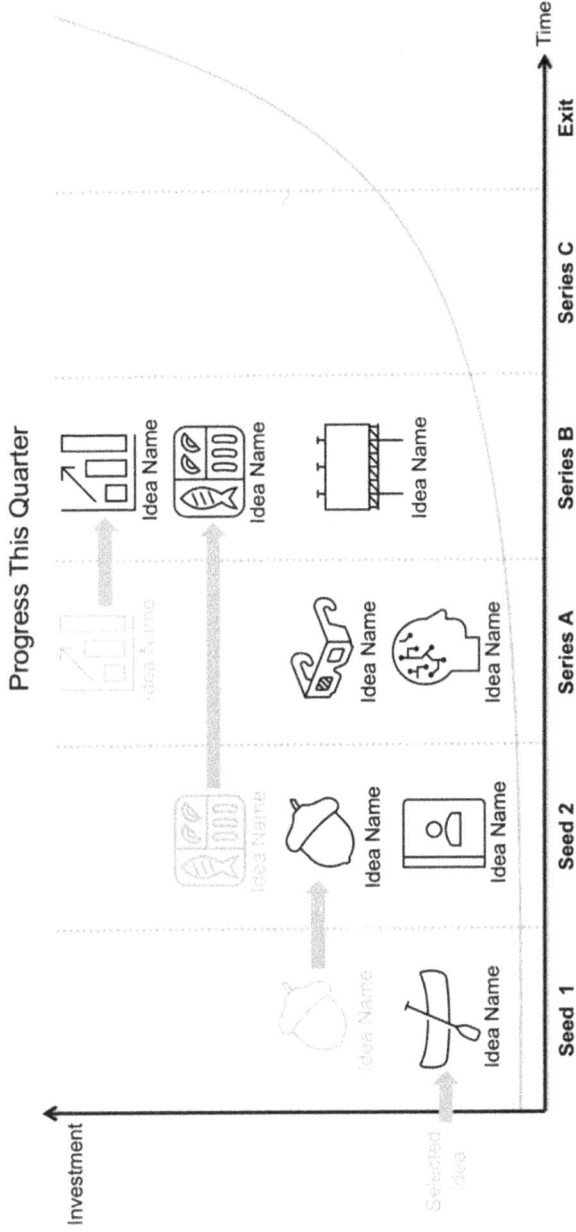

APPENDIX 3 TOOLS AND ARTIFACTS

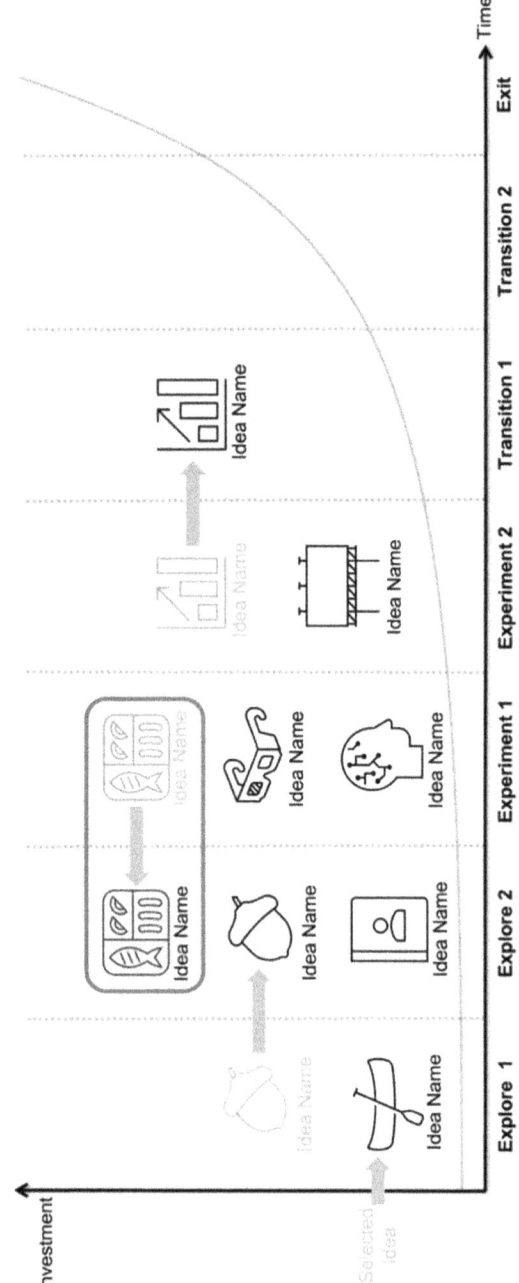

APPENDIX 3   TOOLS AND ARTIFACTS

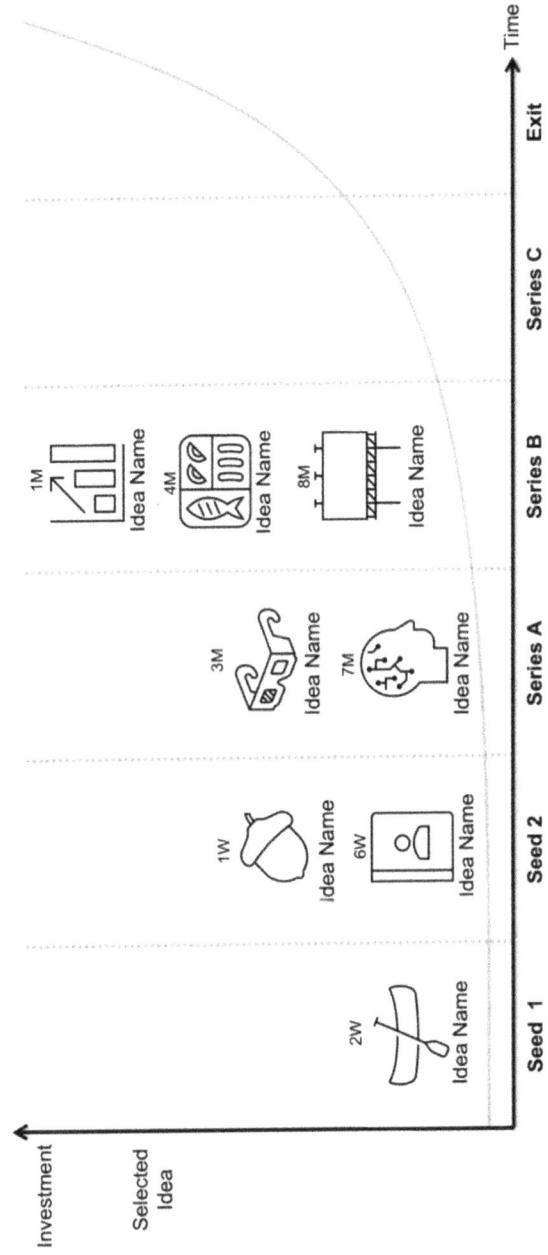

APPENDIX 3   TOOLS AND ARTIFACTS

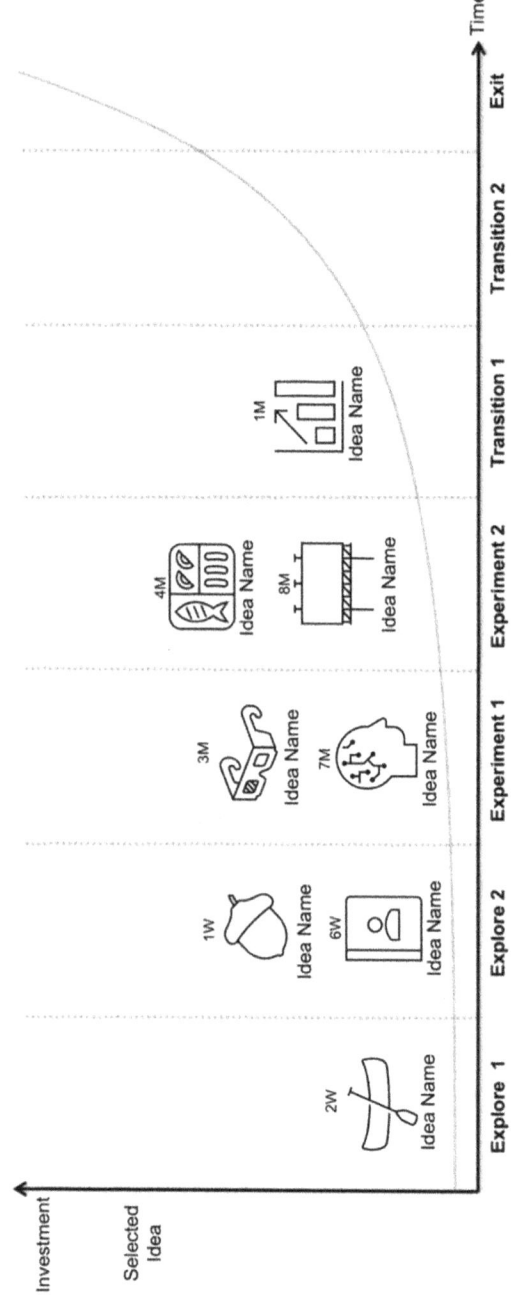

APPENDIX 3 TOOLS AND ARTIFACTS

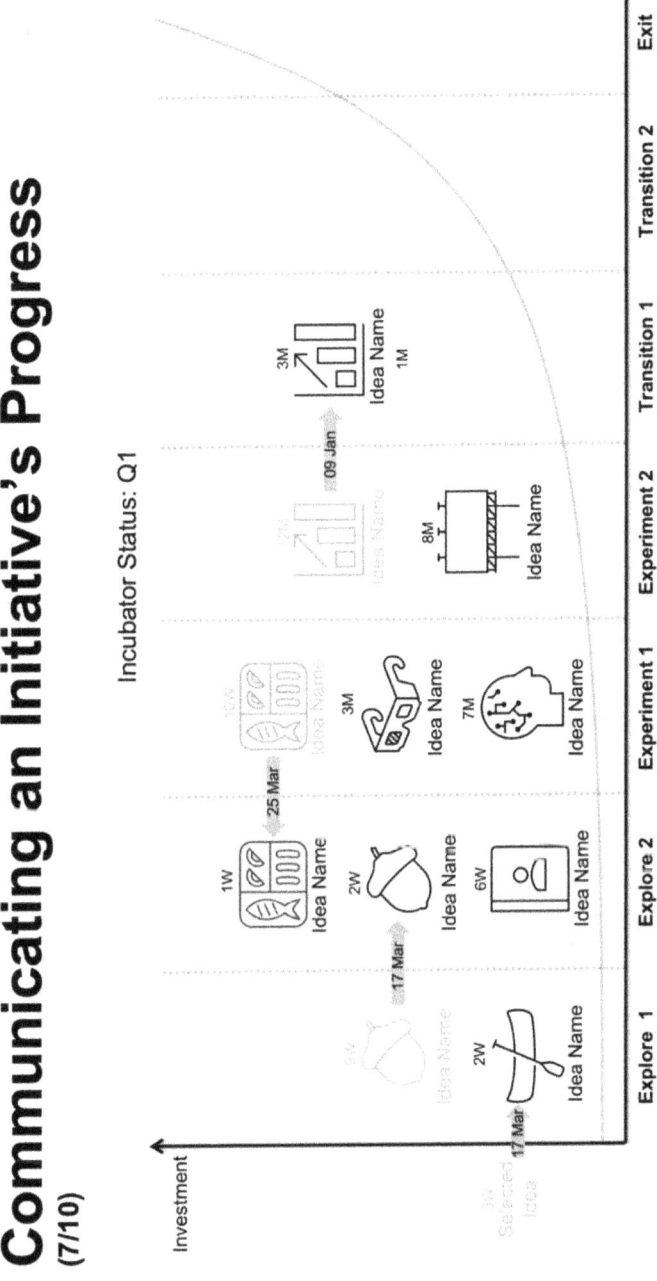

APPENDIX 3   TOOLS AND ARTIFACTS

Communicating an Initiative's Progress
(8/10)

APPENDIX 3   TOOLS AND ARTIFACTS

Communicating an Initiative's Progress (9/10)

Pitches (FY)	Entry	Seed 1	Seed 2	Series A	Series B	Series C	Exits and Pauses (FY)
12	1	2	3	3	0	0	0
Name	Description	Technology	Current Stage	Entered Stage	Entered Initiative	Patents Filed	Next Steps / Comments
Amazing Idea	AI engine for medical diagnoses	AmazingAI GPT, Neural Net, LLM7	Series A	January 2099	September 2098	5	450 active users, 91% retention rate after 6 months, transition to Series B targeted for February 2100
---	---	---	---	---	---	---	---
---	---	---	---	---	---	---	---
---	---	---	---	---	---	---	---

739

APPENDIX 3   TOOLS AND ARTIFACTS

Communicating an Initiative's Progress
(10/10)

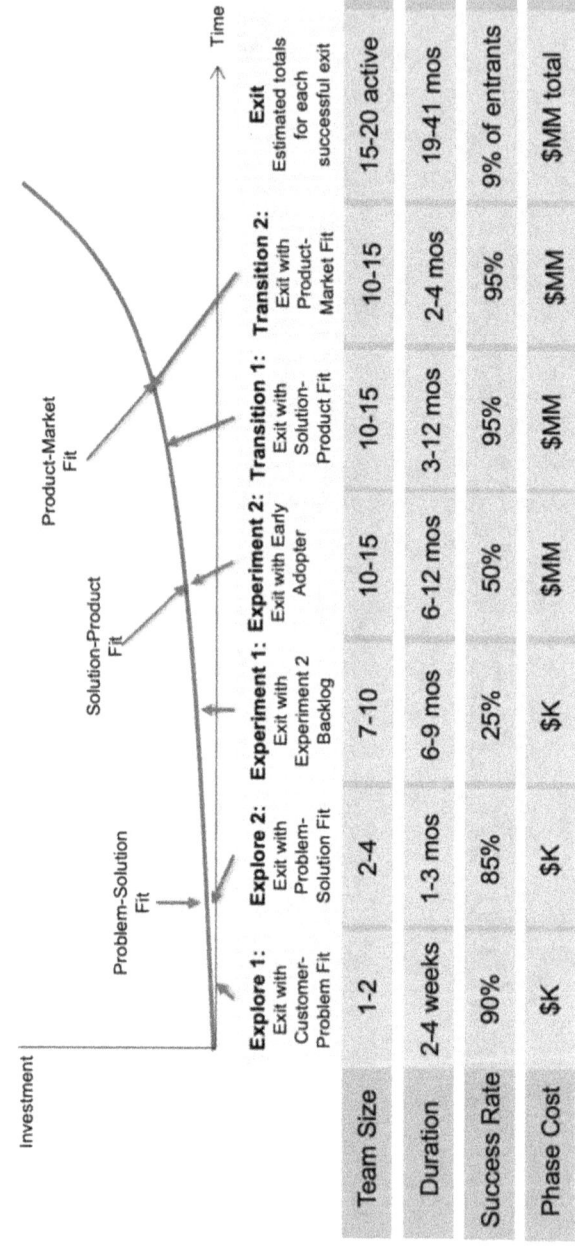

10 Most Common Lean Canvas Problems Public Sector Lean Canvas

1. The problem statement does not describe a problem
2. The problem statement is "my intervention (solution) does not exist" (or is not available…), which may or may not be a problem
3. The problem statement is exactly the same as the interventions statement, just worded differently
4. Existing alternatives are not enumerated, including doing nothing, existing workarounds, and competition
5. The customer or beneficiary referenced on the canvas does not actually have the problem presented in the problem section

10 Most Common Lean Canvas Problems Public Sector Lean Canvas

6. The customer or beneficiary is not well defined, is too broad, or lists all of the mature business' existing customer or beneficiary classifications or segments (often indicates a cut-and-paste approach to customers)
7. There is no early adopter hypothesis, or it is too broad
8. The impact is not described in terms of the value the stated customer or beneficiary receives if the stated problem is solved using the proposed interventions
9. The layout of the canvas is changed
10. The stated benefit is that the solution or interventions exist

APPENDIX 3 TOOLS AND ARTIFACTS

10 Most Common Lean Canvas Problems Private Sector

1. The problem statement does not describe a problem
2. The problem statement is "my solution does not exist" (or is not available...), which may or may not be a problem
3. The problem statement is exactly the same as the solution statement, just worded differently
4. Existing alternatives are not enumerated, including doing nothing, existing workarounds, and competition
5. The customer referenced on the canvas does not actually have the problem presented in the problem section

APPENDIX 3 TOOLS AND ARTIFACTS

10 Most Common Lean Canvas Problems Private Sector

6. The customer is not well defined, is too broad, or lists all of the mature business' existing customer classifications or segments (often indicates a cut-and-paste approach to customers)

7. There is no early adopter hypothesis, or it is too broad

8. The unique value proposition is not described in terms of the value the stated customer receives if the stated problem is solved using the proposed solution

9. The stated unfair advantage can be easily bought or copied by others, so it is not an unfair advantage

10. The stated unfair advantage is "we are <your company name here>"

Index

A

Advisors, 346
Advisory Team, 345, 348, 362
  building, 349
  candidates, 348
  time requirement, 349
AI focused initiative, 219
Alignment, 267, 287–289
Approach, 210, 214, 216, 231, 241, 248
Archetypes, 210, 211, 215, 254
Artifacts, 210, 215, 241, 246–247
Artifact summary, 715
Artificial intelligence (AI)
  engine, 260
Assessment, 9, 113, 115
  benefits, 116, 125
  bias, 121
  change, 118, 122, 123
  cross-purposes, 123, 124
  definition, 114
  and estimation, 115
  and evaluation, 115
  Finding Themes, 710–714
  Frequently Valuable Interview Questions, 675–677
  Goal Examples, 668–669
  goals, 126, 127
    mammoth task, 129
    organizational transformation, 128
    primary contact, 128
    soliciting information, 128
  information, 113
  initiative, 114, 116
  initiative's outcomes, 124
  Interview Guide
    Sample Guide, 681–697
    Sample Structure, 678–680
  interviews, 121, 132
  Interview Tips, 703–707
  Interview Topics, 673–674
  issues and opportunities, 120
  landscape, 118
  learning, 118
  learn stories, 121
  nuances, 122
  organization, 114
  participants, 123
  past/current state, 115
  people for change, 122
  pockets of excellence, 120
  purpose statement, 130, 132
  Pre-Interview
    Checklist, 698–702

INDEX

Assessment (*cont.*)
    relationships, 122, 123, 125, 128
    Report Structure, 708–709
    Schedule, 672
    secondary research, 132, 134
    sources of research
        information, 135
    stories, 121
    team's ability, 114
    themes and priorities, 118
    time requirements, 136, 138
    trust, 124, 128
    vocabulary, 118, 119
    what is an assessment, 114–116
    why, 111, 116
Assessment interviews, 10
    assessment's findings, 194
        additional considerations,
            204, 205
        analysis and theme
            development, 199
        appendix, 195, 196
        brain-heavy exercise, 198
        challenges and
            opportunities, 206, 207
        detailed findings, 195, 197
        executive summary, 195
        finalize findings, 203, 204
        one-page summary, 195
        progressive
            disclosure, 198
        review, reduce and
            repeat, 197
        summary (theme), 195
        themes and
            discovery, 200–204
    automatic transcription
        services, 191, 192
    back up data, 188, 189
    body language, 180
    controversial/challenging
        questions, 181
    conversation, 177, 180
    ethics, 185, 186
    interview participants, selection
        adjust interview guide/
            reset, 161
        beware of bias, 158
        expand list, 156
        feedback, 160
        finalize participant list,
            159, 160
        first interview, 160, 161
        get permission, 159
        12 to 15 interviews, 156
        number of participants, 155
        open and transparent, 157
        open-ended qualitative
            analysis, 154
        quality and diversity, 158
        saturation, 156, 157
        seek experience, 157
    interview preparation
        bias, 167
        ensure environment,
            168, 169
        eye contact, 174
        initial hypothesis, 167

INDEX

interview guide, 168
learn, organization and people, 165–167
rehearsal, 164, 165
schedule interviews, 162–164
video assessment interview checklist, 169–173
listening techniques, 179
"pedagogical" interview stance, 177
positivity, 178
primary contact/stakeholder, 193–195
respect participants' time
 be early, 176
 end on time, 176, 177
respect participants' time, 176
review and clean up interview notes, 189–191
scheduled period, 178
take notes, 182, 183
thank participants, 185
types of information, 184, 185
use pseudonyms, 186, 187
Automatic transcription services, 191, 192
Automating data capture, 442–447

B

Backup, 171, 172, 187–188
Beneficiary-problem fit, 116, 235
Be Opportunistic, 504
Bias, 120–122
 familiarity principle of attraction, 66
 HiPPO-centric, 65
 mere-exposure effect, 66
 unconscious, 64, 66
Brainstorming exercise, 490
Brand contribution, 457
Broader organization, 456
Brand glow, 457
Brand halo, 457
Budget, 366
 expense types, 358
 preparing, 371
 requirements, 354
Budgeting, 355
Budget requirements
 allowances, 356, 358
 benefit, 358
 bonuses, 359
 overhead allocation, 356
 payout or bonus plan, 360
 personnel, 355
 recruiting, 358
 subscriptions, 358
 travel, 357
Buy-in, 287–289

C

Cadences, 283–287
Calculating Governance Team Time Requirements, 728
Ceremonies, 244–246
 Fire Drill, 618–632

747

INDEX

Ceremonies (*cont.*)
    Introspection, 633–648
    Pitch, 569–572
    Pivot, Pause, Persevere
        (3P), 573–593
    Retrospective, 594–617
    Role Clarification, 649–660
    summaries, 241, 245, 246
Checklists, 240, 241, 243–244, 252,
    254, 258, 262
    explore 1, 399, 400, 403
    incubating team entry, 399
    initiative team entry, 399
    pause, 399, 400
    seed 1, 396, 399, 400, 403
Cloud service, 188
Cohorts
    benefits, risks,
        drawbacks, 408
    impacts, 406
Committed bets, 26, 50, 104, 455
    contrast with traditional
        approaches, 101
    explained, 104–106
    innovation CPR, 104
    vs. lean entrepreneurship, 105
    revived, 104–106
Communicating an Initiative's
    Progress, 731–740
Communicating Idea
    Placement, 723–725
Communication, 292, 378, 385,
    408, 503–506
    assistance, 299
    audience, 292, 294, 299, 304,
        305, 314
    case study, adjusting your
        style, 302
    deliberate approach
        celebration, 293
        employee groups, 294
        external groups, 294
        feedback, 294
        initiative insiders, 294
        learning, 294
        message, 294
        promotion, 293
        recruitment, 293
        senior executives, 294
        stakeholder
            management, 293
        status, 293
    existing communication
        channels, 298, 299
    formal and informal
        communication, 297, 298
    help, 299–300, 312, 313
    informal, 292, 297–298
    informal plan, 312
    initiative's communication
        needs, 296
    a lean entrepreneurship
        approach removes risk, 13
    massive communications
        team, 298
    need, 295–299

INDEX

overoptimism, 310
plan, 295, 296, 301, 307, 313–315
to preempt threats, 307
    be transparent, 308
    beware of overoptimism, 310
    chaotic and
      unimpressive, 311
    healthy competition, 308
    personality traits, 309
    reorganizations, 311
    unhealthy competition, 308
proactively communicate
    progress (*see* Proactive
    communication)
simple communication plan
    worksheet, 296
skills, 299, 300
strategy and plan, 312–315
where ideas are best
    incubated, 302
Communication Plan, 721
Communication Plan (Relationship
    Oriented), 722
Competition
    healthy, 308
    unhealthy, 307, 308
Convergence Keynote, 22, 23
COVID-19 pandemic, 169
Cross-Team Engagement
    Model, 717–719
CTO's Fireside Chats, 385
Customer-problem
    fit, 37, 116, 231

D

Data capture
    automating, 442–447
Definition of Done, 666–667
Design
    approach, 209–264
    decisions
      decision 1: toolkit, framework,
        or initiative?, 215
      decision 2: what will enter
        the program?, 218–226
      decision 3: what will exit the
        initiative?, 226–229
      decision 4: select a
        structure, 239–240
    detailed, 240–253
    inputs
      what to include and exclude,
        219–224, 240–241
    outputs
      what will exit, 226–229
    questions
      what will enter the
        initiative?, 218–226
      what will exit the
        initiative?, 226–229
      which approach is best?, 216
    workshop
      step 1: capture learning in an
        initial model, 248–250
      step 2: expand the details and
        refine the model, 250–252

INDEX

Design (*cont.*)
  step 3: socialize and fine-tune the model, 252–253
Design artifacts, 10
Design process
  ceremonies, 244–246
  design workshops, 248
    capture learning, 248–250
    over-engineered model, 253
    socialize and fine-tune, 252, 253
    stages in detail, 250, 251
  detailed checklist, 240
  detailed stage checklists, 243, 244
  one page overview, 240
  stage overview, 242, 243
  summary of ceremonies, 241
  tools
    and artifacts, 241, 246, 247
    and techniques, 246, 247
Design Workshop Layout, 716
Desirable, 230, 234
Desirability, 26, 236, 238–240
Detailed stage checklists, 243
Development stage, 373
Do you have to do everything in the book?, 4–7
Drift, 508

E

Early adopters, 231, 232, 236
Early incubator–accelerator design workshop, 217
Early lean entrepreneurship-style incubator–accelerator, 217
Earlyvangelists, 232
Employee opinion survey metrics, 455
Employee performance, 455
Entrepreneurship concepts, 8
Established organizations, 8, 17, 21, 83, 108
  bad timing/inconsistency, 41
  bottom line, 38
  business case, 33–35
  business case templates, 36
  classic management trap, 29
  consistent approach, 43
  deliberately, 42
  estimates, 34, 35
  executive/sponsor interest, 44
    alignment, time requirements, 47
    battle fatigue, 49
    budget pressure, 47
    cognitive overload, 45
    committed bets, 50
    common vocabulary, 46
    communication, 46
    innovation's messy nature, 49
    internal competition, 50, 51
    measurements/incentives, 45
    quarterly cadence, 45
    reorganization, 48
  failure ecosystem, 51

good ideas failure, 27
heavyweight processes, 30
hero culture myth, 31, 32
innovation failure, 82
innovation pageantry, 40, 41
innovative ideas, 53
innovators, 34
internal process, external supplier, 38, 39
NoOp, 36, 37
process pageantry, 30
projections, 34, 35
Project Sisyphus, 27, 29, 42, 44
root causes, 29
teams, 36
technological overviews, 33
toolkit, 54
Ethics, 185–186
Executives, 26
Existing communication channels, 298
Exit, 217, 226–229, 232, 253, 254, 256, 257
Exit types
  impact, 226, 254–257
  structure, 256, 257
Expectations
  setting long-term, 304–307
Explore-Experiment-Transition model, 234–236, 238, 239, 241, 432, 433
Explore-Experiment-Transition structures, 237
Extended Governance Team, 344

F

Facilitator, 487
Feasibile, 235, 263
Feasibility
  feasibility-myopic, 26
FAQ posts, *see* "Frequently asked questions" (FAQ) posts
Financial forecasts, 367
Findings
  preparation, 194–197
  progressive disclosure, 196, 198–199
Formal communication, 297, 299
Frameworks, 210–215
"Frequently asked questions" (FAQ) posts, 304
Funding, 211, 215, 234, 263

G

GEFN, *see* Good enough for now (GEFN)
Get help, 503, 504
Good enough for now (GEFN), 324
  advantage, 323
  The power of, 324
Governance, 501, 506, 507
Governance Team, 327, 332, 333, 337, 352, 362, 392, 486, 487
  activities, 335
  characteristics, 338
  directing, 391–393
  guiding, 391–393, 416

INDEX

Governance Team (*cont.*)
    and Initiative Team, 494
    members, 334
    time requirements, 339, 341
Governance Team Off-sites, 483
Group development, 371, 372

H
Habits, 392, 405, 417
Heartbeat, 283–287
Hero culture, 31, 32

I, J
Ideas
    capturing
        ten steps, 379, 380
    selecting, 379–398, 419
Incremental learning, 495
Incubate–Startup–Accelerate model, 238, 239
Incubating teams, 362
    diversity, 455
    guiding principles, 405
    onboarding, 398–408
    leaders, 476
    tools and resources, 404
    welcoming, 401–404
Incubation-specific checklists, 244
Incubation team advisor, 351
Informal communication, 297, 298, 313, 315
Initiative at-a-glance
    Seed-Series, 515–529
    Explore-Experiment-Transition, 547–563
    Incubate-Startup-Accelerate, 530–546
Initiative Role Summary, 727
Initiatives, 214, 215, 219
    exits, 226–229
    foundation, 369
    impact of portfolio, 259–262
    innovation/new idea incubation initiatives, 218
    openness and transparency, 226
    overview diagram, 224, 225
    portfolio of, 258–261
Initiative's structure
    alignment with desirability, feasibility and viability, 238
    Explore–Experiment–Transition model, 234–236
    Incubate–Startup–Accelerate model, 238
    need for new structure, 233, 234
    "Seed-Series" structure, 230, 231, 233
    select structure, 239, 240
    Transition phase, 236, 237
Initiative Team, 326, 361, 482
    advisors, 322
    facilitation and leadership, 323
    and Governance Team, 351
    and incubating teams, 361
Initiative Team's members, 329, 477
InnerSource program, 261

Innovation
  failure
    reasons (should we enumerate each of the 4?), 51
    funnel, 60–64
    funnel fatigue, 64
    pageantry, 40–41
    performative, 41
    problems, 53–82
  Innovation initiative failure
    bias, 64
      cliquetocracies, 66
      HiPPO-centric bias, 65
      perception, 67
    challenges and pitfalls, 82
    common vocabulary, 68
    execution errors
      accountability, 71
      ambiguous ownership, 71
      inspect/adapt, 72
      lack of follow up, 72
      reorganization-proofing, 74
      subservience process, 73, 74
    incubating teams, 75
      bad habits, 79, 80
      insufficient training/support, 80, 81
      MVT, 75–78
      placing people, wrong roles, 78
    innovation funnels
      categories, 61
      challenge, 61
      damage control, 62
      diagrams, 60–62
      executives, 62
      fatigue, 64
      left side, 62, 63
    misalignment, 67
    poor strategic choices
      broad ecosystem, 60
      candidate pool, 59
      casting, 60
      deliberate strategy, 57
      isolation, 60
      limiting entry, 59
      part-time innovation, 59
      wrong type of initiative, 58
    strategies, 57
    underinvestment
      budget, 56
      funding, 55
    unhealthy culture, 69
      internal competition, 70
      performative innovation culture, 69, 70
  Innovation metrics, 424, 425, 461
  Innovation programs and contests, 218
  Innovative ideas, 25, 26
  Innovators, 27, 33, 34, 36
  Intentions, 300–303, 309
  Interview
    choosing your first participant, 160–161
    conducting, 160, 161, 168, 175–188

753

Interview (*cont.*)
   data
      backup, 187–188
      cleansing, 189–192
      review, 189–192
   design, 126
   diversity, 156, 158
   guide, 138, 139, 161, 165–168, 174–177, 179, 182, 183, 190, 193
      creating, 138–139
      current approach, 150
      discrepancy, 151
      elements, 139
      example, 149–151
      interview duration, 151
      introduction/context, 150
      introductory statement and context, 150
      landmarks, 148, 149
      options, 151
      prioritizing, 147
      structure, 139–140, 149
         closing, 146
         discovery, 142–145
         opening, 140–142
         questions, 147
      template, 149
      updation, 152
   how many people to interview, 154
   notes, taking, 174, 178, 182–183
   participant selection, 154–161
   preparation, preparing
      configuring your desktop or workspace, 172, 173
      video conference environment, 168
   rehearse, 164–165
   scheduling, 162–164, 190, 191
   synthesis, 198, 199, 203
   when to stop interviewing, 154–161
   whom to interview, 154, 159
Introspection, 488
   benefits
      example, 488
   exercise, 491
   introspective off-site, 490
   workshops
      when we're at our best/when we're not at our best, 490
Investment, 214, 235, 236, 261, 263

K

Kanban function, 443
Key results
   defined, 270

L

Leadership development, 474
   competencies, 475
Lean advantage
   lean navigation, 99–101

INDEX

wilderness navigation, 93, 99
Lean approach, 5
Lean canvas, 314, 381–383, 387, 397
Lean ceremonies, 245
Lean entrepreneurship, 3, 84, 85, 263
　advantages, 101
　alternative/descriptive names, 89
　approach/initiative, 216
　awkward response, 102
　benefits, 93
　　degree, 94
　　errors, 95–97, 99
　　ideas, 99–101
　　risk/waste, 101
　bottom line, 6
　vs. committed bet model, 105
　communication, 11
　customer focus/learning fast/iterating, 103
　feedback, 3
　initiatives, 3, 5, 112
　　fail, 8
　　success, 13
　innovation programs, 8
　language, 89, 90
　launching initiative, 12
　lean advantage, 106, 107
　lean experiments, 86, 87
　　desirablility/feasiblility/viablility, 88
　　pivot/pause/persevere, 87
　lean governance, 91, 92
　learning and improvement, 13
　maniacal focus, 85
　objectives, 10
　the original approach, 85
　overviews and checklists, 14, 84
　participants, 86
　performance and impact, 12
　principles, 9, 90, 423
　recommendations, 15
　seed and series stage names, 89
　solution, 103
　sponsors/stakeholders, 102
　startup, 103
　target, 103
　teams and roles, 11, 12
　timeline, 85
　toolkit, 14, 17
　wasteful committed bets
　　customers, 103
　　follow-up meetings, 103
Lean entrepreneurship, 323, 324, 381
　approaches
　　framework/approach, 210
　　initiative, service and program, 210
　　toolkit, 210
　　tools and techniques, 210
　teams, 86
The Lean Entrepreneurship Toolkit, 14–15
Lean governance, 336–337
Lean innovation
　principle, 423

755

INDEX

Lean mindset, 325
Lean practitioner, 1
Lean public sector canvas, 381, 382
Learn fast and iterate, 89–90
Learning, 502, 509
Leveraging existing events, 385, 397, 420
Leveraging existing resources, 385, 397, 420
Long-term success, 26

M, N

Maker skills, 352
Maker Team, 352, 362
    candidates, 353
Maniacal beneficiary focus, 102
Maniacal customer focus, 102
Measurement
    automating, 442–449
    classes, 423
    continuum, 424–427
    effectiveness, 434, 447, 461
    flow, 428–433, 444
    flow metrics, 434, 437, 448–451
    hypotheses, hypothesis, 426, 427
    impact, 421, 431, 450–457
    impact metrics, 457, 459, 461
    incubating ideas, incubating solutions, 424–429, 445, 446, 449
    innovation metrics, 424, 425, 461
    nascent ideas, 423
    performance, 421, 423, 425, 428–450
    performance data, 434–442
    pirate metrics, 425
    transparency, 445, 446, 460, 461
    validated learning, 424–427, 461
    value, 450–457
    value migration, 457, 458
Metrics, 464, 465
Minimum viable product (MVP), 86, 231–233, 236
Minimum viable teams (MVT)
    dealmaker, 76, 78
    decider, 77, 78
    defined, 75
    designer, 76, 78
    developer, 76, 78
    key personas, 75
    private sector, 78
    public sector, 77
Minimum viable version, 6
Model-at-a-glance, 459
Monday–Friday cadence, 286
10 Most common lean canvas problems
    Lean Canvas, 743–744
    Public Sector Lean Canvas, 741–742
Move fast and break things, 89
MVP, *see* Minimum viable product (MVP)
MVT, *see* Minimum viable teams (MVT)

INDEX

O

Objectives
  alignment
    adjustments, 267
    and buy-in, 288–290
    clarity, communication and confirmation, 267
    defined, 270
    deliberate/intentional, 266
    introspection, 268
  OKRs (*see* Objectives and key results (OKRs))
  ownership, 281
    external ownership, 282
    full-time assignment, 281
    highest priority, 281
    internal ownership advantages, 282, 283
  people/teams working
    at common cadences, 285
    at different cadences, 284, 285
  resett/reconfirm objectives, 267
  set initiative's, 274–280
  setting, 270–274
Objectives and key results (OKRs), 10, 421, 442, 449, 450
  approach, 269
  benefits, 280
  considerations, 274–280
  example, 270, 272, 273
  explained, 270
  horizons, 273–274

  how OKRs work, 270
  incubator–accelerator initiative, 270
  individuals/teams, 270
  objectives management systems, 269
  outcome-focused approach, 268
  ownership, 281–283
  quarterly OKR, 271
  setting, 270–273
Off-site logistics, 483
Off-sites, Governance Team Off-sites
  benefits, 487–488
  introspective, 489
  logistics, 483
OKRs, *see* Objectives and key results (OKRs)
One page stage overviews
  Accelerate 1, 542
  Accelerate 2, 545
  Experiment 1, 555
  Experiment 2, 557
  Explore 1, 551
  Explore 2, 553
  Incubate 1, 534
  Incubate 2, 536
  Seed 1, 519
  Seed 2, 521
  Series A, 523
  Series B, 525
  Series C, 528
  Startup 1, 538
  Startup 2, 540

INDEX

One page stage overviews (*cont.*)
    Transition 1, 559
    Transition 2, 562
Optimum team composition, 327
Organizational programs and
    benefits, 366
Organization's Legal Team, 345

P

Patent program, 261
Patents, 456
3P ceremony, 3P review
    format, 410–412
    scheduling, 413–415
    transition request, 412, 413
People, 501, 503–509
Performance measurement, 422, 423, 425, 428–450
Performance metrics, 449, 450
Personalities
    innovation killing, 309–310
Personality traits, 309
Pipeline
    competitions, 396, 397
    focusing on a domain or technology, 397, 398
    leveraging existing channels, 397
    priming, 396–398
Pirate metrics, 425
Pitch
    accepting, 387–388
    adjudication, 381, 393, 394, 412, 413
    ceremony, 378–382, 388, 390–394, 409
    and entry metrics, 434–437
    events, 379, 380, 383, 388–392, 394, 413, 415
    format, 381, 382, 393
    mechanism, 5
    pipeline
        priming, 396–398
    prepare, 382, 383
    promoting, 380, 384–386
    protocols, 382
    recruiting, 380, 384–386
    requesting, 379, 383, 384, 387, 390
    scheduling, 391–394
    selecting, 388
    sequencing, 388
    team, 395, 396
    triaging, 387–388
Pivot, Pause, Persevere (3P) Review, 399, 400, 403, 409–417, 419, 420
Pivot, Pause, Persist (3P) ceremony, 409
Primary design decisions, 216
Priming the initiative, 368
Private sectors, 10, 44, 84
Proactive communication, 300
    assumptions, 300
    ideas, 301–303

inspect and adapt
    messaging, 303–305
lean entrepreneurship
    approach, 303
potential threats, 307
private sector initiative, 305
realistic expectations, 305
value migration model, 305, 306
Proactive learning
    Failure Mode and Effects
        Analyses (FMEA), 473
    pre-mortem, 473
    techniques, 474, 498
Problem–solution fit, 37, 230, 231, 234, 235
Product-market fit, 231, 232
Product-operations fit, 237
Program, 2
Progressive disclosure, 194, 196, 198
Project Sisyphus, 27, 29, 39, 42, 44
Promoting the initiative, 384–386
Promotion and communications metrics, 434
Protector personality type, 123
Pseudonyms, 186–187
Public sector, 234–237, 264
Public sector internal project exit structure, 257
Public Sector Lean Canvas, 264
Public sector program exit structure, 257
Public sectors, 10, 44, 84

Purpose statement, 662
    example, 130–131
    structure, 130

Q

Qualitative analysis, 154
Qualitative measures, 452
Quantitative metrics, 452
Quarterly OKRs, 270, 271, 273
Quibi, 24, 27
Quick bites, 23

R

Rehearsal, 164
Relationships, 122, 125, 128, 1116
Remote interviews, 168, 169
Reorganizations, 311–312
Research
    primary research, 209
    secondary research, 209
Retrospectives, 471–473, 497
    actions, 471
    analysis, 467
    benefit, 472–473
    ceremonies, 469
    classic, 469
    explained, 465
    follow-up, 469
    forms, 469
    learning and improvement, 468
Rewarding participants, 417–419

INDEX

Risks
    metrics, 458
    organizational, 101
    structural, 44, 51
    talent and education, 67
Robust initiative, 83
ROI, 453
Roles
    alignment, 493
    clarification, 493
    clarity, 492
    workshop
        IS/DOES or IS NOT/DOES NOT, 493

S

Sample stage checklist, 243
Scheduling
    3P ceremonies, 3P reviews, 413–415
    pitch ceremonies, 388–391, 394
    tool, 162–164
Scrooge hypothesis, 1
Scrooge's analysis, 21
Secondary Research, Simple Approach, 670–671
Second order thinking, 363
Seed-Series model, 432
Seed-Series structure, 230, 231, 233
Self-assessments, 475
Seventy-page business case, 33
Software-as-a-service company, 218

Solution–experiment fit, 236
Solution–product fit, 232, 237
Stage Checklists
    Accelerate 1, 543–544
    Accelerate 2, 546
    Experiment 1, 556
    Experiment 2, 558
    Explore 1, 552
    Explore 2, 554
    Incubate 1, 535
    Incubate 2, 537
    Incubating Team Entry, 517
    Initiative Team Entry Preparation, 516
    Pause, 518
    Seed 1, 520
    Seed 2, 522
    Series A, 524
    Series B, 526–527
    Series C, 529
    Startup 1, 539
    Startup 2, 540, 541
    Transition 1, 560–561
    Transition 2, 563
Stage metrics, 437–441
Stakeholder Analysis, 720
Start small, build incrementatlly, 502, 503
Strategizer Mission Model Canvas, 264
Structure
    Accelerate phase
        Accelerate 1, 256
        Accelerate 2, 256

Explore–Experiment–
    Transition, 234–239,
    241, 252
Experiment phase
    Experiment 1, 236, 258
    Experiment 2, 236
Explore phase
    Explore 1, 235, 241–243,
        245–247, 258
    Explore 2, 235, 258
Incubate–Startup–Accelerate,
    234, 237–240
Incubation phase
    Incubate 1, 231
    Incubate 2, 231
    Incubate–Startup–
        Accelerate, 234, 237–240
    Seed-Series, 230, 233,
        237, 252
public sector, 234–237, 256, 257
Seed-Series, 230–233,
    237, 252
    Incubate–Startup–
        Accelerate, 234, 237–240
    Seed 1, 216, 231, 246
    Seed 2, 216, 231
    Series A, 232
    Series B, 232
    Series C, 232
    Startup phase, 231, 232
    Startup 1, 232
    Startup 2, 232
Transition phase
    Transition 1, 237
    Transition 2, 237, 247
"3-2-1" style backup
    strategy, 188
Summits, Founder
    Summits, 478, 480, 482, 498
    agenda, 479
    benefits, 480, 482
    schedule, 479
    topics, 478
Surveys
    pitfalls, 465

T

Teams
    advisory team, 320
    consideration, 328
    diversity, 333
    Governance Team, 342
        extended, 343
        pipeline, 336
    incubating teams, 320
    initiative team, 320
    investment team, 343
    leader's summit, 477
    maker team, 320
    members
        characteristics, 348
    relationships, 353
    size, 371
    time requirements, 339, 349, 352
Testing out, 400, 401

Threats
   to the initiative, 307, 311
   preemptive communication, 307–315
Time requirement, 343
Toolkits, 210–212, 214, 215, 248
Tools, 210, 212, 241, 246–247
Transformation, 127, 128, 134, 138
Transition activities, 254
Transition request, 411–413
Transparency, 309, 313, 445, 446
Trust, 124–125, 128, 177, 181, 185, 192, 206, 218, 226, 284, 288, 309, 314, 504, 505
Tuckman's Stages of Group Development, 374
   forming, 372
   norming, 373
   performing, 373
   storming, 372

U

Unblocking, 408, 409
Unfair advantage, 344, 345

V

Validated Hypothesis Summary, 729
Validated Hypothesis Summary (Extended), 730
Validated learning, 424–427, 461
Value migration, 457, 458
   measuring, 457, 458
   model, 305–307, 726
Viabile, 236
Viability, 26
Video assessment interview checklist, 169–173
Video conferencing software, 170, 172–174
Vocabulary, 114, 117–119

W, X, Y, Z

What's in this book?, 8–15
Why I wrote this book, 3–4
Working Agreement, 664–665

GPSR Compliance

The European Union's (EU) General Product Safety Regulation (GPSR) is a set of rules that requires consumer products to be safe and our obligations to ensure this.

If you have any concerns about our products, you can contact us on

ProductSafety@springernature.com

In case Publisher is established outside the EU, the EU authorized representative is:

Springer Nature Customer Service Center GmbH
Europaplatz 3
69115 Heidelberg, Germany

www.ingramcontent.com/pod-product-compliance
Lightning Source LLC
LaVergne TN
LVHW010331260326
834688LV00036B/650